THE PRISON OF LOVE

Romance, Translation, and the Book in the Sixteenth Century

EMILY C. FRANCOMANO

The Prison of Love

Romance, Translation, and the Book in the Sixteenth Century

UNIVERSITY OF TORONTO PRESS
Toronto Buffalo London

ISBN 978-1-4426-3051-2

Studies in Book and Print Culture

Library and Archives Canada Cataloguing in Publication

Francomano, Emily C., author
The prison of love : romance, translation, and the book
in the sixteenth century / Emily C. Francomano.

(Studies in book and print culture series)
Includes bibliographical references and index.
ISBN 978-1-4426-3051-2 (hardcover)

1. San Pedro, Diego de, active 1500. Cárcel de amor.
2. San Pedro, Diego de, active 1500 – Translations – History
and criticism. 3. San Pedro, Diego de, active 1500 – Adaptations.
4. San Pedro, Diego de, active 1500 – Criticism and interpretation.
5. Translating and interpreting – Europe – History – 16th century.
6. Books and reading – Europe – History – 16th century.
7. Spanish literature – Classical period, 1500–1700 – History and
criticism. 8. Europe – Intellectual life – 16th century. I. Title.

PQ6431.S4C338 2017   863'.2   C2017-905210-1

University of Toronto Press acknowledges the financial assistance to its
publishing program of the Canada Council for the Arts and the Ontario
Arts Council, an agency of the Government of Ontario.

**Canada Council   Conseil des Arts
for the Arts   du Canada**

ONTARIO ARTS COUNCIL
CONSEIL DES ARTS DE L'ONTARIO
an Ontario government agency
un organisme du gouvernement de l'Ontario

Funded by the   Financé par le
Government   gouvernement
of Canada   du Canada

Canadä

Contents

Contents

Part III: French Remediations

Acknowledgments

This is a book that I have wanted to write since my first semester in graduate school, when I took a seminar on the Spanish Sentimental Romances and learned that the works of Diego de San Pedro and Juan de Flores had been widely translated and used as language-learning tools in the sixteenth century. I am ever grateful to Patricia Grieve for introducing me to these works and for her unfailing guidance as I entered, and stayed in, academia. The idea that had been simmering away on the back-burner of my brain for more years than I wish to number here at last began to take shape with the support of an American Council of Learned Societies research fellowship in 2008, for which I am deeply grateful. The National Endowment for the Humanities summer seminar, "The Reformation of the Book, 1450–1700," in 2009, directed by John King and James Bracken, provided invaluable space, time, and mentorship as the project took on more definite outlines. The Folger Library colloquium, "Early Modern/Renaissance Translation," led by Anne Coldiron in the 2014–15 academic year, was a wonderful forum for testing my ideas as work on the book reached its conclusion. I was immensely fortunate to participate in these programs, which gave me the opportunity to discuss Book History and translation with many extraordinary scholars.

I wish to thank colleagues who so generously shared their expertise, read and commented upon drafts, invited me to give talks, and asked fruitful questions at conferences over the past years, especially Lourdes Alvarez, Heather Bamford, Lucia Binotti, Marina Brownlee, Joyce Boro, Robin Bower, Linde Brocato, Anne Coldiron, Véronique Duché-Gavet, Elizabeth Einstein, Irene Finotti, Leonardo Funes, Ethan Henderson, Gwen Kirkpatrick, Debbie Lesko-Baker, Sarah McNamer, Clara

Pascual-Argente, Peter Pfeiffer, Sol Miguel Prendes, Joanne Rappaport, Jonathan Ray, Isidro Rivera, Ron Surtz, Chris Warner, and Barbara Weissberger. Georgetown University has been generous in its support for this project in the form of several summer grants, a semester of senior research leave, and in securing the publication subvention. I owe many thanks to the Department of Spanish and Portuguese at Georgetown, not least for contributing to the publication subvention, but first and foremost for providing talented research assistants from our graduate programs, some of whom are now colleagues: Tyler Bergin, Yoel Castillo Botello, Inés Corujo Martín, María José Navia, Sacramento Roselló Martínez, Maureen Russo de Rodríguez, Estefanía Tocado Orviz, Martina Thorne, and Jovanna Zujevic. I am also grateful to Allison Brice, who was my undergraduate research assistant in the summer of 2012. I also wish to thank Suzanne Rancourt, at the University of Toronto Press, for sharing my enthusiasm about the book from the time I first pitched it to her and for shepherding it into print.

Heartfelt thanks go to friends and family whose hospitality and company was invaluable during my travels to libraries in England, France, Switzerland, Spain, and the United States: Vivian and Roger Cruise, Nick Francomano, Borja Ibarz, María Ibarz, Lola López Ibarz, Tanya, Steve, Jackson, and Lucy Schlemmer, and Harriet Welch. Above and beyond their unflagging support, I thank my mother, Nina Rulon-Miller, the comma queen, for her willingness to read drafts, and my father, Frank Francomano, for his help with sixteenth-century Italian. There is no way to thank Eugenio and Pablo enough for their patience, encouragement, and readiness to travel with me. Nor can I thank Eugenio enough for reading every page I have written.

Parts of chapter 4 first appeared in "'Puse un sobreescripto' [I wrote a new cover]: Manuscript, Print, and the Material Epistolarity of *Cárcel de amor*," published in *Fifteenth-Century Studies* 36 (2011). Parts of chapter 6 first appeared in "Re-reading Woodcut Illustration in *Cárcel de amor* 1493–1496," in *Titivillus* 1 (2015). Material for chapter 8 and the conclusion first appeared in "Reversing the Tapestry: *Prison of Love* in Text, Image, and Textile," *Renaissance Quarterly* 64, no. 4 (2011). I am grateful to the British Library, the Fondation Bodmer Library, and the Hispanic Society of America for allowing me to reproduce images from their collections in this book without permissions fees.

List of Figures

THE PRISON OF LOVE

Introduction: *A book that could not be read in peace*

> Aquella *Cárcel de Amor*
> que assí me plugo ordenar,
> ¡qué propia para amador,
> qué dulce para sabor,
> qué salsa para pecar!
> Y como la obra tal
> no tuvo en leerse calma,
> he sentido por mi mal
> cuán enemiga mortal
> fue la lengua para el alma.[1]

[That *Prison of Love* / it pleased me to so compose, / how fitting for a lover, / how sweet to the taste, / what a sinner's sauce! / And, since that work / could not be read in peace, / I have felt, for my sins, / just what a mortal enemy / was my tongue for the soul.]

In the late 1490s, the Castilian author and courtier Diego de San Pedro submitted his works to a poetic inquisitorial review, lamenting the danger that his romance, *Cárcel de Amor* (*The Prison of Love*), posed for readers. His self-recrimination, be it sincere or not, aptly captures the fervour with which readers in Spain and across Europe took up this work that, as he wrote, "no tuvo en leerse calma" (could not be read in peace). First composed in the 1480s for the entertainment of the Castilian elite in the Court of the Catholic Monarchs, *Cárcel de Amor* was printed in Seville in 1492. After *Cárcel de Amor*'s appearance in print, multiple Spanish editions and a Catalan translation by Bernadí Vallmanya soon followed. From 1496 on, *Cárcel de Amor* was printed with a continuation by Nicolás Núñez, a poet and reader who found the original ending unsatisfactory. Lelio Manfredi's Italian translation, *Carcer d'amore*, was first printed in 1514 and soon after served as the source for François d'Assy's French *La Prison d'Amours*, first printed in 1525. Drawing upon both *Cárcel de Amor* and *La Prison d'Amours*, John Bourchier, Lord Berners, produced the English *The Castell of Love* in the 1520s or early 1530s, printed in 1548 or 1549. A second French translation, made directly from the Spanish, appeared in the 1550s. Like the Spanish *Cárcel de Amor*, these translations circulated in multiple editions throughout the sixteenth century.[2]

Taken together, these editions form a strikingly diverse array of printed formats including elegant and illustrated prestige editions, tiny pocketbooks, and Spanish-French bilingual editions advertised as language-learning aids. But the romance's sixteenth-century media presence was not limited to print. *The Prison of Love* was read in manuscripts, some hastily copied, others produced as luxury items and richly illuminated. The romance also appeared as a three-dimensional visual narrative in sumptuous tapestry sets created for the French nobility. Indeed, at the end of the fifteenth century when he wrote to repent of its ill effects, Diego de San Pedro had only seen the very beginning of "that *Prison of Love*'s" flourishing, multimedia popularity.

The translations, adaptations, and their diffusion throughout the sixteenth century turned the Spanish *Cárcel de Amor* into an intercultural work, which I call here *The Prison of Love*, and which belonged to a select but growing body of cosmopolitan vernacular fictions, read first by the elites in the princely courts of Europe, and then with the spread of printing and literacy, by ever-wider readerships. For the sake of clarity, throughout this study I use the general title *The Prison of Love* to refer to the work in all of its manifestations, and the specific fifteenth- and sixteenth-century titles, *Cárcel de Amor, Lo càrcer d'amor, Carcer d'amore, La Prison d'Amours* (the first French translation), *La Prison d'Amour* (the second French translation), *L'Histoire de Lérian et Lauréolle*, and *The Castell of Love*, to refer to individual versions.[3] Similarly, I use the protagonists' names as given in each version when discussing individual translations and the Spanish names when referring to *The Prison of Love* generally.

The Prison of Love moved easily across multiple political and linguistic frontiers alongside Giovanni Boccaccio's *novelle*, Baldassare Castiglione's *The Book of the Courtier*, Juan de Flores's *Grisel and Mirabella*, Antonio de Guevara's *Diall of Princes*, San Pedro's own *Arnalte and Lucenda*, and Rodríguez de Montalvo's *Amadis of Gaul*.[4]

The Prison of Love's early circulation in fact both predates and presages that of the better-known *The Book of the Courtier* and *Amadis of Gaul*.[5] As the sixteenth century progressed, these works moved through similar multilingual courtly, diplomatic, and commercial networks. They were translated "radiantly," in a "pattern of transmission, in which one work is translated and printed in multiple languages at roughly the same time, radiating outward from one culture into several others."[6] Their physical diffusion was radiant as well, extending even to the Americas.[7]

Such wave-like, multilingual movement does not fit neatly into national-linguistic literary histories or descriptions of sources and influences.[8] Despite the importance of *The Prison of Love* and other transnational fictions that worked across European culture, vernacular translators and literary translations, no matter how popular or influential, have been, if not wholly hidden from view, generally relegated to the margins of literary study, regarded as "unoriginal," secondary, and thus non-representative of national literary character and genius. Yet the history of Western languages and literatures is a history of translations, of continuity and adaptation rather than radical change.[9] In addition, in the fifteenth and sixteenth centuries, early print culture drew its lifeblood from translation. Peter Burke, for example, associates *The Book of the Courtier* with the "Europeanization of Europe,"[10] and Lucien Febvre and Henri-Jean Martín likewise observe how sixteenth-century vernacular-to-vernacular translation and printing "helped to preserve the homogeneity of European culture at a time when national vernacular literatures were being born."[11] As Anne Coldiron sums it up, printing and translation were "transformative co-processes" in literary culture.[12]

Because *The Prison of Love* reached such wide audiences in so many varied forms, its transmission is ideal for a case study of how notions of authorship, reading, translation, books, and of literature itself were continually renegotiated in the period. Yet *The Prison of Love* is seldom studied as anything other than *Cárcel de Amor*, a fifteenth-century Spanish work. Although each of the individual translations has been studied in relative isolation within the context of critical editions, little has been written about the romance's long afterlives, even though the history of its reception clearly points to its lasting, cosmopolitan reach, and material adaptability. Moreover, as Barbara Fuchs observes in her study of seventeenth-century English appropriations of Spanish literature, the importance of Spain and Spanish fiction itself in the development of Renaissance literature has been largely occluded due to an "intellectual

'Black Legend.'" *The Prison of Love* is an early example of not only the English but also a continental "literary fascination with Spain."[13]

This book, *The Prison of Love: Romance, Translation, and the Book in the Sixteenth Century,* will be the first study of *The Prison of Love* as a transnational work and of the material evidence of its reception. It studies how *The Prison of Love* travelled through networks of readers, writers, editors, and printers, and adopting new material forms to match each cultural context of its transmission. It also explores the reasons, both literary and historical, which favoured its long-lasting cultural presence. Some stories are highly adaptogenic, as Linda Hutcheon observes, likening narratives and their transmission to genes and adaptive mutations. They "get retold in different ways in new material and cultural environments; like genes, they adapt to those new environments *by virtue* of mutation – in their 'offspring' or their adaptations. And the fittest do more than survive; they flourish."[14] The "fitness" of *The Prison of Love* to mutate into multiple textual and material forms that each palimpsestically retain likenesses to *Cárcel de Amor*, lies in its genetic-generic content, its *matière*.

The Prison of Love begins with an allegory of lovesickness: the narrator, called the "Author," who is travelling home from "last year's war" through an imaginary geographical location where the Spanish Sierra Morena adjoins Macedonia, comes upon a strange sight. A hirsute wildman, brandishing a flaming image of a woman, holds a young man captive. The wildman introduces himself to the Author as Desire, head servant of the house of Love, and the young man as Leriano, the son of a duke. Desire leads the Author to the eponymous Prison of Love, an edifice built upon the rock of Leriano's faith and constructed from other aspects of his impassioned emotional state. Inside, while tormented, Leriano is treated to a sad meal of his tortured thoughts, washed down by tears. Leriano explains this extravagant allegory point by point: each architectural and comestible detail represents a facet of his passion for Laureola, the princess of Macedonia.

The Author promises to help the suffering noble youth by acting as a go-between and then goes to the court. A stranger in Macedonia, the Author learns the local language and charms his way into the centre of court society – in part by regaling Laureola about the marvels of his homeland, Spain – in order to act as a go-between. The Author convinces Laureola to receive and answer letters from Leriano, even though she – rightly – fears for her honour. Letters are exchanged: Leriano begs for a "remedy" for his suffering and to be recognized as

Laureola's love-servant; Laureola refuses to do anything more than pity him and begs him to protect her honour.

Leriano, temporarily cured of his lovesickness, travels back to the court with the Author. There, Leriano kisses Laureola's hand, causing Persio, who is also in love with the princess, to become jealous. Persio promptly accuses Leriano and Laureola of meeting secretly in her bedroom, causing King Gaulo to imprison his daughter. According to the custom of the land, Persio challenges Leriano to a judicial duel in a *cartel* (letter of challenge), to which Leriano responds in kind. Just as Leriano, having cut off the hand of his rival, is about to prove his and Laureola's innocence, Gaulo calls an end to the battle in order to save Persio's life. Persio then produces false witnesses to convince Gaulo. Despite the wise counsel of the Cardinal, the impassioned supplications of the Queen, and a letter from Laureola, King Gaulo refuses to release his daughter, and orders her execution. Leriano raises an army and attacks the city, liberating Laureola and entrusting her to the care of her uncle in order to safeguard her honour. After a rousing speech to his men and much bloodshed, Leriano forces the false witnesses to recant and at last convinces the king of Laureola's innocence. She is returned to court, from where she sends Leriano a final letter stating her refusal to have anything more to do with him, at least until she inherits the throne and will be in a position to recompense him with riches and honours. Leriano, now lovesick unto death, delivers a lengthy discourse in praise of women in response to his friend Teseo's attempt to convince him that women are evil and thereby cure him of his malady. Leriano's mother then delivers a plaint at her son's bedside. Finally, Leriano tears up Laureola's letters, mixes the pieces with water, swallows them, and dies. His death is accompanied by general mourning. The Author returns to Spain to offer the story to his lord.

Deep preoccupations with rhetorical performances, honour, and gender roles are immediately apparent, even in a brief summary of the romance, as are its metafictive qualities. Throughout, *The Prison of Love* portrays its central characters engaging in multiple linguistic performances, through which they seek to fashion their discursive identities and fame. Leriano seeks to define himself as the perfect courtly lover, military leader, and champion of women by means of his letters and speeches; Laureola's letters display her desire to assert her political power and to control the estimation of her honour, while also manifesting the fear that her letters will circulate and destroy her good name. The Author presents himself as the true interpreter and editor of their words and actions.

Formally hybrid and polygenous, *Cárcel de Amor* and, by extension, all of the versions of *The Prison of Love* draw upon varied literary and rhetorical models that were familiar to late-medieval and early modern audiences, including Ovidian and humanist epistles, Ciceronian oration, Senecan *controversiae*, Boccaccian *novellas*, allegorical dream visions, romances of chivalry, courtesy books, the arts of love and of memory, literature of confession, penitence, and consolation, and the *querelle des femmes*, blending them into a remarkable fictional composition that clearly captivated generations of readers. Furthermore, as this catalogue of genres and intertexts suggests, the late fifteenth-century Spanish context of *Cárcel de Amor*'s composition was not isolated from Italian or continental literary tastes.[15]

Due to its hybridity and allusivity, much work has been devoted to *Cárcel de Amor*'s generic affiliations and its place within a group of "obras cortas de tema amoroso y desenlace triste" (short works on the theme of love, with unhappy endings) and set in courtly milieus, written in the fifteenth and sixteenth centuries, many of which blend poetry and prose, and include epistolary sections.[16] Early Hispanists Pascual de Gayangos and Marcelino Menéndez Pelayo describe *Cárcel de Amor* as a *novela sentimental-caballeresca* and a *novela sentimental*, respectively, terms they used to describe relatively short Spanish fictions blending chivalric romance and Italian *novelle* that developed in the fifteenth century and were imitated in sixteenth. Menéndez Pelayo also remarked upon the importance of letters in the construction of the *novelas sentimentales*. Both Gayangos and Menéndez Pelayo sought to point out a division between the virile genre of chivalric romance and the sentimental romances, devoted to the feminine concerns of "amor y galanteos" (love and gallantry). For Menéndez Pelayo, *Cárcel* and other sentimental romances sought to portray psychological interiority in the pre-modern absence of psychological analysis, which meant that no sentimental romance could ever reach the status of a masterpiece.[17] If *Cárcel de Amor* was not masterpiece material in Menéndez Pelayo's opinion, it certainly was accorded high status among its historical readers and has firmly entered the canon of medieval Spanish literature in academia today.

Following the initial generic outlines of the *novela sentimental* proposed by Menéndez Pelayo, Keith Whinnom's *The Spanish Sentimental Romance, 1440–1550: A Critical Bibliography* provides a list of twenty-one texts that have come to serve as the basis for considering the *novela sentimental* as a cohesive genre. Successive studies have argued for expanding and contracting the temporal, linguistic, and formal limits established by Whinnom, and even for doing away with the notion of a sentimental genre. For instance, Barbara Weissberger has argued against the notion of a clear division between sentimental and chivalric romance, pointing out that it results from the patriarchal nature of traditional literary history and the customary association between women, love, and "minor" literary genres.[18] In more recent scholarship the term *novela sentimental* is often replaced by *ficción sentimental* due to the associations of *novela* with the later novelistic tradition. Nevertheless, the denominations of *novela sentimental* and *ficción sentimental* and their English translations, "sentimental romance" and "sentimental fiction," have proved enduring, if problematic. In this group marked almost as much by diversity as likeness, Juan de Flores's *Grisel y Mirabella* (*Grisel and Mirabella*) (1470–86) and *Grimalte y Gradissa* (*Grimalte and Gradissa*) (1470–86), and San Pedro's two romances, *Cárcel de Amor* and *Arnalte y Lucenda* – all composed roughly contemporaneously and for the same initial circles of historical readers – do in fact share many commonalities of form and content. Indeed, the four romances by San Pedro and Flores form an intertextual nucleus around which scholars group varying numbers of works when describing the genre.

In this study, I have chosen to use the term "romance" for its wide semantic fields of reference, which incorporate medieval and early modern stories of love, battles, and the world of the court, to refer to *The Prison of Love*. This study tables the question of the existence or non-existence and limits of a sentimental genre, focusing on the uses and reception of a romance that formed part of a sixteenth-century cosmopolitan literary canon, approaching the "practical genre" of *The Prison of Love* in terms of audiences, institutions, physical forms, and use that "arise[s] out of attempts to fulfill some culturally authorized task."[19]

Just as the issue of genre has sparked debate, *The Prison of Love*'s ambiguities and allusivity have led to divergent interpretations. Some scholars have read *Cárcel de Amor* as a medieval work brimming with nostalgia for a lost idealized chivalry and courtly culture, while others have seen it as a parody. Sol Miguel-Prendes, for example, has studied how *Cárcel de Amor* and other sentimental fictions depend upon the standardized readings of fifteenth-century elite education, in order to ironically imitate works of moral consolation championing reason over passion.[20] Robert Folger, further developing the love casuistry in *Cárcel de Amor*, reads it as a harbinger of a new post-medieval concept of subjectivity.[21]

Moving beyond the "sentimental," or the psychological and amatory preoccupations of the plot and characters, several scholars have analysed the political valences of *Cárcel de Amor*, which appeared in print for the first time in the charged political context of 1492, when the Catholic Monarchs completed their conquest of Granada and the Expulsion of the Jews. It was also the year in which the Spanish Empire began its expansion into the West, and the year that Antonio Nebrija published his *Gramática de la lengua española*, where he famously stated that "siempre la lengua fue compañera del imperio" (language has always been the handmaiden of empire).[22] Francisco Márquez Villanueva interpreted *Cárcel de Amor* as a critique of unbridled and irresponsible monarchal power, composed by a *converso* at a time when the Catholic Monarchs sought to strengthen their supremacy and, in so doing, persecuted *conversos* and crypto-Jews through the powerful political tool of the Inquisition. Weissberger argues that the romance reflects the shifting political allegiances produced by the war of succession that followed Enrique IV's death and the ascension to the throne of Isabel I. E. Michael Gerli, turning to contemporary accounts of the Catholic Monarchs' administration of harsh justice, argues that *Cárcel de Amor* dramatizes how "judicial practices come into conflict" and the "historical rivalry between the feudal aristocracy and rising monarchical power but also to a more modern forensic practice that politicizes the search for truth and justice."[23]

These readings all study the historical context of the *Cárcel de Amor*'s composition and first printing in Spanish at the end of the fifteenth century. However, the romance, with its opening reference to a recent, yet unnamed, war, suggests its own specific historical context while also allowing "last year's war" to connote almost any war from the recent memory of particular translators and readers. While the late fifteenth-century situation of the Catholic Monarchs and the Castilian aristocracy inspired *Cárcel de Amor*'s political allegories, the romance's view of court life, tyranny, and the distortion of justice could easily be read as relevant to numerous sixteenth-century political situations.

My own interpretation of *The Prison of Love* builds upon the by no means mutually exclusive readings of parody, nostalgia, and political allegory, and upon the work of those scholars who have seen in *Cárcel de Amor* a reflection of vernacular humanism and a fictional tour de force of rhetorical precepts, and the *ars dictaminis* in particular.[24] *The Prison of Love*'s focus on the protagonists' rhetorical performances, all intended to persuade one another to pursue various courses of action, and its self-consciously multilayered and mediated discourses signal its participation in vernacular humanist and diplomatic poetics, two intersecting early modern literary modes.[25] Humanist poetics draws upon the formal study of rhetoric, particularly the creation of narrative around issues akin to those presented in *controversiae, suasoriae*, and *quaestio comparativa*. Consequently, humanist fictions are dialogic, often presenting audiences with contradictions, arguments *in utramque partem*, and they "can be read as serious or ironic, as simply contradictory or profoundly paradoxical, as undecidable or the occasion for a decision," inviting their audiences to ponder their controversies and debates along with their imagined characters.[26] *The Prison of Love* and other humanist fictions of the fifteenth and sixteenth centuries reflect and model rhetorical performances in action. Unlike the manuals that proliferated in the sixteenth century, however, fictions offer more than a set of tools and instruction for orators and writers; they "scrutinize the discourse of rhetoric even as they repeat it," engaging readers in their reflections upon the power and corruptibility of persuasion.[27]

Scenes of linguistic mediation, such as the Author's ferrying of messages and letters, also point to the romance's diplomatic poetics. Observing that the new "political tool of diplomacy and the emerging culture of secular literature shape each other in important ways," Timothy Hampton considers how fifteenth- and sixteenth-century literary works stage "scenes of diplomatic negotiation, delegation, and representation as part of their exploration of the relationship between political rhetoric and the emerging sphere of secular literature." Drawing upon works on the professionalization of diplomacy in the period, Hampton studies how the diplomat's role as a "maker and reader of fictions, as an exchanger of signs and constructor of narratives," parallels literary fictions.[28] The Author, who serves as an ambassador for Leriano, represents Spain in the court of Macedonia, and then carries the news of Leriano's death back to his homeland, is a travelling, diplomatic mediator of signs and stories.

The Prison of Love represents rhetoric as a political tool of self-definition, while also dramatizing the troubling dependence of verbal persuasion upon the emotions and passions. The dynamics of humanist and diplomatic poetics in *The Prison of Love* are continually in play, especially in the portrayal of the Author as a go-between and, ultimately, as the inscribed author of the romance itself. San Pedro and the early sixteenth-century translators all belonged, in some sense, to the European corps of diplomatic professionals, serving as courtiers and secretaries to the nobility. The translators were of course avid readers of the romance, demonstrating its appeal to their peers. The female readers addressed by the romance were also intercultural agents, noble women who travelled as brides and on other diplomatic missions. As such they were all well poised to be nexuses of contact, "people who for reasons of institutional livelihood ... engaged in the transfer of cultural products across borders."[29]

To tell the story of *The Prison of Love* as it travelled as a series of material, literary, and social texts, I approach the romance from diverse angles, drawing upon the "materialist hermeneutics" of the pioneering bibliographical critics Fernando Bouza, Roger Chartier, Jerome McGann, and D.F. McKenzie, who famously coined the term "the sociology of texts" to describe the use of material books as empirical evidence in "the historical study of the making and the use of books and other documents."[30] Although book history has often turned a blind eye to the literariness of books, materialist hermeneutics offers an alternative by reading the texts and material books as "mutually constitutive and ultimately indissoluble."[31] Following this reconciliation of the literary and the material, I read the material forms and texts of *The Prison of Love* as symbiotically connected in the transmission and reception of the romance. As Chartier puts it, "readers, in fact, never confront abstract, idealized texts detached from any materiality ... they hold in their hands or perceive objects and forms whose structures and modalities govern their reading or hearing, and consequently the possible comprehension of the text read or heard."[32] All books are in this sense intermedial, blending visual, tactile, and textual communication. Materialist hermeneutics help us to read – see, peruse, hold – "with the period eye," that is, to hypothesize about historical reception, with the material books leading the way.[33]

The Prison of Love's metamorphoses were achieved through the work of translation, in the dual senses of the word, that is to say through linguistic transfer, and also through *translatio*, literally a "carrying over" of the story from one place and material shape to another. *The Prison of Love* arrived in readers' hands and before their eyes in their own languages, and in a multitude of material forms that each reflect the romance's relationship to its audiences, from quickly prepared manuscript copies, to tapestries and illuminated manuscripts requiring intense labour, elegant illustrated print editions, and tiny pocketbooks. Hutcheson's description of narrative mutation recalls McGann's definition of "the textual condition" itself as one of continuous change and shifting embodiments.[34] This book is, consequently, a study of textual transformation, of textualterity, the "temporal and spatial peregrinations that works of art and literature undergo,"[35] and of remediation, the material refashioning of narrative.[36] In this way, it departs from the norms and *modus operandi* of literary scholarship, where close readings of presumably fixed texts prevail. I do not wish to do away with close reading, but rather bring the material and social conditions of textuality into close readings of a work whose texts were continually in flux. If we stand back from the authorized text in critical editions, the work becomes all the richer in its verbal and material *mouvence*; we can, to borrow Franco Moretti's metaphor, see the wave for the trees. When using the term "work," I do not refer to an ideal text representing an authorial ur-text, but rather to the romance as a literary entity recognizable in each of its material forms, even as it changed according to particular social and technological conditions: the work is both transhistorical *and* historically contingent. Such a "work-centered approach," as Paul Eggert argues, attends to the survival and study of texts "published over many decades or centuries," but also to the work as a series of historical processes, "bringing the history of works in their material and textual forms together with the receptions of those forms."[37]

I have also adopted strategies from microhistory, the "analysis at extremely close range, of highly circumscribed phenomena," in order to "reconstruct the contours" of subjects and objects previously hidden from view. Microhistory, by eschewing grand narratives to focus instead upon the histories of particular individuals or things, however, can lead to a better understanding of broader cultural contexts.[38] The natural affinity between microhistory and book history, noted decades ago by Armando Petrucci,[39] points to the similarly fruitful pairing of materialist hermeneutics with microhistory, as both focus on the shape of material evidence in relation to context. I take *The Prison of Love* and the material objects in which it reached readers as "small places" in which to pursue "large questions" about sixteenth-century book cultures.[40] Study of *The Prison of Love* as a "small place" is useful for understanding key aspects of sixteenth-century book culture and literary history writ large. The large questions that underpin this study, however, never stray far from the literariness of *The Prison of Love*. They concern the relation of narrative matter to material form, the coexistence of textual and human agencies in late fifteenth- and sixteenth-century material books, and, in the case of the tapestries, narrative objects. The romance and its multilingual paratexts – titles, dedications, epilogues – reveal historical configurations and reconfigurations of authorship that

trouble the author-work paradigm while also showing just how important author-functions were for sixteenth-century readers and translators.
The importance of women readers, patrons, and author-figures also
comes to the fore when *The Prison of Love* is studied in its European
contexts, where it entered into the fray in the *querelle des femmes*.

The material book has become increasingly visible in medieval and
early modern studies, and with it, the social, technological, and economic conditions within which every book comes into being. Book historians have duly noted that *Cárcel de Amor*, a work first published in
the incunable period in Seville, and a veritable bestseller among Spanish
readers, played an important role in the development of print culture
in Spain. Yet, "the concept of the book as object can obliterate the traces
of its fragmentary and more volatile constituents," namely, the written
text, as Ana Gómez Bravo observes.[41] In a similar vein, Leah Price points
out that book history "has come to stand for a materialist resistance to
theory, to idealism, even to ideas ... bibliographers' failure to account
for the specificity of the literary is all the more striking given how often
their raw materials are borrowed from a canon established by literature
departments."[42] Just as the methods of book history can elucidate literary history and criticism, the corollary holds true: bringing literariness to
studies of material books is a way of rethinking the sociology of books.
In Leslie Howsam's words, book history can be used "as a way of rethinking and re-writing literary criticism"; bibliographic, literary, and
historical approaches are mutually enlightening.[43]

Chapter Outline

This book contains eight chapters, organized in three sections: "Authors,
Translators, Networks," "Materialities," and "French Remediations."
The three chapters of the first section concern the shifting authorial
figures and networks of patronage through which *Cárcel de Amor* and
The Prison of Love travelled during the first, and most courtly, stages of
its diffusion, from the last decade of the fifteenth century to the early
decades of the sixteenth century. Appendices containing the full texts
of the paratexts composed by each translator (A), known editions of
The Prison of Love (B), and extant manuscripts of *Cárcel de Amor* and *La
Prison d'Amours* (C) follow the three main sections.

Chapter 1, "*Cárcel de Amor, an Accessus ad Auctores*," introduces Diego
de San Pedro and analyses the metafictive relationship created between
the romance's first and extratextual, historical author and the Author as

character. It also discusses the images of social authorship and scribal publication created by the romance's depiction of the creation and circulation of letters. Even from the first instance, where Diego de San Pedro's authorship and intentions are celebrated, the romance envisions its own composition as a shared social endeavour in which the writer is only one of a large cast of contributing creators. Importantly, *The Prison of Love* imagines a female writer, Laureola, taking part in the dynamics of social authorship. Lastly, this chapter turns to the first revisionary author of the romance, Nicolás Núñez, and his continuation. Núñez is a representative of *Cárcel de Amor*'s historical readership, drawn into the open, humanist poetics of the work and inspired to resolve its ambiguities. He is also the first reader-writer of the romance to insert himself into the metafictive relationship between extratextual author and the *Cárcel de Amor* in the paratextual framing of his *cumplimiento*.

Chapter 2, "Translating Authorship," explores the introductions and paratexts that Bernadí Vallmanya, Lelio Manfredi, François d'Assy, and Lord Berners composed to frame their translations of the romance, in order to elucidate how the dynamics of adaptation, authorial appropriation, and cultural brokering all play a part in its radiant translation. Modern practices tend to render the translators of popular literature invisible, as ciphers through which transcendental meaning is seamlessly transferred from one language to another. In stark contrast, the early modern translators of *The Prison of Love* all strove to make themselves highly visible. In *The Prison of Love*'s transmission across languages, the translators' visibility goes hand in hand with patronage and intended readership, demonstrating how authorship could be both social and aggregative in the period. Their successive dedications, valedictions, and author portraits advertise literary redeployment and translation as courtly services worthy of favour. Moreover, the importance of the Author as a character in *The Prison of Love* facilitated the translators' self-inscription into the metafictive relationship between historical author and the world of the romance. The translators' appropriations of *The Prison of Love* show how the work lent itself to open authorship, due in part to its lack of *auctoritas*, the intellectual cachet of the classics. The translators presented *The Prison of Love* as "a little book" (*questo picciolo volume; ce petite livret;* lytle presente treatyse), referring at once to its physical size and to its place in the generic horizons of expectation within which they read and translated.

Chapter 3, "'Easie Languages': The Free and Faithful Translation of *The Prison of Love*," turns from the high visibility of translation and authorship to what Manfredi's, d'Assy's, and Berners' paratexts tell us about the emerging intercultural literary field of vernacular-to-vernacular translation. Scholarly editors of the translations of *The Prison of Love* have, by and large, focused upon granular linguistic comparisons between the Spanish source and the texts in the target languages. Rather than focus on the linguistics of translation, my interest here is to study, on the one hand, the philosophy of translation that emerges in radiant translation, and, on the other, how the translations and material books in which they travelled were experienced by their historical audiences. In an age when European vernaculars were coming into view as languages of international cultural authority but "horizontal" translations from one vernacular to another had yet to be defined as a literary category, the translators of *The Prison of Love* were developing a language to express their tasks and methodologies.

The paratexts that accompany and frame *The Prison of Love* are more than "thresholds" that allow the "text to become a book and to be offered as such to its readers," in Gerard Genette's classic definition.[44] The paratexts also express emergent ideologies of horizontal, vernacular-to-vernacular translation at a time when humanistic discussions of translation were almost wholly dedicated to the vertical translation from classical languages into vernaculars. They partake of both the material and social aspects of textualterity, as spaces where contact between languages and between writers and readers are defined and transacted. The fortunes of *The Prison of Love* also show how book objects can reflect and express a text's obsession with linguistic mediation, rhetoric, and material textuality. What is more, *The Prison of Love*'s adaptation in French manuscripts and tapestries shows how a work translated from the language of an imperial enemy, could be made to function as a political allegory quite distinct from its origins.

While the first section of this book explores the networks of writers and readers and their acts of linguistic mediation – authorship, translation, patronage – that "set the world of the written word in order,"[45] the second section, "Materialities" moves further into realm of material hermeneutics. Chapter 4, "Textual Material: Allegory and Material Epistolarity in *The Prison of Love*," turns to the literary and rhetorical practices of ordering the world through the written word. The romance, which continually reminded its audiences of the materiality of texts, begins with the extended allegory that combines with ekphrasis in the description of the Prison of Love and the multitude of personifications – the concrete representations of intangible emotions – that inhabit Leriano's emotional landscape.

A veritable theatre of memory, the allegory abounds in images meant to be conjured up by the mind's eye, taking on physical form, if only in the imagination.

From the allegorical materialization of words, the plot moves to the concretization of emotions in writing, in the exchange of letters between Leriano and Laureola, enacted through the Author's intercession. Throughout, the romance focuses on the creation and consumption of hand-written texts, culminating in a final scene where Leriano swallows Laureola's letters and dies. The presence of textual material culture within the text of *Cárcel de Amor*, which would be translated into all of the versions of *The Prison of Love*, creates a textual image of manuscript culture and scribal publication, resulting in a remediation – the representation of one medium in another – that reflects the era in which the romance circulated in both print and manuscript.

In chapter 5, "Prisons in Print: The Material Books," I survey the printed books in which *The Prison of Love* reached readers in Spain, Italy, France, England, and the Low Countries, in order to analyse how the literary compositions of San Pedro, d'Assy, Manfredi, and Lord Berners became "the physical and commercial objects we call books."[46] The cosmopolitan transmission of *The Prison of Love* depended upon two institutions that are closely related in the sixteenth century, yet which also became somewhat distanced from one another as print cultures developed: the well-established system of courtly and diplomatic gift-exchange and the newer, rising institution of printing are the motors of *The Prison of Love*'s radiant diffusion. The convergence and distancing of these institutions frame the two main phases of *The Prison of Love*'s transmission in the sixteenth century. From 1492 to the 1540s, the romance circulated in carefully printed editions bearing dedications to elite readers. In the second half of the century, however, the majority of the printed editions of *The Prison of Love* no longer vaunted connections to courts or famed nobles.

The Spanish *Cárcel de Amor* was printed in over forty editions by printing houses in Spain, Antwerp, Venice, and Paris, between 1492 and 1600. From 1552 on, it was often anthologized with another romance, *Questión de amor*, and in the bilingual format mentioned above. All of the translations, with the exception of the Catalan, also appeared in multiple editions produced in rapid succession, attesting to the high popularity of *The Prison of Love* among transnational audiences. *Carcer d'amore* was printed ten times between 1514 and 1546. *La Prison d'Amours* appeared in six editions between 1525 and 1533. Three editions of the

English *Castell of Love* were printed between 1548 or 1549 and 1555. In the 1550s, the second French translation, attributed to Gilles Corrozet, was published in facing-page bilingual editions with the Spanish text, advertised as an aid "pour ceux que voudront apprendre un de l'autre" (for those who desire to learn one [language] from the other). At least eighteen bilingual French and Spanish editions were printed in Antwerp, Lyon, and Paris between 1552 and 1650.[47]

The material configurations of books reflect the intended readership, horizons of expectation, and printers' marketing strategies. *The Prison of Love* was often a small book, printed in octavos, a format associated with vernacular fiction, during the first phase of its transmission. In the second phase of its transmission, *The Prison of Love* appeared in even smaller formats – duo- and sextodecimos – produced for ever-widening audiences. Moreover, many of the extant copies of *The Prison of Love* contain the marks left by their sixteenth-century authors, translators, patrons, editors, printers, and readers, marks which survive in the absence of their producers and intended audiences as the material evidence of reception and use. They show how readers throughout the sixteenth century were drawn to the language and style of *The Prison of Love*, how the *querelle des femmes* figured prominently in the marketing of the romance, and how the romance's genre was understood during the period. The networks of patronage and printing through which *The Prison of Love* moved in the sixteenth century are closely related to the material forms that shaped its transmission and reception, and, when we begin to look at the many material books in which the texts of *The Prison of Love* circulated, the ways in which the romance's obsession with the materiality of languages influenced its physical manifestations become apparent. Moreover, the material books demonstrate how translation is not only a textual process but is often built into the architecture of printed pages.

After size, decoration and illustration are two of the most visible material aspects of books related to their literary meanings and textual contents. The interplay of illustration with narration is particularly intricate in material books, and all the more so in *The Prison of Love*; consequently, chapter 6, "Visual Rhetoric: Reading Printed Images in *The Prison of Love*," offers an intermedial reading of the illustrated editions of *Cárcel de Amor*, *Lo càrcer d'amor*, and *Carcer d'amore* produced from 1492 to 1546, when the romance was printed with two sets of woodcuts designed *ex profeso* for its illustration. The intensely visual opening scenes and prevalence of textual images meant to be conjured up by the mind's eye no doubt inspired the rich iconographic tradition that arose in the wake of the first readings of *The Prison of Love*. The woodcuts, though designed after and in response to the composition of the text, became integral to audiences' experience and reception.

Allegories, which privilege the sense of sight and the power of words to create concrete images, are frequent subjects of illustration in both manuscripts and printed books. The illustrated versions of *The Prison of Love* all feature images of The Prison, Desire, and the flames of passion. However, the majority of the woodcuts as well as many of the manuscript illuminations depict the characters' rhetorical performances: writing, reading, and orating. The conjoining of narrative and illustration intensifies the metafictive *mise en abyme* created by the textual depiction of the creation of narrative and persuasive discourses; the visual images made to accompany these scenes stage rhetoric, gestures, and actions that engage the body, revealing the performative nature of the romance. The design and inclusion of these images moreover, indicate that printers, editors, and booksellers sought to market the work as, on the one hand, allegorical and edifying, and, on the other, as a rhetorically sophisticated humanist fiction.

In addition to *The Prison of Love*'s impressive presence in print culture, one early sixteenth-century manuscript copy of *Cárcel de Amor*, and no fewer than eleven manuscripts of d'Assy's French translation, all dating from the 1520s, are extant. Further, while *La Prison d'Amours* was circulating in print and manuscript in the 1520s, a tapestry workshop in Northern France or Flanders produced perhaps the most striking material translation of *The Prison of Love*, known by the names of the central protagonists as *L'Histoire de Lérian et Lauréolle*. *The Prison of Love* was perhaps even more popular among French audiences than Spanish, and the court of Francis I adapted the romance textually and materially more than any other network of elite audiences. The two chapters in the third and final section, "French Remediations," reflect this intense interest, which inspired the transformation of *The Prison of Love* into luxury objects.

In the 1520s, when *Cárcel de Amor*, *Carcer d'amore*, and *La Prison d'Amours* all circulated in print, bearing the prestige of the celebrated dedicatees, the French court redefined the romance by commissioning its remediation in luxurious manuscripts and tapestries. Chapter 7, "*La Prison d'Amours* Illuminated" studies the remarkable proliferation of early sixteenth-century manuscripts of *La Prison d'Amours* and provides ample evidence of the circulation of the romance among an elite coterie of men and women who were just as interested in the book as an object as they were in the provocative tale held within their costly copies. Beyond illustrating the distinctions that can be drawn between printed copies and deluxe, bespoke manuscript production, the French manuscripts of *La Prison d'Amours* suggest that, for a time, a lavishly produced personal manuscript copy was a much sought-after accessory of political and social prestige, one which memorialized the fraught relations between the French Crown and the Holy Roman Empire in the first decades of the sixteenth century.

Chapter 8, "From Text to Textile: *L'Histoire de Lérian et Lauréolle*," analyses the extant tapestry panels of the *L'Histoire de Lérian et Lauréolle*, which are rarely considered as part of *The Prison of Love*'s literary transmission, an omission that obscures just how deeply the romance had penetrated into French culture. The manuscripts are not only examples of the persistence of manuscript culture in the sixteenth century and its intersections with print culture, but also of the production of distinctive handwritten and hand-painted manuscripts as foils for printed books. Like printed books, tapestries were mechanically reproducible, and at least three sets of *L'Histoire de Lérian et Lauréolle* chamber were made; each reproduction of a tapestry chamber would have required an extravagant investment in materials, time, and labour, far more than a printed book or even an illuminated manuscript, resulting in a luxury item affordable by only the wealthiest of buyers. The tapestries are a three-dimensional and life-sized translation of the romance, designed to clothe the walls of a large room and so envelop their viewers within the fictional world of the romance. Moreover, they recreated *The Prison of Love* within a visual world that closely resembled the French court and transformed it from the *petite livret* that François d'Assy had translated into a dazzling spectacle. Close ties to the court and family of Francis I are clearly indicated in several of the manuscripts, and one set of the tapestries was given by the king to his sister-in-law Renée upon her marriage to Ercole II d'Este in 1528. Both material forms turned *La Prison d'Amours* into sumptuous material objects designed to represent the power, wealth, and refinement of the elite.

The transmission of *The Prison of Love* in French in the early decades of the sixteenth century – in print, manuscript, and tapestry – provides a fascinating case for the critical reconsideration of the divisions between textual and material approaches to literary and cultural history, as well as those traditionally drawn between print and manuscript studies. As Julia Crick and Alexandra Walsham point out, the traditional scholarly paradigm equates "the boundary between 'script' and 'print'" with "the barrier between the medieval and early modern eras."[48] However, as the work of many scholars over the past two decades has shown, the division between print and manuscript studies is not only unnecessary, an "unhappy separation," in David McKitterick's words, but also an obstruction to understanding how texts and images circulated and were received in the fifteenth and sixteenth centuries.[49]

Romance is capacious and malleable, two defining characteristics of the genre that contribute to its protean adaptability in the hands of readers and revisionary authors, and also to its reflection of multiple audiences' desires and historical situations over time. *Cárcel de Amor*'s omnifariousness and its corresponding openness to interpretation, be it historicized, rhetorical, psychoanalytic, or material, have brought it into the critical canon for Hispanists. For many of the same traits, for almost one hundred years, from its first appearance in print in 1492 throughout the sixteenth century, *The Prison of Love*, known under its many titles, was also one of the most widely read vernacular works in Western Europe.

The Prison of Love was not without its detractors. Diego de San Pedro, as we have seen, vilified it as a "mortal enemy to the soul." Juan Luis Vives, writing at the behest of Catherine of Aragon in his *De Institutione Feminae Christianae* (1524), lists *Cárcel de Amor* among the "libris pestiferis" (pestiferous books) from Spain, "whose absurdities are infinite," and that young women should never read.[50] As Charles Fantazzi and C. Matheeussen note, however, the list of forbidden books altered with translations.[51] The Spanish translation, *Instrucción de la muger Christiana*, printed by Jorge Coci in 1528, omits *Cárcel de Amor* from the list of "libros vanos" (foolish/worthless books) from Spain, perhaps because Coci had printed many editions of *Cárcel de Amor* and did not want to jeopardize sales. Francisco de Osuna's *Abecedario espiritual* (Spiritual ABC) (1525–7) contains similar censure of *Cárcel de Amor*, as does Juan de la Cerda's *Libro intitulado vida política de todos los estados de mugeres* (Book of the governance of women of all ranks) (1599). Antoine Du Saix includes *La Prison d'Amours* in his list of the unedifying works that typify the bad reading habits of courtiers in his *L'esperon de discipline* (The spur of discipline) (1532). The English moralist Edward Dering lumped *The Prison of Love* in with other "unchaste fables" that wiled readers away from Scriptures: "Yea some have ben so impudent, as new borne *Moabites*, which wallow in their own vomit, and have not bene ashamed to entitle their bookes, *The Court of Venus*, *The Castle of*

Love, and manye such other as shamelesse as these" in his *A briefe and necessary instruction* (1572).[52] In 1632, *Cárcel de Amor* was added in its entirety to the Spanish Inquisition's *Index of Forbidden Books* when the rationale for prohibition expanded to include books "que tratan, cuentan, y enseñan cosas lascivas, de amores" (that concern, narrate, and teach lascivious things, about love/sex), in addition to those containing heresies and "errors of faith."[53] The inclusion attests to *Cárcel's* lasting popularity among Spanish audiences, even though it was no longer printed with frequency in the seventeenth century.

Throughout my research on *The Prison of Love* and sixteenth-century book cultures more generally, I have been inspired and fascinated by books' quite magical ability to be both physical objects in the world and, when transformed by acts of reading, imaginative, mental entities.[54] It is my hope that this book will open up new avenues of enquiry by peeling *The Prison of Love* away from its traditional, if contentious, generic and academic home among Iberian late medieval and sixteenth-century fictions, while also making the Spanish *Cárcel de Amor* itself better known. Here, reading *The Prison of Love* as an intercultural work will show how its meanings and generic affiliations broadened and were reconfigured as it appeared before the eyes of successive networks of readers and writers and in successive material guises. Hispanists will find new ways to read *Cárcel de Amor* and readers approaching this book from other disciplinary perspectives too will discover new approaches to translations and material books that bring diverse archival materials and texts to light and into dialogue.

PART I

Authors, Translators, Networks

Cárcel de Amor, an Accessus ad Auctores

Diego de San Pedro's palinode, repenting for the "book that could not be read in peace," concisely reflects a conundrum of authorship: once a work enters into circulation, the author loses any semblance of control over its interpretation, and yet, he is to blame for its effects upon readers. Nevertheless, when *The Prison of Love* became a sixteenth-century cosmopolitan work, San Pedro need not have worried about his fame or blame spreading. His name, his intellectual ownership, and consequently his responsibility for the "sinners' sauce," disappeared as the romance travelled during the decades after its first appearance in Spanish. In the case of radiant translation, continuation, and adaptation, a revision of the traditional text-author paradigm, or *accessus ad auctores* convention, where textual authority is vested in a single figure, is in order. Authorship mutates and diffuses along with *The Prison of Love* itself. Notions of authorship are further expanded and complicated in the romance due to the pivotal role played by the inscribed author-figure and narrator-protagonist, the Author, who oscillates quite self-consciously between first- and third-person narration, and between uncertainty and omniscience, as he relates the story of Leriano and Laureola. To make the textual construction of authorship all the more elaborate, the letter-writers Leriano and Laureola (and, to a lesser extent Leriano's rival Persio), are also depicted as the inscribed authors of parts of the romance.

While many scholars acknowledge that for medieval and early modern readers, book producers, and booksellers, author-functions were different from the post-Romantic ideal of the lone inspired genius, the practice of literary scholarship continues to value the personal circumstances of historical authors and the attribution of literary works to an

individual intellect, talent, and character. Heather Hirschfeld characterizes this state of affairs as a "concurrent dismissal of and obsession
with the status and meaning of the author."[1] This seemingly contradictory stance is in fact useful for thinking about authorship in the case of
highly adaptogenic works like *The Prison of Love*, where one historical
individual after another claims the status of an author deserving recognition for his intellectual labour and for his special relationship to his
intended readers, yet not one of these individuals presents the romance
as the original product of his sole genius because of the social nature of
literary production.

Diego de San Pedro was most likely unknown to the majority of
sixteenth-century readers of *The Prison of Love*. His name does not appear
in any of the translations other than Vallmanya's. Nor does it appear in
the bilingual French-Spanish editions printed in France and the Low
Countries in the second half of the sixteenth century. Consequently,
and true to Hirschfeld's summation, this chapter will be devoted to the
meaning of "the author" in *The Prison of Love* and, at the same time, like
many of the romance's historical readers, will ultimately disremember
Diego de San Pedro. That is to say, here, as in the sixteenth century,
he will be dropped from the authorial roles and fade from view, but
only after he has been given his due as the first, historical author of
The Prison of Love.

My approach to authorship in *The Prison of Love* is informed by the
Foucauldian-inflected work of scholars of early modern book cultures
such as Roger Chartier, Natalie Zemon Davis, Alexandra Gillespie, and
Harold Love, who have sought to historicize definitions of authorship
in order to include the collaborative writerly and readerly "repertoire
of practices ... and functions" that combine to locate texts "within time,
place, a culture, a genre, an institution."[2] Noting that distinct author-
functions, or *authemes*, are often distributed among different individuals involved with the creation of a work, Love proposes a typology to
identify the "varieties of individual agency" expressed by the single
term *authorship*, upon which I will draw in order to disentangle the
many authorial functions woven into *The Prison of Love*.[3] Redefining
authorship, however, does not imply the disappearance of the "author,"
a figure that "named or unnamed, *has always been* a way for those who
produce texts ... and those who use, read, censor, or celebrate them to
describe the place of those texts in the world."[4] Such a figure, whether
historical or fictional, serves the "primordial" author-function of "guar-
anteeing the unity and coherence of the discourse."[5] This construction

of author-function is arguably as old as literature itself. In this chapter, my primary concern will be with diegetic and extra-diegetic textual constructions of authorship, and not the author-functions of the translators, printers, editors, illustrators, and other bookmen involved in the transmission of *The Prison of Love,* to whom I will return in chapters 3 and 5.

In *Cárcel de Amor* criticism, the titles of a remarkable number of studies contain the phrase "*Cárcel de Amor* de Diego de San Pedro" or "Diego de San Pedro's *Cárcel de Amor*," reflecting the continued focus on and belief in the individual author's intellectual ownership of *his* work.[6] Indeed, much of the scholarship on *Cárcel de Amor* amounts to attempts to complete what remains a sketchy *accessus* to Diego de San Pedro, his *intentio auctoris,* and the *utilitas* of the romance. Even though the Spanish, Catalan, Italian, French, and English versions of *The Prison of Love* have not been considered as part of a unified literary system, but rather as distinct elements of national traditions, modern literary histories, library catalogues, and inventories attribute the work, in all its incarnations, to Diego de San Pedro. In large part, this is due to bibliographic conventions, academic estimation of the translators as something less than authors, and a tendency to read translations and adaptations as lesser, supervenient beings compared with "original" texts. Aesthetically, the translations and adaptations may well be worse – or even better – than *Cárcel de Amor,* but such comparisons were immaterial to the great majority of *The Prison of Love*'s sixteenth-century readers, who nevertheless appear to have cared deeply about the individual author-figures whose names circulated with each version of the romance.

The paratexts that frame *Cárcel de Amor* and each successive iteration of *The Prison of Love* – titles, title pages, dedications, epigraphs, and, in one case, a continuation – are the primary spaces where authemes and the "facts of collaboration" are announced.[7] They are the loci of authorization, self-advertisement, and claims of recognition through writers' "self-inscription" as authors.[8] Above all, the dedications textually invent "the fundamental relationship that dominated literary activity until the mid-eighteenth century: the connecting of an author ... to a protector from whom he expected support and gratification," as Chartier has observed.[9] Davis points to a shift in the quality of dedicatory paratexts from manuscripts to printed books. In contrast to the paratexts and presentation pages of manuscripts, which, while flattering to their dedicatees, would be limited in circulation, "The printed epistle now carried the patron's praise far and wide ... adding to value of the gift to the recipient," while, at the same time, maintaining some of the aura of exclusivity and gift-exchange expressed in manuscripts.[10] The dedications, as threshold texts, "establish a context for the subject of the book," as a circle where "the spirit with which the book should be read and its contents [were] discussed."[11]

The paratexts prepare audiences to read, situating them in a particular relation to the romance, and "enable a text to become a book and to be offered as such to its readers and, more generally, to the public."[12] Yet, in addition to establishing authorial intention, Renaissance paratexts, as Helen Smith and Louise Wilson write, "operate in multiple directions, structuring the reader's approach not only to the text in question but to the experience of reading, and of interpreting the world beyond the book ... [the paratext] both frames and inhabits the text."[13] The paratexts framing and inhabiting each version of *The Prison of Love* introduce a network of historical and fictional personages that bring the text to life and into the hands of readers. Moreover, the authorial paratexts demonstrate how *The Prison of Love* passed from one group of interconnected readers – friends, clients, and patrons – to another, moving wave-like across the porous geographical, linguistic, and political frontiers of European courts. The movement of *The Prison of Love,* as it was composed, evaluated, adapted, and redeployed in Spanish, Catalan, Italian, French, and English, is an example of how fluidly vernacular fictions and authorship could be recontextualized in the first decades of the sixteenth century. Each of the writers has left different traces in the historical record, but their dedications reveal similar strategies for presenting and repackaging the romance for their readers.

San Pedro, Vallmanya, Manfredi, d'Assy, and Berners all dedicated their *Prisons of Love* to specific noble readers, rather than to a generic "reader." Dedicated books, be they in print or manuscripts, are the "bearers of relationships" and "public gifts" that proclaim the patron's greatness, largesse, and intelligence, as well as the book's and dedicating writer's worthiness of an exalted readership.[14] As the "privileged site[s] of transaction for self promotion, flattery, or even discreet criticism,"[15] titles, dedications, prologues, and epilogues also construct multiple relationships, including those between writers and readers and between translating and translated writers. The prologues of *The Prison of Love* seek to establish and define such interpersonal relationships and also imagine the kinds of relationships each of the above-mentioned producers and receivers of texts will forge with the book presented.

Diego de San Pedro and *Cárcel de Amor*

From its first known appearance in print, in 1492, *Cárcel de Amor* was advertised as the product of readerly desires. The Spanish editions begin with the statement of the work's title, intended readership, and the name of the writer responsible for its composition: "El seguiente tractado fue hecho a pedimiento del señor don Diego Hernandes, alcaide de los donzeles, y de otros cavalleros cortesanos; llámase *Cárcel de amor*. Conpúsolo San Pedro" (The following work was written at the request of Don Diego de Hernández, master of the Light Cavalry, and of other gentlemen of the court; it is called *The Prison of Love*, and was composed by San Pedro) (3).[16] We can appreciate how the title itself begins to distribute author-functions. San Pedro appears as the "executive" and "declarative author," respectively defined as "the maker or *artifex* ... the deviser, the orderer, the wordsmith," and the individual "appearing in the public sphere as the work's creator ... shouldering the responsibilities and accepting the benefits from this."[17] The incipit of the first known edition of *Cárcel de Amor* presents San Pedro as the wordsmith accountable for the contents of the work, making clear what Chartier calls the author's "literary paternity" (fig. 1).[18] At the same time, this title also confers a kind of god-parentage upon the dedicatee, and the court itself.

The conventions of title page formats and the information they contained were developing at the time when *Cárcel de Amor* began to circulate in print. Some of the earliest editions are graced with cover pages containing only a woodcut image of the eponymous *cárcel* and the short form of the work's title, *Cárcel de Amor*, reproduced xylographically (fig. 2); others, such as the title page of a 1523 printing attributed to Jorge Coci's workshop in Zaragoza (fig. 3) contain the full text of the title.

San Pedro left ample evidence of his literary productivity. In addition to *Cárcel de Amor*, he authored another short romance about a doomed lover, *Arnalte y Lucenda*, an *ars amandi*, the *Sermón*, and some thirty poems, including the *Pasión trobada* and *Desprecio de la fortuna*. Despite this rich textual corpus, we have little information about the historical San Pedro's life. His extant works all date to the final decades of the fifteenth century, and, although he is known to have been alive in 1501, the dates of his birth and death are unknown. The dedications of his works suggest that San Pedro frequented the court of the Catholic Monarchs and was associated with two of the great aristocratic families

Figure 1. Title Page. *Cárcel de Amor*. Burgos: Fadrique de Basilea, 1496. London, British Library, IA.53247. © British Library Board.

El seguiente trac
cho apedimiēto del senc
diego herrnãdes:alcay de de
los donzeles y de otros caua
lleros cortefanos: llamafe car
cel de amor. Conpufo lo fan
Pedro.comiença el prologo
affi.

Muy virtuofo feñor.

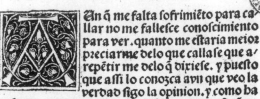

An ŷ me falta fofrimiēto para ca
llar no me fallefce conofcimiento
para ver.quanto me eftaria meior
preciarme delo que callafe que a
repetir me delo ŷ dixiefe. y puefto
que affi lo conozca avn que veo la
verdad figo la opinion.y como ba
go lo peor nunca quedo fin caftigo porque fi có ru
deza yerro có vergüeça pago. Uerdad es que enla
obra prefente no tengo tanto cargo pues me pufe
enella mas por necefidad de obedefcer ŷ có volun
tad de efcreuir.porŷ de vueftra merced me fue di
cho ŷ deuia hazer algüa obra del eftilo de vna ora
ció ŷ enbie ala feñora doña Marına Manuel por
El   ij

Figure 2. Incipit. *Cárcel de Amor*. Seville: Cuatro Compañeros Alemanes, 1492. Madrid, Biblioteca Nacional de España, INC 2134.

of his day, the Fernández de Córdoba and Téllez Girón. He is thought to have served Juan Téllez Girón, Count of Ureña, as a *letrado*, in some kind of secretarial capacity for twenty-nine years. It is possible that San Pedro was a *converso* or of *converso* origins. Due to the reference to a recent war in the opening lines of *Cárcel de Amor*, it is believed that San Pedro may have accompanied the Count of Ureña in the wars of Granada in the

¶ Carcel de amoz Compuesto poz
Diego de sant Pedro a pedimiéto del señoz
don Diego hernandez alcayde delos donze
les z de otros caualleros coztesanos: Nueua
mente hiztoziados y bien cozreydo.

Figure 3. Title Page. *Cárcel de Amor*. Zaragoza: Jorge Coci, 1523. London,
British Library, C.63.e.15. © British Library Board.

1480s. San Pedro's works, in particular the dedication of the *Desprecio de
la Fortuna*, the poem containing San Pedro's famous disavowal of *Cárcel
de Amor*, are the main sources used for constructing his biography and
the date of *Cárcel de Amor*'s composition.[19]

The title rubric naming composer and patrons is followed by San
Pedro's dedicatory letter, which explains the circumstances of the

work's composition in greater detail. The dedication, a highly self-reflexive missive, epitomizes authorial positioning in early modern literary culture. It resounds with authorial self-consciousness and merits quoting at length to demonstrate how San Pedro piled one conventional expression of modesty upon another, identifying multiple authemes and the dependence of the work presented upon a specific literary milieu where readers and writers actively collaborate:

Muy virtuoso señor: Aunque me falta sofrimiento para callar, no me fallesce conoscimiento para ver quánto me estaría mejor preciarme de lo que callase que arepentirme de lo que dixiese; y puesto que assí lo conozca, aunque veo la verdad, sigo la opinión; y como hago lo peor nunca quedo sin castigo, porque si con rudeza yerro, con vergüença pago. Verdad es que en la obra presente no tengo tanto cargo, pues me puse en ella más por necesidad de obedescer que con voluntad de escrevir. Porque de vuestra merced me fue dicho que devía hazer alguna obra del estilo de una oración que enbié a la señora doña Marina Manuel, porque le paresçía menos malo que el que puse en otro tractado que vido mío. Assí que por conplir su mandamiento pensé hazerla, haviendo por mejor errar en el dezir que en desobedecer; y tanbién acordé de endereçarla a vuestra merced porque la favorezca como señor y la emiende como discreto. (*Cárcel* 3)

[Most virtuous lord: Although I lack the forbearance to hold my tongue, I am not so ignorant that I cannot understand how much better it would be for me to take pride in what I had left unsaid rather than to repent for what I had. And, while I know this to be so, although I see the truth, I follow my own council; and since I am taking the worse course, I will never go unpunished. If my ignorance causes me to fail, I will pay with humiliation. Truly, I am not so much to blame for this present work, since I dedicated myself to it more out of the need to obey you than from my own desire to write. For it was said to me by your lordship that I should compose some work in the style of a sermon which I sent to the Lady Marina Manuel, since she deemed that style not as bad as the one I used in another romance of mine that she had seen. So, to carry out her bidding, I decided to write it, believing it better to err by my words than by my disobedience; I also resolved to dedicate it to your lordship, so you might favour it with your patronage, and correct it with your wisdom.]

San Pedro begins by voicing his expectation of evaluation and punishment, effectively presaging one of Foucault's definitions of author-function, as the naming of an individual to whom not only intellectual ownership can be attributed, but also blame and punishment for transgression.[20] Beyond San Pedro's topical articulation of the fear that making his writing public will have negative repercussions, the dedication also works to distance San Pedro from his authorial position, by claiming that although he has composed the work, he is not to blame ("no tengo tanto cargo en ello" [I am not so much to blame, for the present work]). He is blameless because he writes at the command of his patron, who in turn has communicated to San Pedro that doña Marina Manuel desires to read a new a text by him, one that will deliver the same kind of experience as his *oración*, the *Sermón*, which was "menos malo" (not as bad), in her opinion, as his *tratado*, *Arnalte y Lucenda*. Consequently, San Pedro alone should not be blamed for any displeasure or censure caused by *Cárcel de Amor*. Nevertheless, San Pedro does stake a decisive claim to the status of executive and declarative author when he writes of his prior work, the *tractado mío*, which is recognized as his own even if it did not please Marina Manuel. *Cárcel de Amor*, although it revisits many of the themes and situations of *Arnalte y Lucenda* – often considered as something of a rough draft for the later work – will do so more in the rhetorical style of the *Sermón* and as an exemplum of the arts of love preached therein put into practice. In *Cárcel de Amor*, the arts of love are thwarted by the politics of court life, which pit love against honour, leading Leriano to seek the only possible solution that accords with the laws of love, death. In situating and presenting *Cárcel de Amor* within the tissue of texts that he has authored and by putting his own *ars amandi* into narrative practice, San Pedro acts as an "*auctor* exercising his *auctoritas*," according to Joseph Chorpenning.[21] Nevertheless, while San Pedro is clearly asserting his position as an author and as a recognized authority on the arts of love, the dedication continually tempers any claims to *auctoritas* by continually reminding readers that San Pedro is not a long-dead and revered *auctor*, but a writer working within the confines and at the command of his courtly circle.

The dedication and title reveal that the romance is a socially authored product of a courtly network that comes into its audiences' hands as a mediated work rather than directly from Diego de San Pedro, as declarative author. Diego de Hernández (or Fernández) de Córdoba, a well-connected noble and hero of the wars against the Kingdom of Granada; Marina Manuel, lady-in-waiting to Queen Isabel and member of a similarly highly placed family; and the unnamed *otros caballeros* are all depicted as readers who know just what kind of book they desire from San Pedro, who is already well established as an author among them.[22] As collective patrons who desired something new from San Pedro's hand, don Diego and doña Marina are what Love defines as "precursory authors," individuals whose influence "makes a substantial contribution to the shape and substance of the work."[23] Moreover, San Pedro's joining Diego de Hernández and Marina Manuel as the *compadres* of his work is a political act. San Pedro's employers, the Téllez Girón family, were stout opponents of the crown and defenders of the rights of the aristocracy during the reigns of Enrique IV and Isabel I, who had also supported the claims to the Castilian throne of Isabel's rival, Juana de Castile. Although Juan Téllez Girón had served the Catholic Monarchs on the battlefield in the campaign to conquer Granada, his position, and by extension San Pedro's own, characterizes the political climate of shifting allegiances during a "delicate junction in [the] social and political hegemony" of the land-owning *grandes* of Castile.[24] Diego de Hernández, a hero rewarded by Isabel and Fernando for his performance in the wars of Granada, held an official position in their court, but had married into the Téllez Girón family. *Cárcel de Amor* was part of a campaign of ingratiation with the Catholic Monarchs on the part of San Pedro's patrons; the dedication proffers an amicable connection between the Téllez Grión and the court of their monarchal rivals to whom they owed allegiance.

San Pedro continues to position himself simultaneously as executive and obeisant author when he employs the *topos* of authorial doubt in the second half of his dedication, alleging the temerity and timidity of one who wishes to make his own words public, and reiterating his anticipation of censure:

> Comoquiera que primero que me determinase estuve en grandes dubdas; vista vuestra discreción, temía; mirada vuestra virtud, osava; en lo uno hallava el miedo y en lo otro buscava la seguridad; y en fin escogí lo más dañoso para mi vergüença y lo más provechoso para lo que devía. (*Cárcel* 3)

> [When I first decided (to comply with your request) I was beset by grave doubts; considering your refined taste, I feared, seeing your virtue, I dared; in the one I found fear, and in the other I encountered safety; and in the end, I chose the course most harmful to my reputation and most befitting my duty.]

Here, San Pedro's parallel figures of opposition, a signature of his style, highlight one of the key rhetorical strategies of the letter by once more shifting some of the responsibility for *Cárcel de Amor* onto the shoulders of his primary dedicatee. As he concludes the letter, San Pedro declares that he is risking his reputation by writing and begs that the work be appreciated more for the spirit in which it is offered to the reader than for its literary merits: "Suplico a vuestra merced, antes que condene mi falta juzgue mi voluntad, porque reciba el pago no segund mi razón mas segund mi deseo (I beg your lordship to judge my will rather than my shortcomings, so that I may be rewarded for my desire [to serve you] rather than for my talent) (*Cárcel* 4).

San Pedro's dedicatory letter takes recourse to many familiar commonplaces, such as statements of false modesty, authorial doubt, fear of censure, being urged to write by others, the need for the support of his dedicatee, and the shared responsibility of declarative and precursory authors. More than mere and empty *topoi*, however, the conventions reveal some of the central notions of authorship at the time that *Cárcel de Amor* was composed and began to circulate. San Pedro's dedication deftly shows how the writer, dedicatees, and other inscribed readers all participate in the repertoire of literary practices that shaped, first, *Cárcel de Amor*, and then the later manifestations of *The Prison of Love*, as courtly texts fitting for high-ranking and discerning audiences.

The paratexts, title, and dedication of *Cárcel de Amor* place San Pedro within a coterie where authorial functions are located at different points within a late fifteenth-century Castilian courtly network and construct the work as a courtly service rendered by San Pedro primarily to don Diego and other men, but also to Marina Manuel and perhaps, through her, to Queen Isabel. As Leonardo Funes points out, the relationship of literary and courtly service between San Pedro and his precursory authors and intended readers created by the dedication mirrors that between an enamoured courtly lover and his beloved.[25] Leriano's first letter to Laureola explaining his own hesitation to write echoes San Pedro's dedication: "antes que lo començase tove conmigo grand confusión; mi fe dezía que osase; tu grandeza que temiese; en lo uno hallava esperança y por lo otro desesperava" (Before I began to write I was in great confusion. My love bade me be bold; your high estate told me I should be fearful; in the one I found hope, in the other despair) (*Cárcel* 18). Like a lover spurred to great deeds by his lady, San Pedro claims that, inspired by honour and duty to the court, he overcame his trepidation in order to perform his literary feat. The triangular relationship between San Pedro, don Diego de Hernández along with the gentlemen of the court, and Marina Manuel in the dedication, also thus presages the literary relations between the characters of the *Auctor*, Leriano, and Laureola in the story that follows, where both Leriano and the *Auctor* take on challenges, the former driven by love and the latter by honourable duty. Indeed, the historical circle of readers and writers suggested by the paratexts finds its own parallel in the relationships formed among the inscribed authors in the romance.

We cannot know to what extent doña Marina, don Diego, and the court were pleased with the work they demanded of the compliant, courtly author portrayed by the dedication, but we can conjecture that it pleased many readers in and outside of their immediate sphere. The printed editions of *Cárcel de Amor* that quickly followed upon the first, between 1493 and 1546, all reproduce San Pedro's dedication advertising the work as a public gift bearing the noble imprimatur of don Diego, doña Marina, and the court of the Catholic Monarchs. San Pedro would soon disappear from the Italian, French, and English versions of *The Prison of Love*, as all but one of the translators lay claim to the positions of declarative and executive authors in his stead. And, as we shall see, Manfredi, d'Assy, and Berners also went on to appropriate San Pedro's well-turned expressions of authorial modesty. Their names, along with the names of their dedicatees, became those associated with the multiple authorial functions depicted in *The Prison of Love*'s paratexts as the romance travelled outside the Iberian Peninsula.

The *Auctor* and Inscribed Authorship

The speaking, pronominal "I" of the declarative author, directly associated with San Pedro in the dedication, smoothly transitions into the *Auctor*'s first-person narration of *Cárcel de Amor*'s opening allegorical vision: "Después de hecha la guerra del año pasado, viniendo a tener el invierno a mi pobre reposo, pasando una mañana ... vi salir a mi encuentro, por entre unos robledales do mi camino se hazía, un cavallero assí feroz de presencia como espantoso de vista, cubierto todo de cabello a manera de salvaje" (Last year's war ended, as I was travelling back to spend the winter in my humble home ... I saw a knight coming towards me, whose bearing was as ferocious as his visage was frightening, coming out of an oak grove. He was covered from head to toe with hair, like a savage) (*Cárcel* 4). Throughout the narrative, the *Auctor* witnesses, records, and narrates Leriano's passions and the chivalrous, bellicose deeds he performs – judicial combat and all-out war – to restore Laureola's honour. The *Auctor* is also Leriano's ambassador to the Macedonian court, where he learns the language and manners of the courtiers in order to insinuate himself into the princess's good graces and intercede for the lovesick hero.

The tasks set for the *Auctor* are to act as saviour, messenger, and interpreter: he must seek out the "remedy" for Leriano's suffering, relate to Laureola all that he has seen, and then report Laureola's reactions back to Leriano. Leriano appeals to the *Auctor*'s virtue and honour, reminding him that though there may be no reward or even gratitude for his intervention on behalf of the lovesick nobleman, "que mayor virtud es redemir los atribulados que sostener los prósperos" (It is a greater virtue to redeem those who suffer than to help those who prosper) (*Cárcel* 11). Later, in similar terms, the *Auctor* will remind Laureola that she, as the woman who has set Leriano aflame, has both the power and the obligation to remedy his suffering.

When he is first prevailed upon to aid Leriano, the *Auctor*'s words echo the claims of modesty so familiar from prologues of the day and the courtly service offered in San Pedro's own dedication:

> Mándasme, señor, que haga saber a Laureola quál te vi, para lo qual hallo grandes inconvenientes, porque un onbre de nación estraña ¿qué forma se podrá dar para negociación semejante? Y no solamente hay esta dubda, pero otras muchas: la rudeza de mi engenio, la diferencia de la lengua, la grandeza de Laureola, la graveza del negocio ... tanto me ha obligado amarte tu nobleza, que avría tu remedio por galardón de mis trabajos. (*Cárcel* 12)

> [You command me, sir, to make known to Laureola the state in which I found you, but in this I see great difficulties because I am a foreigner. What shape can such negotiations possibly take? And not only does this worry me, but also many other doubts: the dullness of my wit, the difference in language, the high rank of Laureola, the gravity of the undertaking ... your nobility has obliged me to love you so much, that I will accept your cure as a just reward for my labours.]

The *Auctor*'s pledge to Leriano attests to a bond of emotion and honour between the two men, for despite his fears and foreignness, he offers to serve Leriano with such loyalty that it will be "como si oviese seído tuyo después que nascí" (as if I had been your liegeman all my life) (*Cárcel* 12).

The *Auctor* proves to be an adept and something of a chameleon, as all courtiers and diplomats must be. He explains that he arrived at the court and studied the "trato y estilo de la gente cortesana" (bearing and style of the courtiers) and that he quickly became so well attuned to the culture and manners of the Macedonian court that "en poco tienpo yo fui tan estimado entrellos como si fuera de su natural nación, de forma que vine a noticia de las damas; y assí de poco en poco ove de ser conocido de Laureola" (in a short time I was held in such esteem among the courtiers that it was as if I was a native, and in this way I was noticed by the ladies and came to be known to Laureola), whom he entertains with tales of the "cosas maravillosas de España" (marvels of Spain) (*Cárcel* 13).

The *Auctor* soon becomes the go-between who ferries the secret correspondence between Leriano and Laureola. He interprets the letters, to which he has privileged access, and controls the manner and timing of their delivery. The *Auctor* also interprets the emotional states of the two protagonists, reporting Leriano's suffering to Laureola and, less successfully, attempting to divine Laureola's feelings, although he is not always completely trustworthy and indulges in what E. Michael Gerli terms "partisan editorializing."[26] At one point, the *Auctor* falsifies the cover on one of Leriano's letters so that Laureola accepts it despite her stated desire to receive nothing more from Leriano. At another, he decides to hold back one of Laureola's letters to Leriano, in order to protect the secrecy of the correspondence, but also to manipulate Leriano's reaction.

At times, the *Auctor*'s own feelings are the subject of his narration and he becomes not just Leriano's emissary, but yet another subject caught up in the turmoil caused by Leriano's unrequited desire: "Tanta confusión me ponían las cosas de Laureola, que quando pensava que más la entendía, menos sabía de su voluntad; quando tenía más esperança, me dava mayor desvío; quando estava seguro, me ponía mayores miedos ... En el recibir la carta me satisfizo; en el fin de su habla me desesperó" (Laureola's behaviour confused me so much that just when I thought I understood her best, I realized I knew nothing of her real feelings; when I held the greatest hopes, she withdrew her favour; when I was most sure, she gave me reason to fear greatly ... Her acceptance of the letter gave me satisfaction; the meaning of her words caused me to despair) (*Cárcel* 22). While the *Auctor* appears to have complete access to and understanding of Leriano's emotions, Laureola is harder to read, and he suffers the same kinds of hope and despair that might characterize a courtly lover. The *Auctor* also moves easily between Leriano's allegorical world and the court, and he is even able to muster up a brigade of allegorical personifications to accompany him when he returns to the Prison of Love bearing news of Laureola.

The *Auctor*'s first-person narration gestures back into the reality of his dedicatees at the very end of the romance:

> Lo que yo sentí y hize, ligero está de juzgar; los lloros que por él se hizieron son de tanta lástima que me parece crueldad escrivillos ... acordé de partirme. Por cierto con mejor voluntad caminara para la otra vida que para esta tierra; con sospiros caminé; con lágrimas partí; con gemidos hablé, y con tales pasatienpos llegué aquí a Peñafiel, donde quedo besando las manos de vuestra merced. (*Cárcel* 79)

> [It is easy to imagine all that I felt and did then; the lamentations they all made for [Leriano] were so piteous, that it seems to me it would be a cruelty to write them down ... His funeral honours were such as befitted his station. When they were completed, I decided to take my leave. Truly, I would have rather gone to my death than into this land; sighing, I walked; weeping, I took leave; moaning, I spoke; and so, with such diversions, I came here to Peñafiel, where I now stand before your worship to kiss your hands.]

It is generally assumed that the *vuestra merced* mentioned in the *Auctor*'s final words is a reference to the Count of Ureña, San Pedro's historical employer, whose lands included Peñafiel. Here, the *Auctor*'s role as envoy who carries the secret correspondence between Leriano and Laureola shifts and he becomes the messenger who delivers the entire work into the hands of his lord, and, from there, to its readers. This metafictive elision, noted by many scholars, highlights the play between fiction-making and historical reality in the relationships between *Cárcel de Amor*'s paratexts, narrative frame, and plot.[27] There is general critical consensus regarding the *Auctor*'s role as a "metafictional surrogate" for San Pedro.[28] The *Auctor* has also been read as functioning simultaneously as Leriano's alter ego, and as the only character "free to create his own role," bound neither by vassalage to the King, nor by lovesickness, nor by the strictures of honour, able to move between the "irreconcilable worlds of passionate love and honor."[29] An additional rhetorical effect of the *Auctor*'s framing narration is the binding together of the disparate units of the narrative.[30] Thus, the *Auctor*, in his clear relation to San Pedro as declarative author, performs the "primordial author-function," while the textual portrayal of the author-figure "reinforce[s]" the notion that the writing is an expression of individuality that gives authenticity to the work."[31]

The *Auctor*'s presence as a bridge between the extratextual world in which *Cárcel de Amor* circulated and the fictional world of Leriano and Laureola creates a sustained metafiction, clearly inviting the audience to lend attention to his roles as narrator, messenger, and protagonist. And yet, just as the paratexts distribute author-functions beyond San Pedro's declarative and executive authorship, so does the story inscribe other authemes. Other characters write letters and craft speeches, most notably Leriano and Laureola, but also Persio, the Cardinal, the Queen, and Leriano's own mother. Leriano and Laureola are the inscribed and implied authors of the epistolary sections, and the metafictive side of their roles in the romance is brought into high relief by the woodcuts featured in the 1493, 1496, and 1523 editions, which are the subject of chapter 6 of this book. Curiously, the *Auctor* himself is only once depicted in the act of writing, when he falsifies the cover of Leriano's letter. Rather, as we read, and when the work was read aloud, the *Auctor*'s first- and third-person narration is delivered when he speaks directly to the other characters and as if he were addressing the audience as well. The romance envisions social authorship within the limited circulation of scribal publication.

The image of social authorship in *Cárcel* is produced by the profoundly metafictive verbal and visual images of Leriano and Laureola engaged in collaboratively authoring the dialogue that is then carried to Peñafiel by the *Auctor*. Leriano and Laureola, along with Persio and all of the other rhetorically active protagonists, are also the *Auctor*'s precursory authors. The *Auctor*, in turn, is their "literary executor,"[32] who turns their letters, speeches, and actions into a narrative that will be delivered, with all due reverence to the *vuestra merced* of the *Auctor*'s colophon. In Love's terms the *Auctor* is a revisionary author, "a second writer or editor [who] remodels" and publishes the letters and discourses of the ill-fated lover, the honour-bound princess, the scheming jealous courtier, and all the rest, thus producing the romance.

The dedicatory missive and the representation of writers engaged in crafting epistles in *Cárcel de Amor* echoes, if somewhat bitterly, the "dulce comercio y pasatiempo por escriptura" (sweet exchange and pastime through writing) that Fernando de la Torre describes in his mid-fifteenth-century compilation of letters and poetry prepared for Leonor, countess of Foix.[33] Such *dulce comercio* refers to the exchange of vernacular letters in a style similar to the humanistic epistolary ideal, that is to say, letters more familiar and spontaneous than, but not entirely removed from, the formal Latin *ars dictaminis*.[34] Collections of such letters became a popular literary genre in the fifteenth century and contributed in no small part to the development of prose fiction and romance.[35] As Jeremy Lawrance asserts, the practice of crafting epistles in this familiar, yet lettered, style is an important index of humanism's reach into the vernacular in Castilian letters, for the correspondents of such letters were not professional humanists, but rather nobles who had received some rhetorical training, including women.[36] Julian Weiss further observes that Fernando de la Torres's anthology "presents literary composition as an emphatically social act, a means of establishing an extended network of friendships bound together by the love of letters."[37] In Petrarch's estimation, letters written in the familiar, but eloquent, style were capable of providing a "mirror of the writer's soul," and also a stand-in for the interlocutors' physical presence.[38] Humanistic epistles inscribe specific readers and writers, suggesting particular interpersonal relationships, yet simultaneously private and public, they were also composed as documents destined for distribution among wider readership and entertainment.

The vernacular epistolary genre first circulated through the coterie dynamics of scribal publication, but was also one of the vernacular genres to be printed in the incunable period, as the 1500 edition of Fernando de Pulgar's *Letras* shows.[39] Importantly for the continued appeal of *The Prison of Love*, the romance envisions a vernacular space for women's participation in humanist social cultural production, where at least one woman is portrayed as having a "rhetorical life," an educated and intelligent voice, capable of marshalling the available means of eloquence and persuasion, though her experience epistolary exchange is less than sweet.[40] The coterie of readers and writers imagined by the text expands to include the historical women and men who promoted its circulation. And, as the romance moved from one community of readers to another, the paratexts of the translators attribute precursory authorship to women outside the Castilian court and context.

A rotating cast of historical declarative, revisionary, and precursory authors would repeat these dynamics as the romance circulated from one set of readers to another in the first decades of the sixteenth century. In fact, "the Author" and his small circle of inscribed epistolary writers are the only constant author-figures in *The Prison of Love*'s European transmission. The translators, as revisionary and declarative authors, appropriated the metafictive elision that San Pedro first established in

Cárcel de Amor, and, in this way, they also share "primordial author-function" with the central, lettered, and ambassadorial protagonist.

Before turning from *Cárcel de Amor* to the translations, however, yet another historical author-figure intervenes in the majority of the early modern Spanish editions of the romance. From the 1496 edition, printed in Burgos by Fadrique de Basilea onwards, *Cárcel de Amor* was published with Nicolás Núñez's continuation. Núñez, of whom we know little apart from the *cancionero* poetry attributed to him and his *Tratado que hizo Nicolás Núñez sobre el que Sant Pedro compuso de Leriano y Laureola llamado Cárcel de amor* (The work which Nicolás Núñez wrote concerning that which San Pedro composed about Leriano and Laureola, called *Prison of Love*), describes himself as an attentive yet actively dissatisfied reader: "Leyendo un día el tratado del no menos virtuoso que discreto de Diego de San Pedro que fizo de *Cárcel de Amor* ... me parecía que lo dexava en aquello corto" (As I was one day reading the romance called *Prison of Love*, composed by the no less virtuous than wise Diego de San Pedro ... it seemed to me that he had left the story incomplete) (*Cárcel* 83).

Núñez provides us with a splendid example of a historical reader drawn into the dynamics of vernacular humanist fiction. The open and unresolved issues in *Cárcel de Amor* inspired him to respond actively to the romance by creating his own new text, which offers an imaginative correction that seeks to fill in the gaps left in San Pedro's narrative. What most rankled Núñez, and perhaps reflects the responses of other early readers, was the ambiguity of Laureola's feelings, and his central concern is to establish that Laureola did in fact love Leriano and now suffers deep remorse for causing his death. In this way, the *cumplimiento* simultaneously opens and closes the work to new readings, as some readers may have read the continuation as an invitation to imitate Núñez and concoct their own endings, while others may have approved of Núñez's interpretive closure. [41]

Núñez, whose dedication addresses unnamed "virtuous gentlemen" (perhaps meant to include the same *caballeros de la corte* mentioned in *Cárcel de Amor*'s title), is careful to preserve San Pedro's status as author and the important relation between the romance and its noble dedicatee, but also expressly faults San Pedro for not finishing the romance, leaving it "corto" (incomplete) because of his other duties. As if accepting San Pedro's request that the dedicatee correct whatever he found lacking, on Diego de Hernández's behalf, Núñez interposes himself as a declarative revisionary author. Núñez, reading a seamless union between San Pedro and the *Auctor*, explains that San Pedro must have been too busy to write the ending that the story required, in which he should have returned to the Macedonian court to report Leriano's death to Laureola and see if she felt any repentance for her mortal cruelty, which caused his death, and if perhaps she would bestow posthumously upon Leriano "algún galardón, pues en la vida se lo havía negado" (some favour, since she refused him any favour while he lived) (*Cárcel* 83).

Despite his pairing of the *Auctor* with San Pedro, Núñez readily takes up the *Auctor*'s first-person narration in his continuation, blending his authorial appropriation with a conventional bow to modesty and a resisting reading of Leriano's love-martyrdom: "acordé fazer este tratado (que para la publicación de mi falta fuera muy mejor no hazello), en el qual quise dezir: que desque el autor lo vido morir ... se fue por do Laureola estava y le contó la muerte del injustamente muerto" (I decided to write this continuation [although it would have been much better not to do so, for I hereby demonstrate my own inadequacies], in which I have attempted to relate how, after the author saw him die ... he went to Laureola and informed her of the death of he who did not deserve to die) (*Cárcel* 83).

In the first part of the continuation, the *Auctor* visits Laureola to announce the death of Leriano, accusing her, "A él hiziste morir, y a su madre porque no muere, y a mí que biviendo muero" (you made him die, his mother suffer because she does not die, and gave me a living death) (*Cárcel* 85). As in the main body of the text, the *Auctor*'s role is still that of an emotionally engaged messenger, loyal to Leriano and witness to events. However, Núñez then changes this role by concluding the continuation with a dream sequence in which Leriano appears before him "como si vivo" (as if alive) to absolve the *Auctor* of any guilt for having brought him the letter bearing Laureola's last rejection. Then, Laureola also appears in the dream to admit that she did in fact love Leriano and repent of her cruelty to both the *Auctor* and to Leriano's ghost. San Pedro's *Auctor*, who suffers "tanta confusión" (such great confusion), is at a loss to interpret Laureola's words and actions.

Núñez revises Laureola into a character who speaks and acts unambiguously; her words, as scripted by continuation, serve as an explanation of the attitudes that confused the *Auctor* in *Cárcel de Amor* and now leave no doubt about her feelings. The *Auctor*'s revisionary dream vision also brings Leriano and Laureola into direct contact, where they may speak together rather than correspond through a go-between.

But it is all a dream, and consequently, the depiction is all the more mediated by the *Auctor*'s interventions. Núñez appears to have desired a more prominent framing device for the central actions of the plot; the appended dream sequence neatly bookends the vision in *Cárcel de Amor*'s opening scenes, so that the allegory and the continuation oneirically frame the relative realism of the narrative. While the *Auctor* retains his identity and function as the narrator who shapes the story, in the dream sequence his role changes substantially. He has transformed back into his bewildered state when first he saw the Prison of Love, the narrator of a vision, and the inventor of events stemming from his imagination rather than an eyewitness reporter of the happenings at the Macedonian court.

Casting the dream vision as a prosimetrum, Núñez envisions both Leriano and Laureola as splendidly dressed figures to be read: Leriano's clothes are embroidered with eleven *letras* or short poems and Laureola's with nine. The *letras* echo words spoken in the text of *Cárcel de Amor* proper. Leriano's pointy-toed shoes, decorated with "unas letras en ellos muy menudas que dezían: 'Acabados son mis males / por servicio / de quien negó el beneficio'" (verses written in very small letters that said: "my suffering caused by serving one who withheld favour is now at an end") (*Cárcel* 92), which elaborate upon his dying words, "Acabados son mis males" (my suffering is now at an end) (79). Replicating the stance of the interested reader, only after Núñez's *Auctor* deciphers "lo que las letras dezían y la firmeza y pezar que señalavan" (what the verses meant and the steadfastness and pain that they expressed) (92) does Leriano begin to speak. The *letras* adorning his body, and later those on Laureola's, are a poetic retelling of the plot, an appropriative adaptation on Núñez's part, linking the protagonists to the world of courtly spectacle and to *cancionero* poetry. Moreover, Núñez concludes his continuation with the *Auctor*'s own poetic performance text, "tomé una viyuela y ... comencé a dezir esta canción y villancico" (I took up the vihuela and began to sing this song and carol) about the pains of love and the release from pain that death brings (103). His verses clearly recall the double entendre of "death" and "consolation" in fifteenth-century courtly poetry: "Comiénçate a consolar, / no muestres fuerça vencida, / que lo que mata la vida / con muerte se ha de sanar" (Take consolation, do not be defeated, for what kills life, is cured by death) (103). *Cárcel de Amor* not only inspired Núñez to compose a revisionist continuation, it also placed the work within the horizons of expectation of *cancionero* poetry. Such genre cross-polination can also be seen in the

Carcel

El lloro que hazia su madre de leriano crescia la pena a todos los que enella participauan. E como el siempre se acordasse de laureola:de lo que alli passaua tenia poca memoria: y viendo que le quedaua poco espacio para gozar de ver las dos cartas que della tenia no sabia que formase diesse con ellas. Quãdo pensaua rasgallas parescia le que ofenderia a laureola:en dexar perder razones ãto precio. Quando pensaua poner las en poder de algun su portemia que serian vistas de donde para quien las embio se esperaua peligro. Pues tomando de sus dudas lo mas seguro:hizo traer vna copa de agua: y hechas las cartas pedaços echo las enella. E acabado esto mando que le assentassen enla cama. y assentado beuio se las enel agua y assi quedo contenta su voluntad.E llegada ya la hora de su fin: puestos en mi los ojos dito. Acabados son mis males. y assi qdo su muerte en testimonio de su fe:lo que yo senti y hize ligero esta de juzgar. Los lloros que por el se hizieron son de tanta lastima que parece crueldad de escriuillos. Sus onrras fueron conformes a su merecimiento: las quales acabadas acorde de partir me. Por cierto cõ mejor voluntad caminara para la otra vida que para esta tierra:Con sospiros camine:cõ
lagrimas parti con gemidos hable:y
con tales passatiempos llegue
aqui a peña fiel.donde que
do besando
las manos de vuestra
merced.

¶ Aqui se Acaba el
Cercel de Amor.

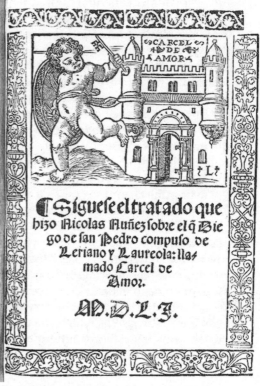

¶ Siguese el tratado que hizo Nicolas Nuñez sobre el q̃ Diego de san Pedro compuso de Leriano y Laureola: llamado Carcel de Amor.

AÑ.Ð.L.I.

Figure 4. Colophon and Title Page. *Cárcel de Amor.* Zaragoza, Esteban de Nájera, 1551. New York, Hispanic Society of America.

Cancionero musical de Palacio, which contains a *villancico* attributed to Juan Ponce, "La mi so la Laureola / la mi sola sola sola / yo el catiuo Leriano, / aunque mucho estoy ufano, / herido de aquella mano / qu'en el mundo es vna sola" (*La mi so la,* my only, lone, alone, Laureola. I, captive Leriano, for all that I strive, am wounded by the hand that is the only one in the world).[42] The integration of song in the romance and the romance in song represents another facet of humanist rhetoric in that the historical audiences of the romance found inspiration for their own writing in the text. Francisco Rico has suggested that some of the so-called sentimental romances of the period are at times little more than pretexts and vehicles for poetry.[43] Núñez does, in fact, present the dream vision as a narrative frame for his *letras, villancico,* and *canción.* However, the two formal genres are intimately linked, Núñez's poetry depends on the narrative and vice versa. As interpretive continuations, both are imitative hypertexts, spin-offs of *Cárcel de Amor.*

While Núñez's emendation became the constant companion to *Cárcel de Amor* in print, the structure of the books in which they appear together presents the two texts as separately authored and as two distinct works in dialogue. In the Spanish editions, the continuation follows the *Auctor'*s declaration at the very end of *Cárcel de Amor* that he has returned to Peñafiel to kiss the hands of his patron. The edition containing the first printing of the continuation gives no indication that Núñez's *tratado* is included on its title page or in the prologue, but appends the continuation in a new quire following the verso of the page containing the *Auctor'*s valediction. In later editions, the *cumplimiento* is advertised on title pages, and in the 1551 edition printed in Zaragoza by Esteban de Nájera, the continuation is even introduced by an illustrated title page that follows San Pedro's conclusion (fig. 4). Although Núñez's continuation would be printed in all of the sixteenth- and seventeenth-century Spanish editions of *Cárcel de Amor,* only one of the sixteenth-century translations would include the *cumplimiento.* And, as we shall see in chapter 3, Lord Berners's adaptation of the continuation is one of the signal instances of translational freedom that he takes in *The Castell of Love.*

Chapter Two

Translating Authorship

"Fame is for the inventors of the works, not for the *traduttori*."

Domenico da Prato

Translators' visibility or lack thereof has been central to translation studies in the wake of Lawrence Venuti's influential *The Translator's Invisibility* and *The Scandals of Translation*, which critique translation practices that render the cultural origins of a given translation and the very act of translation invisible, creating an "illusion of transparency." In this way, he argues, translations "domesticate" and reify the foreign, obscuring cultural difference in the interests of fluency.[1] While visibility, transparency, and domestication are, in my view, useful concepts for looking at early modern European vernacular translations, the visibility of the early modern translators for their contemporary audiences contrasts directly with the practice of modern literary history, just as the disappearance of Diego de San Pedro for *The Prison of Love*'s sixteenth-century readers is ignored in modern bibliographic cataloguing, which lists all versions under his name and authorship.[2] Fame, according to the paratexts of *The Prison of Love*, was for the translators and not for the inventor, whom the translators, with one early exception, did not regard as an *auctor*. At the time *The Prison of Love* began to circulate throughout Western Europe, some contemporary authors, such as Castiglione and Erasmus, were beginning to garner something akin to the status of the ancient *auctores*, as had the famed progenitors of vernacular eloquence, Dante, Petrarch, and Boccaccio. Although Diego de San Pedro was well known among his fellow members of the court of the Catholic Monarchs and was read and published in the Italian peninsula, such authority was not bestowed upon him by his translators, and he did not become "an author" in the Foucauldian sense of representing a mode of thought or discourse until *Cárcel de Amor* entered Hispanic Studies' academic canon in the late twentieth century.

The "asymmetries, inequities, relations of domination and dependence" between translated sources and translations are certainly at work in early modern translation, but they are constructed differently from the national, linguistic, and cultural divides that structure more recent translation theory.[3] Anthony Pym's concept of interculturality in translations breaks down the binary between domestication and foreignization in order to understand the horizontal dynamics between languages and between the translators who worked within networks "in a geometry that is neither culture-specific nor universalistic" in medieval and early modern Europe. Translation, he argues, "can thus be studied in terms of concrete transcultural networks instead of ideally specific cultures."[4] Pym's model is apt for considering *The Prison of Love*. The horizontality of the vernaculars through which it radiated, however, did not erase asymmetries of power. On the one hand, the transcultural network in which the romance travelled, along with a select group of other international fictions, contributed to the courtly elite's vision of its own cultural capital and power. On the other, the courtly networks in which *The Prison of Love* circulated were structured by rivalries and internecine conflicts, as well as by a shared love of humanist poetics.

The first translation of *Cárcel de Amor* appeared quickly upon the heels of the first known Spanish edition of 1492. *Lo càrcer d'amor* was printed in 1493 in Barcelona by Johan Rosenbach.[5] Although it was the first translation, *Lo càrcer d'amor* is the only one that does not have a long history of editions. To our knowledge, it was never reprinted during the sixteenth century. The title, however, tells a story about authorial attribution.

Vallmanya, like San Pedro, was a poet and also served as secretary to a member of the high nobility. *Lo càrcer d'amor* extends San Pedro's dedication, announcing that it was "Composta y hordenada per Diego de Sant Pedro a petició y pregàries de don Diego Ferrandis, Alcayt de los Donzeles, y altres cavallers de la cort del Rey d'Espanya nostre senyor. Traduït de lengua castellana en estil de valenciana prosa per Bernadí Vallmanya, Secretari del spectable Conte d'Oliva" (written and composed by Diego de San Pedro at the behest and request of don Diego Fernandez, Master of the Light Cavalry, and other knights of the court of our lord, the King of Spain. Translated from the Castilian language into prose in the Valencian style by Bernardí Vallmanya, Secretary to the honourable Count of Oliva) The reference to the Count of Oliva is to Serafín de Centelles y Urrea, a staunch supporter of Fernando the Catholic and patron to many writers, including Erasmus.[6] Vallmanya highlights Serafín de Centelles y Urrea's loyalty to the king while at the same time including the Count of Oliva in the courtly network that inspired the Castilian *Cárcel de Amor* by association.

Minervini observes that by the time Vallmanya's translation of *Cárcel de Amor* appeared in print, he had already begun to make a small name for himself in the literary world. Some verses and two other translations by Vallmanya have come down to us.[7] Vallmanya, as the translator responsible for bringing the romance, in his native tongue, into the count's hands, could hope to bolster his position within the count's literary and courtly circle.[8] Despite Vallmanya's recasting of the network in which the romance would travel in *estil de valenciana prosa*, the translation retains both San Pedro's name and dedicatory letter to Diego de Hernández, no doubt because the membership of the two circles, that of the courts of the Catholic Monarchs and Serafín de Centelles y Urrea's in Valencia, intersected. At least two printed editions of *Cárcel* were circulating by the time that *Lo càrcer d'amor* appeared in print bearing the name of a new patron as well as of the old.

We need go no further than the title page of the first edition of the Italian translation, printed in 1514, to see how attributions of authorial functions fluidly transferred from one figure to another: *"Carcer d'amore del magnifico messer Lelio de Manfredi"* (*Carcer d'amore* by the noble gentleman Lelio de Manfredi). While the Spanish origin of the texts and Manfredi's activities as translator are clearly stated in the dedication to Isabella d'Este and in some of the later titles, such as that of the 1521 edition published by Bernandino de Viana in Venice, *Carcer d'amore traduto dal magnifico Meser Lelio de Manfredi, Ferrarese*, Manfredi is publicized as the party responsible for the text readers held in hand.

Manfredi's role as author is reconfirmed in the 1515 edition by the woodcut in which a writer sits with a pensive mien in his book-lined study as an angel crowns him with laurels (fig. 5). The image of the author in his *studiolo*, a private refuge for contemplation, study, and communing with the muses, positions the composition of *Carcer d'amore* within an Italianate, humanist domestic space. Prior to its appearance in *Carcer d'amore*, the author portrait had represented Bernardo Accolti Aretino, one of the interlocutors featured in *The Book of the Courtier* (1528), known as "l'Unico Aretino" (the one and only Aretino).[9] The recycling of Aretino's portrait suggests on the one hand that the book

Figure 5. Title Page. *Carcer d'amore*. Venice: G. de Rusconibus, 1515. London, British Library, 12470.b.4. © British Library Board.

did not rate highly enough for the printer to commission a new cut *ex profeso*, but, on the other hand, the association of Manfredi with the celebrated wit also supports his bid for inclusion as author and client among intellectual circles of Isabella d'Este, as well as *Carcer*'s connections to the work of widely admired humanist authors.

As Roger Chartier observes, author portraits "reinforce the notion that the writing is the expression of an individuality that gives authenticity to the work."[10] The portrait in *Carcer d'amore* is directly associated with Manfredi's appearance as declarative author in the title and also visually inscribes the learned, humanistic readers to whom the work is addressed.[11] Manfredi's and the later translators' prologues, unlike Vallmanya's, do not include the circumstances of the romance's composition in Spanish, which were, as San Pedro explains, shaped by the reception of his previous works and status within the court as a writer. Joyce Boro observes in her study of Berners's translation methods that "such material was irrelevant to the French translator and to Berners, and so they do not follow it."[12] More than simply irrelevant, the inclusion of San Pedro would have interfered in the relationship between writer and dedicatee that each translator celebrated in his respective paratexts.

Lelio Manfredi (d. c. 1528), active at the courts of Ferrara and Mantua in the first decades of the sixteenth century, was an aspiring humanist and writer from a family that had once been quite powerful. Astorre III Manfredi was the Lord of Faenza from 1488 to 1501 and the Condottiero for the Republic of Florence. However, the family lost the lordship when Cesare Borgia deposed and imprisoned Astorre in the Castel Sant'Angelo in 1501 and had him killed in 1502. According to Libanori's *Ferrara d'oro imbrunito* (1674), Lelio Manfredi studied law and travelled extensively in Europe, learning many foreign languages in the process.[13] Manfredi is also remembered in Cassio da Narni's continuation of *Orlando Furioso, La morte del Danese* (1521), where he appears grouped with other writers who worked within Isabella d'Este's sphere:

> Lelio dui libri, uno per man, teneva
> da lui tradutti ne la lingua toscha:
> l'un *Carcer d'amore* chiamar faceva
> l'altro *Tirante*, ognun credo el conosca.
> Questo a Fedrico marchese leggeva
> che in lingua externa, prima obscura e foscha
> Visto l'havea, et per tal exercitio
> L'avea premiato di bon beneffitio.[14]

[Lelio translated the two books into Tuscan, one for each hand: one was called *Carcer d'amore*, the other *Tirant*, I believe everyone knows it. However, when at first Marchese Federico tried to read them, he found the original language obscure and murky. When he saw the result of Lelio's efforts, he richly rewarded him.]

In addition to translating *Cárcel de Amor* and *Tirant lo Blanch* into Italian, Manfredi composed several original and less successful works. Moreover, the Italian translation of Juan de Flores's *Grisel y Mirabella*, *L'historia de Aurelio et Isabella*, advertised in print as the work of one Lelio Aletiphilo, is generally attributed to Manfredi as well. The change of the female protagonist's name from Mirabella to Isabella is likely due to the desire on the part of the translator to please Isabella d'Este.[15]

Although Manfredi makes no mention of San Pedro, he translates parts of the dedication to *Cárcel de Amor* in order to repeat its expressions of conventional modesty, declaring that the exalted status of his dedicatee, Isabella d'Este, caused him to fear writing, but that his knowledge of her virtues gave him the courage to persevere:

E, benché io stessi in gran dubio prima ch'io me determinassi, perché, vedendo la sublimità e intelligenzia Sua, io timevo, mirando la prudenzia e virtute, io avevo ardire: in l'una trovavo il timore, ne l'altra cercavo la sicurezza. Infine ellessi il più dannoso per la mia vergogna e 'l più utile per il mio debito. (*Carcer d'amore* 170)

[Even though at first I had great doubts, when I considered your sublimity and intelligence I feared; yet thinking of your prudence and virtue, I took heart: in the former I had reason to fear, in the latter confidence. And so, I chose the course of action more hazardous to my reputation and the one more appropriate to duty.]

Manfredi goes on to lavish praise upon Isabella, whom he calls, among other accolades, a "living flame of virtue" (vivo lume de la virtute), "shining gem" (lucida gemma), and "home of the nine muses" (abitaculo de le nove muse) (*Carcer d'amore* 169). As Lucia Binotti points out in her work on the reception of Spanish romances in Italy in the first decades of the sixteenth century, Manfredi's preface enshrines Isabella d'Este as an inspiration to humanist scholarly and artistic endeavours and, by choosing her as dedicatee, he inscribed the work's intended courtly, humanistic readership.[16]

Manfredi also wrote a closing epistle to Isabella, with which he replaces the authorial valediction in *Cárcel de Amor*, where the identities of the *Auctor* and San Pedro fuse together and the story is presented by the narrator to his dedicatee in Peñafiel. Manfredi's epilogue carries the metafictive elision between narrator and historical author even further, stressing that the courtly service offered in the dedication of the book to Isabella should be understood as an extension and imitation of Leriano's service to Laureola: "Ebbe questo fine il sfrenato desire, la ostinata voglia e il fedele amore di Leriano, illustrissima ed excellentissima madona, in laude de la cui constanzia ne' futuri lustri restarà questo picciolo volume, per exempio de la mia servitude dicato a Vostra Excellenzia" (The unbridled desire, the stalwart will, and the loyal love of Leriano all came to this end, most illustrious and excellent Lady; may this small volume in praise of his constancy be proof for future generations of my service to Your Excellency) (*Carcer d'amore* 269).

By casting the romance as a celebration of a martyr to courtly love, Manfredi equates his own presentation of *Carcer d'amore* to the loyal love offered by the constant Leriano. He then proceeds to compare his cultural and courtly service to Isabella to that of a much more successful writer, Mario Equicola (1470–1525), the humanist, courtier, and diplomat of high standing in Mantua who served as her private tutor and later as tutor to her son Federico. Manfredi contrasts his "picciolo volume" (little book), *Carcer d'amore*, with the more important cultural work and humanistic studies that Isabella d'Este pursued with Mario Equicolo, "de le cui laudi meglio è chiuder le labra che non parlare a suffizienzia" (of whom I would rather remain silent than risk not praising sufficiently) (*Carcer d'amore* 269).

Equicola was also the author of two works that would ostensibly dialogue well with central themes in *The Prison of Love*. In 1501, as part of his own campaign to enter into Isabella's service, Equicola published a treatise in defence of women, *De mulieribus*, and later, a Latin treatise on the nature of love, the *De natura d'amore*, in 1525. Leriano's impassioned defence of women in the final chapters of *The Prison of Love* may have inspired Manfredi's own translation and presentation of *Carcer d'amore* to Isabella, as catalogues of famous women and works concerning the nature of women and their courtly roles were in demand at the time.[17] Consequently, the composition of such pro-feminine works had become an important element of humanist literary prestige.[18]

In Manfredi's final words to his dedicatee, Equicola appears as both rival for Isabella's patronage and as an intended reader. As tutor to Isabella, Equicola's role as cultural mediator was paramount, and Manfredi no doubt hoped his work would be pleasing to the courtier as well as to the noble patron. Manfredi also praises Equicola in the introduction to the translation of *Tirant lo Blanch*, dedicated to Federico Gonzaga, and also most effusively in a poem where he places Equicola on a par with Dante and Petrarch.[19] Manfredi's dedication echoes the triangular relationship between San Pedro, Diego de Hernandez, and Marina Manuel, and his epilogue makes the parallelism between the declarative author's courtly service and Leriano's desire to serve Laureola all the more patent.

The paratexts of *Carcer d'amore*, as well as correspondence between Isabella d'Este and Manfredi, offer further insights into the ways in which the networks of readers and translators functioned in the travels of *The Prison of Love*. Manfredi evidently desired to enter fully into the Gonzaga circle, and the translation and presentation of *Carcer d'amore* was part of a concerted effort on his part to gain patronage. In 1513, Manfredi wrote to Isabella concerning his translation of the Spanish romance and his desire to dedicate it to her.[20] Later that year, Isabella acknowledged the receipt of the translation in manuscript. She wrote that she judged "la traducione bella" (the translation good) and was sending Manfredi a small amount of money to help with the printing expenses. *Cárcel de Amor* was already known to Italian readers, and the inventory of Isabella d'Este's books indicates that she owned a copy in Spanish; as Stephen Kolsky argues, the translation of the popular romance was in keeping with her interest in rare and new cultural works, a more general interest in Spanish letters in the courts of Ferrara, Mantua, and Milan, and also an interest in the rivalry between Isabella and Lucrecia Borgia as patrons of culture.[21]

Moreover, in addition to rendering a service to Isabella, Manfredi no doubt bargained that her presence in the Italian paratexts would foster the wider circulation and acceptance of his work beyond the court at Mantua.[22] According to the letters, Manfredi ordered twelve luxury copies of the first edition of *Carcer d'amore* to be printed on vellum, but the copies were damaged. In lieu of the luxury presentation copy of *Carcer d'amore*, Manfredi sent Isabella an original work also dedicated to her, the *Palazzo di Lucullo*, a description of an ancient villa.[23] Once again, in this work Manfredi praises Equicola, "suo virtuoso et doctissimo preceptore al cui juditio e castighatione sempre mi rimetto volontieri" (Your talented and most learned tutor to whose opinion and teachings I always willingly submit).[24]

At least one of the vellum copies printed in Venice by Giorgio Rusconi in 1514 has survived.[25] The ink is smudged on some of the pages, marring what had been intended as an elegant presentation copy, and

Manfredi's printed dedication is preceded by three handwritten lines: "Ala segnora mia dolce diua: uita Per cui uiuo e senza cui ogne altra uita e morte. Viua felice. A." (To my Lady, sweet divinity, and life for whom I live and without whom any living would be death to me. May you live happily, A.) (1v). It is impossible to know with certainty if the handwritten lines are Manfredi's autograph and if the *dolce diva* is Isabella d'Este. The "A" may refer to Aletiphilo, Manfredi's presumed pseudonym, used in the Italian translation of *Grisel y Mirabella*.

Presentation copies on vellum and containing personalized inscriptions alter the nature of the "public gift" represented by a printed book dedicated to an illustrious reader. The gift, already made at once personal and public by the dedication, is brought back into a more circumscribed sphere of reception by the manuscript note declaring an even more intense courtly reverence for the intended female reader than the dedication itself. Ironically, Manfredi, who faced formidable competitors for Isabella's favour, and like Leriano in pursuit of Laureola's love, ultimately failed in his quest for social and financial advancement in the court of Isabella d'Este and her son Federico Gonzaga.

Shortly after the printing of *Carcer d'amore*, Manfredi also corresponded with Federico Gonzaga concerning his translation of another popular Spanish romance, *Tirant lo Blanch*, and of Ramon Llull's *Libre de l'orde de cavallería*.[26] Manfredi had less success with Federico than with his mother. Federico was not interested in the treatise on chivalry, and the Italian translation of *Tirant lo Blanch*, *Tirante il Bianco*, would not be printed until after Manfredi's death. *Carcer d'amore* was a success, but it never won him the level of patronage from the Gonzaga and d'Este families that Equicola had attained. The patronage system, as Kolsky remarks, did not reward Manfredi, and his work as a translator did not, in fact, offer him much opportunity for intellectual display. Manfredi also sought the patronage of Francis I of France, with, it seems, even less success.[27] Ten editions of *Carcer d'amore* were printed between 1514 and 1546, and the translation became the basis for future new translations. However, and not withstanding Cassio da Narni's assurance that Manfredi had received "bon beneffitio" from Federico Gonzaga, Manfredi died in relative obscurity and poverty. [28]

Manfredi's *Carcer d'amore* was the direct source for d'Assy's *La Prison d'Amours*. The dedication of the French translation adds ties of friendship between writers and a diplomatic context to the courtly networks and routes of circulation displayed by the titles and dedications of the Spanish, Catalan, and Italian versions of *The Prison of Love*. *La Prison*

d'amours laquelle traicte de l'amour de Lerian et Laureole faict en espagnol
puis translate en tusquan et naguere en langage françois, Ensemble plusieurs
choses singuliers a la louenge des dames (The Prison of Love, which tells
the story of the love of Leriano and Laureola, written in Spanish and
then translated into Tuscan and now into French, containing many singular things in praise of women) first appeared in print in 1525, but
it was probably composed and circulated in manuscript some years
earlier, during Francis I's successful Italian campaigns. D'Assy's translation was printed by the bookseller Galliot du Pré, who was known
for publishing well-designed books that would appeal to a range of
buyers, including nobles, merchants, and lawyers who passed by his
stalls in the Palais de Justice. Moreover, the title makes a clear bid for
female readership. The French translator is not named in the printed
editions, but his authorial presence is asserted by the dedication of
La Prison d'Amours to an unnamed "trés vertueuse et trés prudente
dame" (most virtuous and most prudent lady) as well as by an author
portrait following the dedication (fig. 6).

François d'Assy is somewhat less well documented than Lelio
Manfredi, but he was a member of the French nobility and served as
secretary to King Henri d'Albret of Navarre, Louise of Valentinois,
and Charlotte of Valentinois. François d'Assy also translated the
Il Pelegrino (1508), a romance written by Jacopo Caviceo and first
dedicated to Lucrezia Borgia, into French. The title page of d'Assy's
Dialogue très élégant intitulé le Peregrin, which was also dedicated, like
La Prison d'Amours, to an unnamed lady, announces that he was the
"Contreouleur des briz de la maryine en Bretagne, secretaire du roy
de Navarre et de treshalte et illustre dame Loyse duchesse de Valenti-
nois" (Administrator of the fleet of Bretagne, secretary to the King of
Navarre and to the most noble and illustrious lady, Louise Duchess of
Valentinois).[29] He also appears in the *Catalogue des actes de François Ier*
as the Seignior of Ervau in 1523.[30]

While Manfredi's paratexts and correspondence reveal how the translation of a courtly text was seen as a tool for entrance into a fashionable
and potentially lucrative cultural network, d'Assy's offers a vision of
how travel and alliances made between courtiers representing different courts could be parlayed into cultural capital and courtly service.
Giving *La Prison d'Amours* a linguistic genealogy, d'Assy writes that "ung
ferraroys mon bon et singulier amy" (my good and particular friend from
Ferrara) had translated the "petit livret" (little book) from Spanish into
Italian and had given him a copy when d'Assy accompanied Francis I to

Figure 6. Author Portrait. *La Prison d'Amours*. Paris: Galliot du Pré, 1526.
London, British Library, C.33.f.1. © British Library Board.

Lombardy.[31] This story of transmission is an indication of textual communities that formed irrespective of languages of origin.

D'Assy refers to Francis I's Italian campaigns in the War of the League of Cambrai, including the French victory at the battle of Marignano in 1515, which seems to have been the context for the friendship forged between Manfredi and d'Assy. At the time, the translation of an Italian and Spanish work into the language of the victorious French would have perhaps taken on the tones of a cultural appropriation. However, by the time that the romance began to circulate in print, the reference to the Italian wars would have taken on a wholly different tenor. The first edition of *La Prison d'Amours* appeared in April of 1525, several months after Francis's disastrous defeat at Pavia in February of the same year, when the king languished in Madrid as Charles V's prisoner. The translation was clearly popular: du Pré printed it three times in 1525 and 1526 – perhaps having underestimated demand – and then it appeared in four more editions printed in Paris and Lyon by 1533.

D'Assy, like San Pedro and Manfredi before him, speaks of the fear that his dedicatee's high status and discernment instil in him, a fear that is outweighed by her prudence and virtue, which give him the courage to translate and present the book to her, despite his claimed "dull wittedness" (espritz mattes) and lack of eloquence:

> Primer que en ce labeur cultiver me determinasse en grande dubiosité et diversité d'ymaginations me trouvay. Car voyant la sublimité et intelligence de ton esperit je craignoye et préméditant la prudence et vertue m'enhardissoye et prenoye vigueur très grande. En l'ung trouvoye la timuer et en l'autre sureté et hardyesse. (*La Prison d'Amours* n.p.)

> [When I first thought of setting to work I found myself in great doubt and divers imaginings. For seeing loftiness and intelligence of your spirit, I feared, and then thinking of your prudence and virtue, I was emboldened and became determined. In the one I found dread and the other assurance and strength.]

Importantly, d'Assy asserts, punning upon his own name, that the romance holds special appeal for women readers because it contains "d'assez belles matières ... pour les jeunne femmes" (most pleasing matters for young ladies) (*La Prison d'Amours*, n.p.) Manuscript copies of d'Assy's translation allow the unnamed "très vertuese dame" to be associated with two historical women readers. The version of *La Prison d'Amours* contained in MS NAF 7552 in the Bibliothèque nationale de France in Paris, a manuscript made at some point in the 1520s, contains a dedication miniature and an acrositic identifying the "très vertuese dame" as Jacquette de Lansac, widow of Alexandre de Saint-Gelais, chamberlain to Louis XII, and mother of one of Francis I's children.[32] This dedication has led scholars to believe that this manuscript is a kind of "first edition" of the romance in French.[33] Nevertheless, another manuscript of *La Prison d'Amours*, Bodmer CB 149, which dates from the same period, contains a dedication miniature of similar composition of that found in BnF MS NAF 7552, and bears the arms of Françoise d'Alançon, the wife of Charles de Bourbon, Duke of Vendôme (fig. 7).[34] The existence of two presentation copies suggests that d'Assy might have sought to maximize the potential benefits of his translation by naming multiple dedicatees. In any case, d'Assy's dedication not only praises the lady whose virtues gave him the strength to write in spite of his lack of skills and eloquence, but also serves as the bearer of the French translator's friendship with Manfredi. The presentation miniature in the Bodmer manuscript visually reinforces the metafictive elision between the character of the Author and the writer who presents the book to his patron, by iconographically identifying *l'Acteur* with the historical author who speaks in the dedication. The artist who painted the miniatures makes no visual distinctions between the kneeling writer presenting the book to the seated lady in fig. 7 and the frequent images of the character depicted in his labours as go-between that illustrate the romance. Chapter 7 will return to these French manuscripts, their decoration, and receptive dynamics in greater detail.

John Bourchier, Lord Berners (1466/7–1533), like d'Assy was a high-ranking courtier who translated and re-presented *The Prison of Love* to a new circle of readers. Berners served in the courts of both Henry VII and Henry VIII, travelled extensively in varied diplomatic missions, including as chamberlain to Princess Mary Tudor upon her marriage to Louis XII in 1514, and, in 1518, he accompanied Henry's ambassador to Spain in order to negotiate an alliance with Charles V. While in Spain, Berners composed detailed descriptions of the manners of the Spanish court for Henry VIII. Berners also served as Henry's Deputy of Calais and as Chancellor of the Exchequer.[35] William Dugdale's *The Baronage of England* describes Berners as "a person not a little eminent for his Learning," having translated Froissart's *Chronicles* at Henry's request and "likewise translated out of French, Spanish and Italian, several other Works, *viz.* the Life of Sir *Arthur*, an Armorican Knight; the famous Exploits of *Hugh* of *Bourdeaux*; *Marcus Aurelius*, and the *Castle of Love*."[36]

Berners was indeed a prolific translator. The works that Dugdale mentions, in addition to Froissart's *Chronicles* and *The Castle of Love*, are *Arthur of Lytell Brytane*, translated from the French *Artus de la Petite Bretagne*; *Huon of Burdeux*, translated from the French *Huon-de-Bordeaux*; and *The Golden Boke of Marcus Aurelius*, a translation of the French

Figure 7. Presentation miniature. *La Prison d'Amours*. Geneva-Cologny, Fondation Martin Bodmer, Ms. 149 f. 2r.

version of Antonio de Guevara's *Libro Aureo de Marco Aurelio*.[37] According to Dale Randall, "no other author is to be credited with a more impeccable example of the influence of English translations from the Spanish."[38] The translations of the *Chronicles* and the *Golden Boke* were Berners's most popular works. Two more works are attributed to Berners, the *Ite ad Vineam* and the *Ordinances for watch and ward of Calais*.[39]

Berners dedicated his translation of *The Prison of Love* to his niece, Lady Elizabeth Carew (d. 1542), lady-in-waiting to Catherine of Aragon and wife of Sir Nicholas Carew (d.1539), a diplomat and courtier who was at one time a close companion of Henry VIII and travelled to France and Italy in the king's service. The Carews were sympathizers of both Catherine of Aragon and her daughter Princess Mary, and Sir Nicholas was eventually accused of treason and executed.[40] *Cárcel de Amor* probably first came to the English court when Catherine arrived with her retinue in 1501 – in addition to the romance's popularity in Spain and circulation at her parents' court, one of Catherine's ladies was a close relative of Marina Manuel – and although Berners does not explain the moment or nature of his coming upon the text, he may have come across the romance in multiple versions thanks to his diplomatic work in Spain and France. It is likely that Berners composed his translation as early as the 1520s after his return from Calais, though *The Castell of Love* was not printed until the decade after his death. As Boro maintains, the humanist elements of the text – its focus on rhetoric, epistolarity, court behavior, and governance – would have been in keeping with the current literary tastes of the Henrican court.[41]

Like Manfredi and d'Assy before him, Berners conflates his own authorial pose of modesty with the nature of the book, calling it, in this instance, a "lyttle present treatyse." He too translated San Pedro's now familiar expression of doubt and fear turned into authorial confidence:

> For or I fyrste entred in to this rude laboure I was brought into great doubtfulnesse and found my selfe in dyvers ymagynacions. For seynge the quycke intellygence of your spyrit, I feared, and agayne the remembraunce of your vertue and prudence gave me audacyte. In the one I found feare, and in the other suertie and hardynesse. (92)

Berners, whose translation makes use of both the Spanish and French versions, adapts both San Pedro's and d'Assy's dedications in order to present the romance to his niece, and by extension the other ladies of the Henrican court. Amplifying d'Assy's assertion that the romance will be particularly pleasing to female readers, Berners affirms the refined nature of the text, for its subject is not only pleasing for "yonge ladyes," but also for gentlewomen. He also repeats San Pedro's desire that the work will be judged by his desire to serve rather than upon its literary merits and concludes with an expression of religious observation: "I desyre the Creatour … long to indure and to encrease your happy prosperite. Amen" (*The Castell of Love* 92).

Although there is no evidence that Berners knew *Carcer d'amore*, like Manfredi, he appends his own authorial valediction to the romance: "And thus I byyde fare well & adew to all true lovers and all ther readers and hearers of this proces, desyryng them where they find faulte to amend it. And I shall pray to God for their prosperyte, and at theyr ende to send them the joyes of paradyce" (187). Berners' authorial leave-taking indicates that he considered *The Prison of Love* to be a story about, and for, "true lovers." As we will see in the next chapter concerning translation methods, Berners's inclusion of Núñez's continuation further imposes this interpretive framing upon *The Prison of Love*. The inscription of lovers as readers also suggests that the translation may have been presented to Elizabeth to mark an important event, perhaps her marriage.

Authorial and Intercultural Agents

In contrast to the fluidity and openness of historical attributions of authemes, one author-figure remained constant in all of the versions of *The Prison of Love*, namely, the narrating character, "the Author." As noted previously, scholars have long seen the *Auctor* as a reflection of Diego de San Pedro's subjectivity as historical author. However, more than simply a figure for San Pedro and the other extratextual authors, the Author, not only by virtue of his role as a bearer of letters, but also as the bearer of the story of Leriano and Laureola to "vuestra merced," presents further affinities with *The Prison of Love*'s cosmopolitan readership. *El Auctor*, who would transform into *lo Auctor*, *l'auctore*, *l'acteur*, and *the Author*, is a foreigner who arrives at the court of Macedonia, learns the local vernacular, and insinuates himself into the inner circle of courtiers so that he is free to come and go as a messenger, address the Princess, King, and Queen directly, and organize the affairs of his patron Leriano in his absence. The Author is a literary avatar of an ambassador and of other courtiers involved in the "newest profession" of the era, professional diplomacy.[42] The romance's image of the Author as ambassador overlaps with that of the translator as an intercultural agent, "engaged in the transfer of cultural products across borders."[43] In his work as translator and transmitter of stories from the Macedonian court, the diegetic Author is not only a figure for San Pedro; in the translations he is also a metafictive twin for each successive historical author-translator.

Torquato Tasso's dialogue *Il Messaggiero* (c. 1580) well describes the image of the ideal ambassador that had emerged in the sixteenth century:

> È necessario che concorrano nobiltà de sangue, dignità e bellezza d'aspetto, modo da spender largamente e senza risparmio, e animo e deliberazione de farlo lietamente, esperienza de le corti e del mondo, cognizione de le cose di stato e de l'istorie e di quella parte de la filosofia almeno ch'appartiene a' costumi e al movimento de gli animi, fede e amor verso il suo prencipe, destrezza d'ingegno e accortezza e facondia e grazia nel spiegar i concetti, gravità e piacevolezza nel conversare, affabilità e cortesia nel favorire gli amici e conoscenti.[44]

> [It is necessary that nobility of blood, dignity, and pleasing looks, the habit of spending with largesse, without economizing, the will and resolution to do so lightly, experience of courts and the world, understanding of affairs of state and history, and at least the branch of philosophy that pertains to moving the emotions, confidence and love of his prince, skilful genius and shrewdness, and eloquence and grace in discussions and judgments, gravity and pleasantness in conversation, affability and courtesy in the cultivation of friends and acquaintances all combine in him.]

It is impossible to find all the qualities of the perfect ambassador in a single man, Tasso's interlocutors concede. The Author of *The Prison of Love*, nevertheless, demonstrates many of the traits of Tasso's perfect legate: he is noble, generous, and has ample knowledge of courtly behaviour and civilized conversation, which he uses to Leriano's advantage when he arrives as a foreign visitor to the court of Macedonia. He also appears to have the rhetorical skill that Tasso outlines, the ability to stir the emotions of his interlocutors, even though he is not always successful, and his persuasion of Laureola to write to Leriano has grievous consequences.

Furthermore, as *Il Messaggiero* explains, a diplomatic representative cannot simply carry and repeat the words his patron wishes to express and the replies he receives. The ambassador must be eloquent, and know how to shape and edit the messages he relays:

E se l'ambasciatore altro non fosse che semplice riportatore de le cose dette, non avrebbe bisogno né di prudenza né d'eloquenza, e ogni uomo ordinario sarebbe atto a quest'ufficio; ma noi veggiamo che i prencipi con diligente investigazione fanno scelta degli ambasciatori. Debbiamo dunque conchiuder ch'altro lor si convenga che portare e riportare semplicemente parole e ambasciate.[45]

[If the ambassador were nothing more than a simple reporter of things said, there would be no need for prudence nor eloquence, and any ordinary man would be apt for this office; yet as we see, princes select their ambassadors with great care. We must conclude, then, that more is required of an ambassador than simply carrying and reporting words and embassies.]

Diplomats, like the figure of the Author in *The Prison of Love* and each of the declarative author-figures compelled and inspired to write by their patrons, mediate and create texts at the instigation of others.

After remarking that oratory can be likened to cooking, Tasso proposes an analogy between legates and pimps, who both mediate, one between lovers and the other between princes: "Paragone non men convenevole di quello mi par si possa fare tra l'arte de l'ambasciatore e quella del ruffiano, percioché l'una e l'altra muove gli animi ... l'uno è congiungitore de gli amanti ne l'amore affettuoso, l'altro de principi ne l'amicizia" (It is no less fitting to make a comparison between the art of the ambassador and that of the pimp, for both move spirits ... the one brings lovers together in heartfelt love, the other [brings] princes together in friendship) (61).[46] The comparison and contrast is particularly apropos in the case of the Author of *The Prison of Love* who is first tasked with uniting Leriano with his beloved and then with negotiating a peace between Leriano and King Gaulo. In *The Prison of Love*, however, all attempts at diplomacy fail. Leriano never wins Laureola and he goes to war and triumphs against the King. On the other hand, the Author is successful as a bearer of the story of his own failure as go-between and legate, and he delivers the tale with appropriate reverence to his extratextual patron in Peñafiel (*Cárcel* 79). Timothy Hampton sees the ambassadorial role in diplomatic fictions as that of a "figure of suture," a "facilitator of contact," but at the same time "a marker of difference" between cultures.[47] The Author in *The Prison of Love* is a figure of suture in both the romance's diegesis, where he brings the story of Leriano and Laureola from afar to

Peñafiel; he also joins the story to its extradiegetic frame; and, as an author-figure who appears in all the translations, bestows upon the disparate versions of the romance a unified status as all representing a single work.

We know little about the historical San Pedro and Vallmanya, and relatively more about Manfredi, d'Assy, and Berners. What they all share, however, is their membership in the class of lettered courtiers, whose duties were likely to include their presence at diplomatic ceremonies and negotiations as well as delivery of missives and verbal messages. The *Autor* of San Pedro's earlier romance *Arnalte y Lucenda* establishes the connection between writing as courtly service and diplomatic journeys when he describes the vision he experiences while travelling, "más por ajena necesidad que por voluntad mía" (due more to another's need rather than out of my own will), echoing the historical author's dedication that he writes to the ladies of Queen Isabel, "más por ageno mando que por premia de voluntad mía" (due to another's orders rather than the satisfaction of my own will).[48] San Pedro and the translators were all courtiers who, like the Author, learned new languages and mores as they travelled among the princely courts of Europe and were conversant with the rules of etiquette. San Pedro, Vallmanya, and d'Assy served as secretaries to the upper nobility, and Berners was a member of the emerging diplomatic corps. They are prime examples of the "pluriemployed" men of letters whose livelihoods combined bureaucratic, political work with literary production, described by Ana Gómez-Bravo in the context of the Castilian court poet-bureaucrats of the late fifteenth century.[49] They are also akin to the French court poets known as the *rhétoriquers* as described by Paul Zumthor, whose "duties, however, cannot be readily classified because of the mobility and overlapping between the various functions of the administrators of the kingdoms and principalities of the fifteenth and sixteenth centuries,"[50] and to the aspiring men for whom writing and translation served as "pleas for advancement" and "advertisement[s] or reminders of their talents," in the court of Henry VIII described by Joyce Boro.[51] Their duties gave them access to the literary tastes and texts of the courts they visited, and the translators, as figures of suture and the creators of fictions, contributed to the creation of a cosmopolitan literary field.

The Prison of Love's mediated and metafictive nature was key to its adaptability and openness to multiple appropriations of authorship. The ubiquity of the metafictional author-figure – *el Auctor*, *lo Auctor*, *l'Auctore, l'Acteur,* and *the Author* – facilitated the translators' self-identification as authors of *The Prison of Love*. In this way, historical individuals and metafictional characters coexisted in the pages of the romance, which was continually recontextualized and rehistoricized by the conjunction.

Chapter Three

"Easie Languages":
The Free and Faithful Translation
of *The Prison of Love*

The courtiers and diplomats who translated *The Prison of Love* into their vernaculars, as we have seen, sought to be visible intercultural agents and authors working within social and diplomatic networks that promoted the romance as worthy of reading and translating. Prefaces, dedications, and other paratexts are the prime spaces where sixteenth-century translators reflect upon the nature of their work. Their paratexts also "package and present" translations as translations.[1] Yet, while Manfredi, d'Assy, and Berners have much to say about authorial roles in *The Prison of Love*'s diffusion and always introduce their versions of the romance as translations originating from a Spanish text, they are quite terse in their direct references as to how they went about translating from Spanish, Italian, and French into *nostra vernacula lingua, nostre vernacule et familiere langue francoise*, and *Englishe*. Vallmanya, as we have seen, makes fewer claims to recognition as an author than his successors, and he says nothing at all about his methods of translating from Castilian to the *estil de valenciana prosa* (Valencian prose style). Nevertheless, and despite their brevity, the translators' remarks about translation, when considered beside their practice and in the context of other early modern discussions of translation, are suggestive of an emerging discourse on vernacular translation. Translation both made possible and reflected the multilingual and supranational literary system in which *The Prison of Love* travelled. As Anne Coldiron observes, vernacular translation provided "something like Latinity's opposite number: a transnational discourse community, reading multiple, locally inflected versions of one work instead of reading the work in one (Latin) version."[2] Manfredi, d'Assy, and Berners all demonstrate how, by the first decades of the sixteenth century, vernacular writers were developing a language to express their tasks and a methodology they saw as fitting to the languages, genres, works, and authors they translated.

Moreover, each translator situated his translation within a new circle of readers and patrons, where *The Prison of Love* would be read in a new, local vernacular. According to Friedrich Schleiermacher's, and later Lawrence Venuti's, distinction between "foreignizing" translations that bring the reader to the text, and "domesticating" ones that bring the text to the reader, the sixteenth-century translators brought *The Prison of Love* to their readers, making much of their own authorial agency in the process.[3] In this light, however, it is important to note that the translators' acts of domestication did not necessarily involve great cultural distances, because the sending and receiving cultures were interrelated by family ties, political allegiances, and reading habits. *Cárcel de Amor*'s frame is geographically anchored in the Castilian territory of the Sierra Morena and Peñafiel, but the action of the plot takes place in a locale equally exotic and distant for Spanish, Italian, and French readers, and perhaps even more so for English audiences, in Macedonia. Similarly, the other romances of Spanish origins that circulated widely in the sixteenth century, *Amadis*, *Grisel y Mirabella*, and *Arnalte y Lucenda*, are also set in far-off and sometimes imaginary lands. Perhaps the clearest form of domestication in the multilingual and continental afterlives of Spanish romances is Nicolas de Herberay's "repatriation" of *Amadis de Gaula*. In his introduction, Herberay states that, since Amadis himself was a Gaul, the Spanish romance must be a translation from a now lost French original.[4]

The vast majority of medieval and Renaissance discussions of translation concern "vertical," rather than the "horizontal," translations that made the developing vernacular literature possible. When Erasmus, Juan Luis Vives, or Etienne Dolet, for example, write of translating well, their concern is for preserving the meaning and motives of ancient authors in languages, "non reduictes encores en art certain et repceu: comme est la Francoyse, l'Italienne, l'Hespaignole, celle d'Allemaigne, d'Angleterre, et aultres vulgaires" (without as yet an undoubted and rich canon. Examples are French, Italian, Spanish, German, English, and other common tongues).[5] Their theories of translation are as much about a perceived inheritance from ancient authority, distanced by time, culture, and geography, as they are about "a lingua in linguam verborum traductio sensu servato" (the changing of words from one language to another while preserving the meaning).[6] Vertical translation was the key technology for *translatio studii*. In addition to transferring knowledge, "down" from the heights of classical antiquity to the target culture's present day, vertical translation was seen as an activity that would enrich the target language, allowing vernaculars, as Joachim du Bellay asserted, to "copiously" and "faithfully" treat "all branches of learning."[7]

On the continuum between word-for-word interpretation, sense-for-sense rendering, and imitation, the rewriters of *The Prison of Love* all practise something very near to direct literalism in their treatments of the diegetic portions of the romance. Each translation of *The Prison of Love* does in fact contain amplifications, abbreviations, syntactic shifts, and misreadings, and the French and English versions also bear the marks of the translators' (or editors') interventions in form and structure.[8] Consequently, each translator can be said to have "taken liberties" with their source texts at particular junctures of the story. Notwithstanding these occasional lexical and interpretive liberties, comparisons of the Spanish, Italian, French, and English versions of *The Prison of Love* show that, in seeking transparency and equivalence, Vallmanya, Manfredi, D'Assy, and Berners worked like the often-maligned *fidus interpretes* described by Horace as one who strives to translate word for word: "Nec verbo verbum curabis reddere fidus interpretes" (Do not worry about rendering word for word, like the faithful translator).[9] Nevertheless, this faithful stance towards the text is counterbalanced by the translators' extreme freedom and high visibility in their paratexts.[10]

Then again, in their domesticating paratexts each translator imitates rather than translates his predecessors, freely borrowing ideas and phrases, but reshaping them, adding material as he sees fit, and erasing elements of the cultural and social specificity of his sources. And it is in this imitative mode that the translators discuss translation itself. In any case, "taking liberties" is a metaphor that only makes sense in a context of fixed intellectual ownership and authority, whereas ownership of *The Prison of Love* was, like the romance itself, open to interpretation. From the perspective of literary history and bibliographic convention, *The Prison of Love* belongs to Diego de San Pedro, the author of *Cárcel de Amor*. Nevertheless, his authorship disappeared with his language and Manfredi, d'Assy, and Berners all stepped into the gap left by San Pedro's absence, presenting themselves as revisionary *and* declarative authors. A contrastive blend of free appropriation and faithful interpretation best characterizes the methodology shared by the translators and revisionary authors of *The Prison of Love.*

Even though, as Karlheinz Stierle remarks, a shift from vertical to horizontal translative dynamics marks the transition from medieval to post-medieval cultural exchange,[11] horizontal translation between vernaculars received much less attention from sixteenth-century humanist writers than was given to the vertical axis. However, two frequently cited passages on the nature of translation do in fact contrast and compare vertical and horizontal translation. In the second part of his adventures, Don Quixote finds himself in a print shop, where he falls into conversation with a writer who has translated an Italian book, *Le Bagatele*, into Castilian. After the two discuss equivalences between Tuscan and Castilian vocabulary, trading Italian and Spanish words, Don Quixote levels the following critique at the translator's craft:

> Pero, con todo esto, me parece que el traducir de una lengua en otra, como no sea de las reinas de las lenguas, griega y latina, es como quien mira los tapices flamencos por el revés, que aunque se ven las figuras, son llenas de hilos que las escurecen, y no se ven con la lisura y tez de la haz; y el traducir de lenguas fáciles ni arguye ingenio ni elocución, como no le arguye el que traslada ni el que copia un papel de otro papel. Y no por esto quiero inferir que no sea loable este ejercicio del traducir; porque en otras cosas peores se podría ocupar el hombre y que menos provecho le trujesen.[12]

> [Mee thinkes, this translating from one language into another (except it be out of the Queenes of Tongues, Greeke and Latine) is just like looking upon the wrong side of Arras hangings; that although the Pictures bee seene, yet they are full of thred-ends that darken them, and they are not seene with the plainnesse and smoothnesse, as on the other side; and the translating out of easie languages, argues neither wit, nor elocution, no more then doth the coppying from out of one Paper into another: yet I inferr not from this, that translating is not a laudable exercise: for a man may bee far worse employed, and in things lesse profitable.][13]

Here, Don Quixote directly opposes vertical to horizontal translation. His, or Cervantes's, seventeenth-century dismissal of vernacular translation may well have been pronounced sardonically, in keeping with one of the dominant registers of Don Quixote's adventures, and as the comparison to "less profitable" activities certainly implies.[14] Yet, the observation about *lenguas fáciles* – the "easie languages" of Thomas Shelton's translation – implies that translating from one vernacular to another is little more than copying text. The languages are simple, easy, and moving between them requires little skill or erudition.[15] Indeed, the discussion preceding the famous dictum of reversing the tapestry suggests that vernacular romance languages are mutually transparent. What is more, the results of vernacular translation are sloppy and obvious; the work of the translator can be seen rather than the vibrant contents that one might see looking at the finished side of a tapestry. The image likens the vernacular translator to an artisan rather than to an artist.

Writing almost a century earlier than Cervantes, and roughly contemporary to the translators of *The Prison of Love*, Juan Boscán also distinguishes between translation from the languages of antiquity and from vernacular tongues in the introduction to his translation of *Il Cortegiano*, a work that shares many of the preoccupations of *The Prison of Love* and that travelled through many of the same networks. Unlike Cervantes, however, Boscán is sceptical about translating from Latin and Greek:

Todo esto me puso gana que los hombres de nuestra nación participasen de tan buen libro y que no dexasen de entendelle por falta de entender la lengua, y por eso quisiera traducille luego. Mas como estas cosas me movían a hacello, así otras muchas me detenían que no lo hiciese, y la más principal era una opinión que siempre tuve de parecerme vanidad baxa y de hombres de pocas letras andar romanzando libros; que aun para hacerse bien, vale poco, cuánto más haciéndose tan mal, que ya no hay cosa más lexos de lo que se traduce que lo que es traducido. Y así tocó muy bien uno que, hallando a Valerio Máximo en romance y andando revolviéndole un gran rato de hoja en hoja sin parar en nada, preguntado por otro qué hacía, respondió que buscaba a Valerio Máximo.

[All this made me wish that men of our nation could read such a good book without fear of misunderstanding it due to a lack of knowledge of the (Italian) language, and so I decided to translate it straight away. Yet although these ideas inspired me to do it, others held me back, principally the opinion I have always held that translating books into Castilian (*romanzar*) to be a presumptuous, vain activity for men of lttle learning, and I have even thought that doing it well is of little worth, seeing that most are done so badly that there is nothing so far from what is translated than its translation. As one man put it so well, when upon reading Valerius Maximus in Castilian, he began turning the page back and forth without ceasing, and when asked what he was doing, he responded, "I am looking for Valerius Maximus."][16]

Boscán's anecdote, a humanistic jibe at those who presume to know Latin and interpret the classics well, has the feel of an old chestnut. At the same time, it indicates the anxieties that a sixteenth-century translator might have experienced when submitting a translation from one of the "Queenes of Tongues" to learned readers and recalls Leonardo Bruni's condemnation of translation by the unlearned as a "scelus inexpiabile" (inexcusable act of wickedness).[17] The story is also a comment on visibility: Valerius Maximus, as *auctor*, has disappeared without a trace, leaving only the all-too-visible work of the bad translator. The reader wanted the translation to provide him with direct access to Valerius, while the translator's pages could only provide evidence of mediation and difference.

Following his anecdote of bad translation from Latin, Boscán turns to the comparatively risk-free endeavour of vernacular translation. At first, in his remarks upon the singular worth and benefit to readers of Castiglione's book, Boscán seems optimistic about the translatability of vernacular works. Using the verbs *romanzar* and *mudar* to indicate the distance between translating from the classical languages into Castilian, on the one hand, and translating between vernaculars, on the other, Boscán declares:

> Viendo yo esto y acordándome del mal que he dicho muchas veces de estos romancistas (aunque traducir este libro no es propriamente romanzalle, sino mudalle de una lengua vulgar en otra quizá tan buena), no se me levantaban los brazos a esta tradución. Por otra parte me parecía un encogimiento ruin no saber yo usar de libertad en este caso y dexar por estas consideraciones o escrúpulos de hacer tan buena obra a muchos, como es ponelles este libro de manera que le entiendan.

> [Considering all this and recalling my frequent criticism of *romancistas* (although translating this book cannot be called romancing [*romanzar*], but rather, transforming/changing one vernacular tongue into another, perhaps just as worthy, language), I could not spur myself to do this translation. But then it seemed to me an ignoble lack of spirit on my part, not to allow myself to translate it and so leave aside my hesitation and scruples concerning doing a good deed for many others by presenting this book in a way that they might understand it.][18]

The choice of the verb *mudar* (to transform, to change, to take on a new form or nature), derived from the Latin *mutare*, to characterize the process of translating between vernaculars suggests that Boscán understood his task as changing in appearance and shape, or remolding, Castiglione's words into a form recognizable to Castilian readers. "Mudalle de una lengua vulgar en otra" (change/transform it from one vernacular tongue to another) also implies a closeness between the source and the target languages; the substance of the book stays the same in the process. In Boscán's metaphor, the material has simply been given new form by the translator. European romance vernaculars are "easie" in relation to one another because of cognate relationships, shared roots, shared grammatical structures, as well as geographical and cultural coexistence.

When sixteenth-century translators speak of translating from one vernacular to another, at times they borrow commonplaces from Ciceronian, Horatian, and Hieronyan theoretical discussions of vertical translation, most frequently justifying or championing sense-for-sense, rather than word-for-word, translation. Boscán, for example, describes his method, taking recourse to the ubiquitous opposition. In contrast to his earlier remarks, it is at this point in his dedication that he acknowledges the potential difficulty of translating from Italian to Spanish:

> Yo no terné fin en la tradución de este libro a ser tan estrecho que me apri-ete a sacalle palabra por palabra; antes, si alguna cosa en él se ofreciere que en su lengua parezca bien y en la nuestra mal, no dexaré de mudarla o de callarla. Y aun con todo esto he miedo que según los términos de estas lenguas italiana y española y las costumbres de entrambas naciones son diferentes, no haya de quedar todavía algo que parezca menos bien en nuestro romance. Pero el sujeto del libro es tal, y su proceso tan bueno, que quien le leyere será muy delicado si entre tantas y tan buenas cosas no perdonare algunas pequeñas, compensando las unas con las otras.

> [It is not my goal in this translation to bind myself so tightly [to the original] that I went word-for-word, rather, if the text presents something that seems good in its language and bad in ours, I will not hesitate to transform or silence it. And even with all this I fear that because the vocabulary and customs of both nations are different, it may not come out well in our vernacular. But the subject of the book is such, and its style so good, that whoever reads it would have to be very fastidious if among so many and such excellent things he does not pardon a few small flaws, taking the former as compensation for the latter.][19]

Cervantes' "easie languages" and Boscán's *mudalle* indicate that for early modern translators, the relations between source and target were gauged by time, authority, and a hierarchy of languages that placed the regal, scriptural, and classical languages of *auctoritas* far above the vernaculars. The difficulty of vertical translation continued to be stressed by translators and theorists, but reverence for this hierarchy was to subside in the second half of the sixteenth century, as vernaculars continued to develop through the work of highly self-conscious writers and translators.[20] Further, their remarks on the "easie languages" and their mutual transparency seem to anticipate literalism as a method of translation and also gesture towards a general optimism about their mutual translatability, despite Don Quixote's stated displeasure with the resulting style of horizontal translations. Boscán's prologue is an early reflection on the ideology of translating between vernacular languages and without the distance of centuries. To translate Castiglione was to translate a close contemporary, but one whose work was arguably as beneficial to readers as those of the ancients.

The sixteenth-century translators of *The Prison of Love* worked in the absence of formal, literary categorization of their task, and in the knowledge that their translations would not form part of prescribed educational programs.[21] The products of their labour would be used for recreation and pleasure. As Lelio Manfredi says in his closing remarks to Isabella d'Este, quoted in the previous chapter, he hopes that she will turn to his *Carcer d'amore* when she is resting after her more worthy and taxing studies with her humanist tutor Mario Equicola. D'Assy and Berners also situate their translations within the realm of reading for pleasure, offering *La Prison d'Amours* and *The Castell of Love* as works containing "matters most pleasing to young ladies."

Manfredi dedicates few remarks to the process of translating in his otherwise verbose dedication to Isabella d'Este. At first, he simply says "ché, avendo cum non poca diligenzia e fatica ridutto questo picciol volume da lo externo idioma in nostra vernacula lingua ... l'ho dedicato, avendo forsi abiuto manco rispetto a la grossezza del mio ingegno e a la inezie de la lingua che a la altezza Sua" (I have, with unstinting diligence and labour, conducted/brought [*ridutto*] this little book from the foreign language into our vernacular tongue ... I've dedicated it, perhaps having failed to take the gracelessness of my wit and my inelegant tongue into account, to your highness) (*Carcer d'amore*, 169–70). Contrasting his labour in Isabella's service to the "little book" he offers her and his supposed lack of literary grace, the term Manfredi uses to describe the kind of labour he has performed in translating is *ridurre*.[22] According to Alberto Acharisio da Cento's *Vocabolario* (1543), *ridurre* is a synonym for *conducere*.[23] Moreover, although *ridurre* derives from the Latin *reducere*, it may have recalled one of the widely used Latin terms for translating, *reddere*, to the ears of early sixteenth-century audiences.[24] Like romance derivations of the Latin *translatio*, the Italian *ridurre* is transitive, indicating that the translator takes something other than his pen in hand when he translates, and that something – the translated work – retains its essence once it has been carried or led from one place to another by the translator.

This conception of the unchanged substance of the translated matter is repeated when Manfredi compares his offering to Isabella to crystalline water carried in the hands of a poor rustic: "Supplico, adunque, a quella che si degni cum ilare volto e benigno animo, di acceptarlo, ricordandogli che già Arthaxerse famossimo Re de' Persi non ebbe a sdegno di gustar le cristalline linfe da un povero e rozo agricultore, cum sincero animo, fra le callose mani, dal translucido fonte tolte" (I beg therefore that in regard to anything one might deem worthy, that one ought to accept it, with a smiling face and a good heart, bearing in mind that Artaxerses the renowned King of the Persians did not disdain to enjoy sincerely the crystalline water drawn from a nymph's lucid fountain even though it came from the calloused hands of a poor, rough farmer).[25] The story serves as an image of translation – and of language itself – the crystalline water signifying the meaning (*res*) transferred intact between languages and Manfredi's words (*verba*), the rough, graceless containers. At the same time, it serves to elevate Manfredi's *matière*. As Maria Tymozco observes, the dominant metaphors of translation in the European tradition of carrying and leading "suggest there should be full semantic transfer between source text and target texts and that protocols for achieving such results are possible." Such metaphors, as Tymozco argues, contribute to a literalistic conception of translation.[26]

The dedicatory epistles prefacing the two other translations from Iberian languages attributed to Manfredi, *Aurelio et Isabella* and *Tirante il Bianco*, contain more extensive meditations on the task of translating from one vernacular to another. In both cases, the inscribed readership is male rather than female, and, in the case of *Tirante*, the subject matter is more elevated than that of the "little volume" dedicated to Isabella d'Este.

In his dedication of *Aurelio et Isabella* to Luigi Scipione Atellano, Manfredi, writing under the pseudonym Lelio Aletiphilo, explains that he has translated this "little work" (operetta) faithfully (fidelmente) from Spanish into Italian. Moreover, "in questa traduttione ho io seguito il comandamento del dottissimo Poeta Horatio, dato a quelli che le cose gre-che fanno latine: quali non curando a ogni parola rendere la simile parola, il piu delle volte le sententie alle sententie rendeno" (I have followed the commandment of the most erudite poet Horace in this translation, given to those who translate Greek matters into Latin: [they should] not do so by trying to render each word with a similar word, but, most of the time, by rendering each meaning with a similar meaning).[27]

Manfredi also points to the difficulty of translating from Spanish to Italian, while acknowledging the stylistic potential of Spanish: "Et ver-amente molto malageuole e una bona cosa spagnuola far buona Italica: et altre si di buona Italica far la buona spagnuola. Et chi non sa che ogni lingua ha le sue propietadi a se cosi proprie, che in altro idioma tradu-tte, cangiano la polidezza et la gratia" (It is truly difficult to turn a good thing in Spanish into good Italian: and also from good Italian to good Spanish. And who does not know that each language has its own fitting manners of expression, so when it is translated into another language, its beauty and grace change).[28] Manfredi, however, explains that the lack of direct equivalence between Spanish and Italian does not pose a problem for faithful translation, assuring his reader that "dalla mente del primo iscrittore mai non ho levata la penna" (My pen has never wavered from the intentions of the first writer), except to correct errors in the printed edition he worked from and to change the "barbarous" names of the protagonists.[29]

The preface to Manfredi's *Tirante il Bianco* reflects the need and occa-sional difficulty of finding the most suitable Italian manner of express-ing the words and meaning of the Catalan source text:

E se vi è mancamento alcuno (come gli è certo) ne è causa in parte de la Barbara lingua, della quale in ogni luogo è imposibile de esprimere bene gli vocaboli: havendo rispetto, non alla grossezza di tale orginatione, ne alla differentia delle sententie, ma alla affettione & al desiderio, ch'io ho continuamente di servire la sublimità vostra.

[And if there be some weakness (as I am sure there is) it is caused by the Barbarous language, from which it is impossible to express words well in every instance: I have respected neither the clumsiness of its [word] order, nor the difference of sense, but rather my strong drive and unceas-ing desire to serve your highness.][30]

While Manfredi characterized both *Carcer d'amore* and *Aurelio et Isabella* as small, or minor, works, *Tirante il Bianco valorosissimo caualiere, nelquale contiensi del principio della caualleria del stato and vfficio suo*, in contrast, is an extensive chivalric romance. By amplifying the main title, which appears on the frontispiece, as well as his chapter titles, Manfredi frames *Tirante il Bianco* as a treatise on chivalry, promising readers that the romance is as much about knighthood as it is about the adventures of Guy of Warwick and Tirant. Manfredi's dedication to Federico Gonzaga likens the story to those "fatti di degni d'eterna memoria" (deeds worthy of eternal memory), as if to place his translation of *Tirant lo blanch* on par with epics and romances of antiquity and stresses the importance of such a work about the heroes and rulers of the past for a contemporary man in power. Here, although the source language is somewhat barbarous, the *matière* is elevated above those of the "little" books, *Carcer d'amore* and *Aurelio et Isabella*.

Manfredi, like Boscán, seems to be searching for ways of describing what Eugene Nida calls "dynamic equivalence," an accurate, fluent translation that will elicit the same response to the text experienced by the translator himself, and which will cause a reader with knowledge of both the source and target languages to say, "that is just the way we would say it."[31] In fact, when Garcilaso praised Boscán as a "muy fiel tradutor" (very faithful translator) in his introduction to the translation of *Il Cortegiano*, he remarked that *El cortesano* did not seem to be a translation at all, "no me parece que le haya escrito en otra lengua" (it does not seem to me to have been written in another language).[32]

Thus, while his translations are for the most part "bound tightly" to the Iberian texts, when Manfredi deems it necessary he looks to the most fitting expressions in the target language and creatively or linguistically domesticates his source. In *Aurelio et Isabella*, Manfredi changes names and in *Tirante il Bianco* he embeds an interpretation of genre into the presentation of the romance. Manfredi's comments on the work of translation also reflect a clear Italian chauvinism, despite the contemporary vogue in Italy for the romances and *cancionero* poetry, suggesting that at times "horizontal" translation may have skewed diagonally. In Manfredi's case, the move from Spanish to Italian was a move upwards, the target language being perceived as superior to the source.

Indini and Panunzio describe Manfredi's method of translating as following the criterion of "massima fedeltà, al limite de la 'letteralità' esente da libertà inventiva, con rari e modesti interventi di carattere esornativo" (utmost fidelity, almost to the point of literalness, free from inventive liberties, containing few and modest ornamental interventions).[33] Manfredi's most frequent "interventions" are amplifications, which, in addition to ornament, at times provide contextual information for Italian readers. For example, Manfredi clarifies the reference in *Cárcel de Amor* to the *Sierra Morena* by adding "la montagna chimata la Sierra Morena" (the mountain called the Sierra Morena), an embedded explanation that would be translated by both d'Assy and Berners as well. Other amplifications often result in doublets: where *Cárcel* envisions Desire as "cobierto todo de cabello," *Carcer d'amore* presents him "coperto tutto di capelli e peli" (covered completely by hair and fur), or when Leriano complains to Laureola of "mis males" in *Cárcel*, in *Carcer d'amore* he laments "li miei mali e fatiche" (my pains and labours).[34] Until the very end of the romance, Manfredi's near word-for-word rendering clearly dominates over his amplifications and occasional syntactical abbreviations, and the handful of misreadings of the Spanish text.[35]

The greatest change Manfredi makes to his source, *Cárcel de Amor*, occurs in his paratexts, where, as we have seen, he not only requests recognition and credit, but also creates a direct relationship between his own service to Isabella and Leriano's service to Laureola. Manfredi's reframing of the romance and insertion of himself into the authorial role required the omission of Diego de San Pedro's valediction, "con lágrimas partí" (weeping, I took leave). The return to *vuestra merced* in Peñafiel is a return to the frame narrative in which San Pedro described the genesis of his tale. Manfredi concludes the narration of *Carcer d'amore* with "La funebre pompa e li onori suoi al merito suo furno conformi" (The funereal commemoration and his honours were such as befitted his station), and then appends his own metafictive valediction, "Ebbe questo fine il sfrenato desire, la ostinata voglia e il fedele amore di Leriano" (And so ended the unbridled desire, the tenacious will, and the faithful love of Leriano), quoted above (*Carcer d'amore*, 269).

This is Lelio Manfredi's most material act of domestication of *Cárcel de Amor*. The two other references to the "Spanishness" of the source text are retained in the Italian version: the Author regales Laureola with tales of "Le cose maravigliose di Spagna" and Leriano's catalogue of famous women lists the same ladies of "la castigliana nazione" as *Cárcel de Amor* – María Coronel, Isabel Téllez Girón, and Mari Gracia – when he turns to modern examples. Given Manfredi's dedication to Isabella d'Este, the catalogue of famous women would seem to have been an excellent opportunity for further locally specific changes to the romance and further praise for Isabella herself and her contemporaries. These "Spanish" details in fact are conserved in all of the translations and consequently the specificity of the romance's fifteenth-century Castilian origins is maintained. Manfredi is a faithful interpreter here as elsewhere in the text and only strays from the path of literal translation in his paratexts and at the very end of the tale.

The Italian *Carcer d'amore* was the source for d'Assy's translation, *La Prison d'Amours* (c1520), and d'Assy, like Manfredi, pursues a course of near-literalism combined with particular acts of amplification, adaptation, and domestication. D'Assy refers to Manfredi's production of *Carcer d'amore* as an act of "conversion," once again recalling Boscán's verb "mudar," and perhaps echoing the Latin *vertere*, with its wealth of associations, while also suggesting that translation is a movement of turning rather than carrying, when he says that his *petit livret* was "jadis conterti de langue castillanne i espaignolle en tusquan florentin" (already converted from the Castilian and Spanish language into Tuscan Florentine). D'Assy then returns to the image of translation as carrying over, when he uses the verbs *metre* and *translater* to describe his own process: "j'ay entreprins mettre et translater du dit ytalien en nostre vernacule et familiere langue françoise et le te dédier" (I undertook to put and translate [this little book] from the said Italian into our vernacular and familiar French language).[36] D'Assy uses the same terms to present his translation of Caviceo's *Peregrino* into French, dedicated to an unnamed *tresmagnanime dame*: "a pleu a vostre excellence me faire de translater ce petit oeuvre intitulé le Pèlegrin et de le convertir de langage et ydiomat italique en nostre vernacule et familière langue françoyse" (It has pleased your excellence to bid me translate this little work titled *le Pèlegrin* and to convert it from the Italian language and dialect into our vernacular and familiar French language).[37] D'Assy's references to the "familiar vernacular" would seem to imply both domestication and the production of a text that would be easy to read.

In the prologue to the *Pèlegrin*, d'Assy also makes an intriguing reference to the importance of literalism and the lack of easy transfer between languages: "Bien certain suis que aucuns me vouldront imputer n'avoir ensuy de point en point l'italique translation. Ce que j'ay faict pour esclarcit aucunes scabreuses et difficiles sentences en accomplissant ce quil vous a pleu de grâce me commander" (I am quite certain that some may wish to accuse me of not having followed the Italian translation point by point. All that I have done [is] to clarify some maladroit and difficult sentences/meanings in the completion of the task that it pleased you to ask of me). Here, d'Assy anticipates censure for not having produced a verbatim translation of his source, suggesting that readers desired the sensation of reading an exact copy of the original, necessitating the translator to be invisible in the translated text.

The textual transmission of *La Prison*, however, is complicated by its simultaneous circulation in print and manuscript. The printed editions and the manuscripts present significant variations in precisely those points that the romance is repackaged and domesticated for its new intended readers. In the six print editions – a clear indication of *La Prison*'s success among French audiences – some or all of the letters exchanged between the protagonists are versified in rhymed couplets.[38] Of the eleven extant manuscript copies, which also date from the 1520s, four contain versified letters, and only five of the manuscripts contain d'Assy's dedication. As Irene Finotti concludes in her collation of thirteen of the manuscript and print witnesses, "après de l'effort initial de traduction du toscan au français par François d'Assy, à un certain point de la transmission une main expérimentée a 'traduit' de prose en rime toutes les épîtres du roman. Ni la source espagnole, ni le texte italien n'avaient osé une telle opération" (Following François d'Assy's initial work of translation from Tuscan to French, at some point of the work's transmission, an experienced hand 'translated' the romance's epistles from prose to verse. Neither the Spanish source nor the Italian text had ventured to do so).[39] The adaptation to verse, much like Manfredi and d'Assy's prose translations, achieves a near word-for-word rendition of the prose letters, using amplification and adjectival doubling in order to create its rhyme scheme. D'Assy himself may have desired to revise his translation by versifying the letters, or, as is more likely, someone else active in du Pré's workshop reworked the letters into rhymed couplets, turning *La Prison* into a prosimetrum in order to add to the book's appeal. These verses, to which I will return in chapter 7 in the context of the French manuscripts, add to the courtly register of the romance by imitating the *épîtres* of the French *rhétoriquers*, and also by recalling Francis I's own verse letters.

Lord Berners faced a different task from Manfredi and d'Assy, who were working between romance languages, and we might expect him to be more forthcoming about his task. Berners's dedication is an adaptation and imitation of d'Assy's. Like Diego de San Pedro, Manfredi, and d'Assy before him, he writes to please a lady, aligning the act of translation with satisfying readerly desire and courtly service, "[it] hathe

pleased me to acomplyshe your desyre as in translatynge this present
boke." With regard to the act of translating from romance to English,
he says "I have enterprised to translate [the presente boke] out of Spanyshe into Englyshe," though in fact he used both French and Spanish source texts for *The Castell of Love*. Berners's description of the act
of translation, for all its brevity, conceptualizes movement of the work
from one container to another, much like that of his predecessors, signalling literalism as a modus operandi. When Berners translates San
Pedro's and d'Assy's expression of hesitation and inspiration he amplifies d'Assy's initial amplification, remarking that, "For or I fyrste entred
in to this *rude laboure* I was brought into great doubtfulnesse and found
my selfe in dyvers ymagynacions" (*The Castell of Love* 91–2, emphasis
added).[40] D'Assy had introduced the word and concept of *labeur* into
San Pedro's trope of authorial modesty, which had come to him via
Manfredi's translation. Berners qualifies the labour as "rude" and, once
more, like his predecessors, begs his reader to overlook the lack of grace
and elegance in his words. The supposed inelegance of the results of
Berners's translating labour would find an echo in Don Quixote's later
assessment of horizontal translation.

In the prologues to his translations of Froissart's *Chroniques* and
Guevara's *Libro aureo*, Berners takes recourse to the Horatian distinction between word-for-word and sense-for-sense translations, and, in
contradistinction to his presentation of *The Castell of Love*, makes reference to the authors of his sources. For example, in the first volume
of the *Chronicles*, Berners asks "all the reders and herers therof to take
this my rude translacion in gre. And in that I haue nat folowed myne
authour worde by worde: yet I trust I haue ensewed the true reporte of
the sentence of the mater ... I trust I haue nat swarued fro the true sentence of the mater."[41] In *The Golden Boke of Marcus Aurelius Emperour and
eloquent oratour*, Berners takes care to distinguish the distance between
the author and the translator: "I thynke that every wyse man, after he
hathe redde this boke, wyll not saye that I am the principal auctour of
this warke, nor yet to juge me so ignorant to exclude me clene from
it, for so hygh sentences are not found at this presente tyme, nor to so
hygh a style they of tyme past neuer atteyned."[42]

The *Chronicles* and *The Golden Boke* both belong to more elevated genres than *The Castell of Love* and were destined for a similarly elevated
readership.[43] Berners's prologues also stress the utility of these works,
which serve, especially in the case of *The Golden Boke*, as links between
the present and a glorious, enlightened past. The same holds true for

Berners's presentation of the other romance that he translated, *Arthur of Brytayn*, which he offers to readers as a remedy for idleness.[44] Berners does not present *The Castell of Love*, translated for the pleasure of Elizabeth Carew, as a work that will be morally beneficial or didactic, or as a work containing valiant deeds worthy of memory. However, and as we will see in chapter 5, when Andrew Spigurnell edited *The Castell of Love* for a new readership in the early 1550s, he reframed the romance as both morally and rhetorically instructive.

Berners combined readings from *Cárcel de Amor* and *La Prison d'Amours*, resulting in sentences featuring amplifications in the form of frequent doublets, often directly translated from the French, blended with direct translations from the Spanish.[45] He is simultaneously faithful to both the Spanish and French source texts. Keith Whinnom, who translated *Cárcel* into English in 1979, paradoxically describes *The Castell of Love* as a "disastrously bad" translation that somehow manages to deliver the "essential story ... virtually unscathed."[46] Joyce Boro, in her recent work on Berners, strenuously opposes Whinnom's assertion, noting the linguistic, stylistic, and rhetorical sophistication of the translation.

Berners, in contradistinction to the other translators, further amplifies the text by including a translation of Nicolás Núñez's revisionary continuation of *Cárcel de Amor*. However, unlike the editions printed with the *Cumplimiento*, where San Pedro's text is clearly separated from Núñez's by a new prologue critiquing the original ending, Berners melds the two texts together, as if the continuation were an integral part of his source. Consequently, by embedding Núñez's commentary and revision within the main body of the romance, Berners enshrines Núñez's interpretation as part of the intention of the unnamed Spanish author. Berners's reconfiguration of the final scenes suggests that he shared Núñez's interpretation of *Cárcel de Amor* and wished to translate the whole story, not just what Núñez considered San Pedro's truncated tale; Berners, like Núñez, is glossing San Pedro's romance. Berners's rendering of the final scene of the continuation is also the site of one of his clearest domestications of the romance, and one that dovetails neatly with the metafictive elision between the narrator and the paratextual author-figure. Where Núñez's *Auctor* fears that he will never return alive to "Castilla," Berners's *Auctor* laments, "I never thought to come alyve to my countrey" (*Castell of Love* 187).

The Castell of Love is consequently somewhat closer to an adaptation and gloss of *Cárcel de Amor* than *Carcer d'amore* and *La Prison d'Amours*,

even though Berners's primary method is very close to literal translation. By faithfully translating from three different source texts and then
enclosing the result within his own paratexts and metafictive frame,
Berners offers English readers something new. From the perspective
of literary scholarship privileging national origins and the text-author
paradigm, it appears that Berners was taking liberties with a Spanish
masterpiece. In the context of a sixteenth-century translation of a text
that did not carry the weight of authority, on the other hand, such a
liberty was not a trespass and could be taken without explanation or
apology.

The Italian, French, and English paratexts framing the translations
of *The Prison of Love* constitute the articulation of an ideology, or at the
very least a conceptualization, of the nature of translation from one vernacular to another, an emerging discursive mode during a period of
intense vernacular development, rising vernacular literacy, as well as
expanding readership and production of printed books. The turn from
vertical to horizontal translation involves new and different temporal, geographic, cultural, and linguistic relations between source texts
and translations. Vernacular-to-vernacular translation complicates
many received notions about "Renaissance translation" because such
assumptions are generally grounded in studies and treatises on vertical
translation from classical languages and from scriptural authority into
vernacular languages or on humanist imitation, in which vertical translation serves as a source for poetic invention. At the time of *The Prison
of Love*'s widest circulation, literacy no longer depended upon the use
of Latin, the "supra-national verbal medium ... the *lingua franca* of all
educated men."[47]

While Manfredi, d'Assy, Berners may not have found their work
"easie," they evidently conceived of their projects as something sub-
stantively different from the work of translating Virgil or Ovid, and
expressed a greater concern for their relationships to their readers than
to their sources. Horizontal translation drew the translators of *The Prison
of Love* into relationships with a contemporary, non-authoritative text, a
book that was both generically and physically "little" and seen by the
translators as culturally so – this despite the enormous cultural presence *The Prison of Love* would garner thanks to their translations and the
status of their dedicatees – and whose first author lacked the renown
of Castiglione or Boccaccio, let alone that of classical authors. Instead
of conceptualizing their work as forming a connection between translator and *auctoritas*, Manfredi, d'Assy, and Berners all form relationships

with the romance and, through their delivery of the text, with their own domestic readers. Only Vallmanya indicates his relationship to the author of the "original" *Cárcel de Amor.* D'Assy, on the other hand, tells the story of his friendship with Manfredi and thus constructs a vision of the romance circulating among friends in the service of Francis I.

The opposition or assumed distance between source and target languages and between sending and receiving cultures is not immediately translatable in the context of sixteenth-century vernacular translators working within multilingual and intercultural networks. Manfredi, d'Assy, and Berners were not translating culture, but rather building, and building upon, a shared cosmopolitan court literary culture through translation. Moreover, as we have seen, the opposition of visible and invisible does not quite fit the situation of early sixteenth-century translators, who seek visibility as authors, yet also strive for their understanding of "dynamic equivalence" between sources and translations.

Although the translators of *The Prison of Love* cannot be said to have produced anything so miraculous as the Septuagint, the story, sense, and words of the romance remained remarkably constant, or "unscathed," in Whinnom's words, throughout its translational and multilingual travels. *Lo càrcer d'amor, Carcer d'amore, La Prison d'Amours,* and even *The Castell of Love,* with its altered conclusion, are all examples of how, as Theo Hermans has argued, "the literal mode of translation not only survives in specific types of text, with specific functions, but continues to have a considerable impact on attitudes towards translation ... until at least the end of the sixteenth century" in some spheres.[48] The resulting blend of visibility and literalism, which is not anticipated by Renaissance formal treatises on translation, nor by modern theories of translation, along with the translators' brief remarks on their methods, can be explained by the languages they use, the nature of the work translated, and the anticipated use and readership of each version of *The Prison of Love.*

PART II

Materialities

Chapter Four

Textual Material:
Allegory and Material Epistolarity
in *The Prison of Love*

Cárcel de Amor would not have transformed into *The Prison of Love*, nor would the romance have travelled in so many material forms, were it not for its *matière*. *The Prison of Love* begins with the allegorical descriptions of Desire and the eponymous "prison of love," in which personification and ekphrasis concretize emotions and place them before the eyes of readers and listeners. When the romance moves from the allegorical landscape of lovesickness to the world of the court, the plot turns upon the composition, circulation, reception, and eventual destruction of handwritten letters. In *The Prison of Love*, allegory and epistolary fiction are complementary metafictive devices, despite their rhetorical and generic differences. Both continually focus attention on the power of rhetoric to create effects of physical presence that in turn move the emotions: allegory constructs physical bodies and edifices out of verbal images and places them before the eyes of readers and listeners; letter-writing is an embodied activity by which the protagonists produce tangible material texts. In the printed editions of *The Prison of Love*, embodied letter-writing highlights the contrast between typographic and scribal modes of textual transmission and reception.

The allegorical and epistolary discourses in *The Prison of Love* also exemplify two radically different methods for portraying psychological interiority and subjectivity available to writers at the turn of the sixteenth-century. In fact, *The Prison of Love*'s conjunction of allegory and epistolary narrative bridges the medieval and early modern divide in conventional periodization because the first derives from the dream-vision tradition and the second is a mark of the romance's participation in vernacular, humanist poetics. This combination of medieval tradition and the "dulce comercio" of humanist letters is one of the reasons that

Cárcel de Amor has proven so difficult to define and describe in terms of late-médieval literary genres. And yet, it also no doubt contributed to the success and longevity of *The Prison of Love* in its cosmopolitan, sixteenth-century contexts.

Allegory and Textual Materialization

In the first scenes of *Cárcel de Amor*, the *Auctor* describes a vision he experiences one morning as he travels through the Sierra Morena on his way home from the wars, stressing the faculty of sight:

> *Vi salir a mi encuentro,* por entre unos robledales do mi camino se hazía, un cavallero assí feroz de presencia como *espantoso de vista,* cubierto todo de cabello a manera de salvaje; levava en la mano isquierda un escudo de azero muy fuerte, y en la derecha *una imagen femenil entallada en una piedra muy clara, la qual era de tan estrema hermosura que me turbava la vista;* salían della diversos rayos de fuego que levava encendido el cuerpo de un honbre que el cavallero forciblemente levava tras sí. (*Cárcel* 4, emphasis added)

> [I saw a knight, whose bearing was as ferocious as his visage was frightening, coming out of an oak grove. He was covered from head to toe with hair, like a savage. In his left hand, he bore a shield of strongest steel and in his right, the figure of a woman carved from a brilliant stone. The figure was of such great beauty that it troubled my eyes. Many fiery rays shot out from it, keeping aflame the body of a man, whom the knight dragged captive behind him.][1]

The *imagen femenil*, whose rays enflame Leriano's body, is an object of beauty ripe for poetic description, but the statuette also functions as a kind of alleogorization of optical intromission.[2] The savage is none other than Desire, who introduces himself to the *Auctor*:

> "Yo soy principal oficial en la casa de Amor; llámanme por nonbre Deseo; con la fortaleza deste escudo defiendo las esperanças y con *la hermosura desta imagen* causo las aficiones y con ellas quemo las vidas, como puedes ver en este preso que lievo a la cárcel de Amor, donde con solo morir se espera librar." (*Cárcel* 5–6, emphasis added)[3]

> [I am the chief servant in the house of Love and I am known by the name of Desire. With the strength of this shield I fend off all hope and with the

beauty of this figure, I inflame the passions with which I burn lives, as you can see from this captive that I am taking to the Prison of Love, where the only liberation he can hope for is death.]

The description has a doubling effect, for the *Auctor* not only describes the carved image that the hairy savage carries, but also Desire himself, an imagined allegorical image, projected from the inner emotional world of the tortured lover, who in turn explains the power of the image he carries. From the outset of the romance, then, vision is troubled and troubling.

The translations present the troubling dream vision with few alterations, which is not surprising given the translators' methods and desire for transparent equivalence. However, two of the translations intensify the opening ekphrastic vision through interpretive amplification. Vallmanya writes that the dazzling image held by Desire was "de axí bella forma y gentilesa que la vista affalagant torbava" (of such beautiful form and gentility that it pleasingly troubled my sight), thus adding an element of pleasure to the fear and wonderment experienced by the Castilian *Auctor* (*Lo càrcer d'amor* 37). D'Assy's French version also deepens the emphasis on the sense of sight in these scenes by describing how the extreme beauty of the image "me troubloit toute la veue" (troubled the whole of my sight), and how the sight of the prison itself caused *l'Acteur* "fort a esmerueiller" (to marvel greatly) (*La Prison d'Amours* 1v–2r).

The Prison of Love's historical audiences would have been familiar with the motif of a traveller experiencing a dream vision, a narrative mode that was one of the primary vehicles for medieval ekphrasis.[4] Moreover, San Pedro was clearly drawing upon medieval theories of vision and the importance of sight in lovesickness, perhaps best described by Andreas Capellanus: "love is a certain inborn suffering derived from the sight of and excessive meditation upon the beauty of the opposite sex."[5] Leriano's first letter to Laureola affirms the power of feminine beauty: "tu hermosura causó el afición, y el afición el deseo, y el deseo la pena" (your beauty caused my love, and love caused desire, and desire, suffering) (*Cárcel* 18).

The second ekphrasis, describing the huge tower constructed from Leriano's emotions, is monumental in scope, length, and density of detail, once again emphasizing the faculty of sight:

Vi cerca de mí, en lo más alto de la sierra, una torre de altura tan grande que me parecía llegar al cielo; era hecha por tal artificio, que de la estrañeza della comencé *a maravillarme*; y puesto al pie, aunque el tiempo se me ofrecía más para temer que para notar, *miré* la novedad de su lavor y de su edificio. El cimiento sobre que estava fundada era una piedra tan fuerte de su condición y tan clara de su natural qual *nunca otra tal jamás avía visto*, sobre la qual estavan firmados quatro pilares de un mármol morado *muy hermoso de mirar*. Eran en tanta manera altos que me espantava cómo se podían sostener; estava encima dellos labrada una torre de tres esquinas, *la más fuerte que se puede contenplar*. (*Cárcel* 6, emphasis added)

[I saw close by me, at the very top of the mountain, a tower of such a great height that it seemed to reach the heavens. The tower had been built with such wondrous artifice that I began marvel at it; standing at its foot, although my situation gave me more cause to fear than to observe, I saw the novelty of its design and construction. The foundation upon which it stood was a stone so strong in substance and so transparent in quality that I have never again seen anything like it. Upon this stone stood four pillars of purple marble that were very beautiful to behold. The pillars were of such a great height that I was amazed they were able to remain upright, yet a three-cornered tower, the strongest imaginable, had been built upon them.]

The allegory becomes increasingly meticulous. Inside the dark prison lit only by the light shining from Leriano's heart, the lovesick prisoner sits chained in a "silla de fuego" (flaming chair), weeping servants place upon his head "una corona de unas puntas de hierro sin ninguna piedad, que le traspasavan todo el cerebro" (a crown with merciless iron spikes that passed all through his brain), and serve him a meal. All the while Leriano "sienpre se quemava y nunca se acabava de quemar" (ever burned and never ceased burning), receiving blows from a black figure dressed in yellow, as an old man sits head in hand (*Cárcel* 8). Leriano, like Desire before him, performs an exegesis of the vision, explaining how each detail of the prison represents an aspect of his inner experiences of love, elaborating upon conventional colour symbolism: the regal purple of the pillars represents the high status of the four faculties of the soul; the dark and dull colours of the other figures represent the melancholia of lovesickness; yellow represents desperation.

Leriano goes on to explain the meaning of each of the figures the Author sees within the prison and the meal of hopelessness, washed down by a libation of tears, which he is served by the personifications of Evil, Torture, and Pain. Leriano's interpretation of the allegorical vision for the Author is in fact another allegory, the externalized concretization and personification of the ardour, constancy, and pain of love. Leriano's sad meal of tribulation and tears foreshadows the consumptive nature of his lovesickness and his eventual ingestion of Laureola's letters. If, in the allegory, Leriano eats the verbal images of his emotions, on his deathbed he consumes the tangible epistolary evidence of his unrequited love.

The Prison of Love's allegories tightly intertwine ekphrasis and exegesis, showcasing the rhetorical sleights of hand that create effects of material presence. In order for the allegorical devices to work, and in the absence of actual pictorial images, readers and listeners must see with the interior eye and invent *phantasia*, visual images in mind, such as the prison, and *imagines agentes*, or active images, such as Desire. In this sense, *The Prison of Love*'s opening dream vision is an *imagetext*, an "inextricable weaving together of representation and discourse" that creates an "imbrication of visual and verbal experience," in which image and text are combined rather than opposed, and become all the more memorable.[6] However, textual allegory only makes abstract constructs and feelings visible to the mind's eye. Images are part and parcel of the allegorical process, but it is the work of the reader or interpreter to visualize and recall them. Due to such active mental engagement, rhetorical manuals describe ekphrasis as one of the primary devices recommended for achieving the effect of enargeia, the persuasive appeal to the imagination and emotions.[7]

The opening scenes focus on the Author's sense of sight and abound in images meant to be conjured up by the mind's eye, establishing what Sol Miguel-Prendes has called *Cárcel de Amor*'s dynamic of "visual reading."[8] The descriptions of the *cárcel* and its inhabitants typify how visuality is, in fact, and as Marilynn Desmond observes, integral to medieval allegory itself, which frequently "foregrounds the perception of the first-person narrator."[9] Throughout, the allegorical sense of sight gives the Author access to Leriano's interior psychological experiences. Positioned to see through the Author's eyes, readers are treated to his vivid descriptions and, by listening to Leriano's exegesis through the Author's reportage, to the emotions of both lovesick noble and narrator. In addition to making the metaphorical flames of desire and the torturous nature of love concrete and visible, the allegory asserts the otherness of desire. For desire is no longer a feeling within the confines of the lover's heart, but a castigating external force, an edifice that imprisons, and a being who is not only out of the lover's control, but controls him. Such visual imaginings, as Stephen Nichols has observed, have profound ethical ramifications as they inherently problematize the body by "focusing attention on the disjunction between the body as a physical measure of existence within a specific code of courtly conduct and a spiritual existence very much out of sympathy with the prevailing social mode. The point is that both the physical and the spiritual modes are somehow conceived as *visible*, as etched on the body by the acid of experience."[10]

Many modern-day readers have commented upon the juxtaposition of "realistic" and allegorical settings in *Cárcel de Amor*. The allegory of Leriano's lovesickness does not contain the action of the story; in contrast, it is wholly exposition, setting up the *Auctor*'s role and establishing Leriano's lovesickness.[11] However, as Robert Folger and Miguel-Prendes have each argued, following Keith Whinnom's affirmation that San Pedro's description of the Prison of Love should be understood as a theatre of memory, the allegory serves as an interpretive and visual guide for the work's audiences.[12] For Folger, "the initial images will leave a powerful mnemonic image in the mind of the reader trained to visualize literature. Thus, the image of the doomed Leriano as a prisoner of love will be associated in the reader's mind with the narration of the events in Macedonia, guiding his interpretation of the 'facts.'"[13] Miguel-Prendes situates the opening allegory within the framework of a contemplative, enargeistic reading modelled upon devotional reading, and for readerly meditation upon Leriano's suffering in terms of the Passion.[14] Pairing mental images with verbal descriptions is a key element of the arts of memory and San Pedro's readers would have been trained to read contemplatively and to travel through the text in the wake of the Author. In the hands of the faithful translators, the allegories inherited from *Cárcel de Amor* fulfil the same expositional and illuminating roles.

Nevertheless, the hyperbolic *copia* of the allegory and the exegesis that veers back into the allegorical mode has some parodic inflections, and consequently may have struck some readers as humorous and others as heart-rending. *Cárcel de Amor* may be read as the story of a young knight who suffers in vain and never demonstrates that he merits the love of a highly placed lady, ultimately failing to realize the goals of an archetypal romance hero. He is as much a chump at the mercy of his passions and of women – as his friend Teseo wishes to convince him – as a martyr for love. In this light, Miguel-Prendes further argues in a study of how the so-called sentimental romances parodically rework Boethius's moral and stoic consolation, *Cárcel de Amor*'s allegorical scenes and the woodcuts that illustrate them recall glosses of *The Consolation of*

Philosophy in circulation from the mid-fourteenth to the sixteenth centuries in the Iberian Peninsula.[15] In any case, the necessity of compounding allegory and interpretation yet again calls attention to language's ability to create material things and the powers of vivid description.

The psychological landscape of allegory, inhabited by Leriano, the Author, and a host of personifications, fades almost entirely from view in the following episodes of the romance. It is mentioned again when the Author returns to Leriano's prison bearing the first of Laureola's missives and accompanied by a squadron of personifications (*Cárcel* 29), and it is alluded to when Leriano receives the princess's last letter and once again succumbs to the wasting syndrome that is love (*Cárcel* 64). Just as the Author travels from the Prison of Love to the court of Macedonia, the narrative moves from the discursive mode of allegory to the tangible "real" world, in which the inner emotional states of the characters will be made known through letter-writing and speechifying rather than visions, in the following episodes. Rhetorical performances and written documents become the central images of the text. However, oratory, attempts at persuasion, and letters are not so much vividly described as scripted and verbally enacted.

Material Epistolarity and Metafiction

In his third letter to Laureola, Leriano writes, "Antes pusiera las manos en mí para acabar la vida que en el papel para començar a escrevirte" (I would sooner set my hands to suicide than to paper to begin writing to you) (*Cárcel* 40). Allusions to putting pen to paper, taking pen in hand, and the like are familiar conventions in epistolary discourse. However, Leriano's declaration is more than a commonplace of authorial reticence. Rather, when it rhetorically equates taking up the pen with writing, it captures *The Prison of Love*'s deep preoccupation with material texts and with the high stakes of turning thoughts into words. In *The Prison of Love*, the conventions of letter-writing are linked not only to desire, but also to physical danger. In fact, a plot to assassinate Pope Alexander VI, recounted by Johann Burchard, his Master of Ceremonies, suggests that early modern letters could in fact be literally physically dangerous to their readers: "A certain Tomasino of Forli ... had come to Rome with some poisoned letters which he had rolled up in a reed to present to the pope ... Had the pope accepted the letters, he would, after a few days or even hours, with no hope of remedy, have succumbed and died."[16]

The Prison of Love's abundant materially metafictive scenes – references to the physicality of writing and verbal depictions of the creation, circulation, and reception of handwritten letters – create an effect of textual *mise en abyme* that repeatedly invites the audience to imagine the composition of the texts they can physically see on the page. In contrast to the opening scenes' allegories, the letters visualize internal states of mind through the concretization of language as written text. As Thomas Beebee notes, epistolary fictions are often highly self-reflexive, and letters become more than narrative vehicles, "letters are kissed, wept upon, eaten, beaten, held to the bosom, and caressed in place of the lovers who sent them."[17] And in this way, in *The Prison of Love*, letters are more than linguistic texts destined to be read, interpreted, and to provoke action. They are physical extensions of their writers, talismanic objects, and the material currency of the romance's poetic economy.

As Leriano, Laureola, Persio, and the Author negotiate the frustrated desire, court intrigue, bloody revenge, and suicide that mark the progress of *The Prison of Love*'s plot, they continually create, read, and manipulate handwritten documents. Throughout the romance, acts of writing cause physical alteration in the letter-writers and the letters themselves seem to be contagious objects that provoke similar physical effects not only in readers, but in the messenger as well. For example, Laureola, upon reading Leriano's second missive, "Quedó tan enmudecida y turbada como si gran mal toviera" (became as silent and troubled as if suffering from a great illness) (*Cárcel* 26). Laureola's first letter to Leriano, in contrast, arrives accompanied by a small army of personifications – Alegría (Happiness), Descanso (Repose), Esperança (Hope), Contentamiento (Contentment), Holgança (Delightful Leisure), and Plazer (Pleasure) – and effects a temporary cure for Leriano's lovesickness: "quando lo que Laureola le escrivió acabó de leer, estava tan sano como si ninguna pasión uviera tenido" (when he finished reading what Laureola had written to him, he was as well as if he had never suffered any passion at all) (*Cárcel* 30). This reliance on the handwritten word for persuasion, self-realization, and self-fashioning culminates with Leriano's final act, the simultaneous destruction of Laureola's manuscript letters and of himself.

The Prison of Love's portrayal of material texts is particularly intriguing given the period of its print circulation, the interstitial historical period when the culture of the printed book was rising and gradually distinguishing its material conventions from those of manuscript book production. However, print was not wholly eclipsing manuscript communication at the time. Rather, as Fernando Bouza observes in his study of early modern manuscript culture, throughout the period, "la escritura *ad vivum* se presenta como un eficaz complemento o, incluso, un competidor de lo tipográfico, ofreciendo un ágil sistema de copias o traslados" (writing *ad vivum* was an efficient complement or, even, a competitor of the press, offering an agile system of copies and transfer).[18]

Nevertheless, the success of *The Prison of Love* depends largely upon the development of the printed book trade at the end of the fifteenth and in the first half of the sixteenth centuries. It has even been claimed that *Cárcel* was composed *for* the press.[19] Since the date of *Cárcel's* composition can only be estimated, falling between the years of 1483 and 1492, the year of its first publication in print, a firm *terminus ad quem*, this claim lies on rather shaky ground. On the other hand, while I believe that it is likely that *Cárcel* circulated among its first intended courtly readers in manuscript, the absence of any known manuscript witnesses predating the print editions makes it equally impossible to gauge how and if *Cárcel* circulated prior to its printing in Seville by the Cuatro Compañeros Alemanes in 1492. It is certain that a great number of readers encountered *The Prison of Love* in print throughout the sixteenth centuries, and, when they did, they found images of a vibrant, if perilous, scribal culture on the pages of their printed books.

The first act of writing in the romance occurs when the *Auctor* returns from his initial sojourn in the court of Macedonia to the Prison of Love where Leriano languishes, to urge the suffering nobleman to write to Laureola, in the hopes that she will read with some degree of compassion: "díxele que se esforçase a escrevir a Laureola, proferiéndome a dalle la carta, y puesto que él estava más para hazer memorial de su hazienda que carta de su pasión, escrivió" (I told him that he must find the strength to write to Laureola, offering myself as the bearer of the letter, and, although he was then in a state more fitting to the dictation of his last will and testament than writing of his passion, he wrote) (*Cárcel* 18). The result of this writing *in extremis* is the first of four letters that Leriano will send to Laureola in the hands of his devoted messenger, and to which she will pen three responses.

Writing to Laureola, Leriano claims, is a greater liberty than loving her (18), yet he begs her to write back and save him from suffering and dying due to his unfulfilled desire for her. For all its courtly idioms, the missive contains a veiled threat. Leriano writes as a suicidal lover and debt collector, affirming that though he has done her no other service than to suffer in love for her, she has "destroyed him," and "por mucho que me pagues sienpre pensaré que me quedas en deuda" (no matter how much you (re)pay me, I will think you always in my debt) (*Cárcel* 18). Taking recourse to the equivocal meanings of *muerte*, Leriano warns Laureola that "la muerte sin que tú me la dieses yo mismo me la daría ... si tú no hovieses de quedar infamada por matadora" (were you not to give me death, I would kill myself ... if only that would not cause you to be defamed as a murderess) (*Cárcel* 19). Leriano assures her that a letter will be a substitute for the courtly "galardón" or sexual favour that she cannot grant him; his possession of the letter penned by her will in a sense be his possession of her. Yet it is because of this equivalence that her honour is endangered by the very existence of the letters. Leriano concludes with another threat: "Si algund bien quisieres hazerme, no lo tardes; podrá ser que tengas tienpo de arrepentirte y no lugar de remediarme" (If you wish to do me some good, do not delay, for it could be that you will have time enough to repent and none to cure me) (*Cárcel* 19).

Laureola does not respond to the first letter and angrily sends the *Auctor* away. Leriano writes again of his suffering, begging her to write him "por primero y postrimero galardón" (as her first and last favour) (*Cárcel* 26). Knowing that Laureola would not willingly accept Leriano's second letter, having experienced the trauma and the danger of reading his first, the *Auctor* puts pen to paper, for the first and only time in *Cárcel*, and forges the name of another sender: "puse un sobrescrito a su carta, porque Laureola en seguridad de aquel la quisiere rescibir" (I added a new cover to his letter so that Laureola, thinking it safe, would agree to receive it) (*Cárcel* 26). Taken in, Laureola opens the letter and reads, only to become greatly disturbed, as if ill. She decides to give Leriano the great favour that he has requested, but with trepidation because she knows that by writing she risks her unblemished honour.

Laureola's first letter displays an acute awareness of its own material nature. She writes in full awareness of the risk she takes by committing words to paper, sending the document out of her hands and into the world, where it may become material evidence against her, a tangible witness that can only compete with her unseen intentions. Nevertheless, the letter seeks to make her honourable intentions visible. She writes, as she explains, to "redemir tu vida" (redeem your [Leriano's] life) and not "satisfazer tu deseo" (satisfy your desire), and the letter states plainly that her motives in writing come from "intención piadosa" (merciful intention) and not from "voluntad enamorada" (being in love) (*Cárcel* 27–8). Regardless of this careful rhetoric, Laureola also writes that she will be powerless to defend herself against misprision:

"con este miedo, la mano en el papel, puse el coraçón en el cielo" (with this fear, I put my hand to paper and my hopes in heaven) (*Cárcel* 28). San Pedro's use of antithesis clearly marks the act of letter-writing as one in which the spiritual and material realms collapse. Laureola faces the danger that her merciful act of redemption will be interpreted by Leriano and other, unintended, prying readers as an act of lust.

The next epistolary exchange occurs between Leriano and his rival Persio, who, even without the material evidence of the letters, accuses Leriano and Laureola of fornication after seeing Leriano kiss her hands in public. Ironically, Laureola's letters may have saved Leriano from his impending death, but, because they inspired Leriano's visit to court, they are also effectively death warrants. Unlike the letters that passed from the hands of Leriano and Laureola into the *Auctor*'s and then delivered in secret to their recipients, Leriano and Persio exchange public letters, *carteles*. Leriano asserts his and Laureola's innocence: not only have there been no secret midnight trysts but "palabra de amores jamás le hablé" (never did I speak words of love to her) (*Cárcel* 33). Some readers see this statement as a lie on Leriano's part.[20] However, Leriano has never spoken words of love directly to Laureola, therefore, we may also interpret it as an indication of the difference between written and spoken words accorded by the protagonists and by the romance itself.

In order to deliver Leriano's third missive, the *Auctor* must physically manipulate the letter so that it may reach its intended recipient: "doblada la carta muy sotilmente, púsela en una lança, y con mucho trabajo echéla dentro en su cámara" (having carefully folded up the letter, I set it on the point of a lance and with much difficulty pushed it into her cell) (*Cárcel* 42). Here, the letter enters Laureola's prison much in the way that a clandestine lover might enter the chambers of his beloved by scaling a tower wall. The letter, as epistolary stand-in for the lover, penetrates the cell. Laureola throws her response through the bars on her window onto the ground, announcing with grim irony: "'Cataquí el gualardón que recibo de la piedad que tuve'" ("Just look at what a favour I receive for taking mercy [on Leriano]) (*Cárcel* 42). Both the *Auctor*'s delivery and Laureola's casting of the letters through the bars of her prison accentuate the material presence of handwritten documents in the romance.

The characters see the creation of these documents as both dangerous and binding. The exchange of letters between Leriano and Laureola draws the three protagonists into a triangular relationship that the *Auctor* terms "nuestro secreto" (our secret) (*Cárcel* 43). The Author not only insinuates himself into the relationship between Leriano and Laureola; in fact, he is responsible for the triangle. For there would be no connection between the two other than that imagined in Leriano's tortured thoughts, were it not for the Author's attempts to remedy the knight's lovesickness. In this, the Author assumes in part the healing role that the lady is supposed to play in courtly love. Further, only Leriano, Laureola, and the Author may see, read, and touch the letters, and each expresses anxiety that the documents might fall into the wrong hands. For example, recalling the conflation of the material letter and emotion cited above, Laureola begs Leriano, "Por Dios te pido que enbuelvas mi carta en tu fe, porque si es tan cierta como confiesas, no se te pierda ni de nadie pueda ser vista; que quien viese lo que te escrivo pensaría que te amo" (For God's sake I beg you to shroud my letter in your steadfast love; for if your love is as strong as you confess, do not lose the letter or allow it to be seen by anyone; for whoever saw what I have written to you would think that I loved you) (*Cárcel* 28). Leriano likewise explains to the *Auctor* that he will not remind Laureola in writing of what he has done for her "por el peligro que se puede recrecer si la carta es vista" (due to the danger that could ensue if the letter is seen) (*Cárcel* 60).

Throughout, San Pedro not only draws his readers' attention to the "material realities of writing," to borrow a phrase from Roger Chartier, but also to the psychological and physical effects of writing and reading.[21] Moreover, the romance's audience is allowed textual entry into the epistolary triangle created between the *Auctor*, Leriano, and Laureola by virtue of the book held in the hand of an individual reader or seen in the hands of one who reads aloud. The emphasis on secrecy points to the dynamics of reception created by the letters in *Cárcel* and by epistolary fiction more generally. Within the world of the romance, the letters between Leriano and Laureola are clandestine, yet the romance's audience is allowed access, given a sense of entering into the secret passions, doubts, and hopes of the letter-writers. The dual, public and private nature of letters begins in San Pedro's dedication, an open letter, which not only introduces the romance but also establishes the metafictive tie between the speaking "I" in the paratext and the first-person perspective of the diegetic narrator and character, *el Auctor*; the translations repeat both the metafiction and the contrast between public and private writing. In each of the versions of *The Prison of Love*, the romance's material metafictions are framed by the authors' paratexts, which deliver the romance to their successive inscribed readerships.

The materiality of the manuscript letters that circulate in *The Prison of Love* reaches the peak of its intensity in Leriano's death watch. In *Cárcel de Amor*, San Pedro's prose once again emphasizes the confusion of corporeality and spirituality that the letters themselves represent, an effect that all of the translators follow. The letters are the objects of Leriano's rapturous gaze, yet their physical presence is troubling to him: "viendo que le quedava poco espacio para gozar de ver las dos cartas que della tenía, no sabía qué forma se diese con ellas" (seeing that he had little time left to enjoy gazing upon the two letters from her that he had, he did not know what to do with them) (*Cárcel* 79). He considers tearing them to pieces, but does not want to offend Laureola by destroying her "razones de tanto precio" (words of priceless worth) (*Cárcel* 79). Nor can he give the letters to a confidant for safekeeping, because they might be seen by prying eyes. At last, he determines to consume the letters, making his own body the treasure house for Laureola's precious words:

> Pues tomando de sus dudas lo más seguro, hizo traer una copa de agua, y hechas las cartas pedaços écholas en ella, y acabado esto, mandó que le sentasen en la cama, y sentado, bevióselas en el agua y assí quedó contenta su voluntad; y llegada ya la hora de su fin, puestos en mí los ojos dixo: «Acabados son mis males», y assí quedó su muerte en testimonio de su fe. (*Cárcel* 79)

> [So, choosing the surest way amidst his doubts, he called for a goblet of water, and having torn the letters into pieces, threw them in it. This done, he asked to be sat up in bed and once seated he drank them with the water and thus felt contented; his final hour had now arrived and, his eyes fixed . upon me, he said, "My suffering is now at an end," and thus his death was a testament to his faith.]

This scene has understandably aroused the interest of many scholarly readers of *Cárcel de Amor*. It is the first time in the romance that Laureola's letters take on a public role, as Leriano performs his ritual in the company of friends, servants, and mourners. The allusion to Eucharistic ritual seems clear and indisputable, yet there is no reference in the scene to God or an afterlife: Leriano is clearly dying without the benefit of Catholic sacraments. Rather he dies performing a kind of courtly lover's last rites, following a public confession in the form of his defence of women.[22] Once again, the suffering hero is a ripe target for parody, his erotic frustration open to reading as travesty and sacrilege.[23]

Several critical interpretations of the scene share an appreciation for how Laureola's letters have transformed from rhetorical compositions into non-hermeneutic objects; on his deathbed, Leriano gazes upon, tears up, and imbibes, but does not reread or reinterpret the words of the woman who will not love him. Marina Brownlee, for example, reading Leriano's last act through the lens of discourse analysis, concludes, "Leriano's eating of the words serves as an emblem of a 'dead-end' speech situation. Words are presented as sterile objects rather than communication, Laureola's words and their communicative function are reduced to the status as a metonym for Laureola herself – one that displaces and precludes communication – leading to death, that is, silenced words."[24] Nevertheless, and as a Eucharistic reading of the scene would imply, the letters themselves are not reduced to sterile objects. Rather, Laureola's handwritten letters, as material objects, are endowed with special apotropaic virtues in the text, at least in Leriano's eyes. Nicolás Núñez's continuation of *Cárcel* gives an explanation that blends the two ways of conceiving of Laureola's letters as documents containing information and as objects with extra-hermeneutic powers that are in some sense extensions of their writer. As Núñez's – and later Berners's – reincarnation of the Author says to Laureola, "Y en el tiempo de su morir, que más memoria de su alma y de su cuerpo avía de tener, se membró de tus cartas, las quales, hechos pedaços, en agua bevió, porque nadi dellas memoria oviesse, y por llevar consigo alguna cosa tuya" (for when he died where as he shulde have had most memory upon hys sowle and what shuld have ben done with his body, he then remembred more the letters that ye had sent hym, the whiche he toke, and tare in peces, & drank them in water because they shuld never be sene, and bycause he wold cary with hym some thynge that had bene yours) (*Cárcel* 85; *The Castell of Love* 171).[25] Even though both Núñez and Berners agreed that San Pedro had left his romance unfinished, this last drink recalls the meal served to Leriano in the Prison of Love, the "manjares tristes de mis contemplaciones" (sad dishes of my contemplations), feelings rendered materially concrete via allegory and ekphrasis. Thus, the materialization of abstract concepts, which can only become visible through words on the page, comes full circle.

Bouza provides a further and historically persuasive reading of Leriano's last act. The consumption of a handwritten document would have been recognizable to early modern audiences as part of contemporary manuscript culture. In the *Tratado muy sotil y bien fundado de las supersticiones y hechecerías* (Most subtle and well founded treatise on superstitions and spells) (Logroño: Miguel de Eguía, 1529), Martín de Castañega writes, "Assí parece también que deshazer con agua ciertas letras y palabras escritas en el suelo de la taça y bever aquella agua para remediar algunas passiones o para desatar algunos maleficios entre marido y muger no carecen de sospecha de superstición y pacto oculto diabólico" (Thus it seems to be the case as well that dissolving certain letters and written words at the bottom of a goblet and drinking that water in order to remedy certain passions or to undo certain evil spells between man and wife are not free from suspicion of superstition and occult diabolical pacts).[26] Martín de Castañega's description of the sorcerous and sexual power attributed to handwritten texts torn, mixed with water, and consumed suggests that *The Prison of Love*'s readers might have interpreted Leriano's final actions as morally suspicious.

Leriano not only ingests the letters because of their "precious words," written by Laureola, which must be protected from public view, but because they are also *cartas de tocar*, textual objects that function "por contacto y no por un acto racional de lectura" (through contact and not through a rational act of reading).[27] They are part of an early modern manuscript culture in which "escribir podía no tener nada que ver con leer, con la recepción y comprensión de las ideas que se nos proponen" (writing might have nothing to do with reading, with the reception and understanding of the ideas it contained).[28] Castañega's insistence that neither spoken nor written words "pueden tener virtud natural para algún efecto" (can have inherent powers to work any kind of effect) as well as the other Inquisitorial and pastoral references to manuscripts with magical properties analysed by Bouza would seem to affirm a post-medieval belief in the non-hermenuetic power of written words as talismans.[29] The allusion to witchcraft in Leriano's deathbed drama does not preclude the other religious, pyschosexual, and rhetorical resonances of this most intriguing scene. Rather, the connotation heightens the effect of Leriano's desperation at the impotence of the courtly code to function. At the same time, the allusions to the power of *cartas de tocar* and sorcery remind us that early modern readers were very much aware of the materiality of the texts.

In the last episode of the romance, as composed by San Pedro, the Author describes Leriano's thought processes prior to the libation, explaining that Leriano sought to protect the letters and Laureola herself by hiding her words forevermore from prying eyes. Núñez's continuation and the reference to spells and passions that Bouza brings to light in connection with the romance supply other motivations.

Leriano and Laureola are not letter-writers in the continuation. Núñez in fact creates a contrasting effect, but one that also draws attention to the materiality of texts, by turning the protagonists' bodies into texts to be read. In a manner similar to the use of *motes* (mottoes) in San Pedro's early romance *Arnalte y Lucenda* (1491), Núñez dresses Leriano and Laureola head to toe in garments embroidered with texts alluding to their feelings and the tragic death of Leriano. Leriano, for example, wears a belt made of cloth shot with gold, reading "Muy más rica fue mi muerte / que mi vida / si della quedáys servida" (*Cárcel* 91), which Berners renders in sixteenth-century English as "More richer was my dethe then lyfe, if ye wolde be servyd therwith" (*The Castell of Love* 175). Laureola's girdle echoes with regret: "Más rica sería mi gloria, / si el bivir / consintiesse en mi morir" (*Cárcel* 95), which Berners intensifies: "More rather shulde have bene my glory with thy lyfe then with thy deth" (*The Castell of Love* 180).

With the exception of the letters ingested in Leriano's final epistolary act, the general tendency among critics has been to treat all the letters of *Cárcel de Amor* as wholly linguistic entities, and this approach has led to fruitful studies on the nature of language in the Spanish fifteenth-century prose fiction and in *Cárcel de Amor* in particular.[30] *Cárcel* is in many ways, as Dulce M. García argues, a book about how to do things with words.[31] Nonetheless, a purely linguistic or rhetorical approach obscures the importance given in the work itself to texts as material objects.[32] The plot of *The Prison of Love* epitomizes how "the processes that bestowed existence on writing" could become "the very ground of literary invention," leading to what Chartier, referring to early modern print culture, has characterized as the lack of a "sharp distinction between the materiality of the text and the textuality of the book."[33] Reading with an eye to the materiality of textual imagery throughout *The Prison of Love* not only sheds new light on the famous last scene where Leriano destroys and consumes the precious handwritten documents sent to him by Laureola, but also reveals how the romance's metafictions emphasize the power of written language to create effects of physical presence and emotional response.

Despite Leriano's failure to overcome Laureola's resistance – she was perhaps his most resisting reader – historical readers considered his words worthy of remembering.[34] The persuasive power of both Leriano's and Laureola's letters was noted by later readers whose marks and annotations are found in many of the extant copies of *Cárcel* and the translations. A much-cited anecdote concerning a reader imitating

Leriano's well-spoken words appears in Melchior de Santa Cruz's *Floresta española de apotegmas o sentencias, sabia y graciosamente dichas, de algunos españoles* (1574),

> Un gentilhombre escribió a una señora muy avisada una carta sacada de un libro que se llama *Cárcel de amor*, pareciéndole que no sabría de dónde se había sacado. Como ella la leyó en presencia de quien la había traído, tornósele a dar, diciendo:
> – Esta carta no viene a mí, sino a Laureola.

> [A gentleman wrote a letter taken from a book called *Cárcel de Amor* to a very well informed lady, thinking that she would not know where he had taken it from. When she read it in the presence of the man who had delivered it to her, she gave it back to him, saying, "This letter is not for me, but for Laureola."][35]

It would appear that the *gentilhombre*, rhetorical reader and plagiarist, also imitates Leriano's lack of success overcoming his lady's resistance.

In addition to readers' desire to imitate Leriano's eloquence, this entertaining story, which is the last in a short chapter of the *Floresta* titled "De sobreescriptos" [Concerning covers], is often cited as evidence of *Cárcel de Amor*'s enduring popularity, and the role its letters played as models. The anecdote is one of eight concerning handwritten letters, manuscripts that "ran" from hand to hand, like those that form the central nervous system of *Cárcel*. The *Floresta* itself is a miscellany of quips and sketches offered to the reader for quotation and reuse. It is just the sort of book that invited copying by hand for a personal miscellany or *librillo de memoria*, in which letters might be drafted before committed to a clean and more permanent copy.[36] The *gentilhombre* of the anecdote imitated Leriano, whom he may have seen pictured in a printed edition of *Cárcel de Amor*, by writing out one of his letters to Laureola.[37] Like the *Auctor's sobrescrito*, the story about failed amorous plagiarism also reminds us of the troublesome nature of letters in *Cárcel de Amor* and their vulnerability to misprision and misuse. Both Santa Cruz and his *gentilhombre* put *Cárcel* under new cover. Yet, as Santa Cruz's tale reveals, Leriano was too firmly established in both textual and iconographic tradition as the Author of his letters in *Cárcel* for his words to be pirated.

An analysis of the materiality of language and material texts in the plot of *The Prison of Love* lays the groundwork for understanding how book-objects represent textual production and the corporeality of the handwritten word. Part and parcel of the "unhappy separation" of print and manuscript publication has been a generalized critical association of manuscript transmission with corporeality as opposed to the incorporeal nature of print. Jan-Dirk Müller, for example, sees a "deep-rift in the writing culture during the time of early print." The "technically produced" book, he argues can only "simulate the sensual presence that the medieval scribe experienced."[38] Following this current, Robert Folger posits a "disembodied reader" for the printed *Cárcel de Amor*.[39]

While we cannot know if *Cárcel* was originally envisioned as a printed book, *The Prison of Love* is most definitely a work that depicts *escritura ad vivum* as an embodied practice in a world where handwritten documents functioned as both texts and talismans. The powerful documents circulating in the text also recall the "paper politics" and "papering ... of the social and political spheres" in the Castilian courts of the second half of the fifteenth century, where literary and bureaucratic literacy combined, as described by Ana Gómez Bravo.[40] In both manuscript and print, allegory and letter-writing serve to recreate emotion and sensual presence on the page in *Cárcel* and other versions of *The Prison of Love*. Consequently, and in contrast to the presumption of a "deep rift" between print and manuscript cultures in the period, genres, content, and the physical contours of material books have as much, if not more, to do with modes of production and reception than the difference in medium between handwritten and printed text. In the printed editions of *Cárcel* and *The Prison of Love* more generally, scribal culture is portrayed in print, signalling to readers the differences between intimate, handwritten communications of the protagonists and the openness of print to wider audiences, adding a material facet to the play of public and private communication in the romance. And, as we will see in chapter 6, the visual programs of the illustrated editions of *The Prison of Love* deepen the romance's preoccupation with rhetoric, embodied writing, and material texts.

Chapter Five

Prisons in Print:
The Material Books

"Books that look different *are* different."[1] The shape and size of a book, materials used, its title page, colophon, decoration, and the design of its pages are physical paratexts that have much to tell us about how publishers, editors, and printers understood and intended a given work to be read, as well as about how readers encountered it. This chapter and the next are dedicated to the books that transmitted *The Prison of Love* as expressive forms and the agencies at work (and in play) in their creation. The human agency of author-figures, readers, and bookmen[2] coexists with textual agency, the ability of texts to function at a remove from their producers and intended receivers on incunable and sixteenth-century printed pages.[3] These multiple agencies and events involved in the translation, production, and transmission of reading matter make up the "communications circuits" and "whole socio-economic conjunctures" that encompassed the lives of books.[4] Most bookmen – publishers, editors, printers, and booksellers – were not authors, but they designed the architecture and composed the visual language of books. Textual agency, in turn, is closely related to and depends upon the expressive qualities of the material books (and other supports) that allow for the survival of texts. Book-objects exist in symbiotic relationships with literary texts; without material books literary texts are invisible and intangible, but those books only come into existence in relation to the texts.

The array of material books in which *The Prison of Love* travelled throughout the sixteenth century shows how the romance's texts continued to function at generations' removes from their composition, how historical individuals interacted with textual agency and had a hand in reshaping the romance, and how, while generic affiliations and audiences shifted over time, certain aspects of the of the work endured. Throughout, the material forms engage *The Prison of Love*'s literariness, its preoccupation with language and rhetoric, and its imbrication in the *querelle des femmes*. Although many of the copies of *Cárcel de Amor, Carcer d'amore, La Prison d'Amours, La Prison d'Amour*, and *The Castell of Love* that have survived are pristine exemplars, a significant number also contain the marks left by their sixteenth-century readers. Comments penned in the margins, underlinings, and other material traces of historical reception also provide today's readers fragmentary glimpses of how readers responded to texts within their specific material contexts. Illustration, illumination, and textile remediations of *The Prison of Love* will be discussed in chapters 7 and 8, but I will briefly touch upon the incorporation of woodcut illustrations in printed editions throughout this survey of material forms.

The Prison of Love's material profile over time reveals two distinct phases of circulation. During the first phase, from 1492 to roughly the middle of the sixteenth century, the romance was translated, repackaged, and reframed for imagined audiences of elite readers. The first phase is characterized by carefully produced editions in Spanish, Italian, and French that reproduce San Pedro's and the translators' dedications, respectively, and serve as the bearers of the personal relationships each version of *The Prison of Love* forged between author-figures and their intended courtly readerships into the public sphere of print. In the second phase, from the late 1540s until the first decades of the seventeenth century, *The Prison of Love* was transmitted in Spanish and French in small, economically produced books, intended for broader readerships. In this period, *Cárcel* was also anthologized with *Questión de amor* and printed in bilingual Spanish and French editions of *Cárcel de Amor/La Prison d'Amour*, two forms that came to dominate the ways in which *The Prison of Love* reached readers in the later decades of the sixteenth century and into the seventeenth. Although, by and large, books in Spanish were produced by Spanish presses throughout the first decades of the sixteenth century, Antwerp and Venice were notable for their production of texts in Spanish for both domestic consumption and export to Spanish-speaking lands. In fact, from 1546 onwards, *Cárcel* came to be printed more often outside of the Iberian Peninsula than in its linguistic home territories. The expansion of geographical circulation and printing reflects the cultural and political hegemony of the Holy Roman – and Spanish – Empire. Due to the political and technical circumstances of printing in England, Berners's translation is an exception to this general timeline. *The Castell of Love* first appeared in print in three editions containing paratexts that harked back to the early, courtly stages of the transmission of *Cárcel*, *Carcer*, and *La Prison d'Amours*, in 1548 or 1549, 1552, and 1555, after the deaths of the translator, his dedicatee, and Henry VIII.

Cárcel de Amor and Lo càrcer d'amor

Cárcel de Amor was composed at some point between 1483 and 1492 and was first printed in 1492 by the Cuatro Compañeros Alemanes, a printing partnership established in Seville in 1490 by Paulus von Köln, Johann Pegnitzer von Nürnberg, Magnus Herbst von Fils, and Thomas Glockner, printers of German origin who had come to Seville when commissioned by Isabel I to print Alfonso de Palencia's *Vocabulario universal en latin y romance* in 1490.[5] The only known extant copy of this edition is in the Biblioteca Nacional de España in Madrid (BNE), shelfmark INC/2134 (fig. 2).[6] This *princeps* contains fifty leaves in quarto format, wide margins, round Gothic typeface of two sizes, and initials decorated with botanical motifs, and like most incunables, its print design and layout imitate manuscript conventions.[7] The rubrication, initials, and the use of two type sizes all served to organize the text, by pacing and aiding readers' progress through the work. The edition does not have a title page per se, but rather begins with a rubric in the larger typeface that presents the title, the author, and the circumstances of *Cárcel de Amor*'s composition: "El seguiente tractado fue hecho a pedimiento del señor don Diego de Hernandes, alcaide de los donzeles, y de otros cavalleros cortesanos: llamase carcel de amor. Compusolo san Pedro, comiença el prologo assi" (The following work was composed at the behest of don Diego de Hernandes, Captain of the Light Cavalry, and at the behest of other gentlemen of the court: it is called *Cárcel de Amor*). The rubrics in the *princeps* organize the text into rhetorical units and name the narrator *el Auctor*. Consequently, as Carmen Parrilla notes, the role of "el auctor" thus may well be an effect of editorial decisions made in the printing workshop of the Cuatro Compañeros.[8] The elegant design of the *princeps'* pages and its dedication to a noble war hero endowed the book with social distinction and served ·as visual guarantees of quality, suggesting that the Cuatro Compañeros considered *Cárcel de Amor* a good business opportunity that would appeal to buyers who wanted prestige books.

The single exemplar of the *princeps* also contains evidence of an active sixteenth-century reader, who responded to the text by underlining

pithy phrases and making notes in the margins. As is so often the case
with early printed books, and much to the frustration of scholars interested in reader responses, the margins of the book have been trimmed,
and many of the penned notes are smudged, rendering the majority of
the reader's annotations indecipherable. Nevertheless, it is clear that
the reader took special interest in the novel's epistles. His or her most
intense activity took place in the texts and margins of the last two letters written by Leriano and Laureola. For example, the reader underlined "no haze la merced tu voluntad" (your will/heart does not give
me favour) and "me harías merced non segund quien la pedia mas seg-
und tu que la avies de dar" (I thought you would show me favour, not
because of the one who requested it, but because you were duty-bound
to give it) in Leriano's amorous complaint, accompanying each underlining with a marginal note (E6r). The reader also underlined and commented upon the phrase "mucho te ruego que te esfuerces como fuerte
y te remedies como discreto" (I beg you to arm yourself with strength
and to cure yourself with prudence) and the expression of Laureola's
preference for "la crueldad onesta que la piedad culpada" (virtuous
cruelty rather than blameworthy mercy) in her letter to Leriano (E6r).
A couplet in a similar sixteenth-century hand appears penned on the
verso of the last folio: "que ausente de tu luz, así me siento / como
sacado el pez de su elemento" (when I am not illuminated by your
light, I feel like a fish out of water). This playful couplet, which has
the feel of a *ripio*, may reflect the reader's association of *Cárcel de Amor*
with parodies of courtly love. The lower half of the folio has been cut
out, suggesting the prior presence of yet more readerly activity deemed
either unsuitable or worthy of keeping elsewhere by whoever wielded
the scissors.

The underlinings show an appreciation for *Cárcel de Amor*'s mannered
style, characterized by syncresis, comparison, and contrast in parallel
sentence structures. The readerly comments are also indicative of the
widespread practice of "marginating" (*marginar* or *margenar*) while
reading.[9] Notes, comments, and glosses could later be drawn upon in
the creation of a new text or speech of the reader's own devising, such
as Núñez's prosimetrum continuing *Cárcel de Amor* and Juan Ponce's
villancico, "La mi sola." For example, "rhetorical reading" of exem-
plarily eloquent works, such as *Celestina* and Erasmus's *Enchiridión*, is
advised by Miguel de Salinas in the *Rhetorica en lengua castellana*: "Y
quando en ellos o en otros que hablan bien vemos alguna cosa dicha
por buenas palabras, notarla y procurar ponerla en uso escriviendo o

hablando quando oviere ocasión" (And when we find in these works or others that are well-spoken that something is said with good words [we should] note it and aim to use it in writing or speaking when an apt occasion arises).[10] Such reading practices were long established in humanist pedagogy.[11]

However, by noting Leriano's words, the anonymous reader of *Cárcel* also realized Juan Luis Vives's concerns about the dangers of vernacular eloquence and the contamination of humanistic decorum and *copia*. Vives, excoriating *Cárcel*, *Celestina* – one of Salinas's favourites – and all the other "pestiferous books," protests,

¡Qué locura es tomar plazer destas vanidades! Junto a esto, qué cosa ay de ingenio, ni buen sentido, sino son algunas palabras sacadas de los más bajos escondrijos de Venus, las quales guardan dezirlas a su tiempo para mover de quicios a la que ellos dizen que sirven si por ventura es dura de derribar ... mucho mejor les seria hazer libro de alcahuetería, con perdón a los oyentes.

[What madness it is to take pleasure in such vanities! Moreover, what genius or good sense do they contain? They are just some words taken from the basest, secret lairs of Venus, which lovers recall when they desire overcome the defences of a lady, whom they claim to serve, should she resist conquest ... it would be much better to write the arts of flesh-peddling (please pardon my rude words).][12]

The *gentilhombre* mocked in Melchior de Santa Cruz's *Floresta* was also a rhetorical reader, but his attempt to put Leriano's eloquence to work in an "apt occasion" failed. Vives need not have worried about about the efficacy of the romance's venal rhetoric in the case of that would-be seducer.

Three additional Spanish editions, as well as Vallmanya's translation into Catalan, were produced between 1493 and 1500. In 1493, Pablo Hurus (active 1475–99) produced an edition of *Cárcel de Amor* illustrated by a series of woodcuts made specifically for the work, in Zaragoza,[13] followed by the Catalan edition, printed by Johan Rosenbach (active 1492–1530), in Barcelona, which used the same series of woodcut images (BL shelfmark G.10225). Soon after, Fadrique de Basilea (active 1475/6–1517) published *Cárcel de Amor* in Burgos in 1496. This edition is illustrated with woodcuts copied from those in the 1493 editions, and was the first to include Nicolás Núñez's *cumplimiento* (BL shelfmark

IA 53247). In 1500, *Cárcel de Amor del cunplimiento de Nicolás Núñez* appeared, printed by Pedro Hagenbach in Toledo (Huntington Library shelfmark 93515). At the very least, this rapid succession of editions is a clear indication of booksellers' appreciation of the romance as a good economic investment and of *Cárcel de Amor*'s popularity among book-buyers and readers.[14] Hurus's successor Jorge Coci (active 1499 – 1537) and Fadrique de Basilea's successor Alonso de Melgar (active 1518–25) would also publish additional editions of *Cárcel de Amor*. In Seville, Jacobo Cromberger (active 1499–1528), the founder of the Cromberger printing dynasty, produced four additional editions in 1509, 1511/15, 1525, and 1527.[15]

The early editions of *Cárcel de Amor* and *Lo càrcer d'amor* are all quartos, and their page dispositions are strikingly similar, even discounting the presence of illustrations. While the number of folia varies, each edition uses black letter, or Gothic, type of two sizes, and decorated capitals organized in text blocks of a comparable size.[16] The single edition of *Lo càrcer*, printed in Barcelona in 1493, though a translation introduced by its own distinctive paratext, was designed to look almost identical to the Hurus edition of *Cárcel*, printed earlier the same year. Several later editions also follow this model format, and all the extant Spanish editions up until 1522 are quartos, as are several editions printed the 1530s and 1540s.

The uniformity of the incunable and post-incunable editions shows how *Cárcel* took its place within a distinct editorial genre from 1492 to 1545 in the editions of which we have notice.[17] Potential buyers and readers would have recognized the genre in the size, typeface, and decorative style of title pages that one after another printer replicated. In addition to the textual content of *The Prison of Love*, its length, which contrasts with other romances from the chivalric tradition, also facilitated its material transformations and contributed to its translatability. Even after the addition of Nicolás Núñez's *cumplimiento* in 1496, *Cárcel*'s compactness made it relatively economical to produce and to purchase; like other short romances, its printed forms during the last decade of the fifteenth century and first decades of the sixteenth reflect well-defined editorial and commercial strategies. The length of the romance varied little in the translations, allowing for printers in Italy, France, the Netherlands, and England to pursue similar strategies. Other works pertaining to the same editorial genre include the romances *Arnalte y Lucenda*, also by San Pedro, Juan de Flores's *Grisel y Mirabella* and *Grimalte y Gradissa*, and other short, popular fictions such as *Paris y Viana* and *La Doncella Teodor*.[18] As Victor Infantes de Miguel argues, these *libreros* belong to an important generation of bookmen who, although they produced a variety of titles in varied genres, promoted and disseminated vernacular literature, and, in so doing, shaped literary history by putting models of narrative fiction on the market.[19]

With the introduction of woodcut illustrations made specifically for *Cárcel de Amor* in the Hurus edition of 1493, an illustrated frontispiece became de rigueur for advertising the contents of the work (fig. 1), and, until the middle of the sixteenth century, many editions had title pages bearing a woodcut image of the prison described in the first scenes of the romance or a cut portraying a man and a woman engaged in some sort of courtly communication. The image of the *cárcel de Amor*, depicted with a male figure mounting the stairs to enter, was a visual paratext alerting buyers to the allegorical nature of the romance. In contrast, those printers who decided to advertise *Cárcel de Amor* via an image of a pair of courtly lovers, whether due to a *librero*'s interpretive decision or to lack of an image corresponding to the *cárcel* on hand, placed the romance within a slightly different set of generic horizons of expectation by privileging a scene of amorous parlance over the allegorical prison of Love.[20]

By the 1520s *Cárcel* was beginning to be printed in smaller octavo formats, signalling a decline in the prestige of owning the title as it became more economical to print and purchase; such moves to smaller formats were quite typical for works marketed to successive generations of readers. The first octavos of *Cárcel* are two nearly identical editions dated 1523 and attributed to the workshop of Jorge Coci in Zaragoza, who is thought to have previously printed *Cárcel* in a quarto edition, illustrated by sixteen woodcuts, in 1516, although no known surviving exemplar exists.[21] The 1523 printings contain a new series of woodcuts designed *ex profeso* for *Cárcel*. Both are dated 6 August 1523, and the only difference between the two appears in the title page. One bears the title *Cárcel de Amor. Compuesto por Diego de Sant Pedro a pedimento del señor don Diego hernandez alcayde de los donzelles et de otros cavalleros cortesanos: Nuevamente historiados y bien correydo* (*Cárcel de Amor.* Composed by Sant Pedro at the behest of don Diego Hernández, Captain of the Light Cavalry and at the behest of other gentlemen of the court. Newly Historiated and Well-Corrected) and the other title does not mention the new illustrations, only advertising that the book has been "Nuevamente correydo." Although not advertised on the title pages, these printings also include Núñez's continuation. In 1531, Juan

Batista Pedrezano, a Venetian bookseller known at the time for printing medical, philosophical, and legal works in Latin, produced an edition that replicated the size, *mise en page*, illustrations, type, and text of the "newly corrected" Zaragozan *Cárceles* of 1523.[22]

However, it is possible that the 1523 Zaragoza printings of *Cárcel de Amor* were in fact printed in Venice by Pedrezano and bear Coci's name for the purposes of trading upon his fame in Spain.[23] Why Pedrezano, well established in the industry, might have sought to fake an edition and its correction in 1523 remains a subject for speculation. Pedrezano's 1531 *Cárcel de Amor* was part of a venture the printer undertook in the 1530s, during which time he published popular Spanish works for Italian readers and little else, including *Los cuatro libros de Amadis de Gaula* (1533). According to Conor Fahy, Pedrezano's concentrated production of Spanish books was "undoubtedly associated with the presence in Venice from 1528 of a Spanish *converso*, Francisco Delicado, who edited some, possibly all, of Pedrezanos's Spanish publications," and Pedrezano was probably the unnamed printer of the 1528 edition of *La Lozana Andaluza*.[24] The 1531 imprint of *Cárcel de Amor* may well not have been his first Spanish edition of the romance, as the colophon states that it was made "por importuncion de muy muchos señores a quien la obra: y estilo y lengua Romance Castellana muy mucho place. Corecto de las letras que trastocadas estauan" (due to the importuning of many gentlemen to whom the work, its style, and Castilian vernacular language are greatly pleasing. The letters that were transposed have been corrected) (G7v). The woodcuts featured in these printings were reused in several editions of other Spanish works published by Pedrezano, such as the *Tragicomedia de Calisto y Melibea* (1531), the *Libro aureo de Marco Aurelio* (1532), and *Questión de amor* (1533), which all share the same formatting.[25] Pedrezano, like the early Spanish printers, used the material aspects of his editions to signal genre and contents, in this case, books in Spanish whose language and style would be pleasing. While the relationship between Pedrezano and Coci remains obscure, these editions show the interpenetration of the Venetian and Castilian book trades and literary tastes, as well as the existence of a market for books in Spanish in Italy.

The Italian Editions

Lelio Manfredi's *Carcer d'amore* first appeared in print in 1514 (BL shelfmark G.10100; copy printed on vellum, University of Pennsylvania

Kislak Center shelfmark SC Sa538 Ei513m 1514). This was the first of several editions printed by Zorzi di Rusconi, a printer active in Venice from 1500 to the early 1520s, who was known for the high quality and clarity of his type and the artistic value of the woodcuts he commissioned.[26] Nine more editions, all printed in Venice, with the exception of one Milanese imprint from 1515 without a printer's attribution, followed. Rusconi reprinted *Carcer d'amore* in 1515 and 1518; Bernardino I Viani in 1521; Gregorio de Gregorii in 1525; and Francesco Bindoni and Mapheo Pasini in 1530, 1533, 1537, and 1546.[27] As in the Iberian Peninsula, this frequent reprinting signals the popularity of *Carcer d'amore*, which made it an attractive economic proposition.

The Italian editions are all octavos and all include Manfredi's paratexts praising Isabella d'Este as patron of humanist learning and letters, as well as the translator's aspirational references to her tutor, Mario Equicola, discussed in chapter 2. These editions also prominently feature Manfredi's name and status, either affirming his authorship and intellectual ownership of the work – *Carcer d'amore del magnifico msier Lelio de Manfredi, ferrarese* (*Carcer d'amore* by the most noble Lelio de Manfredi of Ferrara) – or his labour as translator – *Carcer d'amore traduto dal magnifico msier Lelio de Manfredi, ferrarese* (*Carcer d'amore* translated by the most noble Lelio de Manfredi of Ferrara). Diego de San Pedro and his noble dedicatee have disappearèd from view, their agency only sensed, palimpsestically, as it were, by readers familiar with the romance in Spanish. Beyond advertising Manfredi's agency in the cultural transfer of the romance, the titles and title pages all underscore the act of carrying the romance over from Spanish to the mother tongue, the nature of *Carcer d'amore* as the product of translation, as a work originally in *idioma spagnolo*, now presented to readers in *lingua materna*.

In the Italian editions, then, the domesticating activity of the translator is mirrored by the material book. The typefaces used by the Venetian printers also belong to the conventions of humanist printing. Paul Grendler's survey of typefaces used for printing romances in Italian in the sixteenth century finds that roman and Gothic types were used for traditional medieval romances, while italic fonts signalled "new" and imported Spanish ones, the typographic differences serving as markers of generic distinction. *Carcer d'amore*, however, does not conform to Grendler's observations, perhaps because it blended humanism with a non-academic vernacularity, thus allowing for editorial experimentation.[28] Rusconi's editions are all printed in round type, as are the Milan edition of 1515 and the editions printed by Bernandino I

Viani and Gregorio de Gregorii. The later editions printed by Francesco Bindoni and Mapheo Pasini all feature roman type for headings and italic type for the body text. Rusconi's, Bernardino I Viani's, and Gregorio de Gregorii's editions all contain decorative features, such as woodcut initials and decorative borders on the title pages. Bernardino's edition of 1521 also reproduces a woodcut illustration of a supine female figure, nude to the waist, about to be pierced by an arrow shot by blind Cupid (BNE shelfmark R/40529). This image was to reappear in the 1528 edition of Francisco Delicado's *La Lozana Andaluza*.[29] The image constitutes a kind of false advertising for the precise contents of *Carcer d'amore*, but would have served to alert or lure potential buyers to the genre of love-casuistry contained within. All of Bindoni and Pasini's editions contained copies of the woodcuts first featured in the 1523 editions of *Cárcel de Amor*.[30]

Carcer d'amore's historical audiences directly associated the romance with the arts of letter-writing, both diplomatic and amorous, recalling Vives's consternation. One of the extant copies, printed by Bindoni and Pasini in 1537, contains evidence of yet another rhetorical reader, whose notes made in the margins throughout the text were all trimmed beyond legibility (BL shelfmark 1084.d.1). This copy was bound at some point with contemporary reprints of three Italian treatises on letter-writing, among them the *Formulario nuovo de dittar lettere amorose* (A new method for composing love letters) by Andrea Zenophonte da Ugubio (Venice: Sessa, 1531) and *Formulario ottimo et elegante il quale insegna il modo del scrivere lettere* (The best and elegant method which teaches how to write letters) by Bartolommeo Miniatore (Venice: Guadagnino & Florio, 1544), which also contains examples of letters by ambassadors.[31]

The Venetian editions of both *Carcer d'amore* and *Cárcel de Amor* were part of a larger boom in vernacular printing concentrated in the city. As Augustus Palotta notes, "From 1490 to 1540 Venice produced more books than any other European city, books that encompassed socio-intellectual concerns much broader in scope than those represented by humanistic learning. Besides Latin and Greek texts, Venetian printers published a broad range of books in the vernacular that enhanced the status of Italian and gave rise to new classes of readers" and became extremely important as a printing centre for Spanish books that served local and international markets.[32] The Venetian printers worked in "an ever-changing constellation of collaborations and informal partnerships" that produced significant amounts of popular, vernacular reading materials, as Rosa Salzburg notes.[33] Their combined production set the parameters for the circulation and reception of *Carcer d'amore*, situating it in relation to other vernacular works that blended the sensibilities of humanist fiction with eroticism and intimate first-person psychological explorations, such as Boccaccio's *L'amorosa Fiammetta*, one of San Pedro's influences, and *Celestina*, which were both also featured titles in Gregorio de Gregorii's, Bindoni's, and Pasini's publication lists at the time.[34]

The Bodleian copy of Bindoni and Pasini's 1533 edition contains the material traces of another historical rhetorical reader, who marked passages salient for their style throughout the text (Shelfmark Lawn f.30). This reader, like the marginator in the *princeps*, found Laureola's reasoning memorable and marked "Quanto meglio me seria esser biasimata per crudele, che maculata per pietosa" (How much better it would be for me to be defamed for cruelty, than slandered for mercy) (17v). He or she was also drawn to examples of *copia*, such as the King's defence of his dubious administration of justice, "pone timore alli iniqui, sustiene li boni, pacifica differenzie, adapta le questioni, excusa le contenzioni, rimove li liti, assicura li camini, onora li populi " (strikes fear in the iniquitous, supports the good, pacifies disagreements, quells quarrels, prevents disputes, resolves suits, secures byways, honours the people) (29r).

The First French Editions

D'Assy's translation, *La Prison d'Amours*, was first published by the Parisian bookseller Galliot du Pré, known for the meticulousness of his editions and the high quality of their illustrations.[35] Du Pré's bookshop in the Palais de Justice was well placed to attract well-educated clients with business to do in the courts and Parliament, characterized by Annie Parent as "tous seigneurs, gentilshommes ou bourgeois ... ils peuvent y acheter arrêts ordonnances et commentaires juridiques, ou se procurer romans et poèms, curiosités scientifiquies, historiques, géographiques, textes philosophiques ou religieux: par leur éducation et leur rôle dans l'Etat, ils prennent part au mouvement humaniste et aux débats religieux qui divisent leur époque" (lords, nobles, or bourgeois, who could buy legal rulings, judicial commentaries, or get novels and poems, scientific curiosities, histories, geographies and philosophical or religious texts there, men who due to their education and role in state affairs were involved in the humanist movement and in the religious debates that raged at the time).[36] Tilley adds that "Du Pré had numerous patrons among princes and nobles ... in his choice of works of publication he doubtless consulted their taste."[37] Du Pré published one edition of *La Prison* in 1525 (in two print runs) and another in 1526, both illustrated octavos.

The title pages of Du Pré's editions advertise *La Prison d'Amours* as a Spanish story of reciprocal love that has an established history of transmission: *La prison d'amours laquelle traicte de l'amour de Leriano et Laureole, faict en Espaignol puis translate en tusquan et nagueres en language francoise. Ensemble plusieurs choses singuiliers a la louenge des dames* (*The Prison of Love*, which discusses the love of Leriano and Laureole, written in Spanish, then translated in Tuscan, and now in the French language. With many singular things in the praise of ladies) (fig. 8).

This subtitle echoing d'Assy's own evaluation of the romance as containing "dassez belles matières ... pour ieunes dames" (many pleasing matters for young ladies) clearly situates *La Prison* within the *querelle des femmes*. In France, as in Italy, the debate on women intersected with humanist rhetorical practices.[38] Signalling this generic affinity on the title page suggested that in *La Prison* readers would find texts similar to Christine de Pizan's *Cité des dames*, first published in 1497 (Paris, Antoine Vérard), *Le miroir des dames*, the French translation of Boccaccio's *De mulieribus Claris*, among others (Lyon, du Bois, s.d.), the anonymous *Dialogue apologétique excusant le devot sexe femenin* (Paris, Fédéric d'Egmont, 1516), and Symphorien Champier's *La nef des dames vertueuses* (Lyon, Jacques Arnoullet, [1503]). Readers' taste for images of love as a prison or place of captivity was well established in French vernacular letters. Pierre Gringore's *Le Chasteau d'amours*, for example, an allegorical colloquy on the nature and vagaries of love, was published at least seven times between 1495 and 1541. It is possible that Galliot du Pré saw the translation of *Carcer d'amore* as a good opportunity to tap into the same market. The popularity of *La Prison d'Amours*, in turn, may have stimulated the later printings of *Le Chasteau*.

The two-colour printing – frequent in du Pré's title pages – signals the importance of the three languages – *Espaignol, tusquan, françois* – underscoring the cosmopolitan nature of *La Prison*, and, in the 1525 edition, the first rubric, while signalling the domesticating work of translation, also renders homage to the role of Lelio Manfredi in his role as a cultural agent, stating "Carcer ou prison damoure traduict par magnifique Lelie Manfredi ferrarese de langage espaignol en langue tuscane et depuis retraduict du tuscan en nostre maternel francoys" (*Carcer or Prison d'Amour*, translated by the *magnifico* Lelio Manfredi of Ferrara from the Spanish language into Tuscan and then retranslated

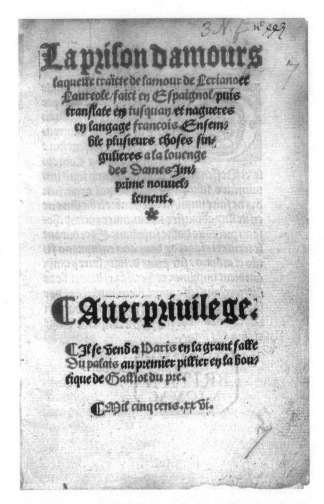

Figure 8. Title Page. *La Prison d'Amours.* Paris: Galliot du Pre, 1526. London, British Library C.33.f.1. © British Library Board.

from Tuscan into our maternal French) (f. 1r) (BnF shelfmark Rés. Y2 2350). Directly below the rubric, and above the opening lines of *l'Acteur,* the French printer inserted a woodcut that recalls the author portrait 1515 Italian edition. However, in the case of *La Prison d'Amours,* where no authorial attribution is provided in print, rather than serve to associate d'Assy with the intellectual authorship of the romance, the picture

provides readers with an image of the diegetic author-figure and narrator. The woodcut portrays a scene of oral transmission, with the author-
figure reading aloud to a group of men (fig. 6).

Du Pré's editions contain tables of contents, a finding aid not included
in the Spanish or Italian printings, but characteristic of du Pré's publications. They also feature woodcuts recycled from other sources, fifteen
in the first edition and ten in the second. While the woodcuts in the two
editions are generally thematically related to the texts they accompany,
the use of recycled cuts leads to some maladroit text-image relations.
On the one hand, both editions reproduce a cut showing a man in bed
speaking with, and perhaps blessing, another kneeling at the bedside,
to illustrate the chapter titled "Lerian au lict malade reprent Theseus
louant les dames" (Lérian, sick in bed reprehends Theseus, [by] praising ladies) (1525, f. 71v; 1526 f. 70r). However, both editions also reproduce a scene of a man and woman sharing a canopied bed, the man
turned away from his bedmate to kiss a second woman at his bedside
to illustrate "L'acteur sur la mort de Lérian" (the Author on Lérian's
death) (1525, f. 76v; 1526, f. 86r). Du Pré's editions also differ in their
presentation of the letters exchanged between the protagonists. The
1525 edition contains versions of all the letters in verse, while those of
1526 only present the final three letters – Laureola's letter to her father,
Leriano's last request for a remedy for his lovesickness, and Laureola's
refusal to communicate any further with Leriano until after her father's
death – in verse. This pattern set in 1526 is followed in all of the suc-
ceeding printed editions of d'Assy's translation.

Two Parisian editions without printers' marks were published in 1527,
also containing recycled woodcuts, perhaps in an attempt to take advantage
of the success of Du Pré's editions, which sold quickly enough for him to
produced three editions in two years. In 1528, Olivier Arnoullet, a printer
active in Lyon from 1514 to 1567, produced another edition of *La Prison*
meant to catch the eye of potential buyers with double colour printing and
a woodcut of a courtly scene depicting a crowned woman embracing a
kneeling man on the title page.[39] Much like the other early printers of *Cárcel
de Amor*, *Càrcer d'amor*, and *Carcer d'amore*, the French printers of d'Assy's
translation followed the patterns established by the first successful editions.
Attractive and decorative title pages, woodcuts, verse, and typefaces that
signalled vernacular literary tradition to French readers combine in these
editions to present *La Prison d'Amours* as a love story reminiscent of the old
romances of chivalry, while at the same time its verses also imitated the
contemporary vogue for the *épîtres* of the *rhétoriqueurs*.

The Prison of Love: 1546–1650

In the second half of the sixteenth century, *The Prison of Love* transformed textually, materially, and generically in print, in step with its circulation beyond its first inscribed and intended readerships. Printing of the Italian translation fell off, while Berners's English translation, composed in the 1520s, appeared in print for the first time. Manfredi, d'Assy, and Berners all refer to *The Prison of Love* as a "little book" in their respective dedications to Isabella d'Este, Jacquette de Lansac, Françoise d'Alançon, and Elizabeth Carew. In the second half of the sixteenth century *The Prison of Love* became literally and physically very small; it was printed most often in duodecimo and sextodecimo formats with few visual embellishments beyond decorated initials. Furthermore, new contexts and paratexts intended to guide readers' reception appeared in both the continental and English editions produced during this period.

Size, or "sheer mass," "is the most readily perceivable piece of evidence" about a physical book and its impact on readers, as Joseph Dane remarks.[40] A book's size often determined the circumstances of its consumption and preservation. Books produced in large folio formats "cannot be read casually" and do not lend themselves to private, informal perusal because they are difficult to transport and too large to be held in readers' hands. Small books can be carried about, and read in private, intimate settings.[41] Menéndez Pelayo associated the size of printed editions of *Cárcel de Amor* with clandestine, gendered reading practices when he remarked that despite its prohibition by Vives, "el librillo de la *Cárcel de Amor*, fácil de ocultar por su exiguo volumen ... continuó siendo leído y andando en el cestillo de labor de dueñas y doncellas" (the little book *Cárcel de Amor*, easy to hide due to its tiny size ... continued to be read and be found in the needlework baskets of ladies and girls).[42]

Genre and format were also often associated in early print culture with legal and canonical works, as well as romances of chivalry, typically appearing in larger, formidable formats. Although not a hard and fast rule, quartos and octavos came to be associated with shorter forms of vernacular literary fiction in the first half of the sixteenth century; novellas and relatively short romances like *The Prison of Love* were seen as "small books," especially when compared with romances of chivalry.[43] Figure 9 shows the relative sizes of small and large formats. The folio pictured measures 35 × 23.5 cm, while the duodecimo only 11.5 × 6.8 cm.

Figure 9. Formats and Comparative Sizes. Booth Family Center for Special Collections, Georgetown University, Washington, DC.

Libraries arranged books according to format, and inventories often categorized books by size, at times omitting individual titles and listing numbers of "small books." The economic significance of editorial choices regarding size, type, layout, and decoration is clear: the larger and more elaborate a book – whether print or manuscript – the greater the cost of its production, the greater its price, and the greater its value as an object of social status and as an object of exchange. Large-format books from the period have a greater survival rate than small ones, which were often damaged and "read to death," which may help to explain why so few exemplars of each of the editions of *Cárcel de Amor* and the translations have survived.[44]

The small-format editions of *The Prison of Love* printed in Spanish and French in the second half of the sixteenth century are not as attractive as aesthetic objects as the elegant, illustrated editions produced by the pioneering bookmen of the 1520s and 1530s, which, though not imposing folios, were objects of prestige consumption, destined for audiences at the upper rungs of the economic and social ladder, that is to say, the "known traditional" market for books.[45] But as new markets for romance reading opened, and as literacy and printing spread, printers sought to print large quantities of certain titles at minimal cost and, in turn, sell to a broader customer base. However, other editorial strategies, including anthologization and the bilingual presentation of the romance in Spanish and French, show how printers and booksellers were purposeful in their repackaging of *The Prison of Love* in the small books they produced. The shift from the publication of larger, illustrated editions proudly advertising the imprimatur of their noble dedicatees points to changing perceptions of books, which were no longer limited in circulation and inscribed readership. The small book had entered common currency.

Anthologies and Agencies

The second half of the sixteenth century was an era of anthologization for *The Prison of Love*, which began to circulate in tandem with *Questión de amor* (1513) as well as with short works that printers and editors considered fitting companions for the romance, and which at times served to fill the final signatures of their editions. In this way, editorial genres, born out of a combination of convenience and literary judgment, continued to reflect and shape literary categories and expectations, as if in anticipation of twenty-first-century booksellers' algorithms that recommend new titles based upon customers' earlier purchases. The sixteenth-century bookmen were just as interested in moving stock, and their title pages were the marketing devices that alerted potential buyers to the "new and improved" contents of their books. Rather than promising newly corrected and illustrated presentations of *The Prison of Love*, as was the case in the 1520s and 1530s, their editions advertised expanded contents, affiliated titles, and new uses. Spanish presses continued to turn out imprints of *Cárcel de Amor* in octavo formats until 1551, when, with the exception of a 1580 duodecimo edition from Salamanca, it would be printed only in Antwerp, Louvain, Paris, and Venice.[46]

In 1546, Martin Nuncio (also known as Martin Nucio and Martinus Nuntius) printed the first of many small-format editions of *Questión de amor y Cárcel de Amor; Cárcel de Amor del cumplimiento* that would be produced in Antwerp in the sixteenth century.[47] Nuncio (active 1540–58), perhaps best known for his editions of the *Cancionero general* and *Cancionero de romances*, was one of several printers in Antwerp who produced popular and widely translated books in Spanish during the reigns of Carlos V and Felipe II and became important figures in the diffusion of Spanish literature and language on the continent and in England.[48] Nuncio also appended three *romances* (ballads) about the Cid to fill the final quire of the 1546 edition; in 1556 he reprinted *Questión/ Cárcel* and included an elegy "sobre la muerte de la fortuna dada por la virtud" (on the death of fortune dealt by virtue) dedicated to Diego de Herrera, to complete the volume (*Questión de amor y Cárcel de amor. Cárcel de Amor del cumplimiento* [Anvers: Martin Nucio, 1556; Hispanic Society of America]).

The anonymous *Questión de amor* is a roman-a-clef that revolves around the question of which courtly lover suffers more, Vasquirán, who enjoyed a passionate relationship with his beloved Violina but lost her to death, or Flamiano, a man suffering from lovesickness who "sirue [a Belisena] sin esperança de galardon" (serves Belisena with no hope of favour) (*Questión* 41).[49] The author, stating that the story takes place during the French king Charles VIII's short reign over the Kingdom of Naples in 1495, declares that he, an eyewitness to the events he will relate, wishes to remain nameless, but that readers can divine the true identities of the *cavalleros* and the *damas* they serve because he has used the first letters of their real names for the names of his protagonists, though he has added to "lo que fue algo delo que no fue" (what was something of what was not) (*Questión* 43).[50]

The introduction to *Questión de amor* promises that readers will find an assortment of literary forms within its pages, "entretexense en esta controversia muchas cartas y enamorados razonamientos" (many letters and enamored discourses are interweaved in this controversy), as well as descriptions of court entertainments (*Questión* 41). The anonymous author concludes his prologue with an invitation to readers to continue the debate: "Sobre lo qual con diversas letras y embaxadas largos dias contienden y al fin hallando se juntos prosiguiendo la question sin dar le fin pendiente la dexan porque los que leyeren sin leer tengan si querran occasion y manera en que altercar y contender puedan" (They argued the question for many days, in divers poems and embassies, and in the end they continued to discuss the question together, without concluding, leaving it unresolved, so that those who might read it, having nothing more to read, would have the opportunity and manner of quarrelling and disputing) (*Questión* 43).

Cárcel de Amor and *Questión de amor* shared comparable horizons of expectation and inscribed readerships, and both first appeared in print in prestige editions. Like *Cárcel*, *Questión de amor* brings readers into a debate about courtly love in the style of a Senecan controversy, with protagonists voicing and dramatizing arguments from both sides, yet leaving the debate inconclusive. Both are composed of hybrid literary and rhetorical forms woven together by the narrating author-figure. The anonymous author of *Questión de amor* may, in fact, have taken his inspiration for Vasquirán's allegorical vision from *Cárcel de Amor*.[51]

The physical proximity of the two works in a single volume is a material reflection of their already strong intertextual relationships, while anthologization is also an expression of how *Cárcel de Amor*'s and *Questión de amor*'s respective textual agencies weave into each other. In the context of the anthology, readings of *Questión de amor* are always informed by *Cárcel de Amor*, and *Cárcel* by *Questión*. Anthologies, as Stephen Nichols and Siegfried Wenzel observe in their work on manuscript culture, create "manuscript agency" by placing individual texts within a single matrix that offers present-day readers a model for understanding the ways that texts drawn together into "could have been read by the patron or public to which [they were] diffused."[52] Clearly, such dynamics are also present in print anthologies, which place individual works into editorial matrices in which the boundaries between one work and another are interleaved while still remaining visible. The result is somewhat paradoxical, as Barbara Benedict remarks, because print anthologies are "more than one work at the same time they are also one work."[53] Author-functions, complex in both *Questión de amor*'s and *Cárcel*'s transmission and textuality, are also transformed in anthologies. No authorial attribution is given on the title pages of the 1546 and later editions of *Questión de amor y Cárcel de Amor*. Nuncio's editions only give the printer's device of two storks and state, "Fue impreso en Enveres en el unicornio doro par Martin Nucio" (Printed in Antwerp at the golden unicorn by Martin Nucio). It appears that *Cárcel de Amor* had originally been intended for sale as a separate edition because it is introduced by a second title page, bearing the title *Cárcel de Amor, del cumplimiento de Nicolás Nuñez*, as well as the printers' device and name. Diego de San Pedro's name only appears in the rubric introducing his dedication to Diego de Hernández. In the case of *Questión de amor y Cárcel de Amor*, however, the fragmenting of authorial subjectivity and perspective is mitigated by the presence of the narrating *Autor* in both texts. This figure may be construed as an intradiegetic inscribed author and an eyewitness to the events and debates on love in both works.

The layout of Nuncio's duodecimo editions of *Questión de amor y Cárcel de Amor*, which would be imitated by successive printers, unquestionably privileges *Questión de amor*. On the title pages, *Questión de amor* appears in a larger roman font than *Cárcel de Amor* and the table of contents gives a detailed description of the first text, while only listing the title of the second. The relegation of *Cárcel de Amor*, and Diego de San Pedro along with it, to the back of book suggests that at the time the printers considered *Questión de amor* of greater appeal to book buyers than *Cárcel*, perhaps due to earlier associations of *Questión de amor* with books of higher status. From 1513 to 1529, *Questión de amor* was often printed in folio editions with elaborately illustrated title pages that also feature two-colour printing, suggesting that its Iberian printers wished to market it as something of greater literary heft and of greater value as an object than the small fictions circulating at the time. *Questión de amor* debuted in a deluxe folio edition printed in Valencia by Diego Gumiel (BL Shelfmark C.57.g.14). However, other editorial strategies had created associations between the two works. Pedro de Castro printed an edition of *Questión de amor* in 1546 and then recycled the woodcut from its title page for the title page of his 1547 edition of *Cárcel de Amor*. The Venetian printer Pedrezano may have been the first to bring the two works into a single editorial genre when he printed an octavo edition of *Questión de amor* in 1533, illustrated with woodcuts recycled from his earlier edition of *Cárcel de Amor* (BNE shelfmark R/8928). Although

Questión de amor was not as widely translated and disseminated as *Cárcel de Amor*, it was highly successful, appearing in twenty-five editions between 1513 and 1598, and translated into French as *Le debat des deux gentilzhommes espagnolz, sur le faict damour* (The debate on love between two Spanish gentlemen), printed in 1541. Whatever the case, *Cárcel de Amor* and *Questión de amor* became closely linked in the Spanish literary field in the second half of the sixteenth century, so much so that the similarities of the two works, along with their shared material contexts in anthologies, led some readers to attribute *Questión de amor* to Diego de San Pedro.[54]

Cárcel de Amor was also published as part of an anthology of Diego de San Pedro's own works during this period. In contrast to the imprints of *Questión de amor* followed by *Cárcel de Amor*, in 1547 Pedro de Castro printed *Cárcel de Amor hecha por Hernando de Sanct Pedro con otras obras suyas va agora añadido el sermón que hizo a vnas señoras que dixieron que le desseauan oyr predicar* (*Cárcel de Amor* by Hernando de Sanct Pedro with other of his works, with the sermon that he wrote for some ladies who said they wanted to hear him preach now added), in Medina del Campo, an edition that highlighted San Pedro's status as author. San Pedro's *Sermón de amores*, a catechism of courtly love that informs Leriano's course of action in the romance, and a lover's complaint in verse addressed to one of Queen Isabel I's ladies, follow *Cárcel de Amor*. The poem's description of lovesickness as a "sacrificio en las llamas del cuidado" (sacrifice in the flames of care), and the lady's rejection and withholding of her *galardón*, which causes the lover's death, concludes the volume by casting San Pedro in the role that Leriano occupies in *Cárcel de Amor*. While elevating San Pedro's authorial status, this edition also continues in the tradition of the earlier printers by drawing readers' attention to the courtly nature and origins of his compositions.

Alfonso de Ulloa edited a reprinting of the anthology, working with Gabriel Giolito de Ferrarii, one of the most productive Italian printers, publishers, and booksellers of the day. Giolito, known for producing popular, vernacular books, published some 850 titles between 1539 and 1578 and had shops in Venice, Naples, Bologna, and Ferrara.[55] Like Pedrezano, Giolito printed many Spanish titles, including *Celestina* and *Questión de amor*, also edited by Ulloa. The only extant copies of Ulloa's *Cárcel de Amor* are from an edition of 1553, with a title page advertising *Cárcel de Amor* and other works by San Pedro, to which "va agora añadido el sermon que hizo [San Pedro] a unas señoras que dixeron que le desseavan oyr predicar" (now with a sermon he wrote for certain ladies, who said they wished to hear him preach) and stating that the text within is "nuevamente con diligencia corregida y emendada" (newly and conscientiously corrected and edited) (BNE Shelfmark R/3238; A1r).

Alfonso de Ulloa, stepping into the role of a revisionary author, rededicated *Cárcel de Amor* to Antonio da Pola, a captain in the Imperial Army, serving under Ferrante Gonzaga. Like the translators of *Cárcel de Amor* who preceded him, Ulloa worked in the world of diplomacy, serving as secretary to Diego de Hurtado de Mendoza, poet, historian, and ambassador for the Empire in Venice. In this position, Ulloa established contact with Giolito and became a promoter, translator, and editor of Spanish literature, an "active mediator between two cultures," who created a Spanish national literary profile for an Italian readership.[56] These books were also exported to the Iberian Peninsula. The increase in Spanish titles printed at Venice at this time coincides with the increase in imported books more generally in the Iberian book trade and a decline in printing output in the Peninsula.[57]

Echoing the dedications of Manfredi, d'Assy, and Berners, Ulloa characterizes *Cárcel de Amor* as reading that his patron will find "muy deleictable y gracioso" (very pleasant and amusing) but "de poco momento" (of small moment) (A2r). The occasion of dedicating the small book also is a celebration of Antonio da Pola and Ulloa's mutual service to Carlos V. Ulloa's dedication, which firmly places his *Cárcel de Amor* within the world of the Spanish Empire and its cultural power, also nostalgically links the triumphs of the mid-sixteenth century to those of the *reconquista*, the "guerra del año pasado" (last year's war) of *Cárcel de Amor*'s opening allegory. Unlike *The Prison of Love*'s earlier revisionary authors, Ulloa promotes San Pedro as an illustrious writer from a celebrated era of conquest, for Spanish readers in Spain, for Spanish-speaking inhabitants of Venice, and for those Italian readers he also imagined as the public for his editions of Spanish literary works.

The copy of Ulloa's edition held by the BNE displays the activities of another rhetorical reader impressed by the eloquence of *Cárcel de Amor*'s letter-writers, much in the style of the marginalizations in the 1492 *princeps*. This reader underlined and placed double vertical lines in the margins beside the expressions and turns of phrase that he found notable, and that Vives would have judged to come from the secret vademecum of Venus, such as "porque quando amor prende haze el coraçon constante" (when love takes hold it makes the heart constant)

(15r), "Y asi quanto yo mas contemplo tu hermosura mas ciego tengo el sentido" (and thus, the more I contemplate your beauty, the more my sense is blinded) (16v).

The images of *Cárcel de Amor*'s early, distinguished dedicatees fade from view, along with Diego de San Pedro in the small-format Spanish and French bilingual editions, published in Paris, Lyon, and Antwerp between 1552 and 1650, in duodecimo and sextodecimo formats. This imprecise number is due to the tangled history of relationships between printers and the difficulty of separating some of the reprintings from editions. In any case, this figure is only rivalled by the number of editions of *Cárcel de Amor* in Spanish printed in the Iberian and Italian peninsulas between 1492 and 1580. The number of known editions, but dearth of extant copies, indicates the popularity and heavy use of these little books.

Cárcel de Amor. La Prison d'Amour. En deux langages, Espaignol et François, pour ceulx qui uouldront apprendre l'un par l'autre

The difference between the two phases of the cosmopolitan circulation of *The Prison of Love* is marked in the French case by two separate translations. At the same time that *Cárcel de Amor*, with its continuation by Núñez, continued to be printed on its own and also as the second fiddle to *Questión de amor*, it began to circulate in its most prevalent late sixteenth-century form, the small-format, bilingual *Cárcel de Amor. La Prison d'Amour. En deux langages, Espaignol et François, pour ceulx qui uouldront apprendre l'un par l'autre* (In two languages, for those who wish to learn one from the other), first printed in Paris by Gilles Corrozet in 1552 (fig. 10).

Giles Corrozet (1510–68) was a polygraph, translator, historian, and publisher, who became active in Parisian book trade around the time when he published his own *Les antiques erections des Gaules* (Architecture of the ancient Gauls) (1531) and *La fleur des antiquités, singularitez et excellences de Paris* (The flower of Parisian antiquities, and unique, distinguished sights) (1532).[58] Corrozet also published several other works in bilingual formats, including *Grisel y Mirabella*, prior to *Cárcel de Amor/ La Prison d'Amour*. Although he was likely aware of d'Assy's translation of *Carcer d'amore*, Corrozet either commissioned a new translation or translated *Cárcel de Amor* himself, directly from a Spanish version close to the text found in the *princeps*.[59] The earlier editions of *La Prison d'Amours* all advertise the Spanish origins and Italian mediation of the

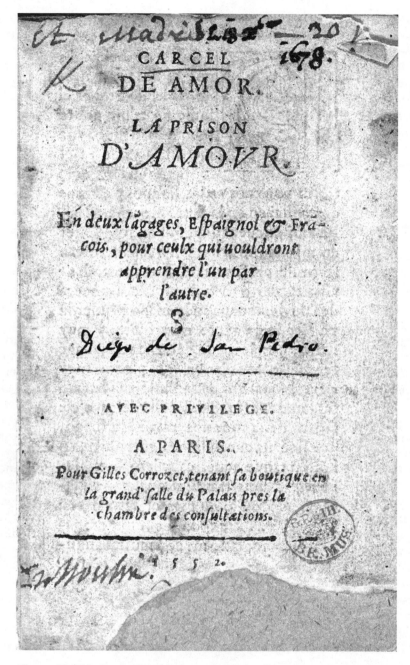

Figure 10. Title Page. *Cárcel de Amor. La Prison d'Amour. En deux langages, Espaignol et François, pour ceulx qui uouldront apprendre l'un par l'autre.* Paris: Gilles Corrozet, 1552. London, British Library, 246.a.30. © British Library Board.

romance and, by reproducing d'Assy's prologue, make the act of translation an act of visible authorship. In contrast, Corrozet's and the other
successive bilingual editions name no authors or translators on their
title pages. Corrozet, moreover, does not address any individual dedicatee, nor does he place himself in the role of author-figure. His claim
for ownership of the work, made on the title page, is that of a publisher,
seller, and architect of the edition.

Language-learning, imitation, and translation were closely related
activities in the Middle Ages and the Renaissance. Students of classical
languages learned by the process of double translation, rendering Latin
or Greek texts into their vernaculars and then retranslating back into
the studied language. During the 1530s and 1540s continental vernaculars had begun to rival Latin as languages of international commerce
and diplomacy, leading to an increased interest in vernacular language
study. Book publishers and language instructors met the demand by
producing multiple language learning texts, polyglot phrase books,
and the like. A great number of these books are small, economical to
print and purchase, and also easily portable. As Louis Kelly observes,
interest in and the growth in publications on language study were
mutually reinforcing.[60]

Cárcel de Amor/La Prison d'Amour, like many bilingual and polyglot
books of the period, presents the texts in parallel, facing-page format,
with verso pages in Spanish and rectos in French, a page layout that
continually reminds readers of translation, linguistic contact, and difference (fig. 11). On the title page and throughout the book, typeface
designates tongue: roman type is used for the Spanish texts and italic
for the French, a distinction that makes concerted used of typographic
interplay, the relationship between the shape of printed words, meaning, textual syntax, and content.[61] As a reader progresses through the
bilingual edition, moving between languages, roman type increasingly
becomes tied perceptually to Spanish, while italic is similarly associated with French. Thus, the bilingual format of the book stages translation and the spatial, visual co-presence of the two languages, while also
typographically signalling their difference.

As Guyda Armstrong argues in her study of sixteenth-century English
translations, the "early modern language manual or translated book is
much more than the text itself: it is a privileged site of cultural transfer
and historic literary and linguistic practices, articulated on the page."[62]
And indeed, in the case of *Cárcel de Amor/La Prison d'Amour*, the material book, like the earlier translators' prologues, expresses an ideology

Espues de hecha la guerra del año passado, viniendo a tener el
inuierno a mi pobre
reposo, passando vna
mañana quando ya el
sol queria esclarecer la
tierra por vnos valles hondos y escuros
que se hazen en la sierra Morena, vi salir ami encuetro por vnos robledales
do mi camino se hazia, vn cauallero taa
feroz de presencia, como espantoso de
vista: cubierto todo de cabello, a manera
de saluaje: lleuaua en la mano izquierda
vn escudo de azero muy fuerte y muy
rezio, y en la mano derecha vna ymagé
feminil entallada en vna piedra muy
clara: la qual era de tan estrema hermo-
fura, que me turbaua la vista delos ojos:
salian della diuersos rayos de fuego,
que lleuaua encendido el cuerpo de vn
hombre, que aquel cauallero forciblemente lleuaua tras si: el qual con vn lastimado gemido de rato en rato dezia.
En mi se sufre todo. Et como emparejo conmigo, dixo me con mortal angustia:

Presque la guerre de
l'an passé fut sinee, ve-
nant tenir mon yuer
en ma pauure maison,
passant vne matinee,
alors que le Soleil cô-
mécoit a illuminer la
terre, je m'en val ombrageux & obscur qui
est en la montaigne de Morienne, vey ve-
uira l'encoire de moy dans vn estroit boys
de chesne ou mon chemin s'adressoit, vn
cheualier auant furieux de presence com
me espouentable de veue, tout couuert de
poil en maniere de sauuage. Il portoit en
la main senestre vn fort escu d'acier tres-
reluisant: & en la main dextre vne image de femme entaillee dans vne pierre tres-
clere: laquelle estoit de tar extreme beaus-
té, qu'elle me troubloit la veue des yeulx.
D'elle sailloient plusieurs rayons de feu qui
tenoient embrasé le corps d'un hôme qui-
celuy cheualier menoit derriere luy par
force: lequel auec lamentables gemisse-
mens continuelement disoit. En ma foy
se souffre tout. Et quand il fut a l'endroit
de moy, il me dit auec mortelle angoiss-
fe.

A. ij

Figure 11. Facing-page Bilingual Opening. *Cárcel de Amor. La Prison d'Amour. En deux langages, Espaignol et François, pour ceulx qui uouldront apprendre l'un par l'autre.* Paris: Gilles Corrozet, 1552. London, British Library, 246.a.30. © British Library Board.

of translation. The books' typographic coding of difference combines with an architecture of likeness. The ideal of translational equivalence is laid out in every opening of facing-page bilingual editions. Such *mise en page* guides readers to move from a line in one language to its corresponding line in another in order to encounter the translational equivalent. In this way, the pages of *Cárcel de Amor/La Prison d'Amour*, in keeping with other language-learning manuals of the period, present linguistic and cultural understanding as attainable.

Moreover, the lateral movement from Spanish to French and back again modelled by the *mise en page* of the bilingual books is a material rendering of horizontal, vernacular translation practised by Manfredi, d'Assy, Berners, and the translator of Corrozet's bilingual editions. As we saw in chapter 3, vernacular translation of fiction was frequently a matter of literal, word-for-word rendering, in contrast to vertical literary *translatio* and imitation of classical texts. The printers replicated the translators' desire for dynamic equivalence, for "easie languages" on the printed page. The visual rhetoric of linguistic relations in *Cárcel de Amor/La Prison d'Amour*, then, presents two vernaculars as mutually accessible and translation as a reversible, transparent process. Pedro Simón Abril, translator and author of a Greek grammar published in 1587, calls this format "la conferencia de lenguas" (the conversation of tongues).[63] Even though the *conferencia* is quickly revealed to be less than exact and less than transparent – once one reads a few passages, the misalignments in the supposedly one-to-one correspondence are evident – the persistence of this kind of layout suggests that the illusion of transparency, exact equivalence, and interlingual ease was a cherished one among printers and readers.

The bilingual editions are also anthologies that draw the Spanish and French texts into a single conceptual and editorial matrix. Yet *Cárcel de Amor* and *La Prison d'Amour* are mutually reflective and interdependent texts within the bilingual structure, interlaced rather than sequentially ordered. A reader, not unlike the character of *El Autor/l'Acteur* learning to translate and interpret the Macedonian language, can move between the two languages, finding the equivalents between Spanish and French vocabulary that can be put into future extra-textual and practical use. However, it is important to note that the relation between French and Spanish in *Cárcel de Amor/La Prison d'Amour* was not as horizontal as the facing-page format might suggest. Each opening is a contact zone between two rival languages with several asymmetries of cultural power.[64] In this case, Spanish hegemony on the continent made learning Spanish both attractive and necessary for the diplomats and merchants that Corrozet and later publishers saw as their primary buyers, and yet at the same time, French readers may have felt pride in the superior eloquence of their own vernacular, which frames the Spanish text. Corrozet's paratexts domesticate the Spanish text, framing it within the desires of French-speaking readers; the title pages of these editions directly interpellate French readers desirous of developing their multilingualism.

Romances, when marketed as texts with practical applications such as *Cárcel de Amor/La Prison d'Amour*, played an instrumental role in this area of book production in the sixteenth century. *Amadis de Gaule* was praised as a superb model for French eloquence, while *Grisel y Mirabella* and *Arnalte y Lucenda* also make frequent appearances in bilingual and polyglot books intended for vernacular language acquisition. By leading readers vicariously through the process of horizontal translation to an understanding of Spanish, the bilingual *Cárcel de Amor/La Prison d'Amour* encourages the reader who "desires to learn one language from the other" to use intuition and experience, building up understanding as they read through the romance; the pleasure of romance offered a stimulus to memory and rhetorical cultivation. Nor did reading the romance with the goal of learning multi-vernacular eloquence mean that readers no longer enjoyed the themes that had spurred *The Prison of Love*'s translation in earlier decades. In 1567, Robert le Mangnier Published *Cárcel de Amor. La Prison d'Amour* followed by "Epitaphes singuliers de plusiers Dames Illustres, traduiz d'Italien en François" (Singular epitaphes of many illustrious women, translated from Italian into French), a choice that, like Du Pré's title pages of the 1520s, signals *Cárcel de Amor/La Prison d'Amour*'s continued association with the *querelle des femmes*.[65]

Some sixteenth-century commentators on language study privileged intuition and literary modelling of language use over formal grammar study, notably Erasmus, who, though he acknowledged the need for learning the rudiments of Greek and Latin, remarked in his *De Ratione Studii* that boys should read literature early in their studies, "For a true ability to speak correctly is best fostered by conversing and consorting with those who speak correctly, and by the habitual reading of the best stylists."[66] Erasmus, of course, was thinking of classical languages and would not have classed *The Prison of Love* among those works to be praised for their eloquence. But, as we have seen above in Salinas's praise for *Celestina*, humanist ideals regarding copia and fluency had found firm footing in vernacular literary culture.[67] Romances, and the translations of San Pedro and Flores's romances in particular, as Joyce Boro has shown, were used as language-learning tools because they are not only models of courtly comportment, but also of vernacular eloquence, "founts of copious sententiae, aphorisms, witty sayings, deliberative and persuasive structures and instances of stylistic prowess."[68] Grace and eloquence, the humanist method suggested, resulted from interest and imitation.

Corrozet does not provide any further instruction to the readers of *Cárcel de Amor/La Prison d'Amour* who desire to learn "one language from the other," other than to point out on the title page that the book is designed for the purpose. Claudius Hollyband's *The Italian Schoolemaister* (London: Purfoot, 1597; BL shelfmark 627c.10) includes a similar, facing-page bilingual English-Italian edition of Diego de San Pedro's other romance, *Arnalte y Lucenda*, at the end of his textbook. On its title page, the *Schoole-maister* promises that the "fine Tuscan historie" is "a verie easie way to learne th'Italian tongue." The romance, Hollyband instructs, should be read after the student has consulted his rules of Italian pronunciation, verb conjugations, article usage, declensions, and "other speciall thinges requisite for the learner of the same tongue." After these preliminary lessons, the student may turn to the *Historie of Arnalt and Lucenda,*

> In the reading whereof, using a good discretion, he maye attayne great profite, as well as for th'understanding of any other Italian booke as for his entraunce to the learning of the same tongue: and maye also gather therein many pretie and wittie phrases, sentences, and devises, agreeable to the same Argumente and apte for the lyke or any other speech or writing. (2v–3r)

Nevertheless, the structure of some of the editions of Hollyband's book place the bilingual text of *Arnalt and Lucenda* before his exposition of Italian pronunciation and grammar, implicitly expecting readers to forego the more formal lessons and, in humanist fashion, learn the language by experiencing its eloquence directly within a literary work.

Some of the extant copies of *Cárcel de Amor/Prison d'Amour* retain the marks of readers' working from one language to another. One historical reader of the 1552 edition, for example, underlined phrases that he or she considered rhetorically memorable – and perhaps "pretty and witty" – especially instances of the figures of opposition that are one of the hallmarks of San Pedro's style, faithfully rendered by the translators, such as "deves tener mas gana de morir, que de hablar" (You must desire death more than speech) (BL shelfmark 246.a.30 B7v). This reader also moved between the two parallel texts in order to identify and translate vocabulary, using underlining and marginal notes as memory aids.

The Castell of Love

The Castell of Love was not printed until 1548 or 1549 and then only twice more, in 1552 and 1555, almost a generation after its translation into English, during a period when the relaxation of printing laws led to the increased production and circulation of romances.[69] And, although the number of editions is limited, the second and third English editions donned new paratexts and an editorial apparatus that was unparalleled by that of the continental editions, providing further evidence of *The Prison of Love*'s continued appeal to rhetorical readers seeking models of eloquence.

All three editions of *The Castell of Love* are octavos, printed in the black-letter type typical of English book production at the time. The edition of 1548 or 1549, printed by John Turke in London, contains very little in the way of decoration (BL shelfmark C.57.aa.36). Two large decorated initials appear at the start of Berners's dedication to Elizabeth Carew and at the beginning of the narrative, respectively. Turke was a London stationer who published ballads in the 1540s, but was tried for his publication of an interpretation of the Gospels and condemned to the Fleet prison in 1543.[70] In 1547, however he seems to have been back in business and printed *A lamentation of the death of the most victorious Prynce Henry the eyght*, and in 1550, *The ryght and trew understandynge of the Supper of the Lord*. Consequently, his publication of *The Castell of Love* seems to be something of an anomaly in his career.

The 1552 edition printed by the prolific Robert Wyer (active 1524–56) contains three decorated initials and five woodcuts, which although recycled from other contexts, are apt for visualizing the action (BL shelfmark G.10332). Of these, one cut features the sort of rhetorical performance that proliferates other illustrated editions of *The Prison of Love* and in the French manuscripts. An image of a woman seated by a castle moat and writing upon a scroll appears between the rubric "The auctor" and the line "When Laureola had endyd her wordes she was so hevye and so full of weepynge that in a maner her paynfull lyfe grevyd me as sore as the death of Leriano" (O6v), illustrating the opening of the last section of Berners's translation of Núñez's continuation. Wyer, like Turke, had also come under ecclesiastical scrutiny for publishing the *Symbolum apostolicum* in 1527, but he went on to publish some 145 popular, inexpensive books over his long and successful career.[71] The third edition, printed by John Kynge (active 1555–61) in 1555, has a title page with decorative borders, but is not illustrated (Huntington shelfmark 27912). Few copies of these editions have survived.

The full title, repeated in all three editions, *The castell of loue, translated out of Spanishe into Englyshe, by Johan Bowrchier knyght, lorde Bernis, at the instance of lady Elizabeth Carew, late wyfe to Syr Nicholas Carew knyght. The which boke treateth of the loue betwene Leriano and Laureola doughter to the kynge of Masedonia*, expresses the importance of the romance's status as a translation from Spanish. In addition to announcing the acts of translation, the title's stress on the romance's Spanishness may also have served as a signal of the rhetorical style readers would find within its pages.[72] There was also undoubtedly a political resonance to the title's announcement of *The Castell of Love*'s Spanish provenance, the courtly origins of the work, and its relationship to the Carews, an allusion, perhaps, to their troubled personal histories as supporters of Catherine of Aragon and to Sir Nicholas's expulsion from Henry VIII's inner circle followed by his execution in 1539.[73]

The Castell of Love's full title highlights female readership, echoing the addresses to Marina Manuel, Isabella d'Este, and d'Assy's unnamed "most virtuous lady," as model inscribed readers. Further, and much like the title pages of *La Prison d'Amours*, the title promises readers a story of reciprocal love. However, unlike the French translation, the English *Castell of Love* leaves readers in no doubt about Laureola's feelings towards Leriano, because Berners chose to include Núñez's continuation, seamlessly weaving it into the romance's conclusion. This interpretation renders Leriano's suffering the direct result of Laureola's cruelty rather than the consequence of unrequited desire, a situation that lends itself to varied readings.

In the second and third editions, Andrew Spigurnell, an otherwise unknown Tudor writer and editor, steps in as a revisionary author-figure, first announcing his edifying presence in a verse prologue inserted between the end of Berners's prologue and the opening of the narrative. Spigurnell's editorial agency is felt throughout the pages of these two editions in the marginal callouts that accompany the text and in the intercalated verses sung by Leriano at turning points in the plot. An additional change found in the second and third editions occurs in

Leriano's speech in praise of women, where the Marian references are altered so that the Virgin Mary is only praised for bearing Christ, rather than as a deliverer of grace in her own right, reflecting the Protestantism of the printer or editor,[74] a textual domestication along doctrinal lines.

Spigurnell's verse prologue intervenes at the juncture between his imagined women readers and his interpretation of Laureola as a *belle dame sans merci*. Depicting himself as one who was tempted to "rede and loke upon" *The Castell of Love* because of its title, Spigurnell says that after he had read it through, he deemed it a "present unworthie" for a lady or a queen, despite the title's reference to Elizabeth Carew's "instance," because the book's "matter" is how the cruelty of a lady caused the death of her lover (93). Women, he says, echoing Leriano's own complaints to Laureola that she was not behaving as a beloved noblewoman should, are specially endowed by nature to be merciful. *The Castell of Love*'s conclusion shows just how "A Lady pyteles and endewed with cruelte / Is to her honour reproach and obloquie [a disgrace]" (93). Nevertheless, Spigurnell concludes that the book can in this way provide counsel to "women in generall" – if not to ladies and queens of exemplary pity, mercy, and grace – concerning how not to behave, since it will teach them the cruel and dangerous effects of "theyr disdayne and lacke of pytie" (93). Affecting the commonplace stance of authorial modesty, Spigurnell claims that he has dared "newly to penne" the book and asks readers to forgive and emend his "rudeness." The claim of "newly penning" *The Castell of Love*, in addition to its appropriation of authorial agency and blame, may also refer to the addition of Spigurnell's three poems and rhetorical apparatus.

The poems, inserted into the episodes where Leriano receives Laureola's first letter, and where he writes his last letter to her, may perhaps be in imitation of the French editions' versifications, or of Núñez's verses in the continuation, though Berners's translation rendered the latter's poetry into prose. Another possibility is that Spigurnell's verses are reflections of the less courtly sort of informal "recreational music making" that urban Tudor book buyers would have recognized.[75] Whatever the case, the performance of the poems adds to Leriano's profile as a perfect courtier, his rhetorical, courtly skills now extending to song and his accomplishments to lute- and harp-playing. The poems also represent the heights of Leriano's hopes of remedy and the depths of his suffering at Laureola's continued rejection even after he has proven her innocence.

The first musical interlude occurs when Leriano's health is restored and the pain of his passion relieved by Laureola's letter and by the personifications of Comforte, Myrth, Rest, Pleasure, and Hope: "when he had rede over the letter he was all hole, as though he hadde never felte passyon" (118). After pledges of friendship and fealty between Leriano and the Author, the lover takes up a lute decorated with the motto "my death causeth by absens … shall be redemyd with presens" and sings a welcome to the healing personifications. The song also takes up the romance's twinned focus on material texts and textual mediation: "Blyssed by the hande that did write, / blyssed be the pen that made the letter, / and blyssed be the memory that dyd indyght, / and blyssed be the paper and the messenger" (118–19). Leriano then sings about the state of the lover sick from unrequited love, who "lives for to die," in verses that repeat the description of his lovesick suffering in the letters he has sent to Laureola (120). Leriano's third and last musical performance, in which he accompanies his song on a black harp, is intended to hasten his death, since "musike to a sorowfull person is as paynful as it is pleasaunte to one that delyghteth in myrth," as Spigurnell, writing in the guise of the Author, explains (149). The verses bemoan Fortune's lack of pity, bid farewell to Hope, Pleasure, and the other life-giving emotions in order to welcome their opposites, and conclude with an apostrophe to Death, who cannot arrive too soon for the singer (150).

Spigurnell invites and guides two types of imagined readers through his revision of *The Prison of Love*. In the prologue he prescribes one interpretation and use of *The Castell of Love* to his imagined lady readers and the dedicatee that he inherited from Berners's own prologue. Ladies, he advises, should read it as a negative exemplum about women's pitilessness and disregard for the men who would love them. Laureola is not a heroine to be imitated. On the other hand, Spigurnell also anticipates "rhetorical readers" who will collect elegant turns of phrase, unpack the individual elements of ekphrasis, and use the epistles and orations as models of persuasive eloquence. His marginal glosses function as a rhetorical scaffolding around the text and draw readers' attention not only to the exemplarity of the plot, but also to *The Castell of Love*'s style and composition. In the opening scenes, Spigurnell's gloss signals readers to note the detail of the description of Desire and the Prison of Love, calling attention to the ekphrastic construction of the *castell*, for example, "The description of the Castell of love outwartle" (B1r) and "the exposicion or declaracion of the castell & of Love" (B4v). In the margin of the scene where Leriano composes his first letter, Spigurnell

commands readers to "Note the writing of Leters," and parses the following letters, drawing readers' attention to their adherence to the *ars
dictaminis* and use of tropes. Call-outs similarly parse each point in Leriano's declamation of the ".xv. poyntes agaynste a them that erreth in
spekynge evell of women, and .xx. other reasones ... wherby we are
bound to say well of all women, with dyverce other amples of theyr
bountie & goodnes" (156). "Note" is printed the margins where Spigurnell's own poems are inserted. Spigurnell's callouts and verses also
provide a visual contrast with the prose text, which directs the flow
of reading and creates pauses in the narration, alerting readers to the
importance of the romance's formal aspects.

Spigurnell's double didacticism would seem to point to gendered
modes of reception. Women, generally encouraged to be "silent, chaste,
and obedient," did not need such rhetorical training unless they occu-
pied very high social positions, as Renaissance experts on their education averred. And, when the plot and the persuasive orations are read
in tandem, it is clear that the noble women in *The Castell of Love* write
and orate eloquently, as did the many historical women involved in
matters of state in the sixteenth century, including some of the women
directly addressed in *The Prison of Love*'s many paratexts. Moreover,
in Berners's translation, eloquence is shown to be more effective than
in *Cárcel de Amor* – when read without Núñez's continuation – and the
other translations, because Laureola is, in the end, persuaded to admit
her love for Leriano. However, with Spigurnell's intervention, Laureola
is above all presented as a negative exemplar for the inscribed female
readers, for she has misused rhetoric in her "cruel" written refusals of
Leriano's love-service. According to the annotated *Castell of Love*, she
should have matched her eloquence with feminine decorum and written
with the mercy natural to women instead of with cruelty, or perhaps, in
the ultimate expression of ideal feminine propriety, just kept her peace.

Like Núñez years before, Spigurnell found the romance incomplete
and sought to remedy the lack through his own assumption of revisionary authorship. *The Castell of Love* modelled ekphrasis, epistles, debate,
lamentation, and oration, yet it still lacked a full complement of rhetorical and literary forms. Consequently, the editor added poetry and
music to the armoury of rhetorical devices modelled in the work. Spigurnell, a rhetorical reader, considered *The Castell of Love*'s other readers
in need of guidance in the form of new, instructive paratexts, and used
the very "pretty and witty" words and tropes that he pointed out to

readers as useful for their own speech and writing in crafting his own verse contributions to the story.

Throughout *The Prison of Love*'s material diffusion, bookmen across Europe created the material look and feel of the romance according to their own interpretations of its meanings and the ways in which it might be placed in book markets. Like the translators, the bookmen who produced *The Prison of Love* in different material forms participated in the process of domesticating the romance for their audiences. Foreignizing and domesticating acts of translation and translation's visibility or invisibility have generally been conceived of in terms of the text alone, as Armstrong observes, yet material book objects also reveal these translational modes.[76] The material books do not just contain the romance, they produce and remediate it in different editorial genres, reflecting what Amadeo Quondam characterizes as the pressure felt by book producers to present old texts in new ways.[77] The bookmen fashioned each of their *Prisons* as a "public artifact," which they released into particular social situations and circuits, promoting *The Prison of Love*'s radiant, wave-like diffusion.[78] At each step of the recursive and iterative process of transmission, the expressive forms in which *The Prison of Love* appeared also asserted their agency, guiding reading and reception. Rhetorical readers responded to these expressive forms in kind, marking "pretty and witty" figures of speech, recording and perhaps inventing verses of their own, as the *princeps* of *Cárcel de Amor* suggests, and plying their pens in the endeavour to "learn one language from the other" in bilingual editions. Readers' underlining, annotating, and inventive writing in the margins turned printed copies into personal objects.

Chapter Six

Visual Rhetoric:
Reading Printed Images in
The Prison of Love, 1493 to 1546

The Prison of Love is a work that inspired illustration. Editions featuring woodcuts designed specifically for the romance began to circulate almost as soon as *Cárcel de Amor* appeared on the printed book market. These woodcuts intensify *The Prison of Love*'s metafictions by remediating romance's internal, textual dynamics of scribal publication and staging of rhetorical performances. That is to say, the cuts refashion and interpret the content of the text in a new, graphic medium.[1] This chapter continues the study of the material books that produced *The Prison of Love* by turning to the relationship between texts and images in the early editions of *Cárcel de Amor*, *Lo càrcer d'amor*, and *Carcer d'amore*, in order, on the one hand, to imagine how late-fifteenth and early sixteenth-century audiences might have *seen* and consequently interpreted the romance, and, on the other, to explore how the books in which *The Prison of Love* was printed engage with material textuality. The woodcuts, as Juan Manuel Cacho Blecua observes regarding the first illustrated editions of *Cárcel de Amor*, are not direct translations or visual adaptations of the romance, rather contemporary readings of the narrative that make it possible to theorize about historical reception.[2] Further, the illustrated editions are evidence of the ways in which printers and booksellers sought to market the romance and capitalize on its popularity and of how woodcut artists added yet more layers of interpretive agency.

Woodcuts, often considered the "poor relations of manuscript miniatures in the study of book illustration," as Martha Driver wryly observes,[3] are also often treated as "extra-literary matter,"[4] or as supervening elements of books rather than integral parts of the narratives they illustrate. While treating xylographic illustration as extra-literary may make sense for studying the life and diffusion of particular cuts, workshops, and artisans, once woodcuts are included in the same material habitat as a literary work, they become integral to the audiences' experience and reception of individual editions. Woodcuts, and especially those cuts designed to illustrate a particular work, are places where the material and narrative aspects of a book meet; they are reminders that books are both objects in the world and imaginative entities. Each illustrated edition of *The Prison of Love* embeds the text within a distinct visual program, and each bookman responsible for the production of these editions performs an authorial function, by revising and repackaging the romance in new material forms.

The sixteen woodcuts designed and first used for the edition of *Cárcel de Amor* printed in Zaragoza by Pablo Hurus in June 1493, reappeared in *Lo càrcer d'amor*, the Catalan translation printed in Barcelona, by J. Rosenbach in September of the same year, and were copied for the third edition of the romance in Spanish, printed in Burgos by Fadrique de Basilea in October of 1496. According to Antonio Gallego, Hurus's workshop produced the greatest number of illustrated books printed during the incunable period in Spain, and although the printer tended to use woodcuts imported from Germany, the use of new and original cuts became necessary with the more frequent printing of works originating in Spain.[5] Until Miguel Ángel Pallarés announced the discovery of thirty-three folios of the second edition of 1493 in the Archivo de Protocolos de Zaragoza, the woodcuts were thought to have been produced for the translation into Catalan.[6] Long considered pre-eminent examples of xylographic art, the woodcuts constitute the beginning of an extensive iconographic tradition that grew in conjunction with the pan-European transmission of *Cárcel de Amor* and *The Prison of Love*.[7] Many of these images are familiar to modern readers of *Cárcel de Amor* due to their frequent reproduction in critical editions and bibliographies.

A second set of seventeen woodcuts was designed to illustrate *Cárcel de Amor* some thirty years later, and first appeared in the two printings dated 1523 and attributed to the workshop of Jorge Coci, in Zaragoza. Much like the images printed for the first time in 1493, this series would also be reused in successive editions and versions of the work. The same cuts appear in the 1531 edition of *Cárcel de Amor*, printed in Venice by Pedrezano; they were subsequently copied and used in four editions of the Italian *Carcer d'amore*, printed by Bindoni and Pasini in 1530, 1533, 1537, and 1546. Some of the images were also recycled for use in other Spanish books printed in Venice by Pedrezano, such as the *Tragicomedia de Calisto y Melibea* (1531), the *Libro aureo de Marco Aurelio* (1532), and *Question de amor* (1533).[8] While the 1493 cuts have received a good deal of previous scholarly attention, the 1523 cuts have not.

Woodcuts, in addition to their ornamental function, provide information, serve to spatially organize and demarcate text, and at times direct the progress of reading.[9] Like other visual elements upon the printed page, woodcuts serve as "points of entry to reading matter," "protocols of reading," and "sites of memory."[10]

In a comparative study of illuminations and woodcuts in the many manuscripts and early printed editions of the *Pèlerinage de la vie humaine*, Michael Camille remarks upon the material likeness shared by printed texts and printed images, where "the image has the same black and white structure as the word," as opposed to manuscript illumination, where paintings may "carry the gaze outside the text" and, consequently, cause "interference" in the reading process.[11] During the early handpress period, xylographic images were often bound together in formes with type in order to be impressed at the same time and with the same ink as text. This shared production of text and image created close material ties and consequently facilitated their reception as collaborating, mutually integral elements in early printed books.

Susan Hagan observes that the interplay of illustrations, graphic designs, and *mise en page* creates a range of *loose* and *tight* perceptual ties between texts and images. Tight interplay links "specific visual information to specific words." Loose interplay and collaboration are produced by "overall thematic relationships between image and text." "Interplay in sequence," on the other hand, is a "directed invitation to look and then read in a particular order." Each of these types can potentially produce "*cross-modal* meaning," which Hagan defines as "shared understanding gained by an audience that must both look and read."[12] While Hagan's observations concern contemporary cognitive theory and visual rhetoric, her categories of interplay are useful for thinking about the relationships between texts and images in early printed books and about how woodcuts function within the material habitat of the narrative text. Early printed books create a further kind of tight interaction, which I call *xylographic interplay*, in order to describe the spatial and syntactic relationships created between printed images and printed type. Xylographic interplay is an important characteristic of many early printed books, and is particularly resonant in the illustrated editions of *Cárcel de Amor*, *Lo càrcer d'amor*, and *Carcer d'amore*. The texts of *The Prison of Love* interlace verbal imagery and visual imagination, particularly through the extravagant allegory of the prison. In these illustrated editions, material image-texts redouble the interplay of reading and seeing, moving from the mind's eye to the material.

These forms of interplay are precisely how woodcuts establish protocols for reading. As Brian McHale, writing about spatial and textual segmentation on the page, notes, "the interaction between narrative and non-narrative organization becomes especially visible whenever textual materials undergo transformation into a different form – for instance in cases of translation and adaptation."[13] The addition of illustrations in new editions of old texts is also an important indicator of how printers and booksellers sought to adapt and refashion books for new audiences.

Reading Printed Images in *Cárcel de Amor* and *Lo càrcer d'amor*, 1493 and 1496

The first series of woodcuts and their placement upon the pages they illustrate provide a good example of the various forms of xylographic interplay at work in the early editions of *Cárcel de Amor* and *Lo càrcer d'amor*. The distribution of woodcuts throughout the three editions – two of *Cárcel de Amor* and one of *Lo càrcer d'amor* – is slightly different due to their textualterity, in this case, the translation to Catalan in September 1493, and the addition of Núñez's continuation in 1496.[14] These three editions, as noted in chapter 5, are a series of lookalikes. The reuse of the woodcut designs was part of the printers' material imitation that made *The Prison of Love* recognizable despite the differences in their language and contents.

It is not surprising that the generically and narratorially hybrid *Cárcel de Amor* inspired a series of images that are at once visually and aesthetically coherent, yet also heterogeneous. The first two woodcuts are large, occupying the full printed space on the pages where they appear. These two cuts are allegorical and ekphrastic: the first depicts the eponymous *cárcel* (fig. 1), the second, the *Auctor*'s vision of *Deseo* leading his captive, Leriano (fig. 12).[15]

Comiença la obra.

Despues de hecha la guerra del año passado: veniendo a tener el yuierno a mi pobre reposo: passando vna mañana quando ya el sol queria esclarecer la tierra.por vnos valles hondos y escuros que se hazen enla sierra morena: vi salir a mi encuentro por entre vnos robzedales do mi camino se hazia.vn cauallero assi feros de presencia.como espantoso de vista:cubierto todo de cabello a manera de saluaje.leuaua enla mano siquierda vn escudo de azero muy fuerte: y enla derecha vna piedra muy clara: la qual era de tan estrema hermosura que me turbaua la vista. faltauan della diuersos rayos de fuego que leuaua encendido el cuerpo de vn hombre que con lastimado gemido de raro en raro destaxen mi se le sufrie todo. y como en parejo comigo: dixo me con mortal angustia. Caminante por dios te pido do que me sigas: y me ayudes en tan grande cuyta yo que en aquella fazon tenia mas causa para temer: que razon para responder. Puestos los ojos enla estraña vision estuue quedo:trastornando en el coraçon diuersas consideraciones. Dexar el camino que leuaua parescia me desuario.no hazer el ruego de aquel que assi padescia:figuraua me inhumanidad. en seguir le: hauia peligro. y en dexar le. flaqueza: con la turbacion no sabia escoger lo mejor. Pero ya que el espanto dexo mi alteracion en algun sossiego. vi quanto era mas obligado ala virtud: que ala vida: y empachado de mi mesmo por la dubda en que estuue: segui la via de aquel que quiso ayudar se

a.iij.

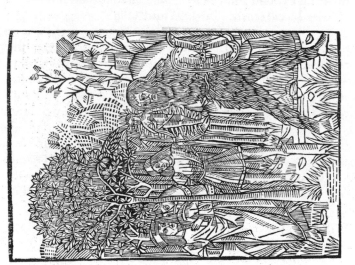

Figure 12. The *Auctor's* vision of *Deseo* leading his captive, Leriano. *Cárcel de Amor*. Burgos: Fadrique de Basilea, 1496. London, British Library, IA.53247. © British Library Board.

Ten smaller cuts depict characters engaging in rhetorical activities: writing, debating, volubly mourning, appealing, and judging. Among these rhetorical woodcuts, four are materially metafictive: they show Leriano and Laureola in the act of producing and destroying the very texts that are reproduced typographically alongside the printed images (figs. 13, 14, and 15).

A third category might be termed genre woodcuts, those images depicting scenes that could belong in other romances, such as the duel, the battle, and the siege (fig. 16).[16]

All but the first two cuts share the text block with type and are the same approximate width of each line of text, indicating that they were printed simultaneously with the text and conceived as part of the overall design of the books they illustrate.[17] Each type of woodcut, by virtue of its *mise en page* and narrative content, inhabits the material book in a particular dynamic of xylographic interplay, presenting different relationships between printed words and images.

The first of the two allegorical woodcuts, the image of the *cárcel* and the *Auctor* mounting the stairs to enter it, appears twice in the editions printed in Barcelona in 1493 and Burgos in 1496, first as the title page, and then on the page facing the *Auctor*'s ekphrasis of the allegorical edifice (fig. 1). The second, which illustrates the *Auctor*'s strange vision of Desire carrying the *imagen femenil* and leading his captive, Leriano, to the Prison of Love, appears just once in all of the editions (fig. 12). The perceptual ties between these two cuts and the texts that they accompany are at once conceptually tight and spatially, or perceptually, loose.

The allegorical woodcuts correspond to the intense visuality of the first scenes in the text, where ekphrasis encourages the conjuring up of images in mind. In this way, the woodcut images visualize materially what the text encourages readers to see with "interior" eyes; they are guides for the imagination and the experience of *enargeia* discussed in chapter 4. Medieval and early modern books frequently concretize verbal allegories by illustrating them. Given the visuality of allegories, so often presented as dream visions, this conventional pairing of rhetorical imagery with pictorial illustration suggests that readers and book designers sought material visual aids for allegorical interpretation. In such illustrations, the allegorical "corporeal similitudes" and edifices that are imagined become the objects of physical sight, transferred back into the realm of material figures. This reconcretization guides readers and viewers to form particular kinds of active images that will, in turn, be stored up in memory.

Carta de leriano a laureola.

S I touiera tal razon para escreuir te: como
para querer te:sin miedo lo osara hazer.
Mas en saber q̃ scriuo para ti se turba el
seso.y se pierde el sentido. z desta causa antes que lo començasse toue comigo gran confusion. mi
fe dezia que osasse:tu grandeza q̃ temiesse. enlo vno ha-
llaua esperança:y por lo otro desesperaua.ytenel cabo a-
corde esto.Mas guay de mi q̃ comence temprano a do
ler me.y tarde a quexar me. Porque a tal tiempo soy ve

Figure 13. Carta de Leriano a Laureola. *Cárcel de Amor*. Burgos: Fadrique de Basilea, 1496. London, British Library, IA.53247. © British Library Board.

otra perſona eneſta vida ſino de mí ſola que poz librar
te de muerte me cargue de culpa. como quiera que eneſta compaſſió q̃ te boue mas bay pena que cargo. pues
remedie como jnocéte.y pago como culpada. pero toda
via me plaze mas la prıſion ſin yerro:que la libertad có
el.y poz eſto abun q̃ pene en ſoffrirla:deſcáſo en no me-
reçer la.yo ſoy entre las que viuen la que menos deuiera ſer viua. Sí el rey no me ſalua eſpero la muerte:ſi tu
me delibzas:la de ti z delos tuyos:de manera q̃ poz vıia

Figure 14. Carta de Laureola a Leriano. *Cárcel de Amor*. Burgos: Fadrique de
Basilea, 1496. London, British Library, IA.53247. © British Library Board.

por ꝓcio de amoꝛ tu vida ſe pudiera cõpꝛar: mas poder
tuuiera mi deſſeo q̃ fuerça la muerte: mas para libꝛar te
della ni tu foꝛtuna quiſo. ni yo triſte pude: cõ doloꝛ ſera
mi biuir. y mi comer. y mi penſar. y mi doꝛmir haſta que
ſu fuerça y mi deſſeo me lieuẽ a tu ſepultura.

El auctoꝛ

Y lloꝛo q̃ hazia ſu madꝛe de leriano creçia
la pena a todos los que enella participa-
uã: y como el ſiẽpꝛe ſe acoꝛdaſſe d̃ laureola

Figure 15. Leriano destroys Laureola's Letter. *Cárcel de Amor*. Burgos: Fadrique
de Basilea, 1496. London, British Library, IA.53247. © British Library Board.

El auctoz

℃Omo la mala fortuna emyidiofa ð los bie
nes de leriano vfaffe conel de fu natural cõ
dició.dio le tal reues quãdo le vido mayoz
en profperidad.fus defdichas caufauã paf
fion a quien las vio. y combidan a pena a quiẽ las oyẽ.
Pues dexãdo fu cuyta para hablar en fu reuto: defpues
que refpondio al cartel de perfio como es efcripto:fabi-

Figure 16. Duel between Leriano and Persio. *Cárcel de Amor*. Burgos: Fadrique de Basilea, 1496. London, British Library, IA.53247. © British Library Board.

In terms of interplay, the two allegorical cuts exist within a relationship of relay and feedback with the text: each visual element in the woodcut images is linked directly to particular words in the text. For example, the *cárcel* in the woodcut depicts the "quatro pilares" (four pillars) upon which rests "una torre de tres esquinas ... en lo alto della, una imagen de nuestra umana hechura" (a three-cornered tower ... atop each an image in our own human form) (*Cárcel* 6). The same sorts of direct ties between the printed words of the narrative and the printed images of the woodcut exist between the second cut readers encountered in the 1493 and 1496 editions of *Cárcel de Amor* and *Lo càrcer d'amor* and the texts it illustrates (fig. 12). The cut depicts the figure of the *Auctor* actively shrinking away from *Deseo*. Although the title page may not reproduce the ekphrasis of the Prison of Love in all its verbal detail, and the second woodcut adds to and interprets the textual description, what I wish to stress here is the very direct relationship drawn in the physical book between the words on the page and the printed image.[18]

The woodcut that serves as title page also offers the first text in the book, reproduced xylographically: "Carcel de Amor" in a phylactery. Thus, the title page, like the text that follows, is an imagetext in which not only are words and images interwoven through interpretive processes, they are also literally and visually linked together upon the material page. The words integrated into the picture serve as "anchors" in Roland Barthes's sense: they focus the readerly gaze and set parameters of perception.[19] Moreover, by integrating text into the picture, the sequential perception of reading printed words is mapped onto the more freely moving spatial focusing of the eye. Discrete pieces of information are all available simultaneously, and sequencing – the focusing and refocusing necessary for looking at an image – depends upon the viewer's habits and horizon of iconographic expectations.[20]

In the first decades of the romance's reception, a title page depicting the allegorical and eponymous Prison of Love was apparently an important printing and marketing convention.[21] Graphic images of the allegorical prison served as frontispieces for many subsequent editions of *Cárcel de Amor* and the Italian *Carcer d'amore*. At least three different woodcuts that graphically reproduce the *Auctor*'s verbal description of the prison were designed for the title pages of five editions dating from 1493 to 1523. Consequently, images of the Prison of Love came to represent the work as a whole and served many of the work's audiences as graphic paratexts and visual protocols for reading. The title pages, blending text and image, establish the metaphorical nature of the tower depicted, leading audiences to expect an allegorical narrative and perhaps a conventional visionary dream narrative.

The second woodcut establishes the *Auctor*'s role as witness and sympathizer to Leriano's enthralment to desire (fig. 12). Desire, holding the flaming image of a woman described in the text, looms larger than the other two figures in the cut, in the foreground of the right side of the frame. Leriano, hands bound behind his back, stands slightly behind Desire, in the middle ground, and the Author is on the left, his body turned away from the other two figures, hands raised to his chest, mouth agape, and his head and eyes turned towards them. The facial features of all three are highly detailed, and the woodcut artist paid particular attention to their eyes and the direction of their gazes. This is a scene where the Author looks and is looked upon: he stares in fear at Leriano, Desire, and the image of the flaming woman. These three figures, in turn, all direct their gazes at the Author. Robert Folger has studied the dynamics of the gaze in this cut, observing that the design of the cut places Leriano and the Author in a mirroring relationship, while at the same time it presents Deseo, the externalized representation of Leriano's desire for Laureola, as his "uncanny double." As the observer of Leriano's captivity and torture, Folger continues, the Author also represents the extra-textual public of Leriano's lovesick performances.[22] Leonardo Funes considers the effect on the extra-textual reader, who in turn gazes upon the figures depicted in word and image, as an extension of the meditative contemplation encouraged by the text.[23] This complicated play of gazes also complements the dialogism of the vision narrative, in which all three male figures speak in the first person.

The enthralling *imagen femenil*, as illustrated in this woodcut, recalls images of Venus and the Virgin Mary, but also may have reminded San Pedro's historical readers of images of Lady Rhetoric wielding the "sword of language," a feminine personification of masculine rhetorical mastery.[24] Consequently, Jill Ross has read this image as an inversion of the *topos* of the "sword of language" controlled by men, who, like San Pedro himself, were trained in the theory and practice of rhetoric. The scene is "an allegorization of the power of the senses to overwhelm reason, to deprive the victim of agency and language," she argues, that in its "yoking of the power of love to that of rhetoric" reflects the deep anxiety about rhetoric in this work where the protagonists' learned attempts to persuade others almost always fail.[25]

The allegories that illustrate – verbally and in woodcut pictures – the first episodes of the romance demonstrate that the *Auctor* has access to Leriano's interior psychological states and, through the *Auctor's* vivid descriptions, which in turn are materialized in the woodcuts, the audience also has Leriano's psychological landscape painted before their eyes, rhetorically, through verbal description, and literally, in the printed image. Nevertheless, a weaker material tie in the physical book tempers this very tight conceptual relationship between the textual narrative and the woodcut images. The allegorical woodcuts are also the only cuts that occupy full pages, without sharing their *mise en page* with blocks of printed text. This disposition of texts and images would have an effect on the pace of reading, because it encourages readers to turn deliberately from one page of a book's opening to another, to pause in the passage from text to picture and vice versa. Such pauses would seem to recall and complement the sense of contemplative, imaginative movement through the allegorical landscape already present in the textual imagery.

Yet the title pages' promises of an allegorical narrative are only partially fulfilled by the Author's initial visions and rallying of his cohort of personifications in order to deliver Laureola's first letter. Just as the opening scenes of *Cárcel* occur in the world of allegory as opposed to the real world of the court, so do the illustrations of the Prison, Desire, and Leriano's suffering at the hands of Desire differ from those depicting later scenes. Importantly, the quality of language itself changes profoundly in the move from the world of allegorical description to narrative action at court. In the latter, words are no longer employed in the service of the interior eyes but for provoking physical action. The change in the quality of language leads to a change in illustration, from allegorical edifices and personifications in which words become tangible, concrete objects in the physical world to scenes of writers composing letters, speakers composing orations, bodies engaged in violent acts, and, lastly, the consumption of a handwritten document.

The *mise en page* of the following illustrations, which were designed to fit within the text blocks of the editions' folia, creating close perceptual ties between text and images, also contrasts with that of the two allegorical woodcuts. All of the woodcuts make physical breaks in the text – they encourage, perhaps even require, the audience to stop and look – to switch from the visual sequential process of reading and turn to the visual process of looking, or in the case of shared readings aloud, to turn from listening and imagining to seeing, if the reader were to pause and show the page to his or her audience. Yet, at the same time, typographic and xylographic interplay on pages, such as those seen in figures 10 through 12 linking printed type to printed woodcuts, make verbal and visual media coextensive.

While the ties between the allegorical cuts and the text link distinct details from the woodcut images to specific words and phrases in the narrative, the other woodcuts depict actions that have no verbal counterpart in the narrative. The texts do not describe, for example, the architectural details of the rooms where Leriano and the *Auctor* meet, the prison in which Laureola is held, the arms of Leriano's men, or the presence of a dog at his bedside. Many of these visual details, in the absence of verbal descriptions, can be explained by the iconographic horizons of expectation of the historical intended audiences of the romance.

If the first two cuts offer the books' audiences visual interpretations of verbal images, the rhetorical cuts offer graphic images of the text delivered *viva voce*, as well as graphic images of the text in the process of mental and manual composition – writing *ad vivum*, followed by the passage of the text from the hand of one protagonist to another. The closest ties between text and image are forged in these metafictive rhetorical woodcuts. In the first such cut, two men talk in a narrow room that is clearly a study, as one wall is flanked by a shelf with three volumes displayed upon it and a book lays open upon a stand (fig. 17). An image that certainly would have lent itself to reuse in other contexts, in the 1493 and 1496 editions the design illustrates scenes in which Leriano and the *Auctor* converse, appearing twice in the extant folia of the Zaragoza edition, four times in *Lo càrcer d'amor*, and five times in the Burgos edition of 1496.

The first appearance of the woodcut illustrating the *Auctor* and Leriano in conversation appears in conjunction with Leriano's exegesis of the Prison of Love and explanation of the unrequited love that brought him there. "Ordenó mi ventura que me enamorase de Laureola, hija del rey Gaulo, que agora reina, pensamiento que yo deviera antes huir que buscar; pero como los primeros movimientos no se puedan en los honbres escusar, en lugar de desviallos con la razón, confirmélos con la voluntad; y assí de Amor me vencí, que me truxo a esta su casa, la qual se llama cárcel de Amor" (My fate was so ordained that I fell in love with Laureola, daughter of King Gaulo, who now reigns; I should have fled rather than pursue the thought, yet since men cannot escape their instincts, instead of using my reason to stop them, I confirmed them with my will, and so was I conquered by Love, who brought me here to his house, which is called the prison of Love) (*Cárcel de Amor* 9). This disquisition provides the rhetorical counterpart to Leriano's physical

Respuesta del auctor a Leriano.

En tus palabras señor has mostrado que
pudo amor prēder tu libertad τ no tuvir
tud.lo qual se prueua:porq̃ segun te veo
deues tener mas gana de morir q̃ de ha-
blar.y por proueer en mi fatiga forçaste tu volūtad:
juzgando por los trabajos passados. y por la cuyta
presente:q̃ yo ternia de venir poca sperāça. lo que sin

Figure 17. Leriano and the *Auctor* converse. *Cárcel de Amor*. Burgos: Fadrique
de Basilea, 1496. London, British Library, IA.53247. © British Library Board.

performance of lovesickness witnessed by the *Auctor* in the previous scenes.

In the cut, the depiction of speech is achieved through gesture: the *Auctor*, dressed in the same long robe shown in the allegorical wood-cuts, holds his hat in his right hand and gesticulates, index finger pointing, with his left; Leriano, dressed in a more fashionable and courtly short robe, also points with the index finger of his left hand. In this cut and others, such as those in which the queen speaks with Laureola and begs for the King's mercy, or when Leriano debates the nature of women from his deathbed, for example, textual oratory is illustrated through posture and gesticulation (fig. 18). These woodcuts stage the fifth canon of rhetoric, *actio*, or delivery. From classical antiquity onwards, rhetoric was taught as a set of physical as well as verbal devices; the orator had to be skilled in both gesture and language in order to move his audiences. Hand gestures and bodily disposition were often used by early modern painters and recall "a generally used, codified repertoire of gesture and expressions that had been in use since classical antiquity" that viewers would have recognized.[26] The woodcuts also use gesture to show the strength of protagonists' feelings, providing visual cues not only for the interpretation of emotions, but also for the performance of reading aloud. Rhetorical invention, delivery, and emotional effects are staged in the repeated images of documents being composed, read, delivered, and destroyed.

The cuts depicting a man and a woman writing are clearly meant to be interpreted as Leriano and Laureola, respectively, writing in private, interior spaces. Leriano is seated on a bench behind a covered table in a room of some architectural complexity. On the table we see, in addition to an oblong sheet of paper half filled with script, pens and an inkwell. The chamber illustrated is scholarly; a book is placed on a stand, conveniently located beneath a window for light. The image alludes to Leriano's skills as a lettered gentleman and casts his writing activities in a humanistic light. Laureola sits in a similar fashion to Leriano, but in a more sumptuous interior setting. She is seated upon a cushion, under a curtained canopy, and her table, in addition to the tools needed for writing, is graced by a small writing desk. She too is depicted in the act of writing, hands upon a half-filled sheet (fig. 14). The book-lined chamber in which Leriano and the *Auctor* converse also appears to be a study or library (fig. 17). The visual program presents both Leriano and the *Auctor* as decidedly bookish men. Leriano's dedication to letters is balanced by the episodes proving his skills at arms, which are

slabanças deuidas:en qual voluntad no hara mudãça
la firmeza çierta: qual se podra defender del contiño se-
guir.por çierto segun las armas con que son cõbatidas
aḥun q̃ las menos se defendieffen no era cofa de marauillar y antes devrian fer las q̃ no puedé defender fe ala
badas por piadofas:q̃ retraydas por culpadas.

Prueua por enremplos la bõdad
delas mujeras.

g.uj.

Figure 18. Leriano's Speech in Defence of Women. *Cárcel de Amor*. Burgos: Fadrique
de Basilea, 1496. London, British Library, IA.53247. © British Library Board.

also illustrated in the woodcuts. In this sense, he is presented to readers as a perfectly educated *caballero*, adept at both arms and letters. The woodcuts staging rhetorical *actio* find their counterpoints in those that depict military action, such as the duel between Leriano and Persio and the battle scenes.

The woodcut of a man writing appears five times in the Barcelona and Burgos editions, and three times in the extant portions of the Zaragoza edition, either between the rubric "Carta de Leriano a Laureola" and the text of a letter or embedded within the text of one of the letters to Laureola and Persio, and, at one point in the Barcelona edition, embedded in the text when the *Auctor* first speaks to Laureola about the possibility of her accepting a letter from Leriano. The woodcut depicting a woman writing appears three times, printed within or next to Laureola's letters to Leriano and to her father the king. The conjunction of the text of the letters with the images of writers at work leaves no doubt that the audience is supposed to understand the woodcuts as visualizations of the production of the very text printed above and below the illustration. Leriano and Laureola, as the inscribed authors of the epistolary sections of the romance, are depicted in the act of composing the words the audience hears, reads, and handles, just as the characters hold the letters they read, write, and hand to one another.

Thus, the two woodcuts, which look like traditional scribal-author portraits, at once function as images of textual creation and of the narrative's vision of scribal authorship, adding to the interplay of authemes already established by the text. The perceptual and referential ties between the cuts and the text are consequently very tight: they recreate the text's metafictional *mise en abyme* and further the sensation that the romance's readers, like the figure of the *Auctor*, have privileged access to the private thoughts and words of the protagonists, and even to their writerly processes of translating their interior states into words on the page.

Although made specifically for *Cárcel*, the two woodcuts are quite stereotypical author portraits based upon familiar visual commonplaces in both manuscript and print cultures. The images of Leriano and Laureola writing are, in a sense, imitations of conventional medieval and humanistic author portraits that serve to anchor the texts as a product of human intellectual and physical labour. The depiction of the author engaged in the work of writing, surrounded by the necessary tools, also functioned as an assurance of authenticity and accuracy of the text associated with the portrait and also "focused readers' attention, before reading, on the voice speaking through the transcribed words."[27] The conventionality of the images suggests that they may have been designed with their potential for reuse and recontextualization in mind.[28]

In addition to visually underscoring the metafiction of the scenes they illustrate, these images also "stand for, substitute for the absent author, but they present a picture of the body while the [text] images the working and production of inner constituents of subjectivity like desire and intellect," as Stephen Nichols observes of author portraits.[29] This effect is not limited to the author-portraits. For not only do we see the inscribed authors of the text at work writing, we see them turning their thoughts into words by speaking and moving theatrically. Each of the rhetorical woodcuts, like the graphic concretization of allegory in the first two cuts, blends mental and physical presences, making a connection between bodies and psychological interiority. And, of course, in the romance, ideas of honour and lovesickness will have direct impact upon the bodies of the protagonists, culminating in Leriano's death, which is heralded by his bodily ingestion of the physical evidence – written letters – of subjectivity, intellect, and desire.

The *Auctor* is never shown with pen in hand in the illustrations; as mentioned previously, although he is the implied author of the entire romance, he writes only when he adds the new cover to Leriano's second letter to Laureola. In the woodcuts, the *Auctor* is shown observing Leriano tortured by Desire, delivering a letter to Laureola, kneeling before Laureola, and speaking with Leriano. As is the case with the image of Leriano writing, perhaps these details in the design are meant to indicate the scholarly character of the *Auctor* and his interlocutor. The books pictured in figures 14 and 17, in addition to suggesting an intended use for the woodcuts beyond *Cárcel*, serve as reminders of the materiality of the text, of books as objects that are part of a particular cultural, lettered milieu.

Four of the sixteen woodcuts used in the 1493 editions of *Cárcel* and *Lo càrcer d'amor* and the 1496 edition of *Cárcel* present us with a printed image of a handwritten document. Of these four, three are used repeatedly throughout the printed books. The last metafictive woodcut to appear in the illustrated editions of 1493 and 1496 depicts Leriano at the key moment when he decides what to do with Laureola's letters (fig. 15). It is the third cut to show Leriano in his deathbed. In the first, Leriano debates the nature of women with Teseo; in the second, he lies unconscious in the bed as his mother weeps in the foreground in the final scene. As Cacho Blecua observes, the chalice into which

Leriano tears the sheet of paper is reminiscent of one that would be used for Communion, reinforcing the already present textual allusions to Eucharistic ritual. If readers did indeed see an additional allusion to spells and the magical properties of the written word for healing sexual ailments, as Fernando Bouza has suggested, the blasphemous nature of Leriano's amorous Communion would have become all the more patent to audiences of the illustrated editions.[30] Moreover, the repetition of these bedside scenes where the sufferer dies disconsolate, rather than restores himself to well-being through reason, as Sol Miguel-Prendes argues, lends itself to parodic interpretation.[31]

Another aspect of the *mise en abyme* created by the woodcuts' representation of the very text that the audience reads or hears is their placement of handwritten and printed texts in complementary roles. Scribal, manuscript culture inhabits the printed image and print becomes a way to preserve the manuscript image, even if – somewhat ironically – handwritten texts are destroyed in the final printed image and last chapter of the text. When Laureola writes, "Por dios te pido que embuelvas mi carta en tu fe, porque si es tan cierta como confiesas no se te pierda ni de nadie pueda ser vista" (For God's sake, I beg you to conceal my letter in your constancy, for if it is as certain as you claim, do not lose it or allow it to be seen by anyone) (*Cárcel* 28), the book's audience "sees" the letter in multiple senses. Not only does the audience, like the *Auctor*, have access to the secret and dangerous correspondence through the texts printed on the page, but also through the graphically reproduced image of the texts in the illustrations. Thus, textually and visually, the romance's audience is allowed entry into the epistolary triangle created between the *Auctor*, Leriano, and Laureola, by virtue of the book held in the hand of an individual reader or seen in the hands of one who reads aloud.

In the play of public and private epistles set up by the romance, Laureola's letters read by Leriano, the *Auctor*, and by the romance's audience are forever unreadable after Leriano consumes them. Neatly reflecting this rhetorical ploy, the intimate, handwritten texts that are depicted by the printed images are legible only in the fictional world of the woodcuts themselves because the woodcut artist has rendered the lines text penned by Leriano and Laureola with marks and lines, not distinguishable as letters and words, but clearly intended to represent them. The woodcuts imitate textuality through the use of their own media-specific means, that is to say, the cut rather than type, producing an image of text and textuality, but an image that renders manuscript textuality illegible. In this way, the woodcuts remediate the text by representing the manuscript text in the xylographic medium, and consequently calling attention to the interplay but lack of congruity between the readable typeface and the illegible handwritten text.

The interplay between text and image is tightly bound in these moments in the printed book, but it is bound in such a way as to highlight the mediated nature of reading – and swallowing – the letters produced in the romance, resulting in a book that is hypermediated.[32] That is to say, the printed book, illustrated by printed images, continually reminds readers of the presence of media and mediation, of print, image, and handwritten texts. Would late fifteenth and sixteenth-century printers, artists, and readers have borne these issues of mediation in mind? The repetition of images of manuscripts and books in the illustrated versions of *The Prison of Love* certainly suggests that some awareness of the metafictive nature of this narratorially hybrid romance guided the choice, composition, and placement of the woodcuts.

Reading Printed Images in *Cárcel de Amor* and *Carcer d'amore* 1523

The second set of woodcuts designed to illustrate *The Prison of Love* imitates the images found in the incunables and consequently performs many of the same narrative and interpretive functions. However, they also present new protocols for interpretation by their increased narrativity, which intensifies the visual metafiction and bodily presences found in the first series. While the first series of woodcuts clearly heightened the romance's textual metafictions, the sixteenth-century series focuses even more fixedly upon rhetorical performances and the composing, reading, and circulating of letters.

Cárcel de Amor ... Nuevamente historiados y bien correydo (*Cárcel de Amor ...* Newly historiated and well-worrected) is one of the two printings of *Cárcel de Amor* attributed to the workshop of Jorge Coci in 1523. The title advertises the inclusion of new illustrations in addition to an improved, corrected text. The very term *historiado* alerts us to the narrative value of the woodcuts, which are advertised as something more than a decorative ornament. The woodcuts are, like the narrative, *historias*, telling their own stories that are intimately related to the story told in and by the text.

The 1523 printings of *Cárcel de Amor* are octavos of forty-eight folia, containing seventeen individual designs, some of which are repeated for a total of twenty-five impressions. In terms of shape and size, there are three different categories of woodcut image in the 1523 editions: a large title-page illustration, two individual scenes, and fourteen more images of the same shape and size, each divided into two square sections in order to show two chronologically consecutive scenes from the plot of the romance.[33] All of the cuts occupy the full width of the text block. The visual content of the woodcuts follows the three categories established by the 1493 designs, with the images of rhetorical *actio* predominating. The episodic structure of many of the cuts, however, allows for the metafictive images to come into close contact with several of the other kinds of scenes.

The 1523 title woodcut depicting the *cárcel* and the author mounting its steep stairs (fig. 3) is smaller than the better-known image, as would be expected in a smaller book.[34] Unlike the title page of the 1493 Zaragoza edition, the 1523 image does not contain the text of the title within the cut, nor is the image impressed a second time to directly illustrate the *Auctor*'s description of the prison he sees.[35] In comparison to the earlier images, this woodcut contains finer lines and detail, as well as a more developed sense of perspective, and this *cárcel* is also pictured within a landscape containing additional architectural elements. The 1523 title page, like the image that predates it, reproduces the text's verbal images of the *torre*, and the title, printed beneath the image, clearly identifies the structure and the book itself as the *Cárcel de Amor*. The title page cut presented the work's potential audience with conventional signs – an isolated traveller, far from the walled towns in the distance, a fantastical structure inhabited by equally fantastical figures – of a visionary narrative. However, unlike the image first used in 1493, this graphic rendering appears only on the title page, in order to advertise the text and attract prospective buyers. In the 1523 and 1531 editions, *Cárcel*'s audience is presented with the allegory only before reading or listening to the text and not a second time as an image facing the textual description of the Prison, as in the editions from the 1490s. Even if the picture was designed to reflect specific verbal images, the visual images are presented to the audience before he or she encounters the text; the tight interplay between text and image is severed spatially by the construction of the material book. Thus, the image of the *cárcel* itself is here only an introductory or framing paratext, an image to be perhaps recalled while reading, if not seen in physical proximity to the text.

The rest of the woodcuts in the 1523 series fit within the pages' text blocks and consequently exist within relationships of tight interplay

with the narrative. Throughout, the woodcuts are placed in close physical proximity to the rubrics, justified in the centre of the text block.
This careful placement in relation to the body of text calls attention to
how the pictures serve as textual markers, dividing and organizing the
texts they accompany. This is true for the second allegorical woodcut
(fig. 19), which shows the *Auctor*, having dismounted from his horse,
gazing with a troubled look upon his face at Leriano, whose hands are
bound behind his back, and at the hirsute figure of *Deseo*, who holds
"un escudo de azero muy fuerte y muy rezio" (a very strong and solid
shield of steel) in his left hand and the "ymagen femenil" (figure of a
woman) in the other. The woodcut does not show the "diversos rayos
de fuego" (divers flaming rays) (*Cárcel* 4) that shoot out from the female
figure and set Leriano aflame, yet, like the earlier design, the figure is
unclothed. Thus Leriano, while shown with his hands behind his back,
is not depicted as if directly suffering from the flames described in the
text. Leriano and the *Auctor* look at one another, establishing their relationship in the first of what will be a series of images in which they
communicate with and gaze at each other.

As in the first set of woodcut designs, the diegetic move from allegorical vision to court is reflected by a change in graphic images. The
first rhetorical woodcut appears beneath the rubric "El preso al auctor"
(fig. 20). The scene is clearly one of active speaking and listening, as
Leriano, on the left, gesticulates with both hands, the signalling with
the index finger of one, while the other is held out, palm open in a
sign of supplication. The *Auctor* holds his hat in one hand and has the
other placed over his heart. The composition of the scene echoes that
of the corresponding image in the 1493 editions, but unlike the earlier
designs, and, as will be the case with all of the following 1523 woodcuts, there are few details of architecture and interior furnishings, such
as the books that lent a scholarly, humanistic air to similar scenes in the
earlier editions.

Here, the two men stand together in a room with a parquet floor; the
depiction of the floor, three windows, and a door creates a strange sense
of perspective, as if the viewer gazed simultaneously from the left and
the right, creating the feeling that the two characters have crossed the
parquet tiles to greet one another. The two protagonists stand face to
face and the *Auctor*, as before, is the direct recipient of Leriano's verbal
performance of lovesickness. While both figures gesticulate in the 1493
cuts, the *Auctor*'s hand-on-heart position is new, adding increased emotional weight to the visual rhetoric of the image. The *Auctor* visually

mas pienso hazer lo: se me offrecen mas cosas para no poder complir lo. Suplico a vuestra merced antes que condene mi falta: juzgue mi voluntad porque resciba el pago: no segund mi razon: mas segun mi desseo.

¶ Prologo deste tratado llamado Carcel de amor.

¶ Al muy virtuoso señor.

Vn que me falta suffrimiento para callar no me fallesce conoscimiento para ver lo q̃ me estaria mejor preciarme de lo q̃ callasse q̃ arrepentir me de lo que dixesse. E puesto q̃ assi lo conozco a vn q̃ veo la verdad sigo la opinió y como hago lo peor: nūca quedo sin castigo. Porque si co rudeza yerro con verguença pago. Verdad es que en la obra psente no tengo tanto cargo pues me puse en ella mas por necessidad de obedescer q̃ con voluntad de escreuir. Porque de vuestra merced me fue dicho q̃ deuia hazer alguna obra del estilo de vna oracion que embie ala virtuosa señora doña Maria manuel: porque le parecia menos malo que el q̃ puse en otro tratado que vido mio. Assi que por complir su mandamiento pensé hazer la. E viendo por: mejor errar en el dezir q̃ en el desobedescer y tābié acorde endereçar la a vuestra merced poq̃ la fauorezca como señor y la emiende como discreto. Como quiera que primero que me determinasse estuue en grandes dudas. Tanto vuestra discrecion temia: mirada vuestra virtud osaua. Enlo vno fallaua el miedo: y enlo otro buscaua la seguridad: y enfin escogi lo mas dañoso para mi verguença: y lo mas prouechoso para lo que deuia. Podre ser reprehendido si enlo que agora escriuo tornare a dezir algunas razones delas que en otras cosas he dicho: delo qual suplico a vuestra merced me salue: porque como vo be fecho otra escritura dela calidad desta: no es de marauillar que la memoria desfallesca: z si tal se fallare: por cierto mas culpa tiene enello mi oluido que mi querer. Sin duda señor considerando esto y otras cosas que enlo que escriuo se pueden fallar: yo estaua determinado de cessar ya en el metro y en la psa por librar mi rudeza de juyzios z mi spiritu de trabajos z parece quanto

¶ Comiença la obra.

Espues de hecha la guerra del año passado: viniendo a tener el inuierno a mi pobre reposo passando vna mañana quando ya el sol queria esclarecer la tierra por vnos valles hōdos y escuros que se hazen en la sierra morena: vi salir ami encuentro por vnos robledales do mi camino se hazia vn cauallero tan feroz de presencia como espātoso de vista: cubierto todo de cabello a manera de saluaje: lleuaua enla mano yzquierda vn escudo de azero muy fuerte z muy rezio y en la mano derecha vna ymagen femenil ental lada en vna piedra muy clara: la qual era de tan estrema hermosura q̃ me turbaua la vista delos ojos: salia della diuersios rayos de fuego q̃ lleuaua encēdido el cuerpo de vn hōbre q̃ aql cauallero forciblemente lleuaua tras si: el ql con vn lastimado gemido de rato en rato dezia. En mi fe se suffre todo. E como emparejo comigo dixo me con mortal angustia: camiāte por dios te pido q̃ me sigas z me ayudes en tā grā cuyta. Yo q̃ en aqlla sazō tenia mas causa p̄a temer q̃ razon p̄a parecer

B 2

Figure 19. The *Auctor's* vision of *Deseo* leading his captive, Leriano. *Cárcel de Amor*, Zaragoza: Jorge Coci 1523. London, British Library, C.63.e.15. © British Library Board.

E ninguna destas cosas pudiera ver segū la escuridad de la to:
re sino fuera poz vn claro resplandoz que le salia al preso del co
raçon que la esclarescia toda El qual como me vio atonito de
ver cosas de tales mysterios:viēdo como estaua en tiempo de
poder pagar me cō habla:lo poco q̃ me deuia poz dar me algū
descāso:mezclādo las razones discretas con lagrimas piado/
sas començo enesta manera a dezir me.

                        ¶ El preso al auctor.

Lguna parte del coraçō quisiera tener libre de sentimiē
to poz doler me de ti segun yo deuiera z tu merescias.
Pero ya tu vees en mi tribulacion que non tengo poder pa
ra sentir otro mal sino el mio. Pido te que tomes poz satisfa
ciō:no lo que hago:mas lo que desseo Tu venida aqui yo mis
mo la cause.El que viste traer preso yo soy z conla tribulaciō
que tienes no has podido conoscer me.Torna en ti tu reposo
sossiega tu juyzio:porque estes atento alo que te quiero dezir.
Tu venida fue poz remediar me:mi habla sera poz dar te con/
suelo:puesto que yo del sepa poco. Quien yo soy quiero dezir
te:delos mysterios que vees quiero infozmarte . La causa de
mi prisiō quiero que sepas:que me libres quiero pedirte si poz
bien lo tuuieres.Tu sabras q̃ yo soy Leriano hijo del duque
Guersio que dios perdone y dela duquesa coleria.zฬ i natura
leza es este reyno do estas:llamado Macedonia.Ordeno mi

Figure 20. "El preso al auctor." *Cárcel de Amor,* Zaragoza: Jorge Coci 1523.
London, British Library, C.63.e.15. © British Library Board.

takes Leriano's words to heart, storing them in his memory in order to transmit them to Laureola, and ultimately to the book's audience. This image is repeated three times throughout the text of the 1523 edition, always in conjunction with a rubric announcing that Leriano addresses the *Auctor* or vice versa.

The next woodcut in the text exemplifies the striking narrative effect of the episodic, two-panel woodcut images, which form a kind of diptych (fig. 21).[36] In the left-hand image, the *Auctor*, on bended knee, appeals with an outstretched hand to Laureola, who stands before him, gesturing with her index figure. On the right, Laureola stands, arms akimbo, an assertive rhetorical posture, especially when enacted by a woman.[37] The image appears directly below the rubric "El auctor a Laureola." The text illustrated by these images relates first the *Auctor*'s recapitulation of Leriano's allegory "Tú, señora sabrás que caminando un día por vnas asperezas desiertas, vi que mandado del Amor levavan preso a Leriano ... supe dél que de todo eso tú eres causa" (Lady, you must know that walking one day through rough, wild terrain, I saw that Leriano was imprisoned under Love's orders ... I learned that you were the cause of all [his suffering]) (*Cárcel* 14), followed by Laureola's rather threatening response, "Si como eres de España fueras de Macedonia, tu razonamiento y tu vida acabaran en un tiempo" (were you a native of Macedonia, as you are of Spain, your speech and your life would both come to an end now) (15), and the *Auctor*'s conclusion that Laureola's speech "aunque fue corta en razón ... fue larga en enojo" (though short ... was long on anger) (16).

As in all of the successive paired images, the temporal and narrative sequence moves from left to right, mirroring the movement of the reading eye through the text, printed in a single column across the page. Moreover, as is the case in many of the following images, the image on the left features a doorway, a graphic threshold leading from the left image into the right, further signalling the temporal relationship between the two episodes. This graphically depicted movement reveals the diegetic nature of the way that these editions have historiated the text. Figure 22, which shows an opening with two facing sets of images, provides an eloquent example of how the woodcut illustrations organize the text and underline the paced progression of the plot, advanced as words are carried from one protagonist to another, first from Leriano's lovesick *voluntad* (will, heart) to the *Auctor*'s heart and mind, to be recorded and relayed to Laureola and back to the suffering hero. The first conversations pictured between the *Auctor* and Leriano and

¶ El auctor a Laureola.

N O les esta menos bié el perdon alos poderosos quan∕
do son deseruidos que alos pequeños la végança quá∕
do son injuriados:porque los vnos se emiédan por honrra:
y los otros perdonan por virtud . Lo qual si alos grandes
hombres es duido:mas τ muy mas alas generosas mugeres
que tienen el coraçon real de su nacimiéto:τ la piadad natu∕
ral de su condicion.Digo a questo señora:porque para lo que
te quiero dezir:halle osadia en tu grandeza:porque no la pue
des tener sin magnificécia. Uerdad es que primero que me
determinasse:estuue dudoso:pero eñl fin de mis dudas tuue
por mejor:si inhumanaméte me quesiesses tratar padecer pe∕
na por dezir:que sufrirla por callar.Tu señora sabras que ca∕
minando vn dia por vnas aspezas de sierras vi que por man
dado del amor lleuauá pso a Leriano fijo del duque guersio.
elql me rogo que en su cuyta le ayudasse.de cuya razon dexe
el camino de mi reposo por tomar el de su trabajo:y dspues
que largamente conel camino vi le meter en vna prision dul
ce para su voluntad y amarga para su vida:donde todos los
males del mundo sostiene:dolor le atormenta:passion le persi
gue:desesperança le destruye:muerte le amenaza:pena le ese∕
cuta:pensamiento lo desuela:desseo lo atribula:tristeza le có
dena: fe no le salua.Supe del que de todo esto tu eres causa:

Figure 21. "El auctor a Laureola." *Cárcel de Amor*, Zaragoza: Jorge Coci? 1523.
London, British Library, C.63.e.15. © British Library Board.

the *Auctor* and Laureola are followed by six more animated rhetorical scenes in quick succession, all of which feature expressive gesturing of hands indicating the speech acts of the text, and four of which depict how the text of the printed *cartas* (letters) are composed by hand by their authors Leriano and Laureola, and then entrusted into the hands of the inscribed author of the entire work, *el Auctor* (fig. 22 A and 22 B).

Paired woodcuts illustrating the episodes in which the Cardinal, Queen, and Laureola herself, try to persuade the King to free his daughter are similarly constructed to show movement and active rhetorical performances. For example, one paring features the Queen kneeling before the King, one hand extended towards him, as if beseeching in the first frame, and then moves to the Queen's plaint. In the second frame, the Queen stands before Laureola's prison window, hands clasped, and Laureola, behind bars, mirrors the Queen's gesture of prayer (F3v). The images exist in a relation of relay with the *Auctor's* narration of the Queen's supplication to the King: "la qual, puestas las rodillas en el suelo, le dixo palabras assí sabias para culpalle como piadosas para amansallo" (the Queen, who, kneeling upon the ground, spoke to the King words just as wise to blame him as they were compassionate to soften him) (*Cárcel* 48) and also with key terms in the text of the Queen's speech to Laureola. The Queen's speech also underlines the futility of such verbal and gestural eloquence: "¡Qué lástima tan cruel para mí que suplicaron tantos al rey por tu vida y no pudieron todos defendella!" (What a cruel agony it is to me that so many pleaded for your life to the King and none could save it!) (50).

In addition to visualizing the clandestine correspondence carried out between Leriano and Laureola through the *Auctor's* verbal and physical mediation, the 1523 woodcuts bring increased attention to the public letters of challenge exchanged between Persio and Leriano and also to Laureola's letter to her father the King. For example, the scene on the right depicts Laureola writing behind bars and the King reading her letter in the second frame, once again visualizing the processes of thought translated to writing, of the written word circulating, and finally, of the written word being read and interpreted by an intended reader (G1r). In this case, however, once again eloquence does not amount to persuasion, but only inflames the King's ire.

The episodic structure of the 1523 woodcuts also allows for rhetorical performances and physical valor to enter into direct relationships, as can be seen in fig. 20. Here, Laureola's rescue and the battle to restore her honour is paired with Leriano's rousing speech to his *cavalleros*,

pues malauenturado fuesse el remedio que a mi libꝛasse de pꝛ/
na: z aꞇ te caußasse culpa poꝛ quitar tales incõuenieꞇtes te su
plico ꝗ̃ pagues tu carta galardon de mis males ꝗ̃ a vn ꝗ no
me mate poꝛ lo ꝗ̃ aꞇ toca: no podꝛe biuir poꝛ lo ꝗ̃ yo tu
fro. E toda via quedarme cõdenada, ſi algun biẽ quiſierⁿe fa
zer no me lo tarde: ſino podꝛa ſer ꝗ̃ tẽgas tiempo de arrepẽ/
tir te z no lugar de remediar me.

¶ El auctoꝛ.

A Un ꝗ Leriano ſ̃ guı̃ su graue ſentimiento ſe qͤxera mas
te eſtender vſando dela diſcrecion z no dela pena no eſ
criuo mas largamente: poꝗ para faze saber a laureola ſu mal
baſtaua lo dicho: ꝗ̃ ꝗñ las cartas ſeuẽ alargar ſere ꝗñ ſe cree
ꝗ ay tal voluntad para leellas ꝗẽ las reſcibe: como para eſcre
uillas quiẽ las embia: y poꝗ̃ eſtaua libꝛe de tal pſuncion no
ſe eſtendio mas en ſu carta. La ꝗ̃l deſpues de acabada recebi
cõ tãta trıſteza de ver las lagrimas cõ ꝗ̃ Leriano me la em
ua : que pude ſentılla mejoꝛ ꝗ̃ cõtalla. Y deſpedido del paꝛ
tı me para Laureola. E como llegue põde eſtaua balle poꝛ
pio tıempo para poder le hablar: z antes ꝗ̃ le dieſſe la carta oꝛ
ꝛe le tales razones.

¶ El auctoꝛ: e laureola.

P Rimero ꝗ̃ nada te diga te ſuplico ꝗ̃ recibas la pena
de aꞇſi catiuo tuyo poꝛ deſcargo dela impoꝛtunidad

¶ Carta de Leriano a Laureola.

S I tuuiera tal razon para eſcriuir te: como para querer
te ſin miedo lo oſara fazer: mas en ſaber ꝗ̃ eſcriuo para
tı ſe turba el ſeſo y ſe pierde el ſentidoꝛ y deſta cauſa antes ꝗ̃
lo comience: ſe ruue comigo gra cõfuſiõ. Mas ſe deſia ꝗ̃ oſaſſe
tu grãdeza ꝗ̃ temıeſſe: en lo vno ballaua eſperãça: y poꝛ lo otro
deſeſperaua: y en el cabo acoꝛdeſto. mas ay de mi ꝗ̃ comence
tẽpano a doler me z tarde a ꝗxarme. poꝛque a tal tiempo ſoꝛ
venıdo: ꝗ̃ ſi alguna merced te mereçieſſe no ay en mi coſa bi/
ua para ſentılla: ſino ſola mi ſe: el coꝛaçõ eſta ſin fuerças y el al
ma ſin poder y el juꝛzio ſin memoꝛia. pero ſi tãta merced gſi
eſſes fazerme ꝗ̃ a eſtas razones te pluguieſſe reſpõder: la ſe cõ
tal bien podꝛa baſtar para reſtituyr las partes ꝗ̃ deſtruyſte yo
me culpo poꝛ ꝗ̃ te pido galardõ ſin auerte ſeruicio algun no pa
ꝗ̃ ſi recibes en cueta del ſeruicio el penar: poꝛ mucho ꝗ̃ me pa
gues ſiempꝛe pẽſare ꝗ̃ me ꝗdas en deuda. podꝛas deſir ꝗ̃ como
penſe eſcriuir te: no te marauilles ꝗ̃ tu fermoſura cauſo el afi/
cio: y el aficiõ el deſſeo: y el deſſeo la pena: z la pena el atreui
mıẽto. E ſi poꝛ lo biẽ te pareçiere ꝗ̃ mereço muerte: mãda
me la dar: ꝗ̃ muy mejoꝛ es moꝛir poꝛ tu cauſa: que biuir ſin tu
eſperãça. Y hablãdo te verdad: la muerte ſin ꝗ tu me la dieſ
ſes: yo miſmo me la daria: poꝛ ballar eſſilla la libertad que en la
vida buſco: ſi tu no quiſieſſes de ꝗdar infamada poꝛ matadoꝛa:
nuea

Figure 22. A. "Carta de Leriano a Laureola" and B. "El auctor a Laureola." *Cárcel de Amor*, Zaragoza: Jorge Coci 1523. London, British Library, C.63.e.15. © British Library Board.

one of the rhetorical tours de force in the romances: "Grandes aparejos tenemos para osar; la bondad nos obliga, la justicia nos esfuerça, la necessidad nos apremia; no hay cosa porque devamos temer y hay mill para que devamos morir" (We have great reason to be bold; goodness obliges us, justice gives us strength, necessity drives us; we have not a thing to fear and a thousand to die for) (*Cárcel* 57). Leriano's ideal, if ill-fated, combination of arms and letters is brought into visual relief and the composition of the cut equates the two activities visually (fig. 23).

The image of Leriano writing is repeated six times in the 1523 editions, and that of Laureola writing also appears six times. Three woodcut designs show the delivery of a letter from the hand of one protagonist to another: one cut, used twice, shows Leriano handing a letter to the *Auctor*; an image of a letter passing between Laureola's and the *Auctor*'s hand appears three times; and an image of the *Auctor* delivering a letter to Leriano appears twice. Further, the 1523 series contains an image of the King reading Laureola's letter of counsel to him, a scene that was not illustrated in previous editions. These repeated images clearly amount to a heightened focus on material texts in circulation and acts of interpretation as well as an intensification of material metafiction.

Cárcel de Amor "nuevamente historiado" is a story retold in a new material form, an adaptation, a new work, recognizably related to the romance first printed in 1492, but substantially altered for a new generation of readers. These readers were Coci's and Pedrezano's imagined audiences, in Spain and Italy, rather than San Pedro's first, imagined readers. The 1523 woodcuts, though smaller and perhaps less artistically accomplished than those first made for the 1493 Hurus edition, were widely diffused in the 1520s and 1530s and thus important elements in historical audiences' experiences of *Cárcel de Amor* and its Italian translation *Carcer d'amore*. The selection of images, followed by their insertion into the story, is one of the ways that printers and editors adapted popular works for new audiences. The effect of this process of selection and presentation was to establish a new visual rhetoric and new protocols for interpretation. The 1523 woodcuts continually invite the audience to focus on rhetorical performances and the circulation of Laureola's and Leriano's written words, extending *Cárcel de Amor*'s verbal metafiction to material and visual metafiction and highlighting the humanist poetics at work in the romance.

The woodcuts produced for early editions are evidence of the way *Cárcel de Amor* was interpreted by its late fifteenth-century audiences, as well as by the publishers and printers who also had an economic

pudo llegar fin que ninguno suyo perdiesse:cosa de gran ma/
rauilla porq con cinco mill hobres de armas venia ya el rey
embuelto coel.El qual muy encedido de coraçe:puso ala ora
cerco sobre el lugar con propofito de no leuantar se de alli ha
fta que del tomaffe vengança. E viendo Leriano que el rey
affentaua real repartio fu gente por eficias fegun fabio guer/
rero.Donde eftaua el muro mas flaco ponia los mas rezios
cavalleros.Donde auia aparejo para dar en el real ponia los
mas fueltos.Donde vera mas difpoficion para entralle por
traycion o engaño ponia los mas fieles:en todo proueya co/
no fabido:y en todo ofaua como varon.El rey como aquel
q penfaua lleuar el hecho a fin mando fortalecer el real z pro
ueyo enlas proueiones:z ordenadas todas las cofas que ala
buefte copia mando llegar las eftancias cerca dela cerca dela
villa:las quales guarnecio de muy buena gente.E parecido
le fegun le acufaua la faña:gran tardaça efperar a tomar a Le
riano por hambre:puefto que la villa fuefe muy fuerte aco/
do fe combatilla:lo qual prouo con tambrauo coraçon q ouo
el cercado bien menefter el efuerço z la diligencia. Andaua
fobrefaliente con cien cavalleros que para aquello tenia depu
tados.Donde vera la flaqueza efforçaua:donde vera coa/
çon alabaua:donde vera mal recaudo prouera. Concluyen/
do poque me alargo: el rey mando aparar el combate con

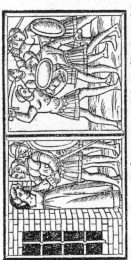

fiempre ella los ojos fafta que de vifta la perdio: la qual fin
ningun contrafte lleuo fu tio a dala fortaleza dicha.pues toz
nando a Leriano como vae el alboroto allego a ordos del rey.
Pidio las armas.E tocadas las trombetas z atabales:armo
fe toda la gente cotellana z dela cibdad.E como el tiempo le
ponia neceffidad para que Leriano fufieffe al cabo começo
lo a hazer esforçando los fuyos có animofas palabras queda/
do fiempre en la reçaga fufriendo la multitud delos enemigos
con mucha firmeza de coraçó.E por guardar la manera hone
fta que requiere al retraer:yua ordenando con menos prieffa
q el cafo pedia.E affi perdiendo algunos delos fuyos z mata/
do a muchos delos contrarios llego a donde dexo los cava
llos:z guardada la orde que para en aquello auia dado fin re/
febir reues ni peligro cavalgarô el y todos fus cavalleros:lo
q por ventura no hiziera fi antes nos proueyera el remedio.
Pueftos todos como es dicho a cavallo tomo adelante los
peones:z figuio fu via de Sufa donde auia partido.E como
fe le acercaua las tres batallas del rey:falido de paffo apreffu
ro el andar con tal concierto z orden que ganaua tanta hôra
en el retraer como en el pelear:yua fiempre enlos poftreros ha
ziendo algüas bueltas quando el tiempo las pedia por entre
tener los contrarios para lleuar fu batalla mas fin congoxa:
en el fin no auiendo andado dos leguas como es dicho fafta fufa

Figure 23. Leriano rallies his troops. *Cárcel de Amor*, Zaragoza: Jorge Coci 1523. London, British Library, C.63.e.15. © British Library Board.

incentive for including images. Both the repetition of particular images and the continued illustration of scenes of textual materiality, moreover, are evidence that the printers considered those episodes to be important ones and worth illustrating. In the case of *Cárcel de Amor*, the choices made in the print shop to repeat images of Leriano and Laureola writing deepens the text's already appreciable preoccupation with the creation of letters and the direct effect of their physical presence upon their writers and recipients.

Cárcel de Amor's engagement with humanist rhetoric is one of the many factors that contributed to the romance's intercultural presence throughout the sixteenth century, when the letters and speeches were received by many readers as rhetorical models and displays of erudition.[38] The iconographic programs first printed in 1493 and in 1523 stage the rhetorical performances of the protagonists, rendering the material metafiction already pronounced in the text by visual means. While the image of a male humanistic author seated at work in his study was an established commonplace in late fifteenth-century and early sixteenth-century books, the author portrait of Laureola has few conventional analogues. *Cárcel de Amor*'s author portraits depict embodied male and female subjects who demonstrate rhetorical mastery. The printed images of Laureola committing her thoughts to writing counter such rhetorical precepts, and reflect how the text opens a vernacular space affirming the possibility of female authorship. Illustrated editions of *The Prison of Love* present visual as well as verbal scenes of scribal publication in which women "have rhetorical lives" and enter into dialogue with male authors.

The depiction of a lettered and literate woman who not only reads "against the grain of courtly texts"[39] but commits her resistant reading to writing creates an "interruption" in "the innumerable interminable, clear examples of public, political agonistic, masculine discourse," and was perhaps one of the most pro-feminine moves *The Prison of Love* made in the eyes of its historical audiences.[40] Laureola's implied authorship and authority were an important aspect of the romance for both readers and editors and no doubt accounted in part for its appeal to such lettered women as Isabella d'Este and Marguerite de Navarre, as it travelled from one reader to another across Europe.

Laureola's written words, which pit honour and the appearance of virtue against love, reveal a keen awareness of her position as both subject and object within the power structure of the Macedonian court and suggest the ineffective nature of Leriano's later defence of women.

In her letters, Laureola points out eloquently the gendered nature of all rhetorical positioning and how the nature of the debate makes it impossible for her to act and circumscribes her actions. It is a debate with no exit and in which every point can be used in *utrumque parte*, just as a skilled rhetor can argue either case successfully. She knows that she is damned if she does and damned if she doesn't give in to Leriano's desire to be recognized as her love-servant. In her last letter she stakes her claim to be his future patroness, instead of his beloved, but this is clearly too close to historical power relations of clientage to satisfy the would-be courtly lover. In the end, Laureola's eloquence is literally consumed, erased, and no longer available to human eyes, when Leriano tears up her letters and ingests them. Still, in an extension of the entire work's conceit of making secret correspondence visible, Laureola's words remained on the page for generations of readers.

Yet the subjectivity of the princess is contested throughout the romance, and we can also read the illustration as a graphic reproduction of the central conundrum of this female protagonist. As Jean Gilkinson observes, Laureola is hard to read because she is both subject and object. Laureola's written language, Gilkinson argues, does not automatically confer upon her the status of subject in the eyes of her diegetic readers, for whom the letters are "publicly available sign[s] ... onto which others project their own meaning," much like the *imagen femenil* carried by the Deseo in Leriano's allegorical Prison of Love.[41] In contrast, the visual rhetoric of the image affirms Laureola's subjectivity, unlike the interpretive gambits of the *Auctor* and Leriano, who insist on defining her as a *belle dame sans merci*. Yet, like Leriano, who was set aflame with desire by her beauty, or so he claims in his letter to her, the audience is also invited by the illustrated edition to gaze upon Laureola as she writes, to look and register her social rank, her literacy and rhetorical mastery, and, insofar as the xylographic medium permits, her beauty.

Nevertheless, and returning to the images of Laureola gesticulating and standing arms akimbo, the woodcuts may have added a touch of misogynist humour to the 1523 and later editions they illustrate. Humanist commentaries on women and rhetoric express a certain amount of ambivalence regarding women speaking publicly. Leonardo Bruni's (in)famous depiction of a speechifying woman "who throws her arms around while speaking, or ... increases the volume of her speech with greater forcefulness ... will appear threateningly insane and require restraint" appears in his treatise instructing Battista Malatesta on her studies and has often been cited as evidence of women's general exclusion from the finer points of humanist rhetoric.[42] The woman described by Bruni is evidently behaving indecorously and reminiscent of the saying that "an eloquent woman is never chaste," but as Virginia Cox shows, the celebrated humanist was making a joke about the misuse of rhetorical precepts that his learned addressee would have appreciated.[43] The joke, with its outrageous female orator, however, stands, and Laureola's broad rhetorical performances in the 1523 woodcuts could certainly have inspired snickers on the part of those readers who sided with Teseo and considered his dying for love and a lady's honour a travesty.

It has been said time and again that the romances grouped together as "sentimental" are not about chivalrous action, but rather focus their narrative attention on the expression of thought and feeling.[44] Indeed, Tobias Brandenberger considers the lack of action to be one of the reasons that so few were illustrated when printed, *Cárcel de Amor* being a notable exception.[45] *Cárcel de Amor* furthermore contains a good deal of chivalrous and bellicose action, which, along with the visuality of its opening episodes, inspired a rich iconographic tradition. Nevertheless, as we have seen, the illustrations do not only depict allegory and combat, but also activities that at first sight may seem static, that is writing, reading, listening and speaking. The visual rhetoric of the woodcuts, like the text itself, showcases rhetorical composition and performance *as* action, reminding us that, for early modern courtiers, the tongue was a weapon and eloquent persuasion akin to a military campaign.[46] The figures represented in the woodcuts move through the pages of the editions bearing these graphic images animatedly gesticulating and speaking, actively turning their thoughts into words, and those words are reproduced typographically on the page. It is very tempting to imagine sixteenth-century readers striking similar poses as they read *The Prison of Love* aloud in groups, perhaps taking on the different speaking roles signalled by the text. In this sense, it is possible that the visual rhetoric of the woodcuts – of both sets, but more so in the second set – reflects what Chartier sees as the characteristic "desire for orality" and for making "the mute page ... capture and retain something of living speech" in sixteenth-century printed books. Like punctuation, the 1523 woodcuts "mark" the written text "to show differences of intensity."[47] In addition to the depiction of the spoken word in so many of the woodcuts, the many depictions of writers and readers engaged in the active composition and reception of written words may reflect a similar desire, the desire for the immediacy and intimacy of manuscript circulation.

Just as the editions including Núñez's continuation offered historical audiences a different experience from the 1492 edition where the story ends with Leriano's death and the *Auctor*'s return to Peñafiel, each illustrated edition of *Cárcel* provided audiences with a substantially different work from the unillustrated first edition, and from each other. Commissioning, designing, and placing graphic images into the text, successive editors adapted the received text for new audiences. The illustrations, to different degrees, reflect the metafictional and intermedial nature of the work; the illustrated books' textual and visual elements of storytelling are combined. The formally hybrid, metafictional, and dialogic romance inspired the visualization of allegorical, rhetorical, and genre scenes. The narrative's insistence on rhetorical performances, particularly letter-writing and debating, is part of *Cárcel de Amor*'s and *The Prison of Love*'s participation in humanist fiction, which became all the more important as the romance travelled throughout Europe in the sixteenth century. The iconographic program of the 1523 editions intimately binds the verbal rhetoric of the romance to graphic visual rhetoric.

In the early printed editions of *Cárcel de Amor*, *Lo càrcer d'amor*, and *Carcer d'amore*, this erasure of the distance between text and image is compounded by the presence of texts – books, half-written documents, delivered messages, and letters about to be destroyed – in the illustrations. In the creation and repetition of these images, *Cárcel*'s publishers constructed and propagated an iconographic program that highlights the importance of handwritten texts as physical, manipulable objects; the letters in *Cárcel* are *cartas de tocar*. Illustrated editions, in their materiality as printed books containing printed images of author-figures writing by hand, evince the coexistence and interplay of print and manuscript culture in the decades following the introduction and spread of printing and the attendant broadening circulation of vernacular fiction.

PART III

French Remediations

Chapter Seven

La Prison d'Amours Illuminated

The editions of *La Prison d'Amours* published between 1525 and 1533 provide solid evidence of the romance's popularity among French audiences. However, interest was even more intense during this short span of time than the already considerable number of printed editions suggests. No fewer than eleven manuscripts of *La Prison d'Amours* dating from the 1520s are extant, ten of which are luxury codices, and five of those ten richly illuminated. Galliot du Pré's, Oliver Arnoullet's, and Antoine de Bonnemere's editions of *La Prison d'Amours* were elegant books, featuring dual-colour printing and woodcuts to add to their decorative appeal. Nevertheless, the prestige of the printed editions pales in comparison to the manuscripts and tapestries. In short, the period witnessed the highly concentrated production of luxury remediations of *The Prison of Love* in French, attesting to its singular appeal in the context of the court of Francis I.

Chapter 6 considered how *The Prison of Love*'s visuality and thematizing of the materiality of narrative inspired illustration, and how woodcut images remediate narrative and, in so doing, can create hypermediated material books that reflect upon their own material natures while also underscoring the theatricality of rhetoric. The French deluxe adaptations of *The Prison of Love* in manuscript and tapestry further develop these aspects of the romance and continually remind viewers of their status as material objects that are distinct from the printed books in which other sixteenth-century audiences experienced the romance.

The illuminated manuscripts and tapestries have been analysed from art-historical perspectives, most notably by Myra D. Orth, who studied the networks of patronage through which the manuscripts and tapestries travelled.[1] Nicholas Guilbert and Fabienne Joubert have traced the tapestries' origins and circulation further, and Irene Finotti has collated and added further precision to Orth's study of the manuscripts.[2] However, Orth, Guillbert, and Joubert only cursorily refer to the romance itself.[3] Yet both the illuminated manuscripts and tapestries are integral parts of *The Prison of Love*'s radiant cultural translation. They also provide us with material evidence for reconstructing the romance's social history and its interpretation by elite sixteenth-century French audiences. Each manuscript and tapestry embodies the central preoccupations of the romance in material form, while also demonstrating how manuscript and tapestry were mediums that lent themselves to domesticating transformations that go beyond textual interpretation and d'Assy's translation of *Carcer d'amore* into "nostre vernacule et familiere langue francoise" (our vernacular and familiar French language).

"Private Treasures"

The illuminated manuscripts of *La Prison d'Amours* produced for French readers form a heterogeneous group, differing in size and design, and reflecting the styles and skills of varied scribes and painters, as well as the desires of individual patrons. The presentation of the text varies as well, suggesting that some of the manuscripts predate the first printed editions, while others may have been copied from one or another of them.[4] Some contain d'Assy's dedication, first printed in 1525, and some reproduce the versified letters. Only one manuscript was copied on paper and, in distinction to the others, appears to have been made as a quick copy for personal use rather than as a luxury item.[5] No doubt because they contain translations rather than a romance of French origin, and also because they belong to what has been termed the "last flowering" of illuminated manuscript production, these manuscripts, singly and as a group, have remained relatively obscure.[6]

In the first decades of the sixteenth century, French painted manuscripts were "exceptional objects," often made to mark special occasions or events.[7] More limited in circulation than most printed books, manuscripts also had the potential to give readers a sense of exclusivity and offered opportunities for individual interpretations and personalization in the celebration of social transmission limited to a given work's most privileged audiences. Printed editions could certainly be personalized, as was the case when illustrated by hand, or printed on velum, such as the presentation copy of Lelio Manfredi's *Carcer d'amore*, but hand copying and painted illustrations, as the *La Prison d'Amours* manuscripts attest, afforded far greater opportunities for adaptation to individual owners.[8] Further, as Sherry Lindquest argues in a study of contemporary manuscripts of Marguerite de Navarre's work, "Illuminated romances revived in the era of printing provided an idiom that drew upon the chivalric, courtly values with which nobles still identified and used to differentiate themselves from other social strata."[9] In the case of *La Prison d'Amours*, the material idiom of the manuscript book, while enhancing the courtly nature of the romance, also reflected its preoccupations with authorship, female readers, and rhetorical performances.

Each of five extant illuminated manuscripts displays an independent iconographic program. Nevertheless, and like the woodcuts designed for the Spanish printed editions of 1493 and 1523, each set of miniatures concretizes the opening allegorical scenes and renders visually the romance's fascination with the materiality of handwritten texts, and the physicality of reading, writing, and orating. Many of the effects of *mise en abyme* created by the woodcuts of the printed editions are also present in the manuscripts. However, since the manuscript miniatures depict reading, writing, orating, and consuming manuscript texts within handwritten and hand-painted books, the material metafiction created by the images is all the more potent. If the illustrated printed editions remediated manuscript culture using the tools of moveable type and woodcuts, drawing readers' attention to the differences between the two media, the manuscripts also create hypermediated book objects by continually and visually reaffirming notions of manuscript culture. The manuscripts are self-reflective, demonstrating what Martha Rust has called "codicological consciousness," the "cultural awareness of both the practicalities of book production and the social and symbolic traditions that books encode as material objects."[10] Such a consciousness is elevated in luxury manuscripts made as alternatives to print for elite audiences, who wished to distinguish their reading habits from those of other social orders.[11]

La Prison d'amours, ou les amours de Leriano et de Lauréole, Bibliothèque nationale de France (BnF) NAF 7552, opens with a presentation miniature depicting a woman sitting beneath a canopy, accompanied by three other female figures, receiving a book from an author-figure on bended knee (f. 1v).[12] The women in the image are presumably Jacquette de Lansac and her daughters, as her family coat of arms is included within the miniature's floral borders, and an acrostic in verse below the miniature contains her name and d'Assy's in blue and red letters, followed by the text of d'Assy's dedication.[13] The first folia of the manuscript also contain Jacquette de Lansac's mottoes, *En bon lieu* (in a good place) and *Sola in patria* (alone/only in the homeland), which appear to refer to the social status of her family, as "bon lieu" is also a reference to the quality of a family line, as well as d'Assy's own motto, *Celer Naper*. D'Assy's motto references secrecy: *celer* means "to hide," or "to dissimulate," and *Nap[p]er* "to ornament," or "to cover." The acrostic reworks many of the courtly appeals from the dedicatory prologue and plays upon Jacquette's *En bon lieu*.

> Illustre dame, franc, séjour de noblesse
> A qui sur toutes je dois honneur sans vice
> En bon vouloir d'affection expresse
> Te présente cy mon petit service
> De vray je scay que c'est faict de novice
> L'an dit pourtant qu'accepter peu de chose
> Sans nul desdaing est de nobles l'office,
> Car (en bon lieu) toute vertu repose.

[Illustrious lady, generous, domain of nobility, to whom above all I must honour without vice. With the desire to express affection, I present my little service to you. Truly I know that it is the work of a novice. It is said, however, that to accept a small thing without disdain is the duty of nobles, for all virtue reposes in a noble place.][14]

Following the presentation miniature and paratexts, the opening of 4v–5r contains two full-page illuminations, the first depicting the initial encounter between *l'Acteur*, *Desir*, and Lérian, with the Prison of Love in the background. *Desir* holds a phylactery reading "En ma foys si soufrireay ie tout" (in my faith, so will I suffer all), the declaration of Lérian's lovesickness. The second illumination depicts Lérian seated in flames and holding a shield to protect himself from the onslaught of his personified emotions. This miniature surrounds this first lines text in the romance.[15] Due to the dedication miniature and the acrostic autograph, this manuscript is considered to be the first and earliest extant text of d'Assy's translation.[16]

Prison d'amour, BnF, Ms Fr. 24382, also opens with d'Assy's dedication and displays d'Assy's *Celer Naper* as well as another, Italian motto, *A che covo*.[17] A smudged coat of arms, a blue sautoir on a gold field, decorates the large initial "R" at the beginning of the dedicatory epistle on folio 3r, the

Figure 24. Miniature of The Prison of Love. Paris, Bibliothèque nationale de France Ms. Fr. 24382, f.5v.

presentation page. A second, smaller heraldic shield containing six open left hands on a blue field is painted in the lower margin, within a frame. Finotti identifies the first coat of arms as belonging to Hugues de Loges, seigneur of La Boulaye and Chailly-sur-Armançon, and a courtier in the service of Francis I, who was the governor of Tornai from 1518 to 1521. The second coat of arms belongs to Charlotte du Mesnil, who married Hugues de Loges circa 1520. These devices suggest that the manuscript was produced in the region of Tournai, at some point after 1521.[18]

Ms. Fr. 24382 illustrates the romance with a series of forty-six highly detailed historiated initials and one marginal painting, rather than a series of independent illuminations, which heightens the intensity of interplay between texts and images in this particular material adaptation. Only the Prison of Love itself seems to have been deemed too large, or perhaps too important, to fit within the confines of an initial: it is envisioned as an elongated structure in the left margin of folio 5v (fig. 24).[19]

The placement of the prison on the edges of the text may also reflect the distance between the allegorical world in which *l'Acteur* first discovers Lérian and the world of the court, in which the greater part of the narrative occurs, and which the majority of the initials depict. The beginning of the text of the romance on folio 3v is historiated in the initial D, which shows *l'Acteur* meeting Lérian and *Desir*. Three of the historiated initials depict Lérian and Lauréolle writing the epistles that the initials commence. Eight initials show the author engaged in his activities as narrator and go-between. A large "R" shows the duel between Lérian and his rival Perseus. Two historiated initials show Lérian and Teseo debating the nature of women, and the points of Lérian's defence are set off by decorated rather than historiated initials, signalling the importance of the debate in the manuscript's matrix, and further intimating that the manuscript's makers or commissioners considered Leriano's defence of women a particular highlight of the text, bearing out d'Assy's promise that the romance contained "dassez belles matières ... pour jeunes dames" (many pleasing matters for young women).

L'Amour de Leriano et de Laureole, Bodmer Foundation Ms. CB 149's nineteen miniatures, are all framed within Italianate gold borders that are often composed of architectural motifs, a common form of presentation in many commemorative manuscripts of the period. Many of these illuminations are painted around the rubrics, creating an effect in which text and image jointly serve to introduce the content of the following sections of the story.[20] Folio 1v bears a large painting of the joint coat of arms of Charles de Bourbon, Duke of Vendôme, regent-governor of Picardy, and his wife Françoise d'Alançon, sister-in-law to Francis and Marguerite by virtue of her first marriage to Charles d'Alançon. The Bourbon arms are repeated in the first initial of the dedicatory letter, just below a presentation miniature on folio 2r (fig. 7).

In the Bodmer presentation miniature, the woman receiving the book from the author-figure's hands is presumably meant to represent Françoise. D'Assy's prologue, with its reference to an unnamed lady, was easily adaptable to repackaging and repersonalizing. Upon receiving the manuscript, Françoise, and perhaps later female owners as well, might have associated themselves with the "très vertueuse et très prudente dame" addressed in the text. The relation of the manuscript to women owners and readers is continued in a seventeenth-century ex-libris on the verso of the third parchment flyleaf: "Ce livre appartien a Jehanne damoiselle de Lausun que feu Monsieur Gra[...] son grand-pere lur a donne" (This book belongs to Jehanne, damoiselle of Lausun, given to her by her grandfather Monsieur Gra[...]).

L'Histoire de Lerian et s'amie Laureole, Bodleian Library, Ms. Rawl D. 591, contains ten multi-episodic miniatures, with individual scenes delineated by architectural motifs painted in gold.[21] The first miniature is a highly detailed depiction of the Prison of Love in which Leriano languishes at the outset of the romance (fig. 25).

Figure 25. Leriano in The Prison of Love. *L'estoire de Lérian et Lauréolle*. Oxford, Bodleian Library MS Rawl D 591, fol. 1v.

Although clearly a deluxe copy of the romance, the Bodleian manuscript bears no heraldry or precise indications of ownership. Hints at provenance may be found in some of the miniatures, which contain lettering embedded in some of the architectural frames, including one that distinctly reads "Monsenor Juan."[22] A further hint at provenance may be found in the final miniature, which contains an image of Saint Catherine of Alexandria, indicating a possible link to Catherine of Aragon, who was associated with the saint in royal pageantry.[23] The manuscript may have been presented to her by someone associated with Francis's court, in the knowledge of La Prison d'Amours's Spanish origins and the connection between queen and saint allows us to imagine Catherine as one of the many intercultural agents involved in The Prison of Love's history of reception. Readerly activity is evident in the corrections scattered throughout the codex and callouts in the margins of the section containing Leriano's defence of women. A note in English on f. 58r in a Gothic hand reads "do never think it strange," which is not a translation of any part of the French text. The note, to which I will return below, indicates that the manuscript was at some point in the sixteenth century in the hands of an English-speaking reader.

The miniatures in both the Bodmer and Bodleian manuscripts are painted in a style reminiscent of the Italianate illuminations produced by the workshop of the Master of the Sacre de Claude de France (c. 1517), identified as Jean Coene IV, an artist affiliated with the Pichore group of French manuscript illuminators. The group was active in the first decades of the sixteenth century, in the production of commemorative volumes for very high-ranking nobles of the French and English courts.[24] In addition to the architectural motifs, the heavily outlined facial features, including lidded eyes, long straight noses, and cheeks reddened by cross-hatching in the Bodmer and Bodleian miniatures, are all hallmarks of this style. The manuscripts containing the Sacré de Claude de France, celebrating the coronation of Francis's first wife (British Library [BL] Ms Stowe 582, c. 1517) and the Pageants for the Reception of Queen Mary of France (British Library [BL] Ms Cotton Vespasian B.II, 1514) as well as Philippus Albericus's Tabula Cebetis (BL Ms Arundel 317, 1507) and the Histoire des guerres des romans (BL Ms Harley 4939, 1515–17), all display similar miniatures to those in the Bodmer and Bodliean manuscripts containing versions of La Prison d'Amours.[25]

Paul Durrieu, and later Orth, disparaged the style of the Pichore Group as "garish" and "mediocre," respectively.[26] However, it is clear that the manuscripts painted by the group were highly prized objects in the first decades of the sixteenth century. For the purposes of this study, however, the affiliation of the codices with well-established genres of illuminated books produced as commemorative objects for members of the high nobility is more important than artistic attribution. The *Pageants for the Entry of Queen Mary* was owned by Mary Tudor, and the *Sacré de Claude de France*, was similarly made for a queen of France. The *Tabula Cebetis* was dedicated to Henry VII of England and the *Histoire des guerres des romans* belonged to Claude de Seyssel, an advisor to both Louis XII and Francis I. Both the Bodmer the Bodleian manuscripts were evidently produced in the same style as the manuscripts commemorating Queen Claude of France's coronation and Mary Tudor's royal entry.

Presentation miniatures of the kind found in Ms. NAF 7552 and the Bodmer manuscript are prime instances of codicological consciousness, in which the books pictured passing from the hands of author to patron are at once symbolic and directly referential, working to establish the courtly nature of the work as a bearer of relationships and of client-age. Such miniatures are images of a ritual, a single repeatable narrative instant, and are also highly formulaic in terms of the positions and gestures of the donor and the receiver: the donor always kneels and the book presented is always in contact with the donor's hands.[27] There is no doubt, consequently, about who is giving and who is receiving; as Erik Inglis notes, "no donor wished to be anonymous in his or her own presentation picture because the gifts commemorated in these pictures established a relationship between the donor and the recipient."[28] The presentation miniatures in the two manuscripts of *La Prison d'Amours* depict formal court encounters, celebrating book ownership as well as social ties. Like d'Assy's textual dedication, the presentation miniatures also place images of the material book in a French setting, in French hands, and before French eyes. The book is not only translated into "nostre vernacule," but visually transported into French ownership. In this way, the presentation miniatures stage the act of translational domestication, as the author-translator-figure delivers *La Prison d'Amours* into the hands of his patroness and reader. The images are reminders of the etymology of translation, of "carrying over," and of the active role of the author-translator as courtier, diplomat, and active agent in the creation and circulation of cosmopolitan literature. Combined portraits of authors, their books, and their inscribed, as well as ideal, readership – in this case circumscribed, courtly, and largely female – presentation miniatures are both metafictive and meta-material.

The very heterogeneity of these manuscripts points to one of the main reasons elite readers desired them over printed books. The adaptogenic *The Prison of Love* could take on the contours of individually designed bespoke productions in which not only the text, but also its illustrations, are domesticated and personalized in the process of translation and presentation. The dedications written by Diego de San Pedro, Lelio Manfredi, and François d'Assy, which all appear in the successive printed editions of *Cárcel de Amor*, *Carcer d'amore*, and *La Prison d'Amours*, all exemplify Natalie Zemon Davis's axiom that dedicated printed books often were the "bearers of relationships." However, one of the clearest distinctions between print and manuscript transmission in the period of *La Prison d'Amours*'s wide diffusion concerns the degree of intimacy and exclusivity of relationship born by a dedicated volume. Although presentation images do often appear in printed books, and each translation of the romance contains a personalized dedicatory text, none of the printed editions of *The Prison of Love*, in any language, contain presentation woodcuts. The presentation miniatures, devices, emblems, and coats of arms in the *La Prison d'Amours* manuscripts demonstrate clearly how the romance was personalized in order to be presented to specific readers.

In the Bodmer manuscript, several illuminations depict *l'Acteur* appealing to Lauréolle to read Leriano's letters and write back. Their composition echoes that of the presentation miniature (fig. 7), with *l'Acteur* on bended knee and Lauréolle seated, flanked by her female attendants (fig. 26). What is more, *l'Acteur* portrayed in the diegetic miniature and the author-figure portrayed in the extradiegetic presentation miniature are almost identical: they share the same hair, facial features, and clothing – a black ermine-trimmed mantle with slashed sleeves, revealing a golden tunic beneath, and red carmignolle (a man's hat with a low crown and an upturned brim). Depictions of Lauréolle, seated in her regal chamber, and the dedication portrait of Françoise also portray nearly identical figures, dressed in black hoods and gowns of the same cut and colour.

Consequently, the presentation miniature and the prose dedication would seem to function as mutually reinforcing paratexts, thresholds that lead the inscribed and visually rendered reader into a familiar visual landscape and encourage her to identify directly with Lauréolle. Indeed, the French court clothing worn by the protagonists painted in BnF Ms. Fr. 24382, Bodmer Ms. CB 149, and Bodleian Ms. Rawl D. 591

ture aussi me tracterent Ilz en peu de temps et suz au-
tant estime entre eulx comme si Jeusse este de leur
propre et naturelle nation de maniere que Je vins a
la notice des dames tellement que peu apres Je fuz
congnu de Laureolle. Et affin davoir plusgrande
participation auec elle Je luy contois des estrangetez
des choses merueilleuses des pays ou auoys este En quoy
prenoit moult deplaisirs. Puis me voyant tracter
delle comme seruiteur me sembla que Luy pourr
oye dire. Ce que Luy wuloye par moy ung Jour
que Je la veys en une salle apart des dames miz
Les genoulx en terre et Luy ce quil sensuit.

Il ne siet moins bien Le pardonner aux
puissans quant sont desserui que au
petiz La vangence quant sont Jniuriez
Pource que les vngs pardonnent par vertu
et les autres se vangent par honneur. Laquelle chose
sc aux grans hommes est deue par plus forte Raison

Figure 26. The Author and Laureola. Geneva-Cologny, Fondation Martin Bodmer Ms. CB 149, f. 9v.

contributes further to the domestication of the romance in illuminated translation. Throughout the three manuscripts' miniatures, the majority of female characters wear the hoods and square-necked gowns with trimmed bombard sleeves fashionable in the French court of the 1520s, while most of the male characters wear the full gowns, round-toed shoes, and low-brimmed hats, or carmignolles, known as "the new style," and in fashion at the time. Although the style of the illuminations is Italianate, the courts imagined in these iconographic programs are determinedly French.

Carcer damour, BnF Ms. Fr. 2150, characterized as a "private treasure" by Orth, contains nine fully painted, full-page miniatures, each framed in a plain gold border.[29] In size, layout, and decoration, Ms. Fr. 2150 is modelled upon the volumes of the *Commentaires de la Guerre Gallique* (BnF Ms. Fr. 13429), which were commissioned for Francis I by his mother Louise of Savoy, and the *Triumphes de Petrarque*, (BnF Bibliothèque de l'Arsenal Ms. 6480), both containing *grisalle* miniatures painted by Godefroy de la Batave.[30]

Ms. Fr. 2150 opens with a double frontispiece, depicting the encounter between *l'Acteur*, Lérian, and *Desir* on folio 1v and the Prison itself on 2r. Both the exterior architecture and the interior happenings are depicted in great detail, following the text's description closely. In a departure from the text, the artist painted two salamanders below the Prison, as direct reference to Francis, who had taken the salamander, a creature thought to be impervious to fire, as a personal emblem symbolizing constancy during trials.[31] The other miniatures, including another double-page spread of the siege and battles to liberate Lauréolle, are all multi-episodic and closely mirror the textual details. The scenes foregrounded include the judicial duel, *l'Acteur*'s receipt of a letter dropped by Lauréolle from her prison window, Lérian's first entry into the court, Lauréolle's liberation, her welcome back to court, and Lérian upon his deathbed. Secondary scenes are painted in the middle ground and within ornate Italianate porticos and window frames.

Although this manuscript was designed in imitation of others belonging to Francis and his emblem is featured in the painting of the Prison, Orth surmised that Ms. Fr. 2150 was copied for his sister, Marguerite de Angoulême, upon her marriage to Henri d'Albret, King of Navarre, in 1527, when she became the Queen of Navarre, noting Marguerite's interest in pro-feminine literature and the fact that d'Assy became Henri d'Albret's secretary in 1526.[32] Given the status of *La Prison d'Amours* in the French court and d'Assy's association with the royal family of Navarre, it is more than likely that Marguerite de Navarre and other women in the extended family figure among the romance's historical readers.[33]

In addition to the direct connection to Francis and his personal library, Ms. Fr. 2150 presents textual variants that place it within a receptive context that differs from the other four illuminated and personalized manuscripts. Unlike the manuscripts made for Jacquette de Lansac, Françoise d'Alançon, and Hugues de Logues and Charlotte du Mesnil, Ms. Fr. 2150 does not contain d'Assy's dedication to the *très vertuese dame.*[34] Moreover, and also in contradistinction to the other illuminated manuscripts, the letters exchanged between the protagonists are rendered in rhyming couplets in Ms. Fr. 2150.[35] If Ms. NAF 7552 is in fact the first, autograph version of d'Assy's translation, it is possible that the rhymed letters in Ms. Fr. 2150 are the work of another writer and that they either provide the models for the verse *épitres* found in the printed editions or were copied from them.

"Vaincu je fuz et rendu prisonnier"

The adaptation of the letters from prose to verse creates the effect that *La Prison d'Amours* is all the more French, a work that could have been written by Francis himself or other writers in his circle. Castilian writers and courtiers engaged in the *dulce comercio* (sweet commerce) of prose letters at the time of *Cárcel de Amor*'s composition. In Francis's court and family, such sweet commerce was also in vogue, but the French royal family and their courtiers often composed their epistles in verse. Manuscript anthologies of court poetry include letters in verse exchanged between Francis, his sister Marguerite, his mother, Louise of Savoy, and his *amye*, Françoise de Foix, his recognized mistress until 1526.[36] These letters are a rich source of information concerning how the family reacted to the events of the day and fashioned their images, individual and corporate. They also provide a wealth of information about how they used literary idioms in crafting responses to Francis's defeat and captivity in Madrid in 1525 and 1526.[37] Louise served as regent during Francis's Italian campaigns from 1515 to 1516 and during 1523–7. Marguerite travelled to Madrid in 1525 and performed an instrumental diplomatic role in the negotiation of her brother's freedom in 1526. The final peace agreement between Francis and Charles V in 1529, the Treaty of Cambrai, was called called the *Paix des dames* or "Ladies' Peace" because it was negotiated primarily by Louise of Savoy and Charles's aunt, then regent of the Habsburg Netherlands, Margaret of Austria. As a result, Francis did not cede Burgundy to Charles, but agreed to give up any claim to Italian territories. Part of the peace negotiations included the marriage between Francis and Eleanor of Austria, Charles's widowed sister.[38]

Francis wrote an extensive narrative, a *triste escripture* (melancholy writing), of his defeat at Pavia in rhymed couplets, addressed to Françoise de Foix, but without a doubt meant for broader circulation. The king laments his fortune and absence from his beloved, "Ne treuve estrange, amye, si le veoir, / qui tant me pleust, a perdu le pouvoir" (Do not think it strange, love, if the vision that so pleased me, has lost its power), yet, he vows that his *doleur* (pain) and *tourmenté desir* (tormented desire) will change back to *plaisir* (pleasure) upon his freedom, when he returns home and may see the lady addressed in the poem.[39] It is quite possible that the English note penned in the Bodleian manuscript is a partial translation of Francis's verse, further suggesting that *La Prison d'Amours* was directly related to his captivity in Spain by contemporary readers.

Francis writes in praise of his armies' chivalry and valour, painting himself first and foremost as a steadfast lover, whose unwavering loyalty and strength of character cannot be broken by the suffering of his imprisonment; he will "nourrir ma vie en ton affection" (nourish my life upon your affection) (*Poésies du Roi François 1er* 38). In reality, Francis became very ill during his time in captivity. Nevertheless, in the narrative reconstruction his imprisonment provides the context for celebrating the captivity of his heart and will, which belong entirely to his *amie* Françoise:

> Quoy qu'il en soit, Amye, je mourray
> En vostre loy, et là je demourray.
> La liberté en prison, sans doubtence,
> En mon vouloir point ne feront d'offence.
> …
> Et si prison il fauldra que j'endure,
> Y finissant mes jours soubz peine dure,
> Si demourray-je en tel travail semblable,
> Comme ay esté, point ne seray muable;
> Mort, ne péril, esloignement d'amys,
> Ny les travaulx à quoy je suis soubzmys,

Indignes sont de leur auctorité
Pour remuer la myenne volenté.

....

Car ton amour, qui tant est asseurée,
en gran travail sera fortifée,
Dont dire pius qu'esgalle peine avons,
Esgalle offrand à Amour nous debvons.

(*Poésies du Roi François 1er* 38–9)

[In any event, my love, I will die in faithfulness to you, and there I will remain. Doubtless, liberty in prison will in no way offend my will … And if I must remain in prison and end my days subject to cruel punishment, if I continue to suffer such trials as I have endured, in no way will I be changeable. Death, peril, distance from friends, the travails to which I am subject, all are stripped of their power to move my will … For your love, which is so secure, will be fortified by great trial. Then, rather than to say that we suffer equally, we owe equal offerings to Love.]

In separate *rondeaux* sent to the lady, Francis plays further on his constrained movement while imprisoned and on his immoveable heart, as well as the freedom in captivity that he enjoys thanks to love (*Poésies du Roi François 1er* 42–3). In his verses on Pavia and its aftermath, all penned to "faire service" (render a service) to his lady, Francis turns his captivity into a labour he will offer up to the God of Love, and military failure transforms metaphorically into martyrdom for love.[40]

Orth, noting the date of the first printed edition of *La Prison* and Francis's captivity, imagined Marguerite de Navarre thinking of her imprisoned brother and her own diplomatic efforts to liberate him as she read the first pages of *Carcer d'amour* in BnF Ms Fr 2150 and looked upon the painted prison as well as Francis's emblem, the salamander, which, like the lovesick Leriano, "adroit e jamais ne consumoit" (burned and never was consumed).[41] The associations between the fictional Prison of Love and the Spanish imprisonment in Madrid go further, however. Francis's poetic transformation from politically imprisoned king to a constant prisoner of love suggests how *La Prison d'Amours* offered an imperfect, if richly evocative allegory to the French court of Francis's suffering in literal imprisonment.

Three of the illuminated manuscripts, BnF Ms Fr 2150, Bodmer Ms CB 149, and Bodleian Ms Rawl D 591, contain highly detailed and, in the case of the Bodleian manuscript, gory illuminations of the battle scene in *The Prison of Love*. In both BnF Ms Fr 2150 and the Bodleian manuscript, moreover, the battle occupies a full opening, pointing to the importance given to the episode in the two iconographic programs.[42] These images, on the one hand, would have resonated with the many reports and visual renderings circulating soon after the Battle of Pavia, but also significantly contrast with images and narratives about the French defeat at the hands of Imperial Spanish forces.[43] Pavia was infamous in its day because of the tactical and symbolic asymmetry between the armoured and mounted French forces and the arquebusiers they faced. More generally in this period, the lances, swords, and hand-to-hand combat of warrior-knights were being superseded by the use of guns.[44] The Spanish *archibugi* at Pavia sprayed "volleys of deadly shot" capable of penetrating two men at arms at a time and their horses as well, leaving "the field covered with the pitiful carnage of dying noble knights as well as with heaps of dying horses."[45] The new firearms, capable of rendering warriors on horseback ineffective, heralded the what some historians have called "end of knighthood"; the armoured knight armed with sword or lance was replaced with the mounted pistoleer in the middle of the sixteenth century, as the wheellock pistol developed and began to be produced in great numbers.[46] Contemporary accounts reveal a keen nostalgia for the older ways, which is one reason for readers' continuing interest in romances like *La Prison d'Amours* that kept the image of the knight on horseback alive.

In the miniatures of the battle scene in the French manuscripts there are cannons, but all of the fighting in these scenes is carried out by armoured, sword-wielding warriors, many on horseback. The images, along with those depicting Leriano's duel, recall the imagined power and strength of *chevaliers* from the past. Reading of the bloody battle with its high body count in *La Prison d'Amours* and looking upon the illuminations, members of Francis's family and court may have been reminded of the many close relations and noblemen killed at Pavia, including Louise of Savoy's husband, Louis de La Trémoille, and Marguerite's first husband, Charles d'Alençon. Of all the manuscripts, however, Ms. Fr. 2150 appears to be most closely associated with Francis and his poetic transformation of defeat at the hands of the Spanish into a victory of love.

"Identifying political allegory is risky," as Ursula Potter notes, "Yet one of the strongest indicators for political allegory must surely be the unusual rise in popularity of a particular tale at certain periods of history."[47] D'Assy's dedication suggests the primary motivation for the sudden and intense interest in *The Prison of Love*. He first read the romance, d'Assy says, during the "primier voyage que le tres chrestien roy francoys premier de ce nom mon souuerain seigneur a fait en lombardie pour la conqueste de son estat ultramontain ay recouuert" (first voyage made by the most Christian king Francis, the first of that name, my sovereign lord, to Lombardy in the conquest and recovery of his territores beyond the Alps). The reference to Francis I's first and successful campaign in the Italian Wars suggests that d'Assy acquired the romance around the time of the French victory at Battle of Marignano in 1515, when the appropriation of a Spanish romance might have been considered something of a literary spoil of war. However, the timing of the printing following Francis's defeat at Pavia and imprisonment in Madrid suggests that the intense interest in *La Prison d'Amours* in the 1520s resonated with a different set of political and royal experiences.

Immediately following d'Assy's dedication, the text of the romance proper begins, "Depuis la guerre faicte et finee de l'an passé" (After the war done and finished last year) (f.1r). The opening lines of the Spanish *Cárcel de Amor* refer to the wars of Granada in the 1480s; in the French context, d'Assy first meant to translate the allusion from Granada to Francis's first and successful campaign of 1515. However, by March 1525, the "war done and finished last year" would have been read as an allusion to Pavia, effectively the end of Francis's Italian campaigns.[48] As mentioned above, many descriptions of the Battle of Pavia were already in circulation when *La Prison d'Amours* was printed in 1525 and 1526. An edition of the Italian *Carcer d'amore* appeared in October of the same year, perhaps reflecting a similar interest in the political associations of Spanish cultural productions.

The proliferation of early sixteenth-century French manuscripts of *La Prison d'Amours* is remarkable in and of itself as evidence of the circulation of the romance among an elite coterie of men and women who desired unique, personalized manuscripts while also enjoying the allusive and provocative tale held within the painted folia of their copies. By illustrating the receptive and social distinctions that can be drawn between printed copies and deluxe, personalized manuscript production, the French manuscripts of *La Prison d'Amours* suggest that the romance had become a much sought-after accessory of political and social prestige among Francis's courtiers, one which commemorated the fraught relations between the French Crown and the Holy Roman Empire in the first decades of the sixteenth century.

In the context of the 1520s, Louise's regency, questioned by many but supported by the Duke of Vendôme, as well as the diplomatic roles played by both Marguerite and Louise, resonate with the gender politics of *The Prison of Love*, where patriarchal imperatives are both questioned and asserted and female readers imagined as the primary readers.[49] The manuscripts of *La Prison d'Amours* commemorated Francis's survival and return after his by turns successful and disastrous campaigns in Italy, and perhaps other events associated with the political climate of the time, and marriages in particular, such as the marriage of Marguerite de Angoulême to Henri of Navarre, who had become something of a war hero after his return unscathed from Pavia. The use of the romance as a text commemorating noble and royal marriages is a possibility that would seem to be supported by Francis's gift of the tapestry set , *L'histoire de Lérian et Lauréolle,* to his sister-in-law Renée of France on the occasion of her marriage to Ercole d'Este in 1528.

Chapter Eight

From Text to Textile:
L'Histoire de Lérian et Lauréolle

Domesticating material translation along with luxury conspicuous consumption reach their culmination in *L'Histoire de Lérian et Lauréolle*, a series of tapestries produced at some point prior to 1528 in a workshop in northern France or Flanders, which transforms *The Prison of Love* into a larger-than-life, three-dimensional narrative object that mirrored and literally enveloped courtly life. At least three individual sets of the series of eight or nine panels were produced in the 1520s, at the same time that the illuminated manuscripts of *La Prison d'Amours* were commissioned and circulated. While not books, the extant *Lérian et Lauréolle* panels are part of the larger cosmopolitan narrative tradition of *The Prison of Love*. Like many of the numerous painted and printed illustrations, the textiles are imagetexts that weave narrative and visual representation together. At the same time, they are also material objects that were interpreted independently from the manuscript and printed versions of the romance.

Tapestries were highly expensive, but also highly useful, domestic objects: furnishings, insulation, and artwork. However, large narrative tapestries were above all displays of the wealth, magnificence, and culture of their owners, capable of warming "an environment both physically and aesthetically."[1] In the sixteenth century tapestry was the "preeminent figurative art form" in royal and noble households.[2] To enter a richly appointed room in a late fifteenth- or sixteenth-century household was to be immediately surrounded by, and immersed in, stories. Every domestic surface, from tabletop and plate, chest and chair-back, to wall and bed-curtain, could be the site for a narrative, for the intertwining of material and literary cultures. This meeting of literature and domestic decoration is particularly clear in large narrative tapestry "chambers," designed to hang from ceiling to floor and wrap around the interior of one or more rooms.

The subject matter of tapestries produced in the sixteenth century varied greatly, from religious subjects to illustrations of court and country customs. Verdures, or panels woven with botanical themes, were more common and less expensive to produce than figural and narrative tapestries, which required greater artistic and artisanal skills at all levels of production, from design to weaving. Biblical and classical narratives were popular, though biblical stories took on the distinct visual tones of sixteenth-century courtly narratives when translated to tapestry.[3] Episodes from the stories of Troy, Aeneas, and Ulysses were also particularly popular. Renderings of contemporary works were far less frequent, though not unknown, such as the now lost chambers of tapestries narrating Christine de Pizan's *Book of the City of Ladies*, and those illustrating episodes from a later international bestseller of Spanish origin, *Amadis of Gaul*.[4] The themes of narrative tapestries were often carefully chosen to create atmosphere, reflect upon their owners, and deliver politically charged messages.

Tools for spatial transformation as well as for image projection, tapestries were important for setting the stage for any sort of momentous political or courtly event, be it the negotiation of a treaty, the visit of a pope, a wedding, or the birth of an heir. Edith Standen notes that "tapestries, like plate and jewels, were primarily sought after as objects of conspicuous display: moreover, like gold and silver treasures, they could be easily transported as the owner moved from one seat to another or set up his tent on the battlefield; they provided instant splendour."[5] And, as Laura Wiegert observes in reference to the tapestries of the Dukes of Burgundy, "By the fifteenth century, the commission and display of tapestries constituted a key component of the public identity that members of the royalty and nobility sought to portray ... The display of tapestries became a requirement in the orchestration of all important ceremonies ... In each case, the medium of tapestry symbolized the status, prestige, and power of a ruler."[6] Checa Cremades similarly asserts that jewels, clothing, and above all tapestries were "los objetos en los que la sociedad cortesana depositaba la manifestación de la magnificencia" (the objects in which courtly society deposited the manifestation of magnificence); tapestries in particular served as "comentario iconográfico a la vida de la corte" (iconographic commentaries on court life).[7] In this context, it is interesting to note that the *Lérian et Lauréolle* chambers were produced at a time when the three most powerful rulers of Europe, Francis I, Henry VIII, and Charles V, all vied to own the most impressive tapestry collection. The owners and commissioners of tapestries were very much aware of their subject matter, and used certain narratives as iconographic "tool[s] of suggestion."[8]

Six panels and fragments of *L'Histoire de Lérian et Lauréolle* have survived, representing five of the original eight or nine designs. The panels originally measured almost five metres in height and width. At present, three panels are conserved in the Musée national du Moyen Âge, Thermes de Cluny in Paris, titled *La Rencontre à la cour* (The Meeting at court), *L'Inflexibilité du roi* (The king's intransigence), and *Le Pardon du roi* (The king's pardon). Another copy of *Le Pardon du roi* is conserved in the Museum of Arts and Crafts in Zagreb. The fifth known panel, *Le Combat de Lérian et Persée* (The knightly combat between Leriano and Perseus), is privately owned, having previously belonged to the Wildenstein collection.[9] A fragment from another panel, *La Libération de Lérian* (The liberation of Lérian), is in the Museé des Tissus in Lyon. The surviving parts of the chamber correspond to concrete episodes in the textual versions and follow the development of the plot line. Although we may surmise that the tapestries' designers included a panel or panels depicting the eponymous Prison of Love, and the Author's initial meeting of Leriano and Desire personified – images always included in illustrated book formats of the romance – no such panels are known to have survived. The extant pieces derive from a single set of cartoons, which does not appear to be directly inspired by, or based upon, any of the extant illuminations or woodcuts.

The panels are all densely woven of silk and wool, allowing for a wealth of details lavished upon the clothing, armour, and faces of the characters. Each of the complete panels contains multiple scenes, divided by architectural images, such as castle and city walls, towers, arches, doorways, and window frames, all set against backgrounds of lush floral and arboreal designs. The sequencing of events is also indicated by perspective, drawing the eye from scenes depicted at a distance and in the upper quadrants of the panels to life-size figures in the centre lower ground. The protagonists and courtiers are all dressed in armour or in opulent French court attire, including robes and gowns trimmed with fur, gems, and chains, and slashed to reveal undergarments of equally costly fabrics.

It is not known if Francis I himself commissioned the textile adaptation of *La Prison d'Amours*, but it stands to reason that he or someone close to him was the original patron of the chamber, and Francis's gift of the tapestries to Renée of France is well documented.[10] According to two sixteenth-century inventories of household furnishings at the Château de Nancy, another chamber belonged to the Dukes of Lorraine, who at the time would have been Antoine and Renée de Bourbon whose marriage in 1515 had also been arranged by Francis I.[11] The provenance of the fragment from one of the tapestry panels now in Croatia is listed as the Counts of Zrinski, one of the ruling families of Hungary at the time of *The Prison of Love*'s translation into French.[12] The depiction of Lérian in the tapestries resembles Jean and François Clouet's portraits of Francis, suggesting that the chamber was meant to function as a kind of royal portrait and as a direct reflection of the king's courtliness and martyrdom to love.

The first scene from the text shown in the extant panels appears in the small fragment, *La Libération de Lérian*. It corresponds to the textual episode in which *l'Acteur* returns to Lérian bearing the letter reluctantly written by Lauréolle, in which she declares, "Car plus pour a ta vie / rémedier t'escripre j'ai prins enuie / que pour au tien grant désire satisfaire" (For rather to save your life than to satisfy your great desire have I taken pains to write to you) (*La Prison d'Amours* 1525, 30r). In the fragment, we see a castle in the background, *l'Actuzer* – labelled *le viateur* in the tapestries – Lérian, and the six personifications Consent, Hope, Comfort, Pleasure, Joy, and Repose. The renaming of the Author as *le viateur* occurs in all of the extant panels.

The plot continues in the panel titled *La Rencontre à la cour*, which depicts Lérian's arrival and reception in the court of the King of Macedonia in the foreground. The French and other textual versions of the scene underline the ceremonial quality of Lérian's entry into the court, and the public nature of his meeting with Lauréolle: "Et sanchant a la court qu'il y alloit tous les grans seigneurs et gorriers de la court, pareillement jeunes courtisans luy vindret au devant pour l recevoir, mais combien qu'il sceust toutes telles anciennes cérémonies, plus de consolation luy donnoit la secrète que le public honneur et ainsi fut acompaigne jusques au palais" (And when it became known at court that he was on his way, all the great lords and gallants of the court, and likewise the young courtiers came out to meet him. But since he was already well acquainted with those old ceremonies, he took greater consolation in his secret glory than in his public honour. And in this way he was accompanied to the palace) (*La Prison d'Amours* 1525, 33r).

The event that will lead to Lauréolle's imprisonment and Lérian's duel unfolds in the upper right: the two protagonists meet in a space crowded with courtly onlookers. This scene corresponds to the first of only two moments in the romance when they come into direct contact, the other being when Leriano rescues Laureola from imprisonment and promptly puts her under the care of her uncle in order to preserve her honour. In the textual versions, the meeting is charged with emotion, as described by d'Assy's *Acteur*: "Quant il baisa les mains de Laureolle survindrent beaucoup de choses a noter ... a l'ung survenoit doubte, et a l'autre dessailloit la couleur, luy ne scavoit que dire, et elle que respondre, car si grande force ont les passions amoureuses que tousiours portent le sens et la prudence soubz les pieds de leur baniere comme je veiz par leur clere experience." (When he kissed Lauréolle's hands, there occurred many things worthy of note ... the one was overcome by doubt, the other drained of colour, he did not know what to say, nor she what to answer, for the passions of love have such great power that they always drag sense and prudence under their banner, and of this I saw there the clearest proof) (*La Prison d'Amours* 1525, 33r).

In the far upper left, Lauréolle and *le viateur* meet alone in a chamber, where he hands her a letter. The visual contrast in *La Rencontre à la cour* between public performative display and private meetings, which echoes the texts' contrasting of Lérian's "public honneur" (public honour) and "secrete gloire" (secret glory), is one of the signature interpretive moves of all the extant panels of the chamber, where heavily populated central scenes border upon smaller, intimate encounters between two or three characters. The viewer, of course, sees both the public and private scenes, just as the readers of *The Prison of Love* in book formats have access to the thoughts and privileged knowledge of the Author as well as to the letters exchanged between Leriano and Laureola.

In *Le Combat de Lérian et Persée*, the duel occupies the middle foreground, depicting the moment in which Leriano amputates the hand of his rival and the king is about to intervene. Perseus's hand lies upon the greenery by the horses' hooves. This central scene is surrounded by smaller episodes leading to the dénouement: Lauréolle taken prisoner, Lérian and Perseus riding to the duel, and the king surrounded by courtiers in a curtained balcony. In the texts, the duel serves as proof of Leriano's pure intentions, nobility, and skill, but also of the negative exemplarity of the jealous rumour-mongering courtier Persio. Moreover, the king, who would interpose his own judgment before God's by suspending the battle of champions, is an object of censure. Nevertheless, Diego de San Pedro and the translators do not dwell on the battle itself. A short passage telling of how the two knights charge at each other, break their lances, and draw their swords concludes with the Author's expressed desire to distinguish his tale from older romances. As d'Assy's *Acteur* remarks: "Finablement pour non estre long en cecy a ce que me semble narration d'histoires anciennes, Lérian couppa a Perseus la main dextre" (In the end, and so as not to extend this narrative, which would seem to me like the telling of an ancient romance, Lérian cut off Perseus's right hand) (*La Prison d'Amours*, 1525, 37v). The tapestry panel brings the abbreviated combat narrative into high relief.

L'Inflexibilité du roi (figs. 27–9), the largest of the surviving panels, depicts six separate scenes following Lauréolle's imprisonment and condemnation to death, in which members of the court react to the princess's plight by attempting to seek the King's clemency, and Lérian prepares for attack. Front and centre, in a garden, the Queen, accompanied by two young attendants and *le viateur*, approaches the King, who is also accompanied by courtiers. In the upper left, an interior scene depicts the Queen and *le viateur*, who kneels before her; behind him stand Gaulio, Lauréolle's uncle, and the Cardinal. Another interior scene portrays the King hearing the petitions of Gaulio and the Cardinal. The image of Lauréolle imprisoned in a tower, in the concrete version of Lérian's allegorical prison, is placed above these scenes. To the right of Lauréolle in the tower, the King receives a letter from the author. On the upper right, Lérian prepares for the battle that will liberate Lauréolle.

In the texts, the Queen's supplication to the King is only rendered in indirect speech:

> "La royne ... mise a genoulx en terre lui dist parolles non moins sages pour le convaincre que piteuses pour le mitigeur. Elle lui disoit la modération que convient aux rois, reprenant la persévérance de son ire, lui recordoit qu'il estoit père, lui notoit raisons autant sages pour noter que pour appassioner pour sentir, le supplioit que si jugement tant cruel disposoit il se voulust satisfaire avecques la mort delle qui desia avoit passe la plus part de ses ans, et laissast a Lauréolle la vie." (*La Prison d'Amours* 1525, 53r)

> [The Queen ... kneeling on the ground, spoke words no less wise for persuading him, than they were heartbreaking for softening him. She told him of the moderation that befits kings, reproving the persistence of his anger; she reminded him that he was a father; she used arguments as noteworthy for their wisdom as they were moving to hear; she begged him that, if he desired so cruel a sentence, he should be satisfied with putting her to death, since she had already lived the greater part of her years, and spare Lauréolle's life.]

Figure 27. Detail, *L'Inflexibilité du roi*. Réunion des Musées Nationaux/Art
Resource.

Figure 28. Detail, *L'Inflexibilité du roi*. Réunion des Musées Nationaux / Art Resource.

Figure 29. Detail, *L'Inflexibilité du roi*. Réunion des Musées Nationaux/Art Resource.

The Cardinal, on the other hand, delivers his counsel in direct speech. The tapestries invert the textual order of importance by foregrounding the Queen and her impassioned plea while relegating the Cardinal to the smaller scenes.

The Queen is also the central figure in *Le Pardon du roi*, a panel measuring some four metres square that relies more heavily on text for its delivery of the narrative sequence it depicts than the others. In fact, the presence of a red banderole at the top of the panel may indicate that it comes from a separate set from the Cluny panel depicting *L'Inflexibilite´ du roi*. The scroll above the scene reads: "Le roi retourne en macedoyne recoit sa fille *Lauréole* / En grant joye chascun lui faict honneur et Lérian demoure / A Suze retourne aux passions d'amour rescript a elle / une lectres par le viateur et elle lui faict response" (The King returns to Macedonia, receives his daughter Lauréolle. With great joy everyone honours her and Lérian remains in Suze. [He] returns to his passions of love, writes to her again [sending] letters to her by the traveller, and she gives him her answer) (fig. 30). This text is not present in any of the printed editions or manuscripts of *La Prison d'Amours*. Nevertheless, its inclusion, much like the labelling of characters and places in all of the panels, serves as a reminder not only of how the tapestry chamber refers back to a known literary work, but also of the imbrication of text and image.

The presentation of narrative progression in *Le Pardon du roi* is more straightforward than in *L'Inflexibilité du Roi*. Here, narrative time moves through three scenes in counterclockwise direction. The central scene, which does not quite reflect the banner's title, depicts Lauréolle's return to the court and to the arms of her mother the Queen, as the King, standing behind them, observes. This foregrounded scene is quite brief in the texts: "Lauréolle ... fut receve du roy et de la royne avec tant d'amour et de larmes de joye comme en estoient espandues de douleur. Le roy s'excusoit, la royne la baissoit, tous la servoient, et ainsi se réintégraient avecques la joye presente de la peine passée" (Lauréolle ... was received by the King and the Queen with much love and as many tears of joy as had been shed in grief. The King apologized, the Queen kissed her, all served her, and so with present joy they were restored of their past sorrow) (*La Prison d'Amours*, 1525 65r). On the upper left, Lérian, wearing an extravagantly plumed helmet, makes peace with the King. The texts of *The Prison of Love* do not recount the battles in great detail, focusing rather on Leriano's tactics and speeches to his followers, but it is easy to conjecture that one of the lost panels contained the sort of crowded

Figure 30. *Le Pardon du roi*. Réunion des Musées Nationaux/Art Resource.

battle scene included in the illustrated books and manuscripts of the romance and hinted at by the depiction of Leriano's army on the march in the upper right corner of *L'inflexibilité du roi*. Also on the upper right, Lauréolle receives Lérian's letter from *le viateur*, who will go on to deliver to Lérian the crushing news of her final rejection.

As the texts make clear, at this point in the plot, Lauréolle is caught in the competing discourses of courtly love and honour: "Moy en prison ma vie tu sauluas / Et a présent que délivrée suis / La condamner tu cherches et poursuys / Se a moy as tant d'affection certaine / Plustost devrois vouloir la tienne peine / Avec le mien honneur sans que

sans coulpe / Que ton remède avec la mienne coulpe" (When imprisoned, you saved my life and now that I am free you seek and strive to
condemn it. If you love me with so much certain affection, you should
sooner desire your own pain and my honour, which cannot be without
shame if it cures you with my shame) (*La Prison d'Amours* 1525 68v–69r).

Several interpretive moves are readily apparent in the adaptation of
The Prison of Love from a book, with or without illustrations, to the tapestry chamber *L'Histoire de Lérian et Lauréolle*. First, unlike the frequent
depiction of solitary reading and writing in the woodcuts and manuscript illuminations in *Cárcel*, *Lo càrcer*, and *La Prison d'Amours*, in the
extant panels no character is depicted alone in the act of reading or
writing. Rather, the tapestries contain multiple scenes of letters changing hands in private chambers, portraying the clandestine nature and
circumscribed readership of such correspondence, as in the scene in
the upper left quadrant of *Le Pardon du roi* where *le viateur* hands Lauréolle a letter (fig. 29). As in the books and their illustrations, material
texts and their circulation continue to be a central theme in the tapestries' rendering of the narrative, but the psychological absorption and
interiority that dominate many of the episodes in the romance are not
woven into the extant panels. This recasting of the production and circulation of material texts in the plot reflects how shifts between verbal,
visual, and intermedial communicative modes, which are embedded in
the material forms of the romance – print, manuscript, and tapestry –
all remediate the narrative according to their respective technological
capacities.

In addition to the move away from psychological interiority, the
physical theatricality inherent in the story is accentuated in the textile
rendering, particularly by the life-size figures duelling, pleading,
and embracing in the foregrounds of the extant complete panels.
Public courtly and military performances are certainly not absent in
the romance, but they are embedded within the story of Leriano's
lovesickness, and interspersed in the Author's narrations with the texts
of the letters composed by Leriano, Laureola, and Persio. In addition
to depicting the central characters writing and reading, the texts dwell
upon the Author's inner emotional states and his interpretation of
those of Leriano and Laureola. The panels that have survived move
us far from the verbalized, interior world of the lovers' suffering and
into the crowded, histrionic world of the court. Nevertheless, while
the tapestries underscore the performative, rather than the verbal,
nature of their courtly activities, the political power of language is by

no means silenced. It is, rather, staged in the many scenes in which the members of the court are shown speaking with one another and before the king.

Moreover, the extant panels foreground scenes of court pageantry and performance in which the public and private lives of the richly arrayed courtiers are portrayed. The tapestries depict courtly negotiations, intrigues, and violence, all ritualized activities in which courtiers jockeyed for position and advantage: the King and Queen listen to the counsel of *le viateur* and others; Lérian is welcomed by a group of courtiers; the Queen has her unfruitful audience with the King; the King passes judgment; Lauréolle is welcomed back into royal favour. In the combat panel, knights joust in front of a crowd of courtiers, illustrating Lérian's prowess in a military exhibition, a time-honoured way of gaining clout in court. It also displays graphically the shameful, humiliating defeat of another courtier. In the world of *The Prison of Love*, the expected outcomes of the joust are reversed: Leriano, the victor, is exiled, and Persio remains in the King's favour.

The pictorial space in tapestries is flexible, allowing for multi-episodic and continuous narrative flow through the panels, an effect of the medium that has important repercussions for the reception of the narrative conveyed. Multi-episodic tapestries, as Laura Weigert observes, "inundate" viewers "with an overflow of visual information": they are "dynamic woven pictures" in which many events transpire simultaneously in a single panel.[13] Unlike the linear progression of a text bound within a book, the tapestries stretch and compress narrative time. A viewer may stand and contemplate an entire panel, his or her gaze progressing through the scenes from centre to margins, from right to left, or in any other fashion. At the same time, as Mieke Bal observes, the theatricality of visual narratives transmits a sense of "unity based on the interaction of figures."[14]

Nevertheless, the panels' designs work to draw the eye back to centre, to the scenes that the now anonymous designer or designers chose to foreground. Textual plot progression in *The Prison of Love* is metonymical and chronologically ordered, which is to say it moves in a line from one connected event to another, even as it moves from the allegorical world to the world of the court. In the romance, which is something of a perfect narratological test case, these related events are bookended, as it were, by the metaphors of lovesickness, uniting *eros* and *thanatos*. In the transference of narrative to this visual format, the metonymy of plot progression is rendered spatially. Related scenes literally touch and border upon one another, an effect of the density of tapestries' narrative depictions, of spatial condensation of plotline, and of crowding of perspective upon perspective.

Yet another significant effect of narrative adaptation to tapestry occurs in focalization. In the written texts, focalization and perspective shift from the first-person narration of the Author to that of the letter writers, to the supplicants on Lauréolle's behalf, and to the debaters. In the tapestries, all of these characters become figures whose actions are depicted in the third person, by virtue of their labels and the banner retelling the main plot points in *Le Pardon du roi*. Like the woodcuts and manuscript miniatures corresponding to the same episode, *Le Combat* turns the two fighting knights into the central objects of focalization, but here in life size and blazing full colour. The panel foregrounds the violence of the duel: Perseus's severed wrist spurts blood, his hand lying limply on the ground, as the King, the Queen, and other courtiers observe from above and and talk among themselves. In the two surviving complete panels from Cluny, the King, the Queen, and Lauréolle are clearly objects of focalization, placed front and centre. In fact, the two Cluny panels give an extraordinary importance to the Queen, who is something of a minor character in the novel in all translations. *L'Inflexibilité du roi* clearly privileges the Queen's attempt at intercession, and *Le Pardon du roi* calls attention to the embrace between mother and daughter, heightening the significance of their reunion.

The Author is central to the metafictive nature of all the textual versions of *The Prison of Love*. Inscribed author-figure and first-person narrator, the Author is a go-between who controls access to the words both readers and protagonists read. A consummate diplomat and wordsmith, in the French context, the Author is a figure for the *noblesse de robe*, whose status was acquired through appointment to court posts.[15] The change from "Author" to "Traveller" was probably inspired by the first scene of *La Prison d'Amours*, in which both Lérian and Desire address *l'Acteur* as such.[16] Whether by the designers' error or by intention, the change is appropriate to the virtual disappearance of literary activities in the extant tapestries and to the role of the Author as a newcomer to the court of Macedonia who must learn its customs, adapt to new situations, new manners, and new expectations if he is to be successful there. However, no longer the source for authorial insights and control, *le viateur* of the tapestries ceases to be a figure in special relationship with the romance's audience.

Reading in Three Dimensions

Narratological and thematic adaptations are clear even when we look at the panels out of context, reproduced in a book, on screen, or hanging in a museum, far removed from their original setting in space and time from the sixteenth-century eye. Although exploring the receptive dynamics further brings us into highly speculative territory, what we know of usage from the period can shed some light upon the ways in which historical viewers engaged with narrative in tapestries in general, and with *L'Histoire de Lérian et Lauréolle* in particular.

In addition to raising the conspicuous consumption of cultural texts to dizzying heights, narrative tapestries offered entertainment and instruction. Fabric, as Clare Sponsler has argued, played "an important role as means of disseminating narratives" in the fifteenth and sixteenth centuries.[17] Thomas Campbell similarly suggests that "in tapestry ... courtiers would have been most directly exposed to the classical and humanistic subjects that replaced medieval romances as the staple literary diet of the sixteenth-century court."[18] And, like the canonical stories they relay, tapestries offered viewers models of correct and reprehensible behaviour.[19]

An early reference to the didactic potential of tapestries occurs in the thirteenth-century French romance *Blanchardyn and Eglantine*, where the young hero's desire for chivalric adventure is roused by his tutor's explanation of a story as told in a tapestry. The romance, which was translated into English and first printed by William Caxton in 1490, hinges on the role of the visual narratives in teaching and learning cultural literacy:

> How Blanchardine walking in his Fathers Pallace accompaned with his Tutor, he perused in the hangings of Tapestrie and Arras, the sack and distruction of the famous Cittie of Troy. It hapened on a day that Blanchardine and his Tutor walking within the Pallace of the King his father, and stedfastly perusing the abstracts and devises in the hangings, demaunded of him what warlike seidge and slaughter of men, that might be which he saw figured in the same: and hearing his Master so to blazon ye warres of the Greekes in this ten yeeres seidge gainst Troy gave more diligent attendance especially when he beheld the valiancie of Hector, Troylus, Paris, Diophoebus, Ajax, and withall, the ingenious capacitie of graue Vlisses: the large circuite of the Cittie, and princely buildings of the same: so that from that time foorth he'e conceiued small delight in any thing, but only in recording the magnanimitie, haughtie courages and the great commendations atcheived by that victorie.[20]

The tutor's explanation simultaneously teaches Blanchardine the foundational narratives of knighthood and inspires him to chivalric deeds.

This tapestry-teaching scene dramatizes the link between visual display and the oral performance of cultural literacy. Like Blanchardine's tutor, a viewer who could decipher the narrative content and retell *l'Histoire de Lérian et Lauréolle* could display his or her mastery of courtly idioms and cultural narratives as well as specific literary works. For historical viewers, such acts of deciphering were perhaps bound up with the pleasure of recognition. Acts of deciphering could also have become acts of transmission, with initiated viewers interpreting for those who had not read the romance. Recounting the story told in tapestry, much like reading aloud, engages the audience in rhetorical theatricality. Such a mode of reading, as Roger Chartier argues, "is not uniquely an abstract object of the intellect: it brings the body into play, it is inscribed in a space and a relationship with oneself or with others. [It has] a dual function of communicating ... but also of cementing the interlocking forms of sociability that are emblematic of private life in the intimacy of the family circle, in worldly conviviality, and in literary circles."[21] The reading of a tapestry, combined with the vocal explanation of its contents, recalls how the medieval romances translated and printed for sixteenth-century readers stem from traditions that blend orality and literacy. The relationship between script, print, and speech "was one of mutual infusion and reciprocal interaction, symbiosis and dynamic continuum. Sight and sound, hearing and seeing, were equally important in the creation of meaning," as Julia Crick and Alexandria Walsham observe.[22] The tapestries further extend the blending of oral narrative, the materiality of the text, and the textuality of the book so characteristic of early printing and manuscript culture, and which was apparent when *The Prison of Love* circulated in its many book formats in the first decades of the sixteenth century.

Much of what has been written about the relationships between words and images in pre-modern representation concerns Gregory the Great's famous dictum that pictures, particularly paintings in churches, were "the books of the illiterate." Armando Petrucci, in fact, suggests that woodcuts in popular printed books served a similar purpose.[23] In contrast, *L'Histoire de Lérian et Lauréolle* was an imagetext for the elite whose meaning was firmly anchored in a courtly literary and ceremonial tradition. Narrative tapestries inspire tellings and retellings of the tales that their patrons and owners deemed worthy of remembrance. However, in the acts of deciphering and retelling, the historical viewers could themselves perform courtly acts of laying claim to cultural capital and courtliness. Through the textile media, living and ceremonial chambers could function as a species of visual dictionary of the historical, biblical, hagiographic, mythical, conduct, and romance narratives that, combined, formed the cultural literacy of the pre-modern elite.

Narrative tapestries also inspired wonder in their contemporary viewers, and sixteenth-century travel narratives remark upon their lifelike nature. For example, Jacques Dubois, one of many visitors impressed by the majesty and opulence of the temporary palace constructed by Henry VIII for his summit with Francis I at the Field of the Cloth of Gold, wrote that Henry had decorated his great hall built for the meeting with "tapestries woven with gold and silk depicting the Creation of Man, all the Old and New Testaments and on the other side how David envied Uriah and took Bathsheba, which appeared to be living."[24] This lifelike effect was produced not just by the figurative images of tapestries, but by their disposition and size. Sets of large panels like *L'Histoire de Lérian et Lauréolle* were made to dress a room or the inside of a tent, often turning corners and covering doors, surrounding viewers and creating a three-dimensional effect that is hard to appreciate in reproductions and museum exhibits that display single panels. As one rapt visitor to the court of the d'Este reported: "The room was dressed in tapestry from its head down to the ground."[25] Moreover, as Weigert has argued, "tapestries offer an alternative to the perspectival spatial construction associated with Renaissance art" because they provide spectators "with a multitude of potential viewing positions, the adoption of which they control."[26] In three-dimensional, enveloping display, combined with multi-episodic panels, perspective becomes a way of drawing viewers in rather than distancing the viewing subject from the viewed object.

Tapestries, especially in chambers that wrapped around rooms, point to a dynamic relationship between subject and object, and the creation of what Ronald Rees describes as "interior landscapes," and Linda Hutcheon calls a "virtual environment."[27] A chamber's design and mode of display encourages a kind of engagement that goes beyond the hermeneutic, that of immersion, which allows viewers to "interact physically and kinesthetically" with the woven images."[28] Another aspect that is difficult to observe in the reproductions is that the figures in the foreground of these tapestries are both life-size and slightly larger-than-life, so that viewers could stand in the same physical plane as the protagonists. In this sense, chambers such as

L'Histoire de Lérian et Lauréolle are specula – full-length mirrors, rather than the mirrors in miniatures, illustrating deluxe manuscripts – that offer reflections of courtiers, both ideal and deficient. Moreover, the mirroring effect may well have created a sort of three-dimensional *mise en abyme* by illustrating and celebrating the very kind of courtly ceremonies occurring within the chambers they decorated, blurring the lines between the worlds of fictional courtly manoeuvring and the real political and diplomatic processes that *The Prison of Love* and other courtly fictions dramatize. It is possible to imagine a flirtatious courtier in Ferrara or the Duchy of Lorraine declaring, "I love you more than Lérian loved Lauréolle," in the manner of the troubadours who boasted they loved more than Flor did Blancheflor, suggesting that the closer real life moved towards the example of fiction, the truer it became. In this way, decorating the walls of a room with tapestries illustrating a work of fiction might have the effect of drawing the room's inhabitants into the fictional world of the characters, offering a physical as well as an imaginative or psychological immersion in fiction. The combination of physical envelopment in the world of the story and recollection of narrative would tend to combine the immediacy of both oral narrative and the presence of figurative art with the interpretive acts of reading romance from a text.

Diego de San Pedro's repudiation of *Cárcel de Amor* branded it a "sinners' sauce" that piqued the sexual appetites of his audiences. The immersion in the world of romance that the tapestries – and some of the illuminated manuscripts – offer allows readers and viewers of *L'Histoire de Lérian et Lauréolle* to wade into the sauce, and perhaps even to imagine himself or herself part of the mix. Lifelike and life-size, the tapestries may have given their sixteenth-century viewers a sense of being transported into the imaginary world of narrative. While the series was on display, the owners and other viewers of the story of Lérian and Lauréolle lived beside the scheming courtier Perseus, the constant chivalric lover Lérian, the irreproachable and falsely accused princess Lauréolle, the irascible King, his piteous Queen, and the diplomatic go-between, *le viateur*. *L'Histoire de Lérian et Lauréolle* stages the precariousness of honour, the importance of diplomacy, secret dealings, and military prowess.

If, at first sight, the plot of *La Prison d'Amours* makes it a curious choice for a wedding present in any format, King Francis's gift to his sister-in-law Renée was in keeping with the current literary and material tastes of his and other princely courts. Both tapestries and illuminated manuscripts were frequently given as wedding gifts that travelled with brides to their new homes, consequently contributing to the development of cosmopolitan cultural tastes and literary systems.[29]

The gift was a performance of magnificence and a testament to Renée's status as a princess of France. By hanging the tapestry chamber in her court at Ferrara, Renée would also have been able to recreate, in some sense, the interior landscape of the French court and recall her brother-in-law's courtliness. Moreover, the chamber's design, which emphasizes courtly performances of reception, intercession, and duelling, set against a background of intrigue, would have been an appropriate tool of iconographic suggestion to send with a bride whose destination was a court where she would, like *le viateur*, need to adapt to new surroundings – in Renée's case, in order to serve the political ends of her own family and to represent France. The tapestries sent to Ferrara were likely to be well received due to the vogue that Spanish romances, and *Carcer d'amore* in particular, were enjoying in the milieu of the d'Este, the Gonzaga, and the Borgia. The French, Italian, and other courtly viewers also knew that the chamber represented both real and cultural capital. Sixteenth-century readership of the many textual editions of *The Prison of Love*, as we have seen, was not limited to the aristocracy, but the tapestries, like the royal bride they accompanied to Ferrara, are the objects of courtly and political currency.

The central role of the Queen certainly suggests that *L'Histoire de Lérian et Lauréolle* interpreted *The Prison of Love* as a story that was as much about the political roles of women as those of men. Barbara Weissberger, writing of *Cárcel de Amor*, suggests that Laureola's resistance to Leriano's advances, made in the impractical language of courtly love, and her rejection of the role of willing object of desire and exchange between men, presented women readers in the Court of Castile with an empowering political image.[30] Laureola's tireless protection of her honour and desire to make her relationship with Leriano one of clientage, in which she wielded power, may also account in part for *The Prison of Love*'s popularity among women readers in the Italian and French courts through which it travelled in the first decades of the sixteenth century. The story also contains a warning in its didactic message, for Laureola and the Queen, like all of the other characters in *The Prison of Love*, live at the pleasure of the King, who is not always just and reasonable and whose power can only be challenged through military might. The romance recognizes that women do indeed have power, but that power is constrained by patriarchal order.

Unfortunately for Renée, her marriage was not only unhappy, but also ceased to be politically relevant after only one year, as Francis' allegiances shifted. Unlike *le viateur*, who successfully mastered the language and customs of a foreign court, Renée surrounded herself with French courtiers (not just with woven images of them) and seems never to have become fluent in Italian. Moreover, the story of a princess caught up in court intrigue and secret, life-threatening correspondence might have had particular additional resonance for the Duchess of Ferrara. Renée, a French princess with Protestant sympathies, married to an Italian duke who needed to maintain his allegiances to Rome, lived in the midst of a complicated and ever-shifting web of political and religious relationships. Renée's court was a known haven for both French and Italian reformers. Letters passed between Renée and Marguerite de Navarre about their shared religious beliefs and the need to protect refugees from persecution. Renée also corresponded with John Calvin, who visited her in Ferrara. At times Ercole turned a blind eye to her manoeuvrings and reformist tendencies, but when he felt pressure mounting from Rome, the duke began to persecute Renée and her court, sending members of her entourage away and attacking known heretics whose presence in Ferrara he had previously tolerated. Eventually Renée was put under the watchful eye of a Jesuit confessor and publicly reaffirmed her Catholicism in 1554. Upon Ercole's death the inquisitional climate in Ferrara further intensified and Renée returned to France, where she continued to support reformers.[31]

The transmission of *The Prison of Love* in French in the early decades of the sixteenth century – in print, manuscript, and tapestry – provides a fascinating case for the critical reconsideration of the divisions between textual and material approaches to literary and cultural history, as well as those traditionally drawn between print and manuscript studies. Many scholars of the history of books and reading have observed that the traditional division between print and manuscript studies is not only unnecessary, but also an obstruction to understanding how the written word circulated and was received in the fifteenth, sixteenth, and seventeenth centuries. Moreover, when the transmission of literature is considered in a "symbiotic" relationship with the material and performative contexts of its reception, the multidimensional culture and nature of reading in the early sixteenth century can be better understood. Both the manuscripts and the textile remediations of *The Prison of Love* draw our attention to some of the elements that made the romance popular among sixteenth-century Europe's elite and the

French in particular, but that are not immediately recognizable to the modern reader of the text. The tapestry chamber's designers evidently read *La Prison d'Amours* as a story about political life at the court of a changeable prince, the theatre of courtly rituals, and the central role of women in such ceremonies.

Francis may not have conquered Milan, but the French court materially made the Spanish romance their own, via its Italian sojourn in Mafredi's translation, and through multiple remediations that turned *La Prison d'Amours* into as series of objects of exclusive consumption, appropriating it as a flattering mirror of court life during a period of political upheaval. Such patronage was not just a "meaningless act of conspicuous consumption," as Myra Orth points out in an important article on the need to incorporate manuscripts into traditional book history.[32] Rather, commissioning manuscripts and tapestries was one way that the ruling elite, along with their clients, staked claims of cultural capital and participated in intellectual movements. For a brief period, *La Prison d'Amours* had become a central cultural text of for the French nobility representing high court culture and magnificence, and functioning as both political allegory and a tool for iconographic suggestion.

Conclusion

This book has mapped the progress – in the sense of movement both ceremonial and practical, rather than teleological – of *The Prison of Love* through the many textual and material forms it took on, from its first appearance in print in 1492 to the end of the sixteenth century. In this radiant movement, *The Prison of Love* entered and contributed to the continuing development of a cosmopolitan literary system that traversed linguistic, political, and social borders with ease, and became common reading for elites in multiple European courts, connected by ties of lineage, amity, and enmity, and by their shared literary tastes and texts. In the first decades of the sixteenth century, the networks through which the romance travelled constitute a veritable *Who's Who* of Renaissance Europe, including, as we have seen, influential women. As the romance travelled, thanks to contacts between intercultural agents, on the tides of translation, diplomacy, and the book trade, its poetics of courtly, humanist fiction, which first delighted elites who saw their own worlds and words reflected in the texts, reached new, expanded readerships for whom *The Prison of Love* offered an aspirational vision of the world of the court, its rhetorical performances, and the "dulce comercio e pasatiempo por escritura" (sweet commerce and pastime of letters).

The itinerary of *The Prison of Love* from the court of the Catholic Monarchs of Castile and Aragon to the princely courts of Italy, and then to those of France, Navarre, and England from 1492 through the 1530s, provides an optimal case for probing questions concerning the social nature of authorship as well as the dynamics of transmission and translation that made cosmopolitan literary culture possible. Throughout the romance's long history, author-functions are social and open:

shared among patrons and writers, and mediated through the narrating author-figure as well as the letter-writing protagonists.

As Bernadí Vallmanya, Lelio Manfredi, François d'Assy, and John Bouchier, Lord Berners, reframed the romance for readers in Italy, France, and England, they declared their roles as translators, and executive and revisionary authors. Manfredi, d'Assy, and Berners redeployed and recontextualized the romance by replacing San Pedro's prologue and Castilian dedicatees with their own paratexts, and by recasting *The Prison of Love* as their public gifts of courtly service. Even Bernadí Vallmanya, whose Catalan translation is the only one to feature San Pedro's name, leaving him intact as originary author, made himself visible as a revisionary author by re-presenting the work to his patron, the Conde de Oliva. Manfredi, d'Assy, and Berners present themselves as the wordsmiths directly responsible for the texts presented and as authors deserving of recognition, and perhaps hoping for recompense, from their dedicatees. The translators's authorship was also established by their direct metafictional relations with the first-person narrator, the Author, who traverses the pages of *Cárcel de Amor*, *Lo càrcer d'amor*, *Carcer d'amore*, *La Prison d'Amours*, *La Prison d'Amour*, and *The Castell of Love*. In *Cárcel de Amor*, and in all of the successive translations and adaptations, authorship is represented as a complex weave of social and textual practices. To pull at the threads of this weave is to reveal the transmission of *The Prison of Love* as a history of authorship, translation, and appropriation.

Bookmen – editors, publishers, printers, woodcut artists – also took on authorial functions, interpreting as they remediated. Prestige and utilitarian editions, manuscripts, language-learning aids, and anthologies all offered readers different experiences of the romance and associated *The Prison of Love* with multiple editorial and practical genres. *Mise en page*, title pages, decoration, and size all serve as material paratexts. The material books that audiences saw and held in their hands were expressive forms that shaped romance-reception: the smaller formats were ideal for private reading and readings that combined education with entertainment. Importantly, they were also accessible to audiences who were not among the romance's imagined readership. Prestige editions and manuscripts, on the other hand, continually signalled that romance reading was an activity for the elite.

This originally Spanish romance was highly adaptogenic because its *matière* was open to interpretation and to authorial appropriation. It was also ripe for parody, lent itself to political allegorization and other forms of domestication, and made for rhetorical reading. Francis and his court turned *The Prison of Love* into a fictionalized, and consequently more palatable, version of the king's suffering. The romance's possible interpretations, including the glorification of lovesickness, the critique of the consolidation of centralized, monarchal power, the protagonism of a knight trying to make his mark in a foreign court, and the concern for women's political and cultural power, clearly resonated far beyond the original political backdrop of the Spanish *Cárcel*.

Readers from Spain to England left their marks in the margins, having found in *The Prison of Love* ample rhetorical models and a register of prose that lent itself to transparent, "easie" translation. San Pedro's, Manfredi's, d'Assy's, and Berners's dedications, prologues, and epilogues are extratextual and metafictive links to many of the romance's central themes, including courtly rhetoric, mediation, and honour. *The Prison of Love* turns on the production and interpretation of courtly and diplomatic words and deeds, despite the ultimate fruitlessness of its protagonists' rhetorical skill and valour. Such doomed virtuoso rhetorical performances were representations of the eloquence and abilities necessary for success in aristocratic circles and the exercise of power, but they also spoke to anxieties about rhetoric. Translation itself was an important skill for the cosmopolitan courtier, and the paratexts of their translations also provide us with critical vantage points from which to study early modern ideas of horizontal, vernacular translation. The translators all produced vernacular versions of *The Prison of Love* in the absence of a formal discourse on horizontal translation. And, although they all found the romance eminently translatable, the translators were also working with an unconsecrated literary genre, short prose fiction that blended allegory, epistles, and debate, one that had been composed for pleasure rather than profit, and inscribed a courtly, heterosocial readership. In each dedication, the translators discuss their roles as cultural intermediaries and present the romance as a token of chivalrous service offered to women envisioned not only as readers and determiners of taste, but also as allies in court and potential patrons.

Publishers followed the example of the translators' offering their "little book" to women, and continued to advertise *The Prison of Love* as pleasing to women, placing the romance within the broader *querelle de femmes*. Discussions of the romance's engagement with the *querelle* have generally been limited to Leriano's lengthy recitation of the commonplace arguments in defence and praise of women and his list of exemplary women. This content prompted French bookmen to add the *louenge des dames* to their titles. Yet in addition to the formal inclusion of the debate, *The Prison of Love* participates in the case for women incidentally, and, more suggestively, in the letters that Laureola writes, with misgivings, to Leriano. No doubt women readers and viewers were not only interested in flattery of the female sex. Its particular appeal to female readers, I would argue, was due as much to Laureola's rhetorical fluency, political behaviour, and resistance to persuasion as to Leriano's gallant display of pro-feminine copia. This direct engagement in the pro-feminine side of the *querelle des femmes* is complemented, but also complicated, by its nuanced analysis of women's power in the figures of Laureola and the Queen. Throughout, Laureola writes not just to Leriano, but also to her father to instruct him on the finer points of honour and kingship, which he seems to have forgotten. Moreover, in her final letter to Leriano, she offers him a relationship of *clientage* rather than love service. Her mother, the Queen, is likewise privileged and able to speak out in court, but powerless to change the course of the King's actions. As Weissberger, writing of *Cárcel de Amor*, sums it up, the romance simultaneously works to legitimize and celebrate "aristocratic masculine power," while also laying bare how the discourses of courtly love and chivalry exalt women and their honour in order to control them.[1] The romance's depictions of female agency are part of its political allusivity in the context of Isabel I and beyond.

The *Prison of Love* deploys the *querelle des femmes*, ever a "hot topic" for humanists and in humanist poetics,[2] within a dialogic frame, inviting audiences to scrutinize its terms and effects. The discourse of misogyny is ineffective and silenced; Leriano is not cured by his friend's diatribe and dies for love. Nevertheless, Leriano's pro-feminine martyrdom seems to suggest that the consequence of defending women may be death. *The Prison of Love*'s denouement is ambiguous: is Leriano a pro-feminine and courtly hero to be applauded, or a failed lover whose vulnerability to women leads to his demise? Is Laureola a *belle dame sans merci* who has cruelly caused the death of a valiant and noble man, or is she the victim of a courtly code that damns her regardless of whether she unsubmissively protects her honour or acquiesces? Reading *The Prison of Love* and other humanist fictions "was *never* a matter of aesthetic enjoyment alone but always an instructive activity that made reading exploratory, an activity in which the reader, responding dialectically to the text, found closure to the text only in his own judgment or interpretation," as Kinney asserts.[3] Nicolas Núñez and Andrew Spigurnell are prime historical examples of readers seeking closure to an open work.

While the translators' and publishers' claims would seem to bear out the general assumption that romances were "women's reading," what is also clear from the authorial paratexts is that men were among the many avid readers of *The Prison of Love*; its circulation depended upon how it was shared between men, first between Diego de San Pedro and the *cavalleros* of the Castilian court, a relationship into which Vallamanya and Núñez inserted themselves as revisionary authors writing for yet more courtiers. Manfredi redeploys the romance as *Carcer d'amore* in order to associate himself with Mario Equicola, and later, according to the dedication of *La Prison d'Amours*, gave the romance to his friend d'Assy, whom he met at some point during their travels in the Italian Wars. The networks of authors, patrons, and translators through which the romance travelled suggests, then, that courtiers whose fortunes depended upon their work as translators, secretaries, envoys, and diplomats were among the first intended readers. Their dedications to noblewomen notwithstanding, Manfredi, d'Assy, and Berners were the epitome of this readership. And, although each version portrays heterosocial images of social authorship, *The Prison of Love*'s authors, like many male romance writers, used their dedications, "pleasing matters," and depictions of women and rhetoric to authorize themselves.[4]

The Prison of Love, an intercultural work deemed worthy not only of textual translation, but also of transmission in illuminated manuscripts, and adaptation to that most expensive and ostentatious of courtly media, tapestry, is ideal for studying the symbiosis between book – and bookish – objects and literary narratives. Given the importance of tapestries in the work's progress through the courts of sixteenth-century Europe, it is tempting to appropriate Don Quixote's evocative metaphor of reversing the tapestry as an optic for understanding its many material and textual translations. However, though his critique of vernacular translation provided a critical point of departure for discussing vertical and horizontal translation, it is not sufficient for discussing the textualterity and material multiformity of *The Prison of Love*, and even less so for its remediations in textile and manuscript. *L'Histoire de Lérian et Lauréolle* and the "private treasures" of the French court are anything but rough reproductions devoid of beauty and style. Don Quixote's warning about the shortcomings and losses of translation constitutes an implicit defence of the role of an original author as the progenitor of a literary text. The translators and retranslators of *The Prison of Love* do not describe themselves as imitating the greater eloquence of literary forebears. Rather, they refer to decorum and the need for elegant language when telling such a story as *The Prison of Love* with its "matters so very pleasing." And, in each incarnation of the romance, the producers responsible similarly repackaged and reshaped the work for their intended audiences, readers, and customers.

Thomas Sackeville, on the other hand, provides a more fitting metaphor likening translation to tapestry in his laudatory poem and letter introducing Thomas Hoby's English translation of *The Book of the Courtier* (1561):

> The prince he raiseth huge and mightie walles,
> Castilio frames a wight of noble fame:
> The king with gorgeous Tissue clads his halles,
> The Count with golden vertue deckes the same,
> Whose passing skill, lo Hobbies pen displaies
> To Britaine folke, a worke of worthy praise.

Here the work of the writer and his translator displays the virtue of the perfect courtier in the way that a king's "gorgeous tissue" displays wealth and might. Sackeville continues:

> Themistocles the noble Athenian in his banishment entertained most honorably with the king of Persia, willed upon a time to tell his cause by a spokesman, compared it to a peece of Tapistrie, that being spread abroad disclotheth the beautie of the workmanship, but folded together, hydeth it, and therefore demanded respite to learne the Persian tongue to tell his own cause.[5]

In addition to praising writing and translation as works of symbolic value equal to the material value of the tapestries of kings, Sackeville commends Hoby's work as an act of revealing and unfolding rather than reversing, a translation that allows "Castilio" to speak for himself in a new language. Like Themistocles unfolding his story before the king of Persia, each translation, material book, woodcut illustration, manuscript illumination, and tapestry panel unfolded *The Prison of Love* before the eyes of their intended audiences, in the idioms particular to each medium and local context.

Following *The Prison of Love* through its textual and material remediations reveals how lively what is usually considered merely the "afterlife" of the fifteenth-century tour de force *Cárcel de Amor* was. *The Prison of Love* was an international book, in many ways emblematic of sixteenth-century literary culture, which was not always confined between the covers of printed books. This book has, I hope, done some unfolding and revealing of its own, by tracing the contours of a small book that transformed into even smaller books, at the same time that it took shape in large manuscripts and expansive tapestries, and a "small" fictional place that was, for a while, ubiquitous within cosmopolitan sixteenth-century literature. *The Prison of Love*'s intercultural appeal and material adaptability cannot be accounted for by any single factor. Part allegory, part exemplary novella, part courtesy book and rhetorical compendium, the "little book" garnered great cultural capital for over one hundred years. Its fortunes do not tell *the* story of the book in the sixteenth century, but rather, a series of stories through which the multifaceted world of sixteenth-century literary and book cultures are refracted.

Appendix A: The Translators' Paratexts

I. Bernadí Vallmanya

Obra intitulada lo Carcer damor.

Composta y hordenada per Diego de Sant Pedro a petició y pregàries de don Diego Ferrandis, Alcayt de los Donzeles, y altres cavallers de la cort del Rey d'Espanya nostre señor. Traduït de lengua castellana en estil de Valenciana prosa per Bernadí Vallmanya, Secretari del spectable Conte d'Oliva. E comença lo pròlech.

Molt virtuós senyor,

Encara que algun comport per a callar me falte, no·m fall coneixença per a veure, què·m seria millor: estimar-me del que poría callar, o del que poría haver dit, penedir-me, y ab tot que axí yo·u conega, encara que, mirant, de la veritat tinga clara coneixença, segueixch la opinió, y, fent lo contrari, nunca sens reprehensió reste; e si erre per ignorància, ab vergonya pagant, ho acabale. És veritat qu·en la present obra tant càrrech no reporte, puix en ella, més per necessitat de obehir que ab voluntat d'escriure he volgut posar-me. Perquè fuy pregat per Vostra Mercè degués fer alguna obra de l'estil de una oració que havia tramès a la Senyora dona Marina Manuel, la qual li semblava seria menys mal que lo que yo havia ja escrit en altre tractat que de mi tenia. Y perquè sos manaments, complidament tingues-sen effecte, delliberí fer-la, havent per millor errar en lo dir que·en la deso-bediència, delliberant d'endreçar-la a Vostra Mercè, perquè li fos, com a senyor, la sua favor prestada, y com a discret, atengués la sua esmena. Ab tot que, ans de determinar-me, dubtava. Car vista vostra singular discre-ció, temia, y mirada vostra noble virtut, en doble ànimo augmentava, y

trobant en la hu temor y en l'altre la seguretat que cercava, he triat a la fi
lo més damnós per a ma vergonya y lo més profitós, per al que fer devia.
E si en lo que ara escrivint ordene tornaré algunes rahons qu·en altres
coses haja escrits, de reprehensió no m'escuse. Del què suplique Vostra
Mercè vulla escusar-me. Que havent ja de la qualitat d'esta obra al[t]ra
hordenada, no serà maravella que la memòria falte, e si tal se troba, per
cert més culpa trendrà en ella l'oblit que la voluntat mia. Per hon senyor
considerant les coses qu·en lo que scrich trobar se poden, yo delliberava
ya cessar de metres y prosa per dellivrar d'ésser ma ignorància jutgada, y
l'esprit meu de treballs quiti, y quant més pense posar-ho en efecte, tant
me occorren més coses per a no poder complir-la, Però suplique Vostra
Mercè, ans que la mia falta no·m condamne, vulla jutjar la voluntat mia
perquè no segons la mia rahó, mas segons mon desig remuneració puga
rebre.   *Lo càrcer d'amor*, 1493, A1v–A2

A work titled the Prison of Love.

Written and composed by Diego de San Pedro at the behest and request
of don Diego Fernandez, Master of the Light Cavalry, and other knights
of the court of our lord, the King of Spain. Translated from the Castilian language into prose in the Valencian style by Bernardí Vallmanya,
Secretary to the honourable Count of Oliva.

Most virtuous Lord,

   Although I may lack the decorum to remain silent, I do not lack the wits
to see that it would be better to take pride in what I could keep to myself,
than to repent for what I might say. Despite all that I know, even though
I understand and have clear knowledge of this truth, I follow my own
council and do the reverse, so I never go unpunished. Therefore, if I err
out of ignorance, in the end, I will pay for it with my shame. It is true that
I do not consider myself fully responsible for the present work, since I set
myself to it more out of the obedience required of me than from my own
desire to write. For I was asked by Your Worship to write something in the
same style of a piece that I had sent to the Lady Marina Manuel, one which
she found less objectionable than another romance I wrote that she had
seen. Consequently, in order to fulfil her commands, I decided to write
it, considering it better to err in what I say, than to err through disobedience, and thinking I would dedicate it to Your Worship, so that it would
have your noble favour, and your wise emendation. Yet before making my
decision, I doubted. For, considering your singular discretion, I feared, yet
seeing your noble virtue, I took great heart. Finding in the former fear and

in the latter the confidence I needed, in the end I chose to do what was most damaging to my reputation, but most advantageous in terms of my duty. I do admit that I may be guilty of having repeated some of the things I said in my other writings, for which I beg you to forgive me. Since I have written something similar to this work before, it will be no surprise if my memory fails. If this is the case, surely it is more the fault of memory than my will. Truly, my lord, considering the faults that can be found in what I have written, I was contemplating never writing anything again in verse or prose, in order to shield my ignorance from judgment and to spare myself pain. Yet, the more I think upon it, the more reasons for not doing so come to mind, so I beg Your Worship, to consider my intentions before you condemn my errors, so that I may be compensated for my desire to serve you rather than for my wit.

II. Lelio Manfredi

A la illustrisima et excellentissima Madona, Madona Isabella Estense da Gonzaga, Marchesana du Mantua, Lelio Manfredi d.s.

E prisci proavi nostri, illustrisima et excellentisima Madona, hebbono in uso non solamente di honorare e cum magnificentissime laude extollere quelli che in proporzione di membri, in venustà di volto, in nova inventione di qualche utile cosa, in gratia, in modestia, o in virtute excedevano gli altri, ma di prestagli il sacro fumo del sabeo incenso e come potentia fuor di natura adorargli. Et a diversi auxilii, ne' bisogni di corpi humani sopraponendogli in favore e aiuto loro, cum pie e affectionate voci gli ivocavono, dandogli – per ricompensa del riceputo benfizio – le spoglie hostili, le primitie di gioveni inserti del fertile agello, del riccho peculio o de lo ingegno loro. La qual consuetudine, per meritar grandissima conmendatione, non senza iustissima causa al presente ancor io ho seguito, ché, havendo cum non pocha diligentia e faticha ridutto questo picciol volume da lo externo idioma in nostra vernacular lingua, a Vostra Excellentia – vivo lume de la virtute, sola beltà de l'unica bellezza, verità aperta del vero, equale bilancia de la iustitia, splendida grandezza de la libertalitade, ferma colonna de la clementia, stabile fortezza del casto pensiero, lucida gemma in oro nitido e pretioso, amenissimo fonte in florido giardino, micante luce ne le tenebre, guida, governo, albergo e habitaculo de le nove muse – l'ho dedicato, havendo forsi habiuto mancho rispetto a la grossezza del mio ingegno e la ineptie de la lingua che a la altezza Sua. Unde, anchora che mi manchasse patientia per tacere non mi manchava cognoscimento per vedere quanto mi era meglio apretiarmi di quel ch'io taccessi che pentirmi per quel ch'io havevo a dire; e, posto che cossì io lo cognoscessi e che anchora ne vedessi apta la veritate, ho seguito la opinion mia. E hauendo operato il peggio, non resto senza punitione: perché cum la vergogna satisso a lo errore che per ignorantia ho commesso. Ma bene è vero ch'io non credo ne la presente opera meritar molto incarico, perché io mi posi più in quella per desiderio di far cognoscere a Vostra Celsitudine la servitù mia che per voluntà di acquistar fama. Da cui mi nacque l'animo grande, il quale sempre sòle causar le gran cose, immaculati li costumi, eximia la humanitate, placida la gratitudine, conspicua la bellezza, faconda la memoria, acuto l'intelletto e retta la voluntate. E benché io stessi in gran dubio prima ch'io me determinassi, perché, vedendo la sublimità e intelligentia sua, io timevo, mirando la prudentia e virtute, io avevo ardire: in l'una trovavo il timore, ne l'altra cercavo la sicurezza. Infine ellessi il più dannoso per la mia vergogna e l'più utile per il mio debito. Supplico, adunque a quella che si degni, cum hylare volto e benigno animo, di acceptarlo, ricordandogli che già Arthaxerse famossimo Re de' Persi, non hebbe a sdegno di gustar le cristalline lynphe da un povero e rozo agricultore, cum sincero animo, fra le callose mani, dal translucido fonte tolte, iudicando prima la voluntà mia che condanni il diffetto. A fine ch'io riceva il premio, non secondo il mio merito, ma secondo il mio desiderio. Et alla bona gratia di, Vostra Illustrissima Signoria umilmente mi racommando.   *Carcer d'amore*, 1514, A1r–2v

To the most illustrious and excellent Lady, Lady Isabella d'Este Gonzaga, Marquise of Mantua, Lelio Manfredi, d.s.

Our first ancestors, most illustrious and excellent Lady, used not only to honour and extol with great praise those who excelled all others in beauty, the invention of some new useful thing, grace, modesty, or virtue, but also to offer them sacred Sabean incense and venerate them as supernatural beings. Our ancestors also raised their pious and passionate voices in prayer, beseeching favour and succour for many of their earthly human needs, offering up the spoils of war, the entrails of the first offspring of the fertile lamb, great wealth, or whatever else they could think of in return for the gods' benevolence. I, too, now have followed that custom, because you deserve great commendation, not without most just cause. I have, with unstinting diligence and labour, brought this little book from a foreign language into our vernacular tongue, to you. Your Highness – living flame of virtue, singular beauty of beauty itself, true portal of truth, balanced scale of justice, splendid greatness of liberality, steadfast pillar of clemency, firm fortress of chaste thoughts, a shining gem in a bright and precious setting of gold, most pleasant fountain in a flowery garden, a sure light in the darkness, guide, ruler, refuge, and home for the nine muses – I dedicate it, perhaps having failed to take the gracelessness of my wit and my inelegant tongue into account. Therefore, even if I have lacked the patience to keep quiet, I did not lack the understanding to see how much better it would have been to value what I kept silent than to regret what I had said; and, even though I knew it and could see the plain truth, I have followed my own council. And, having taken the worse course of action, I am not free from punishment, because the shame I suffer atones for the errors that I have committed. Yet it is true that I do not believe that I am much to blame for the present work, because I wrote it with the desire to express my servitude to Your Highness, and not out of my own desire for renown. From which was born in me the strength of spirit that always tends to cause great things: perfect behaviour, eminent humanity, tranquil gratitude, notable beauty, copious memory, sharp intelligence, and upright will. Even though at first I had great doubts, when I considered your sublimity and intelligence I feared; yet thinking of your prudence and virtue, I took heart: in the former I had reason to fear, in the latter confidence. And so I chose the course of action more hazardous to my reputation and the one more appropriate to duty. I beg therefore that in regard to anything one might deem worthy, that one ought to accept it, with a smiling face and a good heart – bearing in mind that Artaxerses the renowned King of the Persians did not disdain to enjoy sincerely the crystalline water drawn from a nymph's lucid fountain even though it came from the calloused hands of a poor, rough farmer – considering my will to serve you before condemning its faults, so that I may receive recompense for my desire rather than for my merits. I entrust myself to your good graces, most illustrious Lady.

Lelio Manfredi

Hebbe questo fine il sfrenato desire, la ustinata volgia e il fedele amore di Leriano, Illustrisima et excellentissima Madonna, in laude de la cui Constantia, ne futuri lustri restarà questo picciolo volumne, per exempio de la mia seruitute dicato a Vostra Excellentia. La qual se bene è occupata in cose di non poco momento e inportantia – ne li studii, e muse, al sacro fonte de le quale, per via ormai a lei facile e piana, gli ha dimostrato e dimostra continuamente havrire le divine lynphe il dottissimo et eloquentissimo meser Mario Equicolo, de le cui laudi meglio è chiuder le labra che non parlare a suffizientia – si dignarà alcuna volta torlo in mano, et cum quello passar il tempo fastidioso, legiendo pensieri pronti, moti arguti: et effetti amorosi; li quali, quanto mancano di eloquentia, di facondo et ornato parlare, tanto abondano di bono animo, optimo volere e affezionato desiderio di servire, honorare et exaltare Vostra Celsitudine: da la qual impetrando tanto favore e gratia, cumulatamente mi cognoscerò satisfatto de ogni mi fatica.   *Carcer d'amore*, 1514, Q3v–4r

The unbridled desire, the stalwart will, and the loyal love of Leriano all came to this end, most illustrious and excellent Lady; may this small volume in praise of his constancy be proof for future generations of my service to Your Excellency. You are engaged in subjects of no little moment and importance – in your studies, the path to the Muse's sacred fount of wisdom is now made easy and smooth, thanks to the guidance of that most subtle and eloquent Messer Mario Equicolo, of whom I would rather remain silent than risk not praising sufficiently. I will feel the utmost satisfaction for all my labours if you deign at some time to take this book in hand, and with it pass the time reading its lively ideas, clever plot, and amorous doings, which, though lacking the copious and ornate style, is filled with goodwill, the best wishes and affectionate desire to serve, honour, and exalt Your Highness, from whom I beg such favour and grace.

III. François d'Assy

Ce livre a este translaté de langage tusquan florentin en françois e traicte de l'amour de Lérian et Lauréolle, fille du roy de Macedoine.

Remémorant en quante servitute et obligation estoy envers toi, très vertueuse et très prudente Dame, j'ay tenu et obstrainct por le grâces et bien faictz qu'il ta pleu m'octroyer, lesquelz toutesfois comme j'ay peu appercevior n'ont este correspondens a ton magnanime vouloir, l'importunité du temps et saison. Néantmoins n'ay este ne suis ignorant de ta bonne et libéralissime .voulunté, laquelle en c'est endroit justement prens pour effect. Pensant pour iceulx quelque rémunération te faire, non de biens terrestres, car dame Fortune m'en a très mal muny, mais de ce petit livret jadis converty de langue castillanne et espaignolle en Tusquan florentin par ung ferraroys mon bon et singulier amy, des mains duquel en ce premier voyage que le très chréstien roi Françoys premier de ce nom mon souverain seigneur a fait en lombardie pour la conquête de son estat ultramontain ay recouvert. Et voyant que d'assez belles matières traictoit mêsmes pour jeunes dames, j'ay entreprins mettre et translater du dit ytalien en nostre vernacule et familière langue françoise et le te dédier ce que j'ay faict, non

pas de si ornée éloquence comme a ton excellence méritast estre présenté
car mes espritz son trop indécens et mattes. Pour laquelle chose premier
que en ce labeur cultiver me déterminasse en grande dubiosité et diversité
d'ymaginations me trouvay, car voyant la sublimité et intelligence de ton
esperit je craignoye et préméditant la prudence et vertu m'enhardisseoye
et prénoye vigueur très grande. En l'ung trouvoye la timeur et en l'autre
seurete et hardiiesse. En fin je ésluez le plus dommageable pour ma ver-
gongne et le plus utile pour mon devoir. Et se pour ceste cause je tum-
boye en répréhension d'oultrecuidance ou autre vitupère pour n'avoir eu
tant de respect et considération a ta haultesse comme il estoit décent. Mon
affection considérée suis seur d'en échapper pourtant que l'entreprinse
j'ay faicte plus par désir de te faire congnoistre la seruitude et obéissance
que te porte que la voulenté d'acquerir fame et louenge. Par quoy je te
supplie très vertueuse dame que avecque sincère et jucond courage vueisses le petit présent accepter en jugeant la mienne voulenté premier que
le déffaut condamner. Et aussi ayant plus de regard a l'affection et désir
de celluy qui présente que a la valleur de la chose présentée. Te supplie
de réchief que ou nombre de tes très humbles serviteurs me vueisses tous-
jours tenir inscript. Et je prie pour le surplus le plasmateur de la cause
première longuement te conserver heureuse et prospère.

La Prison d'Amours, Paris, 1525, n.p.

This book was translated from the Tuscan Language into French and is
about the love of Lérian and Lauréolle, daughter of the king of Macedonia.

Recalling that I am your most loyal servant and greatly obliged to you,
most virtuous and most prudent Lady, I found myself compelled by the
favours and benevolence that you have seen fit to show towards me –
though I know that my service cannot compare to your magnanimity,
given the vicissitudes of life and time – yet I am not unaware of your good
and most generous nature, which is my motivation for this present work.
Thinking, therefore, that I would like to repay your generosity in some
way, not with any earthly goods, because Lady Fortune has most poorly
rewarded me, but rather with this little book. It has already been converted from the Castilian and Spanish language into Florentine Tuscan by
a Ferrarese, my good and particular friend, from whose hands I received
it, during the first voyage made by the most Christian King Francis, the
first soveriegn lord of that name, to Lombardy in the conquest of his foreign territoritores. Seeing that it treated matters so very pleasing to young
ladies I undertook to translate it from the said Italian into our vernacular
and familiar French language and to dedicate it to you, though I have not

done so with such ornate eloquence as your excellency merits because my wits are too unfit and dull. Consequenly, when I first thought of setting to work I found myself in great doubt and divers imaginings. For seeing loftiness and intelligence of your spirit, I feared, and then thinking of your prudence and virtue, I was emboldened and became determined. In the one I found dread and the other assurance and strength. In the end, I chose the course of action most damning to my honour and most suitable to my duty. I know that I may be criticized for my impudence or else vilified for not having shown the proper respect and consideration for your highness. Considering my affection for you, I am sure that I will escape such censure because I have written out of my desire to demonstrate the service and obedience that I owe you, rather than out of any wish to acquire fame and praisé. Therefore, I beg you, most virtuous Lady, to accept this little gift with a sincere and joyful heart, and to judge it according to my desire to serve you before condemning its faults, and do so also in the knowledge that the gift does not match my affection and desire to serve you. Again, I beg you to consider me forever amongst the number of your most humble servants, and furthermore I pray that the Creator of the First Cause protects and keeps you happy and prosperous for many years.

IV. John Bouchier, Lord Berners

The castell of love, translated out of Spanishe in to Englyshe by Johan Bowrchier, knyght, lorde Bernis, at the instaunce of the Lady Elizabeth Carew, late wyfe to syr Nicholas Carew, knyght. The whiche boke treateth of the love betwene Leriano and Laureola, doughter to the kynge of Masedonia.

For the affeccyant, desyre, and obligacyon that I ame bownde in towardes your ryghte vertuous and good lady, as well for the goodnes that it hath pleased you to shewe me, as for the nyrnesse of consanguinite, hathe pleased me to acomplyshe your desire, as in translatynge this present boke. And though my so doynge, can not be correspondente any thynge to recompence your goodnes, yet not beying ignorante of your wyll and desyre, the whiche in this cause I take for the hole effecte, thynkynge thereby to do you some smale rememoracyon, and also bycause the matter is very plesante for yonge ladyes and gentle women. Therefore I have enterprysed to translate the same out of Spanyshe in to Englyshe, not adorned with so fresshe eloquence that it shulde meryte to be presented to your goodnese. For or I fyrste entred in to this rude laboure I was brought into great doubtfulnesse and found my selfe in dyvers ymagynacions. For seynge the quycke intellygence of your spyrit, I feared, and agayne the remembraunce of your vertue and prudence gave me audacyte. In the one I found feare, and in the other suertie and hardynesse. Fynally I dyd chose the moste unvaylable for myne owne shame, and most utilite in any reprehencion or rebuke for the moche boldenesse in that I have not taken suche respyte as I oughte to have done. Yet in consyderacyon of your gentlenesse, myne affeccyon is always in truste to skape blameles. I have taken this entrepryce on me, more be desyre to have blame thereby then to atteyne by my prayse or laude, wherfore, ryghte veruous lady, maye it please you of your goodnes to accept this lyttle presente treatyse, and to receyve this my good wyll or ye condempne the faulte. And also to have the more affeccyon to the presenter then to the valewer of the thynge presented, requyryng you to holde and repute me alwayes as one of the number of them that always shal be redy to do you pleaure. As for the surplus, I desyre the creatour of the fyrst cause long to indure and to encrease your happy prosperite, Amen.   *The Castell of Love*, 1548? A2r –A3r

And thus I bydde fare well and adew all true lovers and all ye readers and hearers of this proces, desyryng them where they fynd faulte to amend it, and I shall pray to god for their prosperyte and at theyr ende to send them the joyes of paradyce. Amen   *The Castell of Love*, 1548? O7v–O8r

Appendix B: Printed Editions of *The Prison of Love* in Spanish, Catalan, Italian, French, English, and French-Spanish, 1492–1650

Spanish

1. *Cárcel de Amor.* Seville: Cuatro Compañeros Alemanes, 1492. 4°.
2. *Cárcel de Amor.* Zaragoza: Pablo Hurus, 1493. 4°. Woodcut illustrations.
3. *Cárcel de Amor.* Burgos: Fadrique Biel de Basilea Alemán, 1496. 4°. Woodcut illustrations.
4. *Cárcel de Amor.* Toledo: Pero Hagenbach, 1500. 4°.
5. *Cárcel de Amor.* Logroño: Arnau Guillén Brocar, 1508. 4°. Woodcut titlepage.
6. *Cárcel de Amor.* Seville: J. Cromberger, 1509. 4°. Woodcut titlepage.
7. *Cárcel de Amor.* Seville: J. Cromberger, c. 1511–15. 4°.
8. *Cárcel de Amor.* Zaragoza: Jorge Coci, 1516. 4°. Woodcut illustrations. [No known copy]
9. *Cárcel de Amor.* Burgos: Alonso de Melgar, 1522. 4°. Woodcut illustrations.
10. *Cárcel de Amor, nuevamente correydo.* Zaragoza: Jorge Coci, 1523. 8°. Woodcut illustrations.
11. *Cárcel de Amor, nuevamente historiados y bien correydo.* Zaragoza: Jorge Coci, 1523. 8°. Woodcut illustrations.
12. *Cárcel de Amor.* Seville: Cromberger, 1525. 4°. Woodcut titlepage.
13. *Cárcel de Amor.* Burgos: Alonso de Melgar, 1526. 4°. Woodcut illustrations.
14. *Cárcel de Amor.* Seville: Cromberger, 1527. 8°. Woodcut titlepage. *Amor.* Burgos: Alonso de Melgar, 1527. [No known copy]
15. *Cárcel de Amor.* Venice: Juan Batista Pedrezano, 1531. 8°. Woodcut illustrations.

16. *Cárcel de Amor*. Zaragoza: Jorge Coci, 1532. 8°. [No known copy]
17. *Cárcel de Amor*. Toledo: Juan de Ayala, 1537. 4°. Woodcut titlepage.
18. *Cárcel de Amor; De muy subido y gracioso estilo*. Valencia: Francisco Díaz Roman, 1539. 4°.
19. *Cárcel de Amor. Agora nuevamente hecho*. Toledo: Juan de Ayala, 1540. 4°. Woodcut titlepage.
20. *Cárcel de Amor*. Zaragoza: Jorge Coci, 1542. 4°
21. *Cárcel de Amor. Agora nuevamente hecho*. [Seville: Domenico de Robertis?], 1544. 4°. Woodcut titlepage.
22. *Question de amor y Cárcel de amor*. Antwerp: Martin Nucio, 1546. 12°.
23. *Cárcel de Amor hecha por Hernando de Sanct Pedro con otras obras suyas va agora añadido el sermon que hizo a vnas señoras que dixieron que le desseauan oyr predicar; nuevamente impresso*. Medina del Campo: Pedro de Castro, 1547. 8°. Woodcut titlepage
24. *Question de amor y Cárcel de Amor*. Paris: Hernaldo Caldera y Claudio Caldera, 1548. 12°.
25. *Cárcel de Amor y Question de amor*. Zaragoza: Esteban de Nájera, 1551. 8°. Woodcut illustrations.
26. *Cárcel de Amor hecha por Hernando de Sanct Pedro con otras obras suyas, Va agora añadido el sermon que hizo a unas señoras que dixeron que le desseavan oir predicar*. Venice: Gabriel Giolito de Ferrariis y sus hermanos, 1553.
27. *Cárcel de Amor del cumplimiento de Nicolas Nuñez*. Antwerp: Martin Nucio, 1556. 12°.
28. *Question de amor y Cárcel de Amor*. Antwerp: Martin Nucio, 1556. 12°.
29. *Question de amor y Cárcel de Amor*. Antwerp: Phillip Nucio, 1576. 12°.
30. *Questión de amor y Cárcel de Amor*. Salamanca: Pedro Lasso, 1580. 12°.
31. *Question de amor y Cárcel de Amor*. Antwerp: Martin Nucio, 1598. 12°.

Catalan

1. *Carcer d'amor*. Trans. Bernadí Vallmanyà. Barcelona: Rosenbach, 1493. 4°. Woodcut illustrations.

Italian

1. *Carcer d'amore del magnifico meser Lælio de Manfredi*. Venice: Zorzi di Rusconi Milanese, 1514. 8°.

2. *Carcer d'amore traducto dal magnifico miser Lelio de Manfredi.* Venice: G. de Rusconibus, 1515. 8°. Woodcut illustrations.
3. *Carcer d'amore traduto dal magnifico Miser Lelio de Manfredi.* Venice: Gregorio de Rusconi, 1518. 8°.
4. *Carcer d'amore traduto dal magnifico Miser Lelio de Manfredi.* Venice: Bernardino de Viano de Lexona, 1521. 8°. Woodcut illustrations.
5. *Carcer d'amore tradotto dal magnifico miser Lælio de Manfredi. Ferrarese, de Idioma Spanolo in lingua maternal. Novamente stampato.* Venice: Gregorio de Gregorii, 1525. 8°.
6. *Carcer d'amore tradotto dal magnifico miser Lælio de Manfredi, ferrarese, de idioma spagnolo in lingua materna, historiato & nouamente con diligentia corretto.* Venice: Francesco Bidoni and Mapheo Pasini, 1530. 8°. Woodcut illustrations.
7. *Carcer d'amore tradotto dal magnifico meser Lælio de Manfredi Ferrarese, de Idioma Spagnolo in lingua maternal, Hystoriato & novamemte con diligentia corretto.* Venice: Francesco Bindoni and Mapheo Pasini, 1533. 8°. Woodcut illustrations.
8. *Carcer d'amore tradotto dal magnifico meser Lælio de Manfredi.* Venice: Francesco Bindoni and Mapheo Pasini, 1537. 8°. Woodcut illustrations.
9. *Carcer d'amore tradotto dal magnifico meser Lælio de Manfredi.* Venice: Francesco Bindoni and Mapheo Pasini, 1546. 8°. Woodcut illustrations.
10. *Carcer d'amore historiato. Tradotto dal signor Lelio Manfredi ferrarese di spagnolo in lingua italiana. Di nuovo stampato & corretto & di molte figure adornato. Con licenza de' Superiori & Privilegio.* Venice: Ghirardo Imberti, 1621. 8°. Woodcut illustrations.

French

1. *La prison d'amour laquelle traicte de l'amour de Leriano et Laureolle.* Trans. François d'Assy. Paris: Antoine Cousteau pour Galliot du Pré, 1525. 8°. Woodcut illustrations.
2. *La prison d'amours laquelle traicte de l'amour de Leriano et Laureolle.* Paris: Antoine Cousteau vend Galliot du Pré, 1526. 8°.
3. *La prison d'amours.* Paris, 1527. 4°.
4. *La prison d'amour laquelle traicte de l'amour de Leriano et Laureolle.* Paris: Antoine Bonnemère, 1527. 8°.
5. *La prison d'amour laquelle traicte de l'amour de Leriano et Laureolle.* Lyon: Olivier Arnoullet, 1528. 4°.
6. *La prison d'amour laquelle traicte de l'amour de Leriano et Laureolle.* Paris: Pierre Laber and Pierre Sergent, 1533. 8°.

English

1. *Castell of Love.* Trans. John Bouchier, Lord Berners. London: Johan Turke, 1548?. 8°.
2. *Castell of Love.* Ed. Andrew Spigurnell. London: Robert Wyer, 1552?. 8°. Woodcut illustrations.
3. *Castell of Love.* Ed. Andrew Spigurnell. London: John King, 1555. 8°.

French-Spanish

1. *Cárcel de Amor. La Prison d'Amour. En deux langages, Espaignol et François, pour ceulx qui uouldront apprendre l'un par l'autre.* Paris: G. Corrozet, 1552. 12°.
2. *Cárcel de Amor. La Prison d'Amour. En deux langages, Espaignol et François, pour ceulx qui uouldront apprendre l'un par l'autre.* Antwerp: Jean Richart, 1555. 12°.
3. *Cárcel de Amor. La Prison d'Amour. En deux langages, Espaignol et Frãçois, pour ceulx qui uouldront apprendre l'un par l'autre.* Antwerp: Jean Richart, 1556. 12°.
4. *Cárcel de Amor. La Prison d'Amour. En deux langages, Espaignol et Frãçois, pour ceulx qui uouldront apprendre l'un par l'autre.* Antwerp: Jean Richart and J. Steele, 1556. 16°.
5. *Cárcel de Amor. La Prison d'Amour. En deux langages, Espaignol et Frãçois, pour ceulx qui uouldront apprendre l'un par l'autre.* Antwerp: Jean Richart, 1560. 12°.
6. *Cárcel de Amor. La Prison d'Amour. En deux langages, Espaignol et Frãçois, pour ceulx qui uouldront apprendre l'un par l'autre.* Antwerp: Jean Richart, J. Steelsius and Jehan Bellere, 1560. 12°.
7. *Cárcel de Amor. La Prison d'Amour. En deux langages, Espaignol et Frãçois, pour ceulx qui uouldront apprendre l'un par l'autre.* Paris: Robert le Mangnier, 1567. 16°.
8. *Cárcel de Amor. La Prison d'Amour. En deux langages, Espaignol et Frãçois, pour ceulx qui uouldront apprendre l'un par l'autre.* Cologne: Gilles Corrozet, 1569.
9. *Cárcel de Amor. La Prison d'Amour. En deux langages, Espaignol et Frãçois, pour ceulx qui uouldront apprendre l'un par l'autre.* Paris: Robert le Mangnier, 1581. 16°.
10. *Cárcel de Amor. La Prison d'Amour. En deux langages, Espaignol et Frãçois, pour ceulx qui uouldront apprendre l'un par l'autre.* Lyon: Benoist Rigaud, 1583. 16°. Woodcut illustrations.

11. *Cárcel de Amor. La Prison d'Amour. En deux langages, Espaignol et Frãçois, pour ceulx qui uouldront apprendre l'un par l'autre.* Paris: Gilles Corrozet, 1587. 12°. [No known copy]

12. *Cárcel de Amor. La Prison d'Amour. En deux langages, Espaignol et Frãçois, pour ceulx qui uouldront apprendre l'un par l'autre.* Paris: Nicolas Bonfons, 1594. 12°.

13. *Cárcel de Amor. La Prison d'Amour. En deux langages, Espaignol et Frãçois, pour ceulx qui uouldront apprendre l'un par l'autre.* Paris: Gilles Corrozet, 1595. 12°.

14. *Cárcel de Amor. La Prison d'Amour. En deux langages, Espaignol et Frãçois, pour ceulx qui uouldront apprendre l'un par l'autre.* Paris, 1598.

15. *Cárcel de Amor. La Prison d'Amour. En deux langages, Espaignol et Frãçois, pour ceulx qui uouldront apprendre l'un par l'autre.* Lyon: Pierre Rigaud, 1604. 16°.

16. *Cárcel de Amor. La Prison d'Amour. En deux langages, Espaignol et Frãçois, pour ceulx qui uouldront apprendre l'un par l'autre.* Paris: Jacques Bessin, 1616. 12°.

17. *Cárcel de Amor. La Prison d'Amour. En deux langages, Espaignol et Frãçois, pour ceulx qui uouldront apprendre l'un par l'autre.* Paris: Jean II Corrozet, 1616. 16°.

18. *Cárcel de Amor. La Prison d'Amour. En deux langages, Espaignol et Frãçois, pour ceulx qui uouldront apprendre l'un par l'autre.* Antwerp: Jean II Belere, 1650. 12°.

Appendix C: Known Manuscripts of *Cárcel de Amor* and *La Prison d'Amours*

Cárcel de Amor (Fragment)

– MS Trotti 516, Biblioteca Ambrosiana, Milan, Italy.

La Prison d'Amours

– *La Prison d'amours, ou les amours de Leriano et de Lauréole.* MS NAF. 7552. Bibliothèque nationale de France, Paris, France.
– *Prison d'amour.* MS fr. 24382. Bibliothèque nationale de France, Paris, France.
– *Carcer damour.* MS fr. 2150. Bibliotheque nationale de France, Paris, France.
– *L'Amour de Leriano et de Lauréole.* MS CB 149. Fondation Martin Bodmer, Cologny-Geneva, Switzerland.
– *L'Histoire de Lérian et s'amie Lauréole.* MS Rawl. D. 591. Bodleian Library, Oxford, United Kingdom.
– *La Prison d'Amour.* MS 949. Musée Condé, Chantilly, France
– *La Prison d'amour ou Les amours de Leriano et de Lauréole.* MS fr. 186. Bibliothèque de Genève, Geneva, Switzerland
– *L'amour de Leriano a Lauréolle.* MS 3352. Bibliothèque de l'Arsenal, Bibliothèque Nationale de France, Paris, France.
– *La Prison d'Amours.* MS 705. Hispanic Society of America, New York, NY.
– *L'amour de Leriano a Lauréolle.* MS 706. Hispanic Society of America, New York, NY.
– *Amours de Leriano et de Lauréolle.* MS 178. Bancroft Library, University of California, Berkeley, Berkeley, CA.

Notes

Introduction

1 Diego de San Pedro, *Desprecio de la Fortuna*, in *Obras completas III, Poesías*, 276. All translations into English, unless otherwise noted, are my own.

2 A German adaptation, *Gefängnüss der Lieb oder carcell de amor*, by Hans Ludwig von Kuffstein, appeared in the seventeenth century and lies beyond the scope of this book. First printed in 1624, it too was printed multiple times. See also Rohland de Langbehn, "Nicolás Núñez y la tradición alemana de *Cárcel de Amor*," 1–6.

3 In order to differentiate between the two French translations, I use the title from the 1526 printing of *La Prison d'Amours*, which uses the plural *amours*, to refer to the first translation by d'Assy, rather than the title from the 1525 printings, *La Prison d'Amour*. *La Prison d'Amour* will refer to the mid-sixteenth century translation, attributed to Gilles Corrozet.

4 On the movement of vernacular literature more generally in the sixteenth century, see Andrew Pettegree, "Translation and the Migration of Texts." Clive Griffin identifies "international books" as editions of "the classics, legal text-books, theology, and other academic works" intended for international, rather than local, audiences and markets. *The Crombergers of Seville*, 3.

5 *The Book of the Courtier*, first printed in Italian in 1528, began to circulate in translations in the 1530s. *Amadis*, first printed in Spanish in 1508, began to circulate in translations in the 1540s. Peter Burke traces the diffusion of Castiglione's book in *The Fortunes of the Courtier*. On Boccaccio, see Guyda Armstrong, *The English Boccaccio*. On *Amadis* of Gaul in its French contexts, see Paula Luteran, *The Theory of Translation in the Sixteenth Century*, and Marianne Rothstein, *Reading in the Renaissance*. On Juan de Flores, see Barbara Matulka,

The Novels of Juan de Flores and Their European Diffusion, and Francomano, "Introduction," in *Three Spanish Querelle Texts,* 1–51.

6 Anne Coldiron, *Printers without Borders,* 108.

7 "Documentary Appendix," trans. Rolena Adorno, in Irving *The Books of the Brave,* 336–403 (http://ark.cdlib.org/ark:/13030/ft1f59n78v/).

8 I borrow the metaphor of the wave from Franco Moretti, who uses it to describe the diffusion of the modern novel that, as he remarks, is "a wave that runs into the branches of local traditions, and is always significantly transformed by them." "Conjectures on World Literature," 68.

9 On translated works as major contributors to individual national-linguistic literary histories, see Itamar Even-Zohar, "The Position of Translated Literature within the Literary Polysystem (1978)," 240–7. As Susan Bassnett observes, "the development of vernacular languages in Europe was bound up with translation, just as several centuries later, in the Renaissance, the rise of vernacular languages to a status equal to that of classical languages was also accompanied by a ferment of translation activity ... Far from being a marginal enterprise, translation was at the core of the process of transformation of literary forms." "The Translation Turn in Cultural Studies," 437.

10 Burke quotes a concept coined by Robert Bartlett in *The Making of Europe: Conquest, Colonization, and Cultural Change, 950–1350* (Princeton, NJ: Princeton University Press, 1993), *The Fortunes of the Courtier,* 2.

11 *The Coming of the Book: The Impact of Printing 1450–1800,* 274.

12 Coldiron, *Printers without Borders,* 2.

13 *The Poetics of Piracy,* 8 and 5. There are some important exceptions to this occlusion, such as the recent work of Lucia Binotti on the Italian reception of Spanish literature in the sixteenth century, Belén Bistué on Early Modern collaborative and multilingual translations, and Joyce Boro on the diffusion and uses of translated Spanish romances, and particularly *The Prison of Love,* in England. Binotti, *Cultural Capital, Language and National Identity in Imperial Spain.* Bistué, *Collaborative Translation and Multi-Version Texts in Early Modern Europe.* Boro, ed., *The Castell of Love: A Critical Edition of Lord Berners's Romance;* "All for Love: Lord Berners and the Enduring, Evolving Romance," 87–102; and "Multilingualism, Romance, and Language Pedagogy; or, Why were so Many Sentimental Romances Printed as Polyglot Texts?" 18–38.

14 Linda Hutcheon, quoting Richard Dawkins' *The Selfish Gene,* in *A Theory of Adaptation* (New York: Routledge, 2006), 32.

15 The very polygeneity of the texts included among the Spanish sentimental fictions is "lo que permite la agrupación genérica" (what permits their

grouping as a genre), according to Guillermo Seres. "La llamada ficción sentimental y el humanismo vernáculo del siglo xv: un ejemplo," 12. Gustave Reynier, on the other hand, rather disparagingly remarked upon *Cárcel de Amor*'s blending of traditional motifs: "En somme aucun des éléments de la *Prison d'Amour* n'est nouveau. Elle ne marque aucun progrès dans les idées; on pourrait même dire qu'elle recule, puisque, se présentant au seuil de l'âge moderne, elle a tous les caractères d'une œuvre du Moyen Age" (In sum, none of the elements of *The Prison of Love* is new. The work augurs no intellectual progress; one could even say that it regresses, since, appearing at the threshold of the modern age, it has all the characteristics of a medieval work). *Le Roman sentimental avant "L'Astrée,"* 64.

16 Alan Deyermond, "Estudio Preliminar," xxix.
17 *Orígenes de la novela: Introducción; tratado histórico sobre la primitiva novela Española* (Madrid: CSIC, 1961), 3–4. Pascual de Gayangos had previously termed *Cárcel de Amor* a "novela caballeresca-sentimental" (chivalric-sentimental romance). *Libros de caballerias, con un discurso preliminar y un catálogo razonado,* 56.
18 "The Gendered Taxonomy of Spanish Romance," 205–29. For an overview of this scholarly debate, see the collected essays in Marina Brownlee et al., *"Forum*: 'The Genre of the "Sentimental Romance"': Responses to Regula Rohland de Langbehn, 'Una lanza por el género sentimental ... ¿ficción o novela?' (La corónica* 31, no. 1 [Fall, 2002]: 137–41)," *La corónica* 31, no. 2 (2003): 239–319. For views on expanding the limits of the genre, see Antonio Cortijo Ocaña, *La evolución genérica de la ficción sentimental de los siglos XV y XVI*; and Tobias Brandenberger, *La muerte de la ficción sentimental: transformaciones de un género iberorrománico.*
19 Hayden White, "Commentary: Good of Their Kind," *New Literary History* 34, no. 2 (2003), 367.
20 "Otra frontera de la ficción sentimental: la *Consolatio Philosophiae* de Boecio." See also José Francisco Ruiz Casanova, "Introduction," in Diego de San Pedro, *Cárcel de Amor. Arnalte y Lucenda. Sermón* (Madrid: Cátedra, 1995), 9–60; and Dorothy S. Severin, "The Sentimental Genre: Romance, Novel, Or Parody?", and *Religious Parody and the Spanish Sentimental Romance.*
21 *Escape from the Prison of Love: Caloric Identities and Writing Subjects in Fifteenth-Century Spain.*
22 *Gramática de la lengua castellana,* 13.
23 "Conflictive Subjectivity and the Politics of Truth and Justice in *Cárcel de Amor*," 151.

24 The epistolary backbone of the works grouped under the "sentimental" generic heading was first analysed by Charles Kany in *The Beginnings of the Epistolary Novel in France, Italy and Spain*. Marina Brownlee studies the intertextual relations between Ovid's *Heroides* and the Spanish *ficciones sentimentales*, citing epistolarity as a signal defining characteristic of the genre in *The Severed Word: Ovid's "Heroides" and the "Novela Sentimental."* See also Joseph Chorpenning, "Rhetoric and Feminism in the *Cárcel de Amor*," 1–8; Maureen Ihrie, "Discourses of Power in the *Cárcel de Amor*," 1–10; Sol Miguel-Prendes, "Las cartas de la *Cárcel de Amor*," 1–22; and Esther Torrego, "Convención retórica y ficción narrativa en la *Cárcel de Amor*."

25 *Continental Humanist Poetics*, 19.

26 Arthur Kinney, *Humanist Poetics*, 24.

27 Wayne Rebhorn, *The Emperor of Men's Minds*, 18–19.

28 Timothy Hampton, *Fictions of Embassy*, 189.

29 Anthony Pym, *Negotiating the Frontier*, 5.

30 *Bibliography and the Sociology of Texts*, 11.

31 Paul Duguid, "Material Matters: The Past and Futurology of the Book," in *The Future of the Book*, ed. Geoffrey Nunberg (Berkeley: University of California Press, 1996), 78.

32 "Laborers and Voyagers: From the Text to the Reader," 50.

33 I take the concept of "the period eye" from Michael Baxandall, who coined the term to describe the "mental equipment" with which a viewer of art "orders visual experience, which is variable, and much of this variable equipment is culturally relative." *Painting and Experience in Fifteenth Century Italy*, 40.

34 *The Textual Condition*, 9.

35 Joseph Grigely, *Textualterity: Art, Theory, and Textual Criticism* (Ann Arbor: University of Michigan Press, 1995), 1.

36 David Jay Bolter and Richard Grusin, *Remediation*, 272–3.

37 "Brought to Book: Bibliography, Book History, and the Study of Literature," 32.

38 Carlo Ginzburg and Carlo Ponti, "The Name and the Game," 3. Florike Egmond and Peter Mason, *The Mammoth and the Mouse*, 3.

39 *Libri, editori e pubblico nell'Europa moderna*, xvi.

40 Charles Joyner's phrase, "asking large questions in small places," from *Shared Traditions: Southern History and Folk Culture*, has been taken up as the standard of microhistory.

41 *Textual Agency*, 6.

42 "Reading Matter," 10.

43 *Old Books and New Histories*, 40. On further intersections and interactions
    between book history and critical theory, see Eggert, "Brought to Book,"
    and Peter McDonald, "Implicit Structures and Explicit Interactions," 105–21.
44 *Paratexts*, 1.
45 Chartier, *The Order of Books*, vi.
46 Howsam, *Old Books and New Histories*, 38.
47 Ultimately, these numbers must be provisional, as new copies may come
    to light, some bibliographies contain inaccuracies, and at times it can
    be difficult to distinguish distinct editions from reprints. Bibliographic
    indexing and cataloging have become much more inclusive in the
    past few decades, but documentation remains uneven, fragmented,
    and disconnected by the geographical locations of libraries and the
    national origins of printers and authors, despite the development of new
    bibliographic tools, such as the *Catálogo de de obras medievales impresas
    en castellano hasta 1600* (http://comedic.unizar.es/index/index/id/60),
    and the *Universal Short Title Catalogue*, "a collective database of books
    published in Europe from the invention of printing though the sixteenth
    century" (http://ustc.ac.uk). I have arrived at my tallies of extant
    editions in Spanish, Italian, French, and English through the inspection
    of individual copies of many of the editions held in libraries in England,
    France, Spain, Switzerland, and the United States, as well as the archives
    of the *Musée National du Moyen Âge* in Paris, where three of the tapestry
    panels are conserved, and also with the aid of multiple bibliographies and
    databases. To date, to my knowledge, Antonio Cortijo Ocaña and Milena
    Hurtado have published the most comprehensive list of the translations of
    The Prison of Love in "Las obras de Diego de San Pedro. Un éxito editorial,"
    the introduction to their online edition of Leonard Lawrance's English
    verse translation of *Arnalte y Lucenda* (http://www.ehumanista.ucsb.edu/
    publications/translations)).
48 "Introduction," in their *The Uses of Script and Print, 1300–1700*, 3.
49 *Print, Manuscript and the Search for Order, 1450–1830*, 11.
50 *De institutione feminae christianae, Liber Primus*, 44–7.
51 *De Institutione Feminae Christianae, Liber Primus*, xviii.
52 *A briefe & necessary instruction*.
53 "Diego de San Pedro … su *Cárcel de Amor,* que el mismo autor la reprueva"
    (Diego de San Pedro, his *Prison of Love,* which the author himself
    reproves). Antonio Zapata de Mendoza, *Novus index librorum prohibitorum
    et expurgatorum*, xvi and 304.
54 See Walter Ong, "Orality, Literacy, and Medieval Textualization," 2; and
    Janet Esrock, *The Reader's Eye*, 22.

1 *Cárcel de Amor*, an *Accessus ad Auctores*

1 "Early Modern Collaboration and Theories of Authorship," 609.
2 Harold Love, *Attributing Authorship*, 33.
3 *Attributing Authorship*, 50.
4 Alexandra Gillespie, *Print Culture and the Medieval Author*, 15.
5 Chartier, *The Order of Books*, 46.
6 Recent examples include Deyermond, "The Woodcuts of Diego de San Pedro's *Cárcel de Amor*"; Gil Sáenz, "Reading Diego de San Pedro in Tudor England"; Miguel-Prendes, "Remagining Diego de San Pedro's Readers at Work"; Sandra Munjic, "Diego de San Pedro's *Cárcel de Amor*: Allegorizing the Role of Poets in a Well-Ordered State"; and Afredo Sosa Velasco, "La producción del espacio en la *Cárcel de Amor* de Diego de San Pedro: Apuntes sobre el desarrollo de una economía capitalista."
7 "Beyond the Market: Books as Gifts in the Sixteenth-Century France," 87.
8 On "self-inscription" in Renaissance prologues, see Deborah N. Losse, "From *Auctor* to *Aucteur*."
9 *The Order of Books*, 44.
10 Davis, "Beyond the Market," 74.
11 Davis, "Beyond the Market," 78.
12 *Paratexts: Thresholds of Interpretation*, 2.
13 "Introduction," *Renaissance Paratexts*, 6–7. Smith and Wilson further associate the Renaissance paratext with Jacques Derrida's *parergon*, an imagining of the paratextual frame as existing neither inside nor outside the text proper, which "disconcerts any opposition but does not remain indeterminate and it *gives rise* to the work." Derrida, qtd. in Smith and Wilson, 7.
14 Davis is concerned with printed books, but her observation about books as bearers of relationships and public gifts is applicable to works transmitted in manuscript as well, even though printing facilitated broader circulation.
15 Ronald E. Surtz, "The Reciprocal Construction of Isabeline Book Patronage," 70.
16 *Cárcel de Amor* (Sevilla: Cuatro Compañeros Alemanes, 1492). *Cárcel de Amor con la continuación de Nicolás Núñez*, ed. Carmen Parrilla (Barcelona: Crítica, 1995). All quotes from the Spanish are cited in the text and are from this edition, which takes the 1492 *princeps* as its base for *Cárcel*, and the 1496 edition of *Cárcel de Amor*, the first to feature Núñez's emendation, for the text of the continuation. My renderings of *Cárcel de Amor* into English are indebted to Diego de San Pedro, *Prison of Love (1492) together with the Continuation by Nicolás Núñez (1496)*, translated by Keith Whinnom (Edinburgh: Edinburgh UP, 1979). Whinnom rendered *tratado*

as "romance," but nuanced his view in a later article: "The only essential qualifications for a *tratado* are that it should be written down, that it should ... be in prose, and, possibly, that it should be of a certain length"; "Spanish possessed no unequivocal term for prose fiction." "*Autor* and *tratado* in the Fifteenth Century: Semantic Latinism or Etymological Trap?" *Bulletin of Hispanic Studies* 59 (1982): 216.

17 Love, *Attributing Authorship*, 43 and 45.

18 *The Order of Books*, 45.

19 "The only chronological clue available, the textual reference to the 'war of last year' (most likely the Battle of Lucena, 1483), would suggest composition of *Cárcel* between 1483 and the terminus date given, 1492, the year of the first known printed edition." Ivy Corfis, "Introduction," 2. Since both *Arnalte* and the *Sermón* are mentioned in the prologue, it is reasonable to assume they were composed before *Cárcel*. For further notes on San Pedro's biography, see Whinnom, "Introducción," in Diego de San Pedro, *Obras completas* I, 9–25; and Parrilla, "Prólogo," in Diego de San Pedro, *Cárcel de Amor con la continuación de Nicolás Núñez*, ed. Carmen Parrilla (Barcelona: Crítica, 1995), xxxvii–xliv. On his possible *converso* identity, see also Francisco Márquez Villanueva, "*Cárcel de Amor*, novela política"; and Manuel da Costa Fontes, "*Cárcel de Amor* and the Situation of Conversos."

20 "What Is an Author?"

21 "Rhetoric and Feminism," 4. I follow Chorpenning's reading of the relationship between the *Sermón* and *Cárcel*.

22 On the biographies of Diego de Hernández and Marina Manuel, see Parrilla, "Notas complementarias," in Diego de San Pedo, *Cárcel de Amor*, 123.

23 *Attributing Authorship*, 40.

24 Weissberger, "The Politics of *Cárcel de Amor*," 308.

25 "La impronta lírica de la narrativa de ficción sentimental del siglo XV." Sandra Munjic expands upon this reading to argue that San Pedro allegorizes "the mutually reinforcing relationships between lovers and poets in the mimetic relationship between art and reality. Lovers need authors to imitate and recreate through writing their amorous pains ... Authors, in turn, need lovers whose desires to represent." "Diego de San Pedro's *Cárcel de Amor*: Allegorizing the Role of Poets in a Well-Ordered State," 95.

26 "Conflictive Subjectivity and the Politics of Truth and Justice in *Cárcel de Amor*," 167.

27 See, for example, Rogelio Miñana, "Auctor omnisciente, auctor testigo: el marco narrativo en *Cárcel de Amor*," 138.

28 Peter Dunn, "Narrator as Character in the *Cárcel de Amor*," 198. On the identification of the *Auctor* with San Pedro and Leriano, see also Robert

Folger, "'Besando las manos de vuestra merced,'"; and Bruce Wardropper, "Allegory and the Role of *El Autor* in the *Cárcel de Amor*."

29 Dunn, 196. For James Mandrell, the *Auctor* "invites us to consider the activity of the writer San Pedro," who "has discovered how to do an allegory of authorship." "Author and Authority in *Cárcel de Amor*: The Role of *El Auctor*," 198.

30 Esther Torrego, "Convención retórica y ficción narrativa en la *Cárcel de Amor*," 331.

31 Chartier, *The Order of Books*, 52.

32 Margaret Schlauch coins the term "literary executor" to refer to the narrators' roles in both *Arnalte y Lucenda* and *Cárcel*. *Antecedents of the English Novel*, 130.

33 "Una pregunta de mosén Fernando a Ýñigo de Mendoça de la diferençia que ay entre amor e amistad, e su repuesta," in Fernando de la Torre, *Libro de las veynte cartas e quistiones y otros versos y prosas*, 111. The expression "dulce comercio" to describe the exchange of letters was also used by Alonso de Cartagena and may have been commonplace.

34 The humanistic epistolary ideal was inspired, in large part, by Petrarch's discovery and imitations of Cicero's letters. Both Cicero's and Petrarch's letters circulated widely in print by the end of the fifteenth century.

35 Juan Rodríguez del Padrón's *Bursario*, a translation and creative amplification of Ovid's *Heroides*, for example, provided a model of letters on love to vernacular writers.

36 "Nuevos lectores y nuevos géneros: apuntes y observaciones sobre la epistolografía en el primer renacimiento español," 98. On humanist education and the *ars dictaminis*, see Thomas Beebee, *Epistolary Fiction in Europe, 1500–1850*, 21–31; Antonio Cortijo Ocaña, "De amicitia, amore et rationis discretione. Breves notas a propósito de Boncompagno da Signa y el *Siervo libre de Amor*" and "Hacia la ficción sentimental: *la Rota Veneris* de Boncompagno da Signa"; and Pedro Martín Baños, *El arte epistolar en el renacimiento europeo*, esp. chapter 6: "La tradición teórica latina I. Del *ars dictaminis* a Erasmo," 221–303.

37 "What Every Noblewoman Needs to Know: Cultural Literacy in Late Medieval Spain," 1118.

38 "Animi mei effigiem atque ingenii simulacrum" (An image of my soul and a figure of my mind); "alloquor te dum scribo, audio te dum epistolas tuas lego; utrobique te udio, tecum sum" (I speak with you as I write, I hear you when I read your letters; in both cases, I hear you and am with you). Cited in Martín Baños, *El arte epistolar en el renacimiento europeo*, 268–9.

39 *Claros varones: con las letras* (Seville: Stanislas Polono, 24 April 1500).

40 Joy Richie and Kate Ronald, "Introduction," xvi.
41 On Núñez's interpretation of *Cárcel*, see Carmen Parrilla,
    "'Acrescentar lo que de suyo está crescido': el cumplimiento de
    Nicolás Núñez"; and Sun-Me Yoon, "La continuación de Nicolás
    Núñez a *Cárcel de Amor*."
42 *Cancionero musical de Palacio*, 256.
43 "Un penacho de penas. De algunas invenciones y letras de caballeros," in
    Texto y contextos. Estudios sobre la poesía Española del siglo XV, 192.

2 Translating Authorship

1 *The Translator's Invisibility*, 2.
2 Some early modern bibliographies, such as François de La Croix du Maine's
   Premier volume de la bibliothèque (1584), do accord distinction to translators
   and recognize the importance of translated works.
3 *The Scandals of Translation: Towards an Ethics of Difference*, 4.
4 "Alternatives to Borders in Translation Theory." On interculturality and
   intercultural agents, see Pym, *Negotiating the Frontier*.
5 *Lo càrcer d'amor (Traduït d'lengua castellana: en estil de valenciana prosa por*
   B. vallmanya), British Library, shelfmark G.10225. Textual references are
   cited from *"Càrcer d'amor," "Carcer d'amore": Due traduzioni della "novela" di*
   Diego de San Pedro, ed. Vincenzo Minervini and Maria Luisa Indini (Fasano:
   Schena, 1986). Minervini notes the disagreement among scholars with
   regard to whether the adjective "valenciana" in the title's *estil de valenciana*
   prosa refers to a language or a literary school or style and concludes,
   following J. Fuster, that there is not sufficient evidence in the literature
   of the time to affirm either definitively. Curt Wittlin, on the other hand,
   defines "estil valenciana prosa" as humanistic prose written in Catalan, but
   with multiple Latinisms and Castilianisms that were supposed to elevate
   the vernacular. *De la traducció literal a la creació literària: Estudis filològics*
   i literaris sobre textos antics catalans i valencians, 161. Minervini further
   characterizes Vallmanya's language in the translation as characteristic of
   Valencia at the end of the fifteenth century. That is to say, Vallmanya writes
   in Catalan, but with numerous Valencianisms, as well as a good number
   of Castilian elements. "Introduzione," 22–5. Following general academic
   convention with regard to *Lo càrcer d'amor*, I will refer to it as the Catalan
   translation.
6 On the Conde de Oliva and his literary circle, see Oscar Perea Rodríguez,
   "Valencia en el *Cancionero general* de Hernando del Castillo: los poetas y los
   poemas," 231–5.

7   A *troba*, "Por ab glosar, / ardiment e temor," in *Les obres o trobes davall scrites, les quals tracten de lahors de la sacratíssima verge Maria* (Valencia, 1474) is attributed to Vallmanya. He translated Gonzalo García de Sancta María's version of the *Cordiale quatuor Novissimorum* into Catalan as the *Cordial de l'ànima*, printed in Valencia in 1495, and a work by Antoninus of Florence, the *Revelació del benaventurat apòstol sanct Pau*, also printed in Valencia in 1495.

8   Minervini, 20–1.

9   The woodcut appears to be recycled from an edition of works by Pietro Aretino, as the words "Unico Are" have been inked out in a panel below the image of the writer.

10   *The Order of Books*, 52.

11   Binotti, *Cultural Capital, Language and National Identity in Imperial Spain*, 21–4.

12   "This Rude Laboure," 10. Berners used both Spanish and French versions of *The Prison of Love* in the preparation of his *The Castell of Love*.

13   "Manfredi, Astorgio" and "Manfredi, Lelio," *Dizionario biografico degli Italiani*, 707–10.

14   *Dizionario biografico degli Italiani*, 710.

15   For *Aurelio et Isabella*, see Francomano, "Introduction," in *Three Spanish Querelle Texts*, 43–7.

16   *Cultural Capital, Language, and Identity in Imperial Spain*, 19–21.

17   Kolsky, *Mario Equicola, the Real Courtier*, 67–77. On Equicola's *De mulieribus*, see also Kolsky, "Mario Equicola's *De mulieribus* revisited," *Spunti e ricerche* 22, no. 1 (2007): 50–82.

18   Kolsky, "Women through Men's Eyes: The Third Book of *Il Cortegiano*,", 49.

19   *Poema in terza rima*. Biblioteca Trivulziana, Milan, cod. 908 L. 43. Ffs. 40v–41r. cited in Kolsky, *The Real Courtier*, 13n.

20   Kolsky, "Lelio Manfredi traduttore cortigiano: Intorno al *Carcer d'Amore* e al *Tirante il Bianco*," 46.

21   "Lelio Manfredi traduttore cortigiano," 45

22   Kolsky, "Lelio Manfredi traduttore cortigiano," 46 and 48.

23   On the *Palazzo*, see Kolsky, "Lelio Manfredi traduttore cortigiano," 49.

24   Manfredi's other known original works are two humanist comedies, the *Paraclitus* and the *Filadelfia*. Carmelo Zilli, "Notizia di Lelio Manfredi, letterato di corte."

25   *Carcer d'amore* (Venice: Rusconi, 1514), Van Pelt Library, University of Pennsylvania, shelfmark SC Sa538 Ei513m 1514.

26   Isabella d'Este read *Tirant* in 1500, when it was loaned to her, and in 1510 she expressed a desire for her own copy; she must have found one as it is

in her inventory of books. She also asked Nicolo da Correggio to translate *Cárcel* soon after first reading it. Francesco Fiumara, "'Tradotti per hora,'" 35–6.

27 Zilli, "Notizia di Lelio Manfredi, letterato di corte," 40.

28 Stephen Kolsky demonstrates the precarious position of a "second string" intellectual in the humanist and literary circles that gathered round great princes of the early sixteenth century and "traces Manfredi's *iter* as he slides deeper into poverty and discovers that the patronage system only dispenses 'welfare' if the prince is truly entertained or the aspirant has provided a useful service." "Lelio Manfredi traduttore cortigiano," 45.

29 Duché-Gavet XV. The 1531 edition of the *Dialogue très elegant intitulé le Peregrin* can be viewed in its entirety at http://catalogue.bnf.fr/ark:/12148/cb39338048p. Accessed 20 August 2013.

30 *Catalogue des actes de François Ier. Tome V*, 583.

31 *La Prison d'Amours laquelle traicte de l'amour de Lerian et Laureolle faicte en espagnol, puis translate en tusquan et nagueres en langage francois. Ensemble plusiers choses singulieres a la louenge des dames*, (Paris: Galliot du Pré, 1525), n.p.

32 Jacquette de Lansac was the mother of Louis de Lansac, also known as Louis de Saint Gelais. "Lansac (Louis de)," *Dictionnaire de Biographie Française*.

33 Myra D. Orth, "'The Prison of Love': A Medieval Romance in the French Renaissance and Its Illustration (B.N. MS fr. 2150)," 212.

34 BnF MS NAF 7552 is currently in a delicate a state of conservation and its illuminations cannot be reproduced. I was able to inspect it personally in February 2008.

35 Boro, *The Castell of Love*, 3–5.

36 *The baronage of England, or, An historical account of the lives and most memorable actions of our English nobility in the Saxons time to the Norman conquest, and from thence, of those who had their rise before the end of King Henry the Third's reign deduced from publick records, antient historians, and other authorities* (London: Newcomb, 1675), 132–3. EEBO. http://eebo.chadwyck.com. Accessed 1 July 2012.

37 Boro, *The Castell of Love*, 9–10, 13.

38 *The Golden Tapestry*, 42.

39 Boro, *The Castell of Love*, 13.

40 On the Carews' biographies, see R.J. Knecht's introduction to Thomas Wall's *The Voyage of Sir Nicholas Carewe to the Emperor Charles V in the Year 1529*, 1–21.

41 Boro, *The Castell of Love*, 13.

42 G.J. Meyer "The Newest Profession," 350–2.
43 Pym, *Negotiating the Frontier*, 5.
44 *Il Messaggiero*, 72–3.
45 Tasso, 70.
46 Tasso, *Il Messaggiero*, 61, trans. Hampton, *Fictions of Embassy*, 5.
47 Hampton, *Fictions of Embassy*, 8.
48 *Arnalte y Lucenda*, in *Obras Completas I*, 87 and 89.
49 *Textual Agency: Writing Culture and Social Networks in Fifteenth-Century Spain.*
50 "The Great Game of Rhetoric," 493–4.
51 "All for Love: Lord Berners and the Enduring, Evolving, Romance," 97.

3 "Easie Languages": The Free and Faithful Translation
of *The Prison of Love*

1 As Şehnaz Tahir-Gürçağlar observes in a study of twentieth-century
   Turkish translations, paratexts "can be instrumental in bringing to light the
   divergent concepts and definitions of translation in a specific period within
   a culture." Moreover, "it can be safely assumed that our first impressions
   of what distinguishes a translation from a non-translation are shaped not
   by the translation (or non-translation) itself, but by the way the texts are
   packaged and presented." "What Texts Don't Tell: The Uses of Paratexts in
   Translation Research," 44–5.
2 *Printers without Borders*, 9.
3 "On The Different Methods of Translating," trans. Susan Bernofsky, in
   The Translation Studies Reader, ed. Lawrence Venuti, 2nd edition (New
   York: Routledge, 2004), 43–63. Venuti discusses "foreignizing" and
   "domesticating" translations in *The Translator's Inivisibility*, esp. 1–42.
4 "Il est tout certain qu'il fut premier mis en noftre langue Françoyse,
   estant Amadis Gaulois e non Espagnol" (Undoubtedly this romance was
   first written in our French language, given that Amadis was Gallic and
   not Spanish). *Le Premiere Livre de Amadis de Gaule, Mis en Francoys par le
   Seigneur des Essarts, Nicolas de Herberay*. https://archive.org/details/
   premierlivredama00herb. Accessed 20 October 2014.
5 Dolet, *La manière de bien traduire d'une langue en aultre*, 14. "How to Translate
   Well From One Language to Another," 96.
6 Vives, "El arte retórica," 92.
7 "Toutes sciences se peuvent fidelement et copieusement traicter en icelle,
   comme on peut voir en si grand nombre de livres Grecz et Latins, voyre
   bien Italiens, Espagnolz, et autres traduictz en Françoys." For du Bellay,
   imitation of the ancients, above and beyond translation, was the optimal

way to enrich and cultivate the French vernacular. It is interesting to note that du Bellay considers translations from Italian and Spanish as potential contributors to the elevation of French. *La deffence et Illustration de la Langue Françoyse/The Defense and Enrichment of the French Language*, 130–1.

8 For detailed descriptions of the linguistic aspects of each translator's practice and catalogues of variants, see the respective critical editions of *Carcer d'amor, Carcer d'amore, Cárcel de Amor/La Prison d'Amour*, and *The Castell of Love*. To date, there is no critical edition of d'Assy's *La Prison d'Amours*. At the time of this writing, Irene Finotti is preparing a critical edition of d'Assy's translation. "Traduire d'une langue à l'autre, traduire de prose en rime: De la *Cárcel de Amor* à la *Prison d'amour*," *Oeuvres & Critiques* 36, no. 1 (2011): 37–49.

9 *Ars Poetica*, in *Satires. Epistles. The Art of Poetry*, 133–4.

10 Early Modern discussions of translation tend to view Horace's lines as a condemnation of word-for-word translating, which accorded neatly with the Patristic elevation of the spirit over the letter, although, as Glyn P. Norton points out, in context Horace's lines do not condemn word-for-word translation outright, but only for the translation of Homeric poetry. *The Ideology and Language of Translation in Renaissance France and Their Humanist Antecedents*, 58–67.

11 "One might say that the dominance of the axis of vertical translation is basic to the medieval conception of culture and cultural exchange in western Europe. The transition from a medieval to a postmedieval model of culture can be understood as a shift from vertical to horizontal dominance." "Translatio Studii and Renaissance: From Vertical to Horizontal Translation," 56.

12 Miguel de Cervantes, *El ingenioso hidalgo Don Quijote de la Mancha II*, 519. Cervantes was by no means the first author the use this metaphor for translation.

13 *The History of Don Quixote of the Mancha*, 4:196.

14 Belén Bistué reads this moment in *Don Quijote* as the culmination of many parodic commentaries on translation theory and practice made by Cervantes in the work. *Collaborative Translation and Multi-Version Texts in Early Modern Europe*, 147–58.

15 Cervantes was presumably thinking about cognate romance languages and not English. One wonders what Shelton thought about rendering Spanish into English as he translated this passage.

16 *Los quatro libros del cortesano compuestos en italiano por el conde Balthasar Castellon; y agora nueuamente traduzidos en lengua castellana por Boscán.* Barcelona: Montpezat, 1534. Proyecto Boscán. http://www.ub.edu/boscan. Accessed 14 October 2014.

17 "Ex quo scelus quodammodo inexpiabile censendum est hominem non plane doctum et elegantem ad transferendum accedere." *De interpretatione recta, de Leonardo Bruni: un episodio en la historia de la traducción y la hermenéutica,* 66; "On the Correct Way to Translate," trans. James Hankins, in *Western Translation Theory,* 60.

18 *Los quatro libros del cortesano.*

19 *Los quatro libros del cortesano.*

20 Hermans, "Renaissance Translation between Literalism and Imitation," 105. See also Belén Bistué, *Collaborative Translation and Multi-Version Texts in Early Modern Europe,* chapter 1, "Res dificilis," 19–47.

21 Literary translation in the vernacular, as Theo Hermans has noted, "had no place as a recognized literary category." "Renaissance Translation between Literalism and Imitation," 95–6.

22 On Italian terms for translating, see Gianfranco Folena, "'Volgarizzare' e 'tradurre': idea e terminologia della traduzione dal Medio Evo italiano e romanzo all'umanesimo europeo." The *Vocabolario etimologico della lingua italiana* explains that a *traduzione* involves the rendering "nel modo più conveniente all'indole della lingua nella quale si traduce" (in the manner most suiting the nature of the target language), in distinction to a *versione,* which is "più letterale e segue passo per passo la costruzione analitica, tale quella della Sacra Scrittura" (more literal and follows the exact structure step by step, as in the Sacred Scriptures), or a *volgarizzamento,* which "si occupa di volgere le lingue morte rendendo popolari e comuni i soggetti letterari di altre età" (is devoted to turn dead languages into the vernacular, making learned subjects from the past accessible to the unlearned). Ottorino Pianigiani, *Vocabolario etimologico della lingua italiana,* 1451.

23 *Vocabolario, grammatica, et orthographia de la lingua uolgare con ispositioni di molti luoghi di Dante, del Petrarca, et del Boccaccio.* 91. Folger Shakespeare Library Shelfmark 178–427q.

24 *Reddere, vertere, transfere, transponere,* and *translatio* are all commonly used Latin terms used to refer to verbal and literary translations. Glyn P. Norton, *The Ideology and Language of Translation in Renaissance France and Their Humanist Antecedents,* 57. See also Joaquín Rubio Tovar, *El vocabulario de la traducción en la Edad Media.*

25 *Carcer d'amore,* in *Càrcer d'amor/Carcer d'amore,* 171. This anecdote, from Plutarch's *Artaxerxes,* also appears in Johan Andreas de Garisendi's dedication of *Antifilo e Filero* to Lucrecia d'Este. Ludovico Frati, "Andrea Garisendi e il suo contrasto d'amore," 79.

26 "Western Metaphorical Discourses Implicit in Translation Studies," 109.

27 *Historia de Isabella et Aurelio in lingua castigliana composta, et da M. Lelio Aletiphilo in parlare italico tradutta.* Folger Shakespeare Library Shelfmark PQ6390.F67 1534 Cage. Manfredi's translation of *Grisel y Mirabella* would become the source text for the French and English translations. ·

28 *Historia de Isabella et Aurelio.*

29 *Historia de Isabella et Aurelio.*

30 *Tirante il Bianco valorosissimo caualiere, nelquale contiensi del principio della caualleria del stato and vfficio suo.*

31 "Principles of Correspondence," 162–3.

32 Castiglione, *Los quatro libros del cortesano compuestos en italiano por el conde Balthasar Castellon.* Proyecto Boscán.

33 "Modelli e registri nelle traduzioni romanze della *Cárcel de Amor*," 87–8. See also Indini, "Introduzione," 139.

34 *Carcer d'amore,* 172 and 189.

35 Diego de San Pedro, *Cárcel de Amor, con la continuación de Nicolás Núñez,* ed. Carmen Parrilla (Barcelona: Crítica, 1995), 4 and 19. These interventions are cataloged by Indini, "Introduzione," in *Càrcer d'amor; Carcer d'amore,* 139–44.

36 *La Prison d'Amours laquelle traicte de l'amour de Lerian et Laureolle faicte en espagnol, puis translate en tusquan et nagueres en langage francois. Ensemble plusiers choses singulieres a la louenge des dames* (Paris: Galliot du Pré, 1525), n.p.

37 *Dialogue treselegant intitule le Peregrin traictant de l'honnesté et pudicq amour concilie par pure et sincere vertu traduict de vulgaire Italien en langue Françoise par maistre Françoys d'Assy,* f. 6v. http://gallica.bnf.fr. Accessed 13 October 2014.

38 In the first edition all of the letters are versified, but the second edition of 1526, seven letters are in verse and three in prose. Irene Finotti, "Traduire d'une langue à l'autre, traduire de prose en rime: De la *Cárcel de Amor* à la *Prison d'amour*," 42.

39 Finotti, "Traduire d'une langue à l'autre, traduire de prose en rime," 41.

40 *The Castell of Love, A Critical Edition of Lord Berners' Romance,* ed. Joyce Boro (Tempe, ACMRS, 2007). This edition will be cited in the text.

41 *Here begynneth the first volum of sir Iohan Froyssart of the cronycles of Englande, Fraunce, Spayne, Portyngale, Scotlande, Bretayne, Flau[n]ders: and other places adioynynge. Tra[n]slated out of frenche into our maternall englysshe tonge, by Iohan Bourchier knight lorde Berners: at the co[m]maundement of oure moost highe redouted souerayne lorde kyng Henry the. viii. kyng of Englande and of Fraunce, [and] highe defender of the christen faythe,* (London: Pynson, 1523). EEBO. https://eebo.chadwyck.com. Accessed 13 October 2014.

42 *The golden boke of Marcus Aurelius Emperour and eloquent oratour* (London: 1537). EEBO. https://eebo.chadwyck.com. Accessed 13 October 2014.

43 The *Chronicles* were dedicated to Henry VIII.
44 *Arthur of Brytayn The hystory of the moost noble and valyaunt knyght Arthur of lytell brytayne.*
45 Boro, "Introduction," in San Pedro, *The Castell of Love: A Critical Edition of Lord Berners's Romance*, 26–46.
46 "Introduction," in *Prison of Love 1492 together with the Continuation by Nicolás Núñez* (Edinburgh: Edinburgh UP, 1979), xxxii.
47 Helena Mennie Shire, "The Function of Translated Literature within a National Literature: The Example of Renaissance England and Scotland," 178.
48 "Images of Translation," 96.

4 Textual Material: Allegory and Material Epistolarity in *The Prison of Love*

1 For the sake of brevity, textual references in this chapter will be primarily to the Spanish *Cárcel de Amor*, which is the version of *The Prison of Love* studied by the critics cited.
2 Optical intromission is the theory that the eyes see by receiving rays exuded from the object perceived. As Suzanne Conklin Akbari observes in her study of how optical theories function in medieval literature, theories of vision describe the meeting of subjects and objects, and the theory of intromission "stresses the primacy of the object" seen, and consequently, the passivity of the subject who perceives. *Seeing through the Veil: Optical Theory and Medieval Allegory*, 23–4.
3 On the tradition of the *hombre salvaje*, see Alan D. Deyermond, "El hombre salvaje en la novela sentimental."
4 Claire Barbetti, *Ekphrastic Medieval Visions: A New Discussion in Interarts Theory*, 2.
5 *The Art of Courtly Love*, 28.
6 *Imagetext* is a concept that replaces the binary between *word* and *image* and the compulsion to contrast words and images. As W.T.J. Mitchell, explains, drawing upon the work of Michel Foucault and Giles Deleuze, "the interaction of pictures and texts is constitutive of representation as such: all media are mixed media, and all representations are heterogeneous; there are no 'purely' visual or verbal arts." *Picture Theory: Essays on Verbal and Visual Representation*, 5, 83, 152.
7 For example, the effect is described by Quintilian in book four of the *Institutio Oratoria*: "From such impressions arises that ἐνάργεια [enargeia] which Cicero calls illumination and actuality which makes us seem not so much to narrate as to exhibit the actual scene, while our emotions will be no less actively stirred than if we were present at the actual occurrence." 437.

For a discussion of the relations between ekphrasis and enargeia, see Ruth Webb, *Ekphrasis, Imagination and Persuasion in Ancient Rhetorical Theory and Practice.*

8 "Reimagining Diego de San Pedro's Readers at Work," 18.

9 "The Visuality of Reading in Pre-Modern Textual Cultures," 223.

10 "Picture, Image, and Subjectivity," 618. Janet Esrock explains how, counterintuitively, twentieth-century literary criticism, particularly structuralism and the linguistic turn, generally rejected the idea that readers visualize as they read. *The Reader's Eye: Visual Imaging as Reader Response.* Yet, visual imaging and visual imagining in tandem with reading or listening are responses shared by readers across time.

11 As Robert Folger comments, "Although most studies of *Cárcel* address the underlying conception of love when discussing the 'allegorical' portions of the text, they tend to neglect San Pedro's initial description of the phenomenology of love in their analysis of other facets of the text." Folger relates the allegory to medieval medical theories of *amor heroes, philcaptio,* and faculty psychology. *Images in Mind: Lovesickness, Spanish Sentimental Fiction and "Don Quijote,"* 196.

12 See also Wardropper, "Allegory and the Role of *El Autor* in the *Cárcel de Amor*"; Damiani, "The Didactic Intention of the *Cárcel de Amor*"; and Whinnom, "Introduction," in *Obras completas II: Cárcel de Amor.*

13 Folger, *Images in Mind,* 206.

14 "Reimagining Diego de San Pedro's Readers at Work: *Cárcel de Amor.*"

15 "Otra frontera de la ficción sentimental: la *Consolatio Philosophiae* de Boecio," 529.

16 *At the Court of the Borgia,* 167.

17 *Epistolary Fiction in Europe, 1500–1850,* 50.

18 *Corre manuscrito: Una historia cultural del Siglo de Oro* (Madrid: Marcial Pons, 2001), 16–17.

19 Stephen Gilman asserts that it was the first Spanish book of fiction composed for the press. *The Spain of Fernando de Rojas,* 327–8n125. Alan Deyermond similarly asserts "*Cárcel de Amor* was almost certinaly written for immediate printing." "The Woodcuts of Diego de San Pedro's *Cárcel de Amor,* 1492–1496," 513.

20 According to Carmen Parrilla, for example, "Leriano oculta una prueba: el intercambio de cartas." *Cárcel de Amor,* 33n.

21 *Inscription and Erasure: Literature and Written Culture from the Eleventh to the Eighteenth Century,* ix.

22 E. Michael Gerli, "Leriano's Libation: Notes on the Cancionero Lyric, *Ars Moriendi,* and the Probable Debt to Boccaccio," 417. Domingo Ynduráin

surveys numerous literary antecedents in "Las cartas de Laureola (beber cenizas)." Keith Whinnom surveys the range of critical takes on Leriano's death scene in "Cardona, the Crucifixion and Leriano's Last Drink." Some readers assert that Leriano's consumption of the letters is "an act of symbolic cannibalism" in which, via metonymy, the letters are Laureola's body. Joseph Chorpenning further suggests an analogue in the command Ezekiel receives to "eat this book" (Ezekiel 3:1). "Loss of Innocence, Descent into Hell, and Cannibalism: Romance Archetypes and Narrative Unity in 'Cárcel de Amor.'" See also Harriet Goldberg, "Cannibalism in Iberian Narrative: The Dark Side of Gastronomy." Gerli, drawing upon the aforementioned analyses, and calling attention to the imbrication of "language, desire, and death" in *Cárcel* as a whole and its last scene in particular, reads Leriano's libation through a Lacanian psychoanalytic prism. "Leriano and Lacan: The Mythological and Psychoanalytical Underpinnings of Leriano's Last Drink," *La corónica* 29, no. 1 (2000): 113–28, 116.

23 As Miguel-Prendes argues, "Las ficciones sentimentales transforman la frustración amorosa en farsa ... especialmente claro en el caso de Leriano que acaba comiéndose literalmente las cartas de su amada Laureola" (Sentimental fictions transform amorous frustration into farse ... this is especially clear in the case of Leriano, who dies literally eating the letters of his beloved, Laureola). "Otra frontera de la ficción sentimental," 530.

24 *The Severed Word*, 172.

25 Here we see one point where Berners departs from word-for-word translating in order to gloss the Spanish text and explain what he believed was meant by "más memoria de su alma y de su cuerpo avía de tener" (He should have had more care for his soul than for his body).

26 *Corre manuscrito*, 86n. Bouza cites chapter XV of Martín de Castañega's treatise, "Qúales empéricas de los médicos no son supersticiosas ni hechizos" (Which medical treatments are not superticious or witchcraft). 86n.

27 *Corre manuscrito*, 22.

28 Ibid., 108.

29 Castañega, Martín de, *Tratado muy sotil y bien fundado delas supersticiones y hechizerias*, 78–9. For other magical manuscripts, see Bouza, "Tocar las letras, cédulas, nóminas, cartas de toque, resguardo y daño en el siglo de oro," 85–108.

30 In addition to Brownlee, see also Dulce M. García, *Espada, escudo y espejo: el lenguaje como tema en las novelas de Diego de San Pedro*; and Sol Miguel-Prendes, "Las cartas de la *Cárcel de Amor*."

31 *Espada, escudo y espejo*, 22.

32 Beebee mentions the importance of the material presence of Laureola's letters to Leriano in the final scene, but declares that it is the "only" instance in the romance that alludes to the materiality of the letters. Ibid., 53.

33 *Inscription and Erasure*, ix and xi.

34 Barbara F. Weissberger, "Resisting Readers and Writers in the Sentimental Romances and the Problem of Female Literacy."

35 *Floresta española*, 177. The *Floresta*, itself a compilation of pithy maxims and anecdotes compiled from the process of rhetorical readering, was quite popular and, like *Cárcel*, was translated into Italian, French, and English in the sixteenth century.

36 Chartier describes a *librillo de memoria* as a bound book of chemically treated pages that could be written upon with a stylus and then erased, "the primary medium for recoding poems and letters for later copying." *Inscription and Erasure*, x and 22.

37 Weissberger reads this anecdote in the *Floresta* as one that not only attests to female readership of the romance, but which also signals the existence of a historical "resisting" female readership and anxiety about women's reading habits on the part of male moralists. "Resiting Readers and Writers," 176–7.

38 "The Body of the Book: The Media Transition from Manuscript to Print," 33 and 44. See also Gumbrecht, "The Body vs. The Printing Press: Media in the Early Modern Period, Mentalities in the Reign of Castile, and Another History of Literary Forms," *Poetics* 14, no. 3–4 (1985): 209–27.

39 *Escape from the Prison of Love: Caloric Identities and Writing Subjects in Fifteenth-Century Spain*, 124–6.

40 *Textual Agency: Writing Culture and Social Networks in Fifteenth-Century Spain.*

5 Prisons in Print: The Material Books

1 Paul F. Grendler "Form and Function in Italian Renaissance Popular Books," 451.

2 "Bookmen" is something of a catch-all term to refer to those agents involved with the various and overlapping commercial aspects of the book trade. See Darnton, "What Is the History of Books?" and "'What Is the History of Books?' Revisited"; and Manuel José Pedraza Gracia, "La función del editor en el libro del siglo XVI."

3 This definition of textual agency builds upon François Cooren, "Textual Agency: How Texts Do Things in Organizational Settings." Ana Gómez Bravo, defining textual agency as "the agency of the paper ... set in motion" by individuals writing within social and professional networks but that

circulated and signified beyond authorial control, demonstrates how textual agency and authorial agency compete in fifteenth-century handwritten documents and manuscripts. *Textual Agency: Writing Culture and Social Networks in Fifteenth-Century Spain*, 58.

4 For the concept of the "communications circuit," see Robert Darnton, "What Is the History of Books" and "'What Is the History of Books?' Revisited." Thomas Adams and Nicolas Barker extend and rename the "communications circuit" as "the whole socio-economic conjucture" that encompasses the life of a given book in "A New Model for the Study of the Book."

5 The group fluctuated in number, with some imprints produced by only two or three of the *compañeros*, and Pegnitzer also collaborated with his sometime rival Meinardo Ungut on books commissioned by the archbishop of Toledo, Hernando de Talavera. All in all, the *compañeros alemanes* in their various configurations produced thirty to forty incunables in Seville. Many of the printers working in Spain at the time were itinerant craftsmen of German origins. Julián Martín Abad, *Los primeros tiempos de la imprenta en España*, chapter 2, esp. 54–6.

6 The BNE includes a digital reproduction of this edition in the Biblioteca digital hispánica. http://bdh.bne.es/bnesearch/detalle/bdh0000174210.

7 For a full bibliographic description, see Martín Abad, *Catálogo bibliográfico de la colección de incunables de la Biblioteca Nacional de España*, 699.

8 "Notas complementarias," in *Cárcel de Amor*, 130–1. The narrator is first named "El Autor" in the heading to the second episode, "El preso al Autor" (The prisoner to the author), and in all later rubrics referred to with Latinate spelling as "el auctor."

9 Bouza, *Communication, Knowledge, and Memory in Early Modern Spain*, 42–3.

10 *Rhetorica en lengua castellana*, f. 86v. "Rhetorical reading" is a concept most often used to describe the reading habits of sixteenth-century humanists' approach to Latin texts. Robert Black, *Humanism and Education in Medieval and Renaissance Italy*, 22–30; and Anthony Grafton and Lisa Jardine, *From Humanism to the Humanities: Education and the Liberal Arts in Fifteenth- and Sixteenth-Century Europe*, 16–24. However, as Barry Taylor observes, such habits crossed over into humanist reception of vernacular works, which can be seen in the vogue for translations from Spanish in the sixteenth-century English literary market. "Learning Style from the Spaniards in Sixteenth-Century England," 78.

11 Guarino Guarini (1374–1470), for example advised a student, "Whenever you read, have ready a notebook ... in which you can write down whatever you choose and list the materials you have assembled," for future

reference to contents, *loci*, and exemplary language use (qtd. in Grafton and Jardine, *From Humanism to the Humanities*, 16).

12 *Libro llamado instrucción de la muger christiana*, f. xii.

13 The Hurus edition is only extant in fragments, described and published with facsimiles by Miguel Ángel Pallarés, *La "Cárcel de Amor" de Diego de San Pedro, impresa en Zaragoza el 3 de junio de 1493*. The discovery of these fragments revealed that the first illustrated edition of Cárcel was not the Catalan translation, as was previously thought, but the second known edition of the Spanish text.

14 In the absence of formal regulations and privileges, *Cárcel* was at the time in what is now called the public domain. Royal concessions to monasteries to print bulls and indulgences date from 1487, but the first *pragmática* (rules) regarding printing were issued by the Catholic Monarchs in 1502. These rules had more to do with censoring the content of any printed book than with granting monopolistic privilege. See José Bellido, Raquel Xalabarder, and Ramón Casas Valles, "Commentary on Catholic Monarchs' Licensing Rules (1502)," in *Primary Sources on Copyright (1450–1900)*, ed. Lionel Bently and Martin Kretschmer. www.copyrighthistory.org.

15 Cromberger, as Clive Griffin has documented, followed in the footsteps of Seville's first generation of printers of German origins, having worked for a time for Ungut and Stanislao Polono, whose partnership was even more prolific than that of the *Compañeros Alemanes*. Cromberger, who married Ungut's widow in 1499, came to dominate printing in Seville. Famed for his high-quality books, "his editions became so well known that they were imitated not only in other cities of the Iberian Peninsula, but also in Italy." *The Crombergers of Seville*, 41.

16 The text blocks measure between 14 and 15 centimetres in height and 9 and 10 centimetres in width, each block admitting between 29 and 31 lines of type.

17 As Víctor Infantes de Miguel surmises, literary genres were formed by material as well as verbal structures and books circulated within what Víctor Infantes has called "editorial genres," recognizable by their shape, size, and length. "La prosa de ficción renacentista," 472. See also José Manuel Lucía Megías, *Imprenta y los libros de caballerías*.

18 Martín Abad, *Los primeros tiempos de la imprenta en España (c. 1471–1520)*, chapters 2 and 3. See also Juan Casado Delgado, *Diccionario de impresores españoles*; and Martín Abad, *Post-incunables ibéricos*.

19 Infantes, "La prosa de ficción renacentista," 473.

20 Title pages with images of the *cárcel* appear in ten of the extant editions (1493 [2], 1496, 1508, 1509, 1526, 1523 [2], 1525, 1531), while images of

courtly couples are found on the title pages of six (1511, 1522, 1540, 1544, 1547, 1551).

21 Several bibliographies also erroneously attribute a 1511 edition to Coci, but Martín Abad corrects this misapprehension in the updated Spanish translation of James P. R. Lyell's *Early Book Illustration in Spain*, 392. See also Corfis, *Diego de San Pedro's "Cárcel de Amor*," 24–5.

22 *Cárcel de Amor*, Venice, 1531, BNE Shelfmark R/3260. Pedrezano's 1531 edition differs by a repetition of the title and the presence of an inhabited initial "A" containing an author portrait on a2r. *Cárcel de Amor*, Zaragoza? 1523, BNE Shelfmarks CERV.SEDÓ/8642, R/13346 and U/687, BL Shelfmarks C.63.e.15 and C.63.e.16, and Houghton Library Shelfmarks SC Sa535 492cj and Typ 525 23.767.

23 Juan M. Sánchez Fernández, "Salvá apunta la sospecha de que la presente edición no sea zaragozana; por nuestra parte no recordamos haber visto empleados los caracteres tipográficos, con que se halla impresa esta obra, en ninguna otra producción de las que en el largo espacio de medio siglo salieron de los talleres de Jorge Coci en Zaragoza; por esta razón nos inclinamos a creer que su origen sea veneciano con la suplantación de las indicaciones tipográficas, para hacerla pasar como española, amparándola nada menos que con el nombre del impresor más notable de España en aquel timepo." *Bibliografía aragonesa del siglo XVI* (Madrid: Arco, 1991), I. #117, 169. See also Corfis, *Diego de San Pedro's "Cárcel de Amor*," 60.

24 "The Venetian Ptolemy of 1548," 96.

25 BNE shelfmarks R/12435, R/1435, and R/8928, respectively.

26 Contemporary poetry and devotional texts predominate in Rusconi's editions. The USTC lists 256 editions by Rusconi, the majority of which are octavos in the Italian vernacular. On Rusconi's biography, see Fernanda Ascarelli and Marco Menato, *La tipografia del '500 in Italia*, 168; and Ester Pastorello, *Tipografi, editori, librai a Venezia nel secolo XVI* (Florence: Olschki, 1924), 76.

27 On these printers, see Marco Menato, Ennio Sandal, and Giuseppina Zappelli, eds, *Dizionario dei tipografi e degli editori italiani. Il Cinquecento*.

28 "Form and Function," 451–85.

29 Carla Perugini, "Las fuentes iconográficas de la Editio princeps de la *Lozana andaluza*."

30 BL shelfmarks 12470.aa.18 (1530), 12490.b.24 (1533), 12490.b.25 (1546); BNE shelfmark R/40766 (1537), R/14298 (1546).

31 BL Shelfmark 1084.d.1.(1–4.). The third work is Giovanni Antonio Tagliente's *Formulario nuovo che insegna dittar letter e missive*.

32 Augustus Pallotta, "Venetian Printers and Spanish Literature in Sixteenth-Century Italy," 21.

33 "'Per le Piaze & Sopra il Ponte': Reconstructing the Geography of Popular Print in Sixteenth-Century Venice," 120.

34 *La Fiammetta* (Venice: Gregorio de Gregorii, 1525); *Fiammetta amorosa* (Venice: Bindoni and Pasini, 1527). *L'amorosa Fiammetta* was also printed by Rusconi's frequent collaborator, Nicolao di Aristotile detto el Zoppino, in 1525.

35 Established as a bookseller in 1512, du Pré' maintained a stall called the "Gallée d'Or" (Golden Galleon) in the Palais du Justice and from his home in the city. According to his inventories, he had a large stock of almost forty thousand printed books, with about half dedicated to legal texts, and another significant portion to religious titles, although he also stocked romances, histories, and classical texts in Latin and translation, and also books imported from abroad. Annie Parent, *Les métiers du livre à Paris au XVIe siècle (1535–1560)*, 221. See also Paul Delalain, *Notice sur Galliot Du Pré, libraire parisien de 1512 à 1560*.

36 Parent, *Les métiers du livre à Paris au XVIe siècle (1535–1560)*, 222.

37 *Studies in the French Renaissance*, 190.

38 Lyndan Warner, *The Ideas of Man and Woman in Renaissance Print, Rhetoric, and Law*, 223.

39 This edition is available in full-colour, high resolution images on Gallica: http://gallica.bnf.fr.

40 Dane also notes that physical mass is "paradoxically the first thing eliminated in an electronic copy" of a given book. While those of us who learned to read paper books in the twentieth century probably came to associate big books with long texts, in the fifteenth and sixteenth centuries, while size and textual length were not wholly unrelated, the size of a book carried more information than an estimated amount of time it might take to finish reading. *What Is a Book?*, 38.

41 Dane, *What Is a Book?*, 39.

42 *Orígenes de la novela*, 48.

43 As Grendler puts it, popular books were "small and short." *Form and Function in Italian Renaissance Popular Books*, 484.

44 One of the Catholic Monarchs' early rulings made to control book trade in their realms reflects the importance of size in the horizons of expectation and use of early sixteenth-century readers and booksellers. The statute divides books into four general categories of recognition: small and large, vernacular and Latin. The *Diligencias que deben preceder á la impresion y venta de libros del Reyno, y para el curso de los extrangeros*, issued in 1502, states: "Mandamos y defendemos, que ningun librero ni impresor de moldes, ni mercaderes, ni factor de los suso dichos, no sea osado de hacer

imprimir de molde de aquí adelante por vía directa ni indirecta ningún libro de ninguna Facultad o lectura, o obra, *que sea pequeña ó grande, en latin ni en romance*, sin que primeramente tenga para ello nuestra licencia y especial mandado ... ni sean asimismo osados de vender en los dichos nuestros Reynos ningunos libros de molde que truxeren fuera dellos, de ninguna Facultad ni material que sea ni otra obra *pequeña ni grande, en latin ni en romance*, sin que primeramente sean vistos y examinados" (We order and decree that from this day forward, no bookseller, printer of type, merchant, nor agent of any of the above, dare to have printed in type, by direct or indirect means, any book, *be it small or large, in Latin or in vernacular*, without first obtaining our license and particular permission ... nor may they likewise dare to sell in our said realms any printed books that are brought from elsewhere, of any kind or on any subject, be they *small or large, in Latin or in vernacular*, without their first being seen and examined) (emphasis added). In Bently & Kretschmer, *Primary Sources on Copyright (1450–1900)*. www.copyrighthistory.org.

45 Rudolf Hirsch, *Printing, Selling and Reading, 145–1550*, 41.

46 This edition, listed in many bibliographies, is not extant. See Whinnom, "Introducción," in *Obras completas II*, 68; and Corfis, *Diego de San Pedro's "Cárcel de Amor,"* 37.

47 A fifth edition, printed by Roger Velpio in Louvain in 1580, may also have paired *Cárcel* with *Questión*. Corfis, *Diego de San Pedro's "Cárcel de Amor,"* 37.

48 On Nuncio's biography and career, see Peeters-Fontainas, "L'officine espagnole de Martin Nutius à Anvers,"; and Pedro R. León, "Brief Notes on some 16th Century Antwerp Printers with Special Reference to Jean Steelsius and his Hispanic Bibliography." See also Jaime Moll, "Amberes y el mundo hispano del libro."

49 *Questión de amor*, ed. Carla Perugini (Salamanca: Universidad de Salamanca, 1995), 40. Subsequent citations appear in the text and all translations are mine.

50 The protagonists are masks for members of the courts of Naples and Milan. Benedetto Croce, *España en la vida italiana del renacimiento*, 154–9. Perugini hypothesizes that the author may have been the Comendador Escrivá in her introduction to *Questión de amor*, 16–27.

51 Perugini, *Questión de amor*, 32.

52 "Introduction," in *The Whole Book: Cultural Perspectives on the Medieval Miscellany*, 2.

53 "The Paradox of the Anthology: Collecting and Difference in Eighteenth-Century Britain," 232.

54 Perugini, *Questión de amor*, 13.

55 A.F. Johnson, *The Italian Sixteenth Century*, Periods of Typography, 17–22.
56 Binotti, "Alfonso Ulloa's Editorial Project, Translating, Writing and Marketing Spanish Best-Sellers in Venice," 35. On Ulloa's biography, see A. Rumeu de Armas, *Alfonso de Ulloa, introductor de la cultura española en Italia*; and José Solís de los Santos, "Ulloa, Alfonso de."
57 Griffin, *The Crombergers of Seville*, 13.
58 For Corrozet's biography and career, see Suzanne Marie Bouchereaux, *Recherches bibliographiques sur Gilles Corrozet*.
59 Véronique Duché-Gavet, "Introduction," in *La Prison d'Amour. 1552.*, xvii. Many catalogues and bibliographies mistakenly attribute d'Assy's translation to Corrozet.
60 *Twenty-Five Centuries of Language Teaching (500 BC–1969)*, 257. See also Rocío G. Sumillera, "Language Manuals and the Book Trade in England."
61 "Typographic interplay" is a mode of verbal/visual collaboration "that identifies the relationship between typographic shape and its potential meaning combined with textual syntax and its content. On one hand, it can be found in examples as simple as the page you are now reading, in which social conventions concerning typographic shape interact with academic content. On the other hand, typographic interplay can also use shape in ways that that challenge or contradict the ordinary meaning of text for a particular audience." Susan Hagan, "Visual/Verbal Collaboration in Print," 53.
62 "Coding Continental: Information Design in Sixteenth-Century English Vernacular Language Manuals and Translations," 79.
63 Manuel-Breva Claramonte, *La didáctica de las lenguas en el Renacimiento*, 232.
64 Mary Louise Pratt defines "contact zones" as "social spaces where cultures meet, clash and grapple with each other, often in contexts of highly asymmetrical relations of power such as colonialism, slavery, or their aftermaths." "Arts of the Contact Zone," 34.
65 *Cárcel de Amor. La Prison d'Amour. En deux langages, Espaignol et Frãçois, pour ceulx qui uouldront apprendre l'un par l'autre* (Paris: le Mangnier, 1567), BL Shelfmark 12489.a.12.
66 *On the Method of Study / De ratione studii ac legendi interpretationeque auctores*, 661–91.
67 Similar opinions are found in Comenius's *Restuaratio linguae latinae*, who wrote that grammarians depended upon the poets, while his close contemporary, Liebanus, even more adamantly voiced his disdain for formal grammatical basis of study, stating that "grammar repels students and bores the master" (qtd. in Kelly, *Twenty-five Centuries of Language Teaching*, 36–7).

68 "Multilingualism, Romance, and Language Pedagogy," 33. See also Taylor,"Learning Style from the Spaniards in Sixteenth-Century England."
69 On the printing environment in London in this period, see John King, *English Reformation Literature*, chapter 2.
70 *A Century of the English Book Trade*, 159. Turke, according to the *Dictionary of National Biography*, was a nom de plume for Thomas Lancaster, Bishop of Armagh. Henry A. Jefferies, "Lancaster, Thomas (d. 1583)," *Oxford Dictionary of National Biography*, http://www.oxforddnb.com/index/101015965/Thomas-Lancaster.
71 N.F. Blake, "Wyer, Robert (fl. 1524–1556)," *Oxford Dictionary of National Biography*, http://www.oxforddnb.com/view/article/30124.
72 Taylor, "Learning Style from the Spaniards in Sixteenth-Century England."
73 Stanford Lehmberg, "Carew, Sir Nicholas (b. in or before 1496, d. 1539)."
74 Boro, "Introduction," in *The Castell of Love: A Critical Edition of Lord Berner's Romance*, 77.
75 John Milsom, "Songs and Society in Early Tudor London," 236. In this light, it is interesting to note that an English adaptation of *Celestina*, the *Interlude of Calisto and Melibea* (London: Rastell, 1525?), the protagonists also break into song, in this case, four part harmony. I am grateful to Isidro Rivera for this observation.
76 "Coding Continental," 80.
77 "'Mercanzia d'onore / Mercanzia d'utile': Produzione libraria e lavoro intellectual a Venezia nel Cinquecento."
78 Paul Duguid, "Material Matters: The Past and Futurology of the Book," in *The Future of the Book*, ed. Geoffrey Nunberg (Berkeley: University of California Press, 1996), 81.

6 Visual Rhetoric: Reading Printed Images in *The Prison of Love*, 1493 to 1546

1 Jay David Bolter and Richard Grusin define *remediation* as "the formal logic by which new media refashion prior media forms." *Remediation: Understanding New Media*, 273.
2 "Los grabados de la *Cárcel de Amor* (Zaragoza, 1493, Barcelona 1493, y Burgos, 1496): La muerte de Leriano," in *Actas del Xi Congreso Internacional de la Asociación Hispánica de Literatura Medieval* (Universidad de León, 20 to 24 September 2005), ed. Armando López Castro and María Luzdivina Cuesta Torre, 367–79 (Leon: Universidad de Leon, 2005). See also María Carmen Marín Pina, "La *Cárcel de Amor* zaragozana (1493), Una edición desconocida."

3 *The Image in Print: Book Illustration in Late Medieval England and Its Sources*, 1.
4 Joseph A. Dane, *What Is a Book? The Study of Early Modern Printed Books*, 168.
5 *Historia del grabado en España*, 34. Although there are no extant woodcuts in the *editio princeps* printed in Seville by the Cuatro Compañeros Alemanes in March 1492, according to Deyermond, it is possible that its title page, like those of successive editions, was decorated by a woodcut image of the eponymous *cárcel*. "The Woodcuts of Diego de San Pedro's *Cárcel de Amor*, 1492–1496," 513. However, as Christina Ivers remarks, the existence of a now lost title page "seems unlikely considering the lack of images in their workshop's output in general during 1490–92." "Risky Collaboration in Fifteenth-Century Printing and *Cárcel de Amor*," 96.
6 Miguel Ángel Pallarés, *La "Cárcel de Amor" de Diego de San Pedro*. Pallarés identifies the woodcut artist as Tomás Ubert (ix–x).
7 James P.R. Lyell, *Early Book Illustration in Spain*, 44; Gallego, 41–2.
8 Biblioteca Nacional de España shelfmarks R/12435, R/1435, and R/8928, respectively.
9 Driver, *The Image in Print*, 1.
10 Chartier, "Laborers and Voyagers," 55, and "General Introduction: Print Culture," 5–7.
11 "Reading the Printed Image," 283.
12 "Visual/Verbal Collaboration in Print: Complementary Differences, Necessary Ties, and an Untapped Rhetorical Opportunity."
13 "Narrativity and Segmentivity, or, Poetry in the Gutter," 27.
14 For a complete listing of the woodcuts and their disposition in the first three peninsular editions of *Cárcel de Amor* and *Càrcer d'amor*, see Deyermond, "The Woodcuts," 525–6.
15 The image of the *cárcel* measures 154 × 96 mm; the second woodcut is slightly smaller, measuring 139 × 96 mm. The text block, which admits thirty lines of type, is 150 × 97 mm.
16 Deyermond divides the woodcuts into three categories: those that "could only have been produced to illustrate [*Cárcel*]"; *episode-specific* designs that correspond to single points in *Cárcel's* plot, but that depict motifs and actions that "are frequent in other literary works"; and *generic* scenes that could accompany any other text but which also depict actions that are repeated in *Cárcel*. "The Woodcuts," 520.
17 The cuts measure from 95 to 98 mm in width and 104 to 112 mm in height.
18 Folger analyses the woodcut image of the *Auctor's* first meeting with Leriano and Desire as the key to the romance's construction of individual psychology and as emblematic of emerging notions of subjectivity in the Early Modern period. *Escape from the Prison of Love*, 22–111.

19 *Image, Music, Text*, 38–9.
20 Hagan notes that "the physical inability to see all at once is one way that meaning emerges differently from visual versus textual information." "Visual/Verbal Collaboration in Print," 59.
21 The convention was important but not exclusive. Title pages designed or used for *Cárcel de Amor*, Toledo, Juan de Ayala, 1540 (BL Shelfmark C.62.b.13) and *Cárcel de Amor*, Burgos, Alonso de Melgar, 1522 (BNP Shelfmark RES-Y2-855) do not feature the *cárcel*, but rather depict scenes of courtly encounters between a man and a woman, suggesting that some printers wanted to advertise a different kind of book to potential buyers and audiences.
22 *Escape from the Prison of Love*, 78–9.
23 "*Cárcel de Amor*: emoción sentimental en los albores de la cultura impresa," 141.
24 Harvey L. Sharrer, discusses the likeness of the image to Venus and the Virgin Mary in "La *Cárcel de Amor* de Diego de San Pedro: la confluencia de lo sagrado y lo profano en 'la imagen femenil entallada en una piedra muy clara.'"
25 "The Dazzling Sword of Language: Masculinity and Persuasion in Classical and Medieval Rhetoric," 169.
26 Caroline Van Eck, *Classical Rhetoric and the Visual Arts in Early Modern Europe*, 1. See also Peter Burke, "The Language of Gesture in Early Modern Italy."
27 Elizabeth Sears, "Portraits in Counterpoint: Jerome and Jeremiah in an Augsburg Manuscript," 61.
28 The cut representing Leriano writing in *Cárcel* was in fact recycled for use in other books, for example as an author portrait in the 1502 edition of Íñigo López de Mendoza, Marquis of Santillana's *Bias contra Fortuna* printed in Toledo by Hagenbach. Although María Fraxanet Sala remarked that in the woodcut depicting Leriano writing "se crea un espacio y una acción nuevos para representar una escena tan corriente" (new space and action are created in order to represent such a common scene), in the first study of all of the woodcuts in the series, as Fernando Checa Cremades observes, the image of the humanistic author at work was an established convention in the incunable and post-incunable eras. Driver, commenting upon the topical nature of such images, remarks, "Woodcuts of writers at work often feature, like their manuscript counterparts, the writer himself seated in a canopied chair, copying his text, with his books lying open or shut on a shelf or jumbled in a cabinet, and his inkpot and 'penner,' or pencase, beside him." Checa Cremades, "La imagen impresa en el Renacimiento y el Manierismo," 178; Driver, *The Image in Print*, 158.

Fraxanet Sala, "Estudios sobre los grabados de la novela 'La Cárcel de Amor' de Diego de San Pedro," 443.

29 "Picture, Image, and Subjectivity in Medieval Culture," 621–2.

30 *Corre manuscrito*, 86n.

31 "Otra frontera de la ficción sentimental: la *Consolatio Philosophiae* de Boecio," 529.

32 Hypermediacy is "a style of visual representation whose goal is to remind the view of the medium." Bolter and Grusin, *Remediation*, 272.

33 The title cut measures 78 × 92 mm, and the others 76 × 38 mm. Although there are no breaks in the rectangular frames of these images, it is likely that the episodic images were made from two separate blocks; while the blocks are not mixed and matched in this book, several of the blocks appear singly and in combination with factotum figures in later editions by Pedrezano.

34 An initial "F" in the lower right corner might allow for the future identification of the artist.

35 The 1493 woodcut depicting the *cárcel* is an *imagetext*, in which not only are words and images interwoven through interpretive processes, they are also literally and visually linked together upon the material page, creating a relationship of very tight xylographic interplay.

36 The individual scenes within the two squares making up each rectangular illustration are separate cuts. They are not mixed and matched within the 1523 printings and there are no visible breaks in the framing borders. However, single scenes do appear in the editions of the *Tragecomedia*, *Libro aureo*, and *Questión de amor* printed by Pedrezano in Venice in the 1530s, where the printer used designs made for *Cárcel* in conjunction with other factota.

37 On the use of the elbow as a gesture of assertiveness, see Joaneath Spicer, "The Renaissance Elbow."

38 On the use of *Cárcel* as a rhetorical exemplar, see William G. Crane, *Wit and Rhetoric in the Renaissance*, 198; and Joyce Boro, "Multilingualism, Romance, and Language Pedagogy."

39 Weissberger, "Resisting Readers and Writers," 186.

40 Joy Richie, commenting upon Cheryl Glenn's concept of "rhetorical lives," "Introduction," in *Available Means*, xvi.

41 "Language and Gender in Diego de San Pedro's *Cárcel de Amor*," 119.

42 Bruni, qtd. in *From Humanism to the Humanities*, 32–3.

43 "Leonardo Bruni on Women and Rhetoric: *De studiis et litteris* revisited," 47–75.

44 For a critique of this traditional view of the sentimental romances as a genre, see Barbara Weissberger, "The Gendered Taxonomy of Spanish Romance."

45 *La muerte de la ficción sentimental: transformaciones de un género iberorrománico*, 201.

46 Luis Milán's *Cortesano* (1561) typifies how rhetorical performance was considered a martial art in the period, speaking of, for example, the "lengua spade" (tongue-sword) and the "lanza de la conversación" (lance of conversation). On these metaphors and courtly performances, see Ignació López Alemany, *Ilusión áulica e la imaginación caballeresca en "El cortesano" de Luis Milán*.

47 *The Author's Hand*, 22.

7 *La Prison d'Amours* Illuminated

1 "The *Prison of Love*: A Medieval Romance in the French Renaissance and Its Illustration (B. N. MS fr. 2150)."

2 Nicholas Guilbert, "A propos de la tapisserie"; Fabienne Joubert, *La tapisserie médiévale au Musée de Cluny*, 88; Irene Finotti, "Pour une classification des témoines de '*La Prison d'amour*.'"

3 Indeed, references to the romance in manuscript catalogs are often incorrect, and Orth, whose work continues to be an essential reference, nevertheless dismissed *Cárcel de Amor* as a "simple tale" derived from a medieval French love poem. "'The *Prison of Love*': A Medieval Romance in the French Renaissance and Its Illustration (B. N. MS fr. 2150)," 211.

4 Finotti's collations point to close relationships between manuscript and print circulation in the period. "Traduire d'une langue à l'autre, traduire de prose en rime: De la *Cárcel de Amor* à la *Prison d'amour*."

5 *La Prison d'Amour*, Hispanic Society Ms 706.

6 John Plummer, Gregory Clark, and Pierpont Morgan Library, *The Last Flowering: French Painting in Manuscripts, 1420–1530*.

7 Richard H. Rouse, Mary A. Rouse, *Manuscripts and Their Makers: Commercial Book Producers in Medieval Paris, 1200–1500*, 329.

8 Additional motives for manuscript production and publication during this period included readers' desire to copy texts not currently or readily available for purchase in print, the compilation of private miscellanies, the circulation of court poetry, and also to continue the circulation of texts on the margins of recognized written culture, such as personal prayers, recipes, and spells. See, for example, C.M. Bajetta, *Some Notes on Printing and Publishing in Renaissance Venice*, 14; Ana Gómez-Bravo, *Textual Agency*; Armando Petrucci, "Una nueva historia del libro," in *Libros, escrituras, y bibliotecas*, 4; and Brian Richarsdson, *Manuscript Culture in Renaissance Italy*.

9 Sherry C.M. Lindquist, "'Parlant de moy': Manuscripts of *La Coche* by Marguerite of Navarre," 201.
10 *Imaginary Worlds in Medieval Books*, 15.
11 Although manuscripts were commissioned as book-objects to be deliberately distinct from printed editions, sixteenth-century manuscript production often followed some of the conventions of print, reversing the relationship between imitators and imitated (Petrucci, 41). For example, manuscript hands began to resemble printed typefaces, which is the case for the round Gothic and humanistic hands used in the French manuscripts of *La Prison d'Amours*.
12 Ms. NAF 7552 is a parchment manuscript of ninety-three folia, measuring 250 × 172 mm, and written in a round Gothic hand. It contains three illuminations, decorated initials, and the epistolary sections of the romance are transmitted in prose.
13 Jacquette de Lansac's husband, Alexandre de Saint-Gelais, died in 1522, giving the manuscript a *terminus a quo* of the same year (Finotti, "Pour une classification," 70). The dedicatory epistle and text of the romance are written in a very clear French *batârde*, but the acrostic is written in a textura hand, suggesting that the personalizing paratext was added after the romance had been copied.
14 The first letters of each verse, along with the *q* in verse two, all penned in red ink spell *Iaqet*, while the translator's name is found in the conjunction of other words and letters in red: *franc, ois, d'a*, and *cy*.
15 Unfortunately, MS. NAF 7552 is currently in too delicate a state for reproductions to be made.
16 Orth argued that "we are obliged to take this manuscript as a sort of 'first edition'" ("The Prison of Love," 213), and Finotti follows this assertion ("Pour une classification," 70).
17 Ms Fr. 24382 is a parchment manuscript of sixty-eight folia, measuring 270 × 185mm. Written in a round Gothic hand, Ms Fr. 2438245 contains one miniature and forty-five historiated initials. The epistolary sections are all in prose. See also Guillaume De Bure and Joseph Van Praet, *Catalogue des Livres de la Bibliothèque de feu M. Le Duc de la Vallière*, 657.
18 Finotti, "Pour une classification," 70–1.
19 A full reproduction of the manuscript, in black and white, is available through the Bibliothèque nationale de France's *Bibliothèque numerique, Gallica*. http://gallica.bnf.fr.
20 CB 149 is the largest of the manuscripts, measuring 313 × 201mm. It is copied in sixty-four partchment folia, in a round Gothic hand, and contains d'Assy's dedication and the prose versions of the letters. See also *Manuscrits*

Français du Moyen Âge, 161–3. A full colour, high-resolution digitization of Bodmer CB 149 is available on *e·codices*: http://www.e-codices.unifr.ch/en/searchresult/list/one/fmb/cb-0149.

21 Ms. Rawl D. 591 is a parchment manuscript of seventy-five folia measuring 277 × 190 mm. Written in a round Gothic hand, it contains the prose letters and ten full-page miniatures. Ms. Rawl D. 591 has been treated as a "Hispanic manuscript" due to its textual relationship, though filtered through the Italian *Carcer*, to *Cárcel de Amor*. Peter Russell, *A Catalogue of Hispanic Manuscripts and Books before 1700*. See also Otto Pächt,and J.J.G. Alexander, *Illuminated Manuscripts in the Bodleian Library. I. German, Dutch, Flemish, French, and Spanish*, no. 845.

22 I have not been able to identify who this Monsenor might have been, though the name *Juan* suggests that he may have been Spanish.

23 Among other images associating the two Catherines, Emma Luisa Cahill Marrón describes how Saint Catherine figured in the festivities for Catherine of Aragon's entry into London in 1500 for her marriage to Arthur Tudor. The Catholic Monarchs also commissioned a stained glass window featuring images of Arthur and Catherine, with Saint George above the prince and Saint Catherine above the princess. "Arte y poder: negociaciones matrimoniales y festejos nupciales para el enlace entre Catalina Trastámara y Arturo Tudor," 85 and 94.

24 The identification of the Master of the *Sacre de Claude de France* with Jean Coene IV was made by Eberhard König. Jean Coene IV was the successor of a long line of manuscript illuminators, most notably the Parisian painter Jacques Coene, active at the turn of the fifteenth century, who may have been the Boucicault Master (Meiss 5). On the Pichore group, see Caroline Zöhl, *Jean Pichore: Buchmaler, Graphiker und Verleger in Paris um 1500*. See also François Avril and Nicole Reynaud, *Les Manuscrits à peintures en France 1440–1520*, 282–5.

25 Miniatures from these manuscripts are freely accessible online via the British Library's *Catalogue of Illuminated Manuscripts*. http://www.bl.uk/catalogues/illuminatedmanuscripts/welcome.htm.

26 Durrieu, "Les manuscrits à Peintures de la bibliothèque de sir Thomas Phillipps à Cheltenham," 409. Orth notes that the miniatures "would ... seem to belong to the prevalent mediocre Parisian style of the second and third decade" ("The *Prison of Love*," 213n).

27 Inglis, "A Book in the Hand: Some Late Medieval Accounts of Manuscript Presentations," 59.

28 "A Book in the Hand," 70.

29 MS Fr. 2150, written in a round humanistic hand on 106 parchment folia, is the smallest of all the manuscripts, measuring 180 × 120 mm. The manuscript also contains champ initials, and five of the miniatures are also framed by an opaque black field that extends to the edge of their pages. See also Léopold Delisle, *Le cabinet des manuscrits de la Bibliothèque Impériale: Catalogue des Manuscrits Français*; and Orth. A full-colour, high-resolution digitization of Ms. Fr. 2150 is available online, through the Bibliothèque nationale de France's *Bibliothèque numerique, Gallica.*

30 Full-colour, high-resolution digitization of these manuscripts is also available on *Gallica.* Although the paintings in Ms. Fr. 2150 were at one time attributed to Godefroy, Orth concluded that they are rather imitations of Godefroy's distinctive Italiante, à l'antique style painted by at least four different artists. "Progressive Tendencies," 1976, 330–43. See also Orth's posthumously published *A Survey of Manuscripts Illuminated in France*, 117–20 and plates 83–6. Guy-Michel Leproux posits that at least two of the miniatures may be attributed to Noël Bellemare. "Le peintres et l'enluminure à Paris au XVIe siècle," 60.

31 Anne-Marie Le Coq, *François Ier: Imaginaire symbolique et politique à l'aube de la Renaissance française*, 35–52.

32 "Manuscrits pour Marguerite," 90.

33 An exploration of the clear intertextual relations between Marguerite de Navarre's *Heptameron* and the *Prison of Love*, which, in addition to having their participation in the *querelle des femmes* in common, both employ humanist and diplomatic poetics, lies beyond the scope of this study.

34 Two of the other eleven manuscripts contain the dedication: Arsenal Ms. 3352 and Hispanic Society of America Ms. 706.

35 Two other manuscripts, Arsenal Ms. 3352 and Hispanic Society of America Ms. 705, also contain the versified letters, while Hispanic Society of America Ms. 706 contains a mix of letters in prose and in verse. As Finotti notes in her initial collation of the manuscripts, "l'embrouillement de la tradition de *La Prison d'amour* est encore loin d'etre démêlé." "Pour une classification," 78.

36 *Poésies du Roi François 1er*, ix.

37 The letters are "occasional pieces, often written to accompany a gift ... spontaneous, and generally less polished than the other pieces composed by the family members," Leah Middlebrook explains in a study of Marguerite's letters to Francis and Louise. "'Tout mon office:' Body Politics and Family Dynamics in the Verse *Épîtres* of Marguerite de Navarre," 1110.

38 On these negotiations, see Jocelyne Russell, *Diplomats at Work: Three Renaissance Studies*, chapter 3, "Women Diplomats: The Ladies' Peace of 1529," 94–152.

39 Francis, King of France, Louise de Savoie, Marguerite de Navarre, et al., *Poésies du Roi François 1er, de Louise de Savoie Duchesse d'Angoulême, de Marguerite, Reine de Navarre, et correspondance intime du Roi avec Diane de Poitiers et plusieurs autres dames de la cour*, ed. Aimé Champollion-Figeac (Paris: Imprimerie Royale, 1847), 27. All references are to this edition and appear in the text.

40 In addition to the shared rhetoric of love in Francis's and Lérian's verse letters, as Anthony Perry points out, it is easy to see the intertextual ties between Francis's report of how he rallied his soldiers before the battle of Pavia and Leriano's own harangue to his soldiers before attacking the Macedonians. "A French Reading of a Spanish Text: Paratexts in *Prison damour*," unpublished paper read at the 49th International Congress on Medieval Studies, Kalamazoo, MI, 11 May 2014.

41 *Manuscrits pour Marguerite*, 90.

42 See, for example ff. 67v–68r in BnF Ms Fr. 2150. http://gallica.bnf.fr.

43 On such images, see Timothy Wilson, ed., *The Battle of Pavia*.

44 Bert Hill, *Weapons and Warfare in Renaissance Europe: Gunpowder, Technology, and Tactics*.

45 Paolo Giovio, quoted in Hill, *Weapons and Warfare*, 182.

46 Hill, *Weapons and Warfare*, 190–200.

47 "Tales of Patient Griselda and Henry VIII," 25.

48 On the Italian campaigns and their aftermath, see R.J. Knecht, *Renaissance Warrior and Patron: The Reign of Francis I*, chapters 4–13.

49 According to Knecht, it appears that Charles de Bourbon, Duke of Vendôme, was urged to take over the regency in Louise's stead by men in the government who were not happy to have a woman rule in the place of Francis. *Renaissance Warrior and Patron*, 227.

8 From Text to Textile:
L'Histoire de Lérian et Lauréolle

1 Lotus Stack, *The Essential Thread: Tapestry on Wall and Body*, 25. Used indoors for daily and ceremonial decoration, and outdoors for urban festivals and to line the tents of military commanders, tapestries were called "mobile frescoes from the North," due to their portability and the fame of Flemish workshops. Nora Chalmet, *Les Fresques mobiles du Nord: Tapisseries de nos Règions, XVIe –XXe siècles*.

2 Thomas P. Campbell, *Henry VIII and the Art of Majesty: Tapestries at the Tudor Court*, 336–7.

3 The *David and Bathsheba* tapestries now housed at the French Museé National de la Renaissance, Château d'Ecouen, is a complete chamber demonstrating this tendency, as well as the manner in which tapestry chambers were displayed in the sixteenth century.

4 For the *Book of the City of Ladies*, see Susan Groag Bell, *The Lost Tapestries of the City of Ladies: Christine de Pizan's Renaissance Legacy*. For the *Amadis* tapestries, see Simone Pinet, "The Knight, the Kings, and the Tapestries: The *Amadis* Series"; and Elizabeth Cleland, "Oriane Passing the Magical Love Tests in the Magician's Enchanted Garden."

5 "Studies in the History of Tapestry 1520–1790," 6.

6 *Weaving Sacred Stories: French Choir Tapestries and the Performance of Clerical Identity*, 8.

7 "Fiestas, bodas y regalos de matrimonio," 135–6, 141, and 161.

8 Campbell, *Henry VIII and the Art of Majesty*, xiv.

9 This panel is described and reproduced in colour in Joubert, *La tapisserie médiévale au Musée de Cluny*, 127–34; and in Guy Wildenstein et al., *The Arts of France from François Ier to Napoléon Ier*.

10 The order of payment for the gift of the *Lérian et Lauréolle* chamber, as well as for other tapestries given to Renée for furnishing her new home, are in the *Archives nationales*, Paris KK 66, and cited by Jules Guiffrey, "Tapisseries Françaises," 2:81. Joubert argues that the record of Francis I's purchase, rather than commission, of the chamber from a Parisian merchant suggests that it was a series kept in stock, and not a rare or new item. *La tapisserie médiévale au Musée de Cluny*, 88.

11 The first of the two inventories is dated 1552; the second is undated and listed as "late sixteenth-century." Emile Moliner, "Les tapisseries des Ducs de Lorraine," 471–2.

12 Joubert, *La tapisserie médiévale au Musée de Cluny*, 88.

13 "Tapestry Exposed," 784.

14 Bal's discussion of theatricality and absorption in visual narratives is based upon the opposition proposed by Michael Fried. *Reading Rembrandt: Beyond the Word-Image Opposition*, 47.

15 John Adamson, "The Making of the *Ancien-Régime* Court 1500–1700," 15, 20.

16 Lérian and Desire first address *l'Acteur* as "Voyagier" in the printed *La Prison d'Amours*, and as "viateur" in several of the manuscripts, suggesting that the artist or artists who created the models for the tapestries were familiar with at least the beginning of the text. Moreover, if the designs were based upon a particular French text, the use of "le viateur" instead of "le voyagier"

suggests that it was in manuscript rather than printed form. Although some narrative tapestries do include a narrator or author-figure – such as the Author at his desk in the *Infamia* panel of the *Honores* series, which belonged to Charles V – in the case of *Lérian et Laureolle*, the consistent use of the label "le viateur" in scenes corresponding to the beginning, middle, and penultimate episodes of the romance suggest that the character's name did not change throughout the complete chamber of eight or nine panels.

17 "Text and Textiles: Lydgate's Tapestry Poems," 20.

18 "The English Royal Tapestry Collection, 1485–1547," 1:275.

19 On female role models in tapestries, see Susan Groag Bell and Birgit Franke, "Female Role Models in Tapestries."

20 *The moste pleasaunt historye of Blanchardine, sonne to the King of Friz.*

21 *The Order of Books*, 8.

22 "Introduction," in *The Uses of Script and Print, 1300–1700*, 17.

23 *Libros, escrituras, y bibliotecas*, 217.

24 Cited in Campbell, *Henry VIII and the Art of Majesty*, 144–6. See also Clifford Brown and Guy Demarcel for a rich source of sixteenth-century correspondence concerning tapestry use, reception, and patronage in Ferrara. *Tapestries for the Courts of Federico II, Ercole, and Ferrante Gonzaga, 1522–63.*

25 Guiseppe Campori, *L'Arrazeria Estense*, 126. Some museums do indeed display full tapestry chambers much in the way that they would have been situated in the sixteenth century. For example, Hampton Court Palace outside of London, the Musée National de la Renaissance in Ecouen, France, La Granja near Madrid, and the Cloisters in New York City all allow modern viewers to experience something of the three-dimensional immersion effect this study posits. One aspect that even these chamber exhibits cannot preserve is colour. Most panels that have survived from the late fifteenth and early sixteenth centuries have faded drastically. A recent exhibit at Hampton Court Palace projected the bright colours that historical viewers would have seen onto a faded panel depicting the biblical story of Abraham. "Henry VIII's Tapestries Revealed."

26 Weigert, "Tapestry Exposed," 784.

27 Rees, *Interior Landscapes: Gardens and the Domestic Environment*, 25–32; Hutcheon, *A Theory of Adaptation*, 13.

28 Hutcheon, *A Theory of Adaptation*, 13.

29 Cleland, "Oriane Passing the Magical Love Tests in the Magician's Enchanted Garden," 42. See also Checa Cremades, "Fiestas, bodas y regalos de matrimonio."

30 "Resisting Readers and Writers in the Sentimental Romances," and *Isabel Rules*, 163–4.

31 For Renée of France's life, see Bartolomeo Fontana, *Renata di Francia*. On her time in Ferrarra, see Charmarie Jenkins Blaisdell, "Renée de France between Reform and Counter-Reform" and "Politics and Heresy in Ferrara, 1534–1559."
32 "Manuscript Production and Illumination in Renaissance Paris (1500–1565)."

Conclusion

1 "The Politics of *Cárcel de Amor*," 309–10 and 322.
2 Merry Weisner, "Beyond Women and the Family: Towards and Gender Analysis of the Reformation," *Sixteenth Century Journal* 18, no. 3 (1987): 312.
3 *Humanist Poetics*, 45.
4 I am drawing upon Lorna Hutson's work on the symbolic indispensability of women for humanist writers in *The Usurer's Daughter: Male Friendship and Fictions of Women in Sixteenth-Century England*, which is, in turn applied to Lord Berners' work by Joyce Boro in "All for Love: Lord Berners and the Enduring, Evolving, Romance."
5 *The Book of the Courtier*, 1–4.

Bibliography

Primary Works Cited

Acharisio da Cento, Alberto. *Vocabolario, grammatica, et orthographia de la lingua uolgare.* Cento: Alberto Acharisio, 1543.

Arthur of Brytayn The hystory of the moost noble and valyaunt knyght Arthur of lytell brytayne. Trans. John Bouchier. London: Copland, 1560. EEBO. https://eebo.chadwyck.com/home. Accessed 14 October 2014.

Blanchardyn and Eglantine. [*The moste pleasaunt historye of Blanchardine, sonne to the King of Friz; & the faire lady Eglantine Queene of Tormaday, (surnamed) the proud ladye in loue.*] London: E. Allde for William Blackewall 1595. Early English Books Online: https://eebo.chadwyck.com/home.

Boccaccio, Giovanni. *La Fiammetta.* Venice: Gregorio de Gregorii, 1525.

Bruni, Leonardo. "De interpretatione recta." In *Western Translation Theory: From Herodotus to Nietzsche,* edited by Douglas Robinson and translated by James Hankins, 57–60. Manchester: St Jerome, 1997.

– *De interpretatione recta, de Leonardo Bruni: un episodio en la historia de la traducción y la hermenéutica.* Edited and translated by Fernando Romo Feito. Vigo: Univerisdade de Vigo, 2012.

Burchard, Johann. *At the Court of the Borgia. Being an Account of the Reign of Pope Alexander VI written by his Master of Ceremonies Johann Burchard.* Edited by Geoffrey Parker. London: The Folio Society, 1963.

Cancionero musical de Palacio. Edited by Joaquín González Cuenca. Madrid: Visor, 1996.

Capellanus, Andreas. *The Art of Courtly Love.* Translated by John J. Parry. New York: Columbia University Press, 1990.

Castañega, Martín de. *Tratado muy sotil y bien fundado de las supersticiones y hechecerías y vanos conjuros y abusiones y otras cosas al caso tocantes, y de la possibilidad et remedio dellas*. Logroño: Miguel de Eguía, 1529.

Castiglione, Baldassare. *The Book of the Courtier*. Translated by Sir Thomas Hoby. Edited by Drayton Henderson. New York: Dutton, 1937.

– *Los quatro libros del cortesano compuestos en italiano por el conde Balthasar Castellon; y agora nueuamente traduzidos en lengua castellana por Boscán*. Barcelona: Montpezat, 1534. http://www.ub.edu/boscan.

Caviceo, Jacopo. *Dialogue treselegant intitule le Peregrin traictant de l'honnesté et pudicq amour concilie par pure et sincere vertu traduict de vulgaire Italien en langue Françoise par maistre Françoys dassy*. Paris: Antoine Couteau, Alain Lotrian, Jean Saint-Denis, 1531. https://eebo.chadwyck.com/home. Accessed 13 October 2014.

Cerda, Juan de la. *Libro intitulado vida política de todos los estados de mugeres*. Alcala de Henares: Viuda de Juan. Gracian, 1599.

Cervantes, Miguel de. *El ingenioso hidalgo Don Quijote de la Mancha II*. Edited by Luis Andrés Murillo. Madrid: Castalia, 1978.

– *The History of Don Quixote of the Mancha*. Translated by Thomas Shelton. Edited by James Fitzmaurice-Kelly. New York: AMS, 1967.

Dering, Edward. *A briefe & necessary instruction verye needefull to bee knowen of all housholders, whereby they maye the better teach and instruct their families in such points of Christian religion as is most meete*. London: J. Awdely, 1572. N.p. Early English Books Online. https://eebo.chadwyck.com/home.

Dolet, Etienne. "How to Translate Well from One Language to Another [La manière de bien traduire d'une langue en aultre]." In *Western Translation Theory: From Herodotus to Nietzsche*, edited by Douglas Robinson, translated by David G. Ross, 95–6. Manchester: St Jerome, 1997.

– *La manière de bien traduire d'une langue en aultre*. Cognac: Obsidiane, 1990.

Du Bellay, Joachim. *La deffence et Illustration de la Langue Françoyse/The Defense and Enrichment of the French Language*. In *"The Regrets," with "The Antiquities of Rome," Three Latin Elegies, and "The Defense and Illustration of the French Languages": A Bilingual Edition*. Edited and translated by Richard Helgerson. Philadelphia: University of Pennsylvania Press, 2006.

Dugdale, William. *The baronage of England, or, An historical account of the lives and most memorable actions of our English nobility in the Saxons time to the Norman conquest, and from thence, of those who had their rise before the end of King Henry the Third's reign deduced from publick records, antient historians, and other authorities*. London: Newcomb, 1675.

Erasmus, Desiderius. *On the Method of Study / De ratione studii ac legendi interpretationeque auctores*. In *Literary and Educational Writings, 1 and 2*, edited by Craig R. Thompson, translated by Brian McGregor. Collected Works of Erasmus 24. Toronto: University of Toronto Press, 1978.

Flores, Juan de. *Historia de Isabella et Aurelio in lingua castigliana composta, et da M. Lelio Aletiphilo in parlare italico tradutta*. Venice: Bindoni and Pasini, 1534.

Francis, King of France, Louise de Savoie, Marguerite de Navarre, et al. *Poésies du Roi François 1er, de Louise de Savoie Duchesse d'Angoulême, de Marguerite, Reine de Navarre, et correspondance intime du Roi avec Diane de Poitiers et plusieurs autres dames de la cour*. Edited by Aimé Champollion-Figeac. Paris: Imprimerie Royale, 1847.

Froissart, Jean. *The cronycles of Englande, Fraunce, Spayne, Portyngale, Scotlande, Bretayne, Flaunders: and other places adioynynge. Translated out of frenche into our maternall englysshe tonge, by Iohan Bourchier knight lorde Berners*. London: Pynson, 1523.

Gringore, Pierre. *Le Chasteau d'amours*. Paris: Simon Vostre, 1499.

Guevara, Antonio de. *The Golden Boke of Marcus Aurelius Emperour and eloquent orator*. Translated by John Bourchier. London: Thomae Brtheleti, 1537.

Herberay, Nicolas, Trans. *Le Premiere Livre de Amadis de Gaule, Mis en Francoys par le Seigneur des Essarts, Nicolas de Herberay*. Paris: Estienne Groulleau, 1560.

Horace. *Satires. Epistles. The Art of Poetry*. Translated by H. Rushton Fairclough. Loeb Classical Library 194. Cambridge, MA: Harvard University Press, 2014.

Irving, Leonard. "Documentary Appendix." In *The Books of the Brave: Being an Accournt of Books and Men in the Spanish Conquest and Settlement of the Sixteenth-Century New World*, 335–403. Berkeley: University of California Press, 1992. http://ark.cdlib.org/ark:/13030/ft1f59n78v/.

Manfredi, Lelio. Trans. *Tirante il Bianco valorosissimo caualiere, nelquale contiensi del principio della caualleria del stato and vfficio suo*. Venice: Peitro di Nicolino da Sabbio, 1538.

Nebrija, Elio Antonio. *Gramática de la lengua castellana*. Edited by Antonio Quilis. Madrid: Ediciones de Cultura Hispánica, 1992.

Osuna, Francisco de. *Tercer Abecedario espiritual*. Edited by Melquiades Andrés Martín. Madrid: Editorial Católica, 1972.

Questión de amor. Edited by Carla Perugini. Salamanca: Universidad de Salamanca, 1995.

Saix, Antoine du. *L'esperon de discipline pour inciter les humains aux bonnes lettres, stimuler a doctrine, animer a sciēce, inuiter a touttes bōnes oeuures vertueuses et moralles*. Paris 1532.

Salinas, Miguel de. *Rhetorica en lengua castellana*. Alcalá de Hernares: Juan de
   Brocar, 1541.
San Pedro, Diego de. *Cárcel de Amor. Con la continuación de Nicolás Núñez.*
   Edited by Carmen Parrilla. Estudio Preliminar de Alan Deyermond.
   Barcelona: Crítica, 1995.
– *Carcer d'amor*. Translated by Bernadí Vallmanyà. Barcelona: Rosenbach, 1493.
– *Càrcer d'amor; Carcer d'amore: due traduzioni della 'novela' di Diego de San
   Pedro*. Edited by Vincenzo Minervini and Maria Luisa Indini. Fasano, Italy:
   Schena. 1986.
– *Carcer d'amore del magnifico meser Lælio de Manfredi*. Venice: Zorzi di Rusconi
   Milanese, 1514.
– *Castell of Love*. Translated by John Bouchier, Lord Berners. London: Johan
   Turke, 1549.
– *Castell of Love*. Edited by Andrew Spigurnell. London: Robert Wyer, 1550.
– *The Castell of Love. A Critical Edition of Lord Berners's Romance*. Edited
   by Joyce Boro. Medieval and Renaissance Texts and Studies. Tempe, AZ:
   ACMRS, 2007.
– *Gefängnüss der Lieb oder carcell de amor*. Translated by Hans Ludwig von
   Kuefstein. Edited by Gerhart Hoffmeister. Bern: Lang. 1976.
– *La Prison d'Amour: 1552*. Edited by Véronique Duché-Gavet. Paris: H.
   Champion, 2007.
– *Obras Completas I, Tractado de Amores de Arnalte y Lucenda, Sermón*. Edited by
   Keith Whinnom. Madrid: Castalia, 1985.
– *Obras Completas II, Cárcel de Amor*. Edited by Keith Whinnom, Madrid:
   Castalia, 1971.
– *Obras Completas III, Poesías*. Edited by Dorothy Severin and Keith Whinnom.
   Madrid: Castalia, 1979.
– *Prison of Love (1492) together with the Continuation by Nicolás Núñez (1496)*.
   Translated by Keith Whinnom. Edinburgh: Edinburgh UP, 1979.
Santa Cruz de Dueñas, Melchor de. *Floresta española*. Edited by María Pilar
   Cuartero Sancho and Maxime Chevalier. Barcelona: Crítica, 1997.
Tagliente, Giovanni Antonio. *Formulario nuovo che insegna dittar letter e missive,
   & reponnsive con le sue mancioni & sottoscristioni, intitolato Componimento di
   parlamento*. Toscolano: Paganino, 1538.
Tasso, Torquato. "Il Messaggiero." In *Prose*, edited by Ettore Mazzali, 3–73.
   Milan: Riccardo Ricciardi, 1959.
Torre, Fernando de la. *Libro de las veynte cartas e quistiones y otros versos y prosas*.
   Edited by María Jesús Díez Garretas. Segovia: Junta de Castilla y León –
   Fundación Instituto Castellano y Leonés de la Lengua, 2009.

Vives, Luis. *Libro llamado instrucción de la muger christiana,* translated by Juan Justiniano. Valencia: Coci 1539.

– *De institutione feminae christianae, liber primus.* Edited by Charles Fantazzi and C. Matheeussen. New York: E.J. Brill, 1996.

– "El arte retórica: De ratione dicendi." In *Western Translation Theory: From Herodotus to Nietzsche,* edited by Douglas Robinson, translated by Ana Isabel Camacho, 92–4. Manchester: St Jerome, 1997.

– *The Education of a Christian Woman: A Sixteenth-Century Manual.* The Other Voice in Early Modern Europe. Translated by Charles Fantazzi. Chicago: University of Chicago Press, 2000.

Zapata de Mendoza. *Novus index librorum prohibitorum et expurgatorum.* Hispali: F. de Lyra, 1632.

Secondary Sources Cited

Akbari, Suzanne Conklin. *Seeing through the Veil: Optical Theory and Medieval Allegory.* Toronto: University of Toronto Press, 2004.

Akbari, Suzanne Conklin, and Karla Malette, eds. *The Sea of Languages: Rethinking the Arabic Role in Medieval Literary History.* Toronto: Toronto University Press, 2013.

Adams, Thomas R., and Nicholas Barker. "A New Model for the Study of the Book." In *A Potencie of Life: Books in Society; the Clark Lectures, 1986–1987,* edited by Nicholas Barker, 5–43. London: British Library, 1993.

Adamson, John. "The Making of the *Ancien-Régime* Court 1500-1700." In *The Princely Courts of Europe: Ritual, Politics and Culture Under the Ancien Régime 1500–1750,* edited by John Adamson, 7–41. London: Weidenfeld and Nicolson, 1999.

Amos, Flora R. *Early Theories of Translation.* New York: Columbia University Press, 1920.

Areford, David S., Nina Rowe, and Sandra Hindman, eds. *Excavating the Medieval Image: Manuscripts, Artists, Audiences; Essays in Honor of Sandra Hindman.* Burlington, VT: Ashgate, 2004.

Armstrong, Guyda. "Coding Continental: Information Design in Sixteenth-Century English Vernacular Language Manuals and Translations." *Renaissance Studies* 29, no. 1 (2015): 78–102.

– *The English Boccaccio.* Toronto: University of Toronto Press, 2013.

Ascarelli, Fernanda, and Marco Menato. *La tipografia del '500 in Italia.* Biblioteca de bibliografia italiana. Vol. 116. Florence: L.S. Olschki, 1989.

Avril, François, and Nicole Reynaud. *Les manuscrits à peintures en France
    1440–1520*. Paris: Flammarion, 1993.
Bajetta, Carlo M. *Some Notes on Printing & Publishing in Renaissance Venice*.
    Typophile Monograph, New Series no. 16. New York: Typophiles, 2000.
Bal, Mieke. *Reading Rembrandt: Beyond the Word-Image Opposition*. Cambridge:
    Cambridge University Press, 1991.
Balteau, J., Michel Prévost, and Roman d'Amat. *Dictionnaire de biographie
    française*. Paris: Letouzey et Ané, 1933.
Barbetti, Claire. *Ekphrastic Medieval Visions: A New Discussion in Interarts
    Theory*. The New Middle Ages. New York: Palgrave Macmillan, 2011.
Barthes, Roland. *Image, Music, Text*. Edited by Stephen Heath. New York: Hill
    and Wang, 1978.
Bassnett, Susan. "The Translation Turn in Cultural Studies." In *Translation
    Translation*, edited by Susan Petrilli, 433–9. Amsterdam: Rodopi, 2003.
Baxandall, Michael. *Painting and Experience in Fifteenth Century Italy: A Primer
    in the Social History of Pictorial Style*. Oxford: Clarendon Press, 1972.
Beebee, Thomas O. *Epistolary Fiction in Europe, 1500–1850*. Cambridge:
    Cambridge University Press, 1999.
Bell, Susan G. *The Lost Tapestries of the City of Ladies: Christine de Pizan's
    Renaissance Legacy*. Berkeley, CA: University of California Press, 2004.
Benedict, Barbara M. "The Paradox of the Anthology: Collecting and *Différence*
    in Eighteenth-Century Britain." *New Literary History* 34 (2003): 231–56.
Binotti, Lucia. "Alfonso Ulloa's Editorial Project, Translating, Writing and
    Marketing Spanish Best-Sellers in Venice." *Allegorica* 17 (1996): 35–54.
– *Cultural Capital, Language and National Identity in Imperial Spain*.
    Monografías, vol. 311. Woodbridge, UK: Tamesis, 2012.
– "Humanistic Audiences: *Novela sentimental* and *libros de caballerías* in
    Cinquecento Italy." *La corónica* 39, no. 1 (2010): 67–114.
Bistué, Belén, *Collaborative Translation and Multi-Version Texts in Early Modern
    Europe*. Burlington, VT: Ashgate, 2013.
Black, Robert. *Humanism and Education in Medieval and Renaissance Italy:
    Tradition and Innovation in Latin Schools from the Twelfth to the Fifteenth
    Century*. Cambridge: Cambridge University Press, 2001.
Blaisdell, Charmarie Jenkins. "Politics and Heresy in Ferrara, 1534–1559."
    Sixteenth Century Journal 6, no. 1 (1975): 67–93.
– "Renée de France between Reform and Counter-Reform." *Archiv für
    Reformationsgeschichte* 63 (1972): 196–226.
Bolter, David J., and Richard Grusin. *Remediation: Understanding New Media*.
    Cambridge, MA: MIT Press, 1999.

Boro, Joyce, ed. "All for Love: Lord Berners and the Enduring, Evolving Romance." In *The Oxford Handbook to Tudor Literature, 1485–1603*, edited by Mike Pincombe and Cathy Shrank, 87–102. Oxford: Oxford University Press, 2009.

– *The Castell of Love: A Critical Edition of Lord Berners's Romance*. Medieval and Renaissance Texts and Studies. Tempe, AZ: ACMRS, 2007.

– "Multilingualism, Romance, and Language Pedagogy; or, Why Were so Many Sentimental Romances Printed as Polyglot Texts?" In *Tudor Translation*, edited by Fred Schurink, 18–38. New York: Palgrave, 2011.

Bouchereaux, Suzanne M. *Recherches bibliographiques sur Gilles Corrozet*. Paris: L. Giraud-Badin, 1948.

Boutcher, Warren. "The Renaissance." In *The Oxford Guide to Literature in English Translation*, edited by Peter France, 45–55. Oxford: Oxford University Press, 2000.

Bouza Alvarez, Fernando J. *Communication, Knowledge, and Memory in Early Modern Spain*. Philadelphia: University of Pennsylvania Press, 2004.

– *Corre manuscrito: Una historia cultural del Siglo de Oro*. Madrid: Marcial Pons Historia, 2001.

Brandenberger, Tobias. *La muerte de la ficción sentimental: Transformaciones de un género iberorrománico*. Madrid: Verbum, 2012.

Breva-Claramonte, Manuel. *La didáctica de las lenguas en el Renacimiento: Juan Luis Vives y Pedro Simón Abril*. Bilbao: Universidad de Deusto, 1994.

Brown, Clifford M., and Guy Demarcel. *Tapestries for the Courts of Federico II, Ercole, and Ferrante Gonzaga, 1522–63*. Seattle: College Art Association in association with University of Washington Press, 1996.

Brownlee, Marina S. *The Severed Word: Ovid's "Heroides" and the "Novela Sentimental."* Princeton, NJ: Princeton University Press, 1990.

Brun, Robert. *La Typographie en France au seizième siècle*. Recuils Illustrés de la Bibliothèque nationale de France. Paris: Éditions des Bibliothèques Nationales, 1938.

Burke, Peter. *The Fortunes of the Courtier*. University Park: Pennsylvania State University Press, 1996.

– "The Language of Gesture in Early Modern Italy." In *A Cultural History of Gesture*, edited by Jan Bremmer and Herman Roodenburg, 71–83. Ithaca, NY: Cornell University Press, 1992.

Burns, E.J. *Courtly Love Undressed: Reading through Clothes in Medieval French Culture*. The Middle Ages. Philadelphia: University of Pennsylania Press, 2002.

Cacho Blecua, Juan Manuel. "Los grabados de la *Cárcel de Amor* (Zaragoza, 1493, Barcelona, 1493, y Burgos 1496)." In *Actas del XI Congreso internacional de la Asociación hispánica de literatura medieval*, 367–79. León: University of León, 2007.

Cahill Marrón, Emma L. "Arte y poder: Negociaciones matrimoniales y festejos nupciales para el enlace entre Catalina Trastámara y Arturo Tudor." MA thesis. Cantabria, Spain: Universidad de Cantábria, 2012.

Camille, Michael. "Before the Gaze: The Internal Senses and Late Medieval Practices of Seeing." In *Visuality before and beyond the Renaissance: Seeing as Others Saw*, edited by Robert S. Nelson, 197–223. Cambridge: Cambridge UP, 2000.

– "Reading the Printed Image: Illuminations and Woodcuts of the *Pèlerinage De La Vie Humaine* in the Fifteenth Century." In *Printing the Written Word: The Social History of Books, circa 1450–1520*, edited by Susan Hindman, 259–91. Ithaca, NY: Cornell University Press, 1991.

Campbell, Thomas P. "The English Royal Tapestry Collection, 1485–1547." PhD diss., Courtauld Institute, University of London, 1998.

– *Henry VIII and the Art of Majesty: Tapestries at the Tudor Court*. New Haven, CT: Yale University Press, 2007.

Campori, Guiseppe. *L'Arrazeria Estense*. Modena: 1876.

Casado Delgado, Juan. *Diccionario de Impresores Españoles (Siglos XV–XVII)*. 2 vols. Madrid: Arco, 1996.

Casas Rigall, Juan. "El mote y la invención en la estructura narrativa de *Cárcel de Amor*." *Cancionero General* 6 (2008): 33–61.

Chalmet, Nora. *Les fresques mobiles du nord: tapisseries de nos régions, VXIe–XXe siècle*. Antwerp: Gaspard de Wit, 1994.

Chartier Roger. *The Author's Hand and the Printer's Mind*. Translated by Lydia G. Cochrane. Cambridge: Polity, 2014.

"General Introduction: Print Culture." In *The Culture of Print: Power and the Uses of Print in Early Modern Europe*, edited by Alain Boureau, Roger Chartier, and Lydia G. Cochrane, 1–11. Princeton, NJ: Princeton University Press, 1989.

– *Inscription and Erasure: Literature and Written Culture from the Eleventh to the Eighteenth Century*. Translated by Arthur Goldhammer. Philadelphia: University of Pennsylvania Press, 2007.

– "Laborers and Voyagers: From the Text to the Reader." Translated by J.A. González. *Diacritics* 22, no. 2 (1992): 49–61.

– *The Order of Books: Readers, Authors, and Libraries in Europe between the Fourteenth and Eighteenth Centuries*. Translated by Lydia G. Cochrane. Stanford, CA: Stanford University Press, 1994.

Chas Aguión, Antonio. "*Cárcel de Amor*: Hacia la novela moderna." In *Semiótica y modernidad: actas del V congreso internacional de la asociación española de semiótica, La Coruña, 3–5 de diciembre de 1992*, vol. 2, edited by José Angel Fernández Roca, Carlos J. Gómez Blanco, and José María Paz Gago, 91–102. La Coruña, Spain: Universidade da Coruña, 1994.

Checa Cremades, Fernando. "Fiestas, bodas y regalos de matrimonio: Del tesoro principesco al inicio del coleccionismo artístico en las cortes habsbúrgicas de la época de Juana de Castilla (1498–1554)." In *Juana I en Tordesillas: su mundo, su entorno*, edited by Miguel Ángel Zalama Rodríguez, 135–62. Valladolid, Spain: Ayuntamiento de Tordesillas, 2010.

– "La imagen impresa en el Renacimiento y el Manierismo." In *Summa artis: Historia general del arte XXXI*, edited by Juan Carrete, Fernando Checa Cremades, and Valeriano Bozal, 9–200. Madrid: Espasa Calpe, 1987.

Chorpenning, Joseph F. "Loss of Innocence, Descent into Hell, and Cannibalism: Romance Archetypes and Narrative Unity in *Cárcel de Amor*." *Modern Language Review* 87, no. 2 (1992): 343–51.

– "Rhetoric and Feminism in the *Cárcel de Amor*." *Bulletin of Hispanic Studies* 54 (1977): 1–8.

Churchill Candee, Helen. *The Tapestry Book*. London: Constable and Company, 1913.

Cleland, Elizabeth. "Oriane Passing the Magical Love Tests in the Magician's Enchanted Garden." In *Tapestry in the Baroque: Threads of Splendor*, edited by Thomas P. Campbell, 36–42. New York: Metropolitan Museum of Art, 2007.

Coldiron, Anne E.B. *Printers without Borders: Translation and Textuality in the Renaissance*. Cambridge: Cambridge University Press, 2015.

Conley, Thomas M. *Rhetoric in the European Tradition*. Chicago: University of Chicago Press, 1994.

Cooren, François. "Textual Agency: How Texts Do Things in Organizational Settings." *Organization* 11, no. 3 (2004): 373–93.

Corfis, Ivy A. "Introduction and Catalogue of Editions." In *Diego de San Pedro's Cárcel de Amor: A Critical Edition*, 1–50. London: Tamesis, 1987.

Cortijo Ocaña, Antonio. "De amicitia, amore et rationis discretione. Breves notas a propósito de Boncompagno da Signa y el Siervo libre de Amor." *Revista de Literatura medieval* 16 (2006): 23–52.

– "Hacia la ficción sentimental: *la Rota Veneris* de Boncompagno da Signa." *La corónica*, 29, no. 1 (2000): 53–74.

– *La evolución genérica de la ficción sentimental de los siglos XV y XVI: Género literario y contexto social*. London: Tamesis, 2001.

Cortijo Ocaña, Antonio, and Milena Hurtado. *Arnalte y Lucenda*. "Las obras de Diego de San Pedro. Un éxito editorial." In *Arnalte y Lucenda. eHumanista. Sixteenth Century English Translations of Spanish Literature*. http://www.ehumanista.ucsb.edu/publications/translations.

Costa Fontes, Manuel da. "*Cárcel de Amor* and the Situation of Conversos."
    In "*Entra Mayo y Sale Abril": Medieval Spanish Literary and Folklore Studies in
    Memory of Harriet Goldberg*, edited by Manuel da Costa Fontes and Joseph F.
    Snow, 143–60. Newark, DE: Juan de la Cuesta-Hispanic Monographs, 2005.

Cox, Virginia. "Leonardo Bruni on Women and Rhetoric: *De studiis et litteris*
    revisited." *Rhetorica* 27, no. 1 (2009): 47–75.

Crane, William G. *Wit and Rhetoric in the Renaissance: The Formal Basis of
    Elizabethan Prose Style*. Columbia University Studies in English and
    Comparative Literature, vol. 129. New York: Columbia UP, 1937.

Crick, Julia C., and Alexandra Walsham. "Introduction." In *The Uses of Script
    and Print, 1300 – 1700*, edited by Julia C. Crick and Alexandra Walsham,
    1–28. Cambridge: Cambridge University Press, 2004.

Croce, Benedetto. *España en la vida italiana del Renacimiento*. Vol. 2. Buenos
    Aires: Ediciones Imán, 1945.

Damiani, Bruno M. "The Didactic Intention of the *Cárcel de Amor*." *Hispanófila*
    56 (1976): 29–44.

Dane, Joseph A. *What Is a Book?: The Study of Early Printed Books*. Notre Dame,
    IN: University of Notre Dame Press, 2012.

Darnton, Robert. "What Is the History of Books?" *Daedalus* 111, no. 3 (1982):
    65–83.

– "'What Is the History of Books?' Revisited." *Modern Intellectual History* 4, no.
    3 (2007): 495–508.

Davis, Natalie Zemon. "Beyond the Market: Books as Gifts in Sixteenth-
    Century France; The Prothero Lecture." *Transactions of the Royal Historical
    Society* 33 (1983): 69–88.

Delalain, Paul. *Notice sur Galliot du Pré, libraire parisien de 1512 à 1560*. Paris:
    Cercle de la Librairie, 1891.

Delgado Casado, Juan. *Diccionario de impresores españoles*. 2 vols. Madrid: Arco
    Libros, 1996.

Desmond, Marilynn. "The Visuality of Reading in Pre-Modern Textual
    Cultures." *Australian Journal of French Studies* 46, no. 3 (2009): 219–34.

Deyermond, Alan D. "El hombre salvaje en la novela sentimental." *Filología*
    10 (1964): 97–111.

– "Estudio Preliminar." In Diego de San Pedro, *Cárcel de Amor. Con la
    continuación de Nicolás Núñez*. Edited by Carmen Parrilla. Barcelona: Crítica,
    1995. ix–xxxiii.

– "The Woodcuts of Diego de San Pedro's *Cárcel de Amor*, 1492–1496." *Bulletin
    Hispanique* 104, no. 2 (2002): 511–28.

Donovan, Josephine. *Women and the Rise of the Novel: 1405–1726*. New York: St
    Martins, 1999.

Driver, Martha. *The Image in Print: Book Illustration in Late Medieval England and its Sources*. London: The British Library, 2004.

Dunn, Peter N. "Narrator as Character in the *Cárcel de Amor*." *Modern Language Notes* 94, no. 2 (1979): 187–99.

Durrieu, Paul. "Les manuscrits a peintures de la bibliothèque de Sir Thomas Phillipps a Cheltenham." *Bibliothèque de l'Ecole des Chartes* 50 (1889): 381–432.

Eggert, Paul. "Brought to Book: Bibliography, Book History, and the Study of Literature." *The Library* 13, no. 1 (2012): 2–32.

Egmond, Florike, and Peter Mason. *The Mammouth and the Mouse: Microhistory amd Morphology*. Baltimore: Johns Hopkins University Press, 1997.

Eisenstein, Elizabeth. *The Printing Press as an Agent of Change: Communications and Cultural Transformations in Early Modern Europe*. Cambridge: Cambridge University Press, 1982.

Esrock, Janet. *The Reader's Eye: Visual Imaging as Reader Response*. Baltimore: Johns Hopkins University Press, 1994.

Evans, Ruth, Andrew Taylor, Nicholas Watson, and Jocelyn Wogan-Browne. "The Notion of Vernacular Theory." In *The Idea of the Vernacular: An Anthology of Middle English Literary Theory, 1280–1520*, edited by Wogan-Browne, Watson, Taylor, and Evans, 314–30. University Park: Pennsylvania State University Press, 1999.

Even-Zohar, Itamar. "The Position of Translated Literature within the Literary Polysystem (1978)." In *The Princeton Sourcebook in Comparative Literature: From the European Enlightenment to the Global Present*, edited by David Damrosch, Natalie Melas, and Mbongiseni Buthelezi, 240–7. Princeton, NJ: Princeton University Press, 2009.

Fahy, Conor. "The Venetian Ptolemy of 1548." In *The Italian Book: 1465–1800; Studies Presented to Dennis E. Rhodes on his 70th Birthday*, edited by Denis V. Reidy, 89–115. London: The British Library, 1993.

Febvre, Lucien, and Henri-Jean Martin. *The Coming of the Book: The Impact of Printing 1450–1800*. Translated by David Gerard. London: Verso, 1997.

Fernández Valladares, Mercedes. *La imprenta en Burgos (1501–1600)*. Vol. 2. Madrid: Arco, 2005.

Finotti, Irene. "Pour une classification des témoines de *La Prison d'Amour* de François Dassy." *Studi Francesi* 166 (2012): 69–78.

– "Traduire d'une langue à l'autre, traduire de prose en rime: De la *Cárcel de Amor* à la *Prison d'amour*." *Œuvres & Critiques* 36, no. 1 (2011): 37–49.

Fiumara, Francesco. "Tradotti per hora: Mambrino roseo da Fabriano e la diffusione del romanzo cavalleresco spagnolo nell'Italia della Controriforma." PhD diss., Johns Hopkins University, 2006.

Folena, Gianfranco. "Volgarizzare e tradurre: Idea e terminologia della traduzione dal medio evo italiano e romanzo all'umanesimio europeo." In *La traduzione: Saggi e studi*, edited by Bertil Malmberg, 57–120. Trieste: Edizioni LINT, 1973.

Folger, Robert. "'Besando las manos de vuestra merced': Los modos de subjetividad y la emergencia del discurso novelesco en *Cárcel de Amor* y *Lazarillo de Tormes*." In *La fractura historiográfica: Las investigaciones de edad media y renacimiento desde el tercer milenio*, edited by Javier San José Lera, 599–610. Salamanca: Universidad de Salamanca, 2008.

– "Cárceles de Amor: 'Gender Trouble' and Male Fantasies in Fifteenth-Century Castile." *Bulletin of Spanish Studies: Hispanic Studies and Researches on Spain, Portugal, and Latin America* 83, no. 5 (2006): 617–35.

– *Escape from the Prison of Love: Caloric Identities and Writing Subjects in Fifteenth-Century Spain*. Chapel Hill: North Carolina Studies in Romance Languages, 2009.

– *Images in Mind: Lovesickness, Spanish Sentimental Fiction and "Don Quijote."* North Carolina Studies in the Romance Languages and Literatures, vol. 274. Chapel Hill: North Carolina Studies in Romance Languages, 2002.

Fontana, Bartolomeo. *Renata di Francia, Duchessa di Ferrara, sui documenti dell'archivo Estense, del Mediceo, del Gonzaga, e dell'archivo secreto vaticano (1510–1536)*. Rome, 1889.

Foucault, Michel. "What Is an Author?" In *Language, Counter-memory, Practice: Selected Essays and Interviews*, edited by Donald F. Bouchard, translated by Donald F. Bouchard and Sherry Simon, 113–38. Ithaca, NY: Cornell University Press, 1977.

Fowler, Alastair. "The Formation of Genres in the Renaissance and After." *New Literary History* 34 (2003): 185–200.

Francomano, Emily C. "'Puse un Sobreescripto' [I Wrote a New Cover]: Manuscript, Print, and the Material Epistolarity of *Cárcel de Amor*." *Fifteenth-Century Studies* 36 (2011): 25–48.

– "Reversing the Tapestry: *Prison of Love* in Text, Image, and Textile." *Renaissance Quarterly* 64, no. 4 (2011): 1059–1105.

Francomano, Emily C., ed. *Three Spanish Querelle Texts: "Grisel and Mirabella," "The Slander Against Women" and "The Defense of Ladies Against Slanderers," by Pere Torrellas and Juan de Flores. A Bilingual Edition and Study*. Toronto: CRRS/ITER, 2013.

Franke, Birgit. "Female Role Models in Tapestries." In *Women of Distinction: Margaret of York, Margaret of Austria*, edited by Dagmar Eichberger, 155–65. Leuven, Belgium: Brepols, 2005.

Frati, Ludovico. "Andrea Garisendi e il suo contrasto d'amore." *Giornale storico della letteratura italiana* 49 (1907): 73–82.

Fraxanet Sala, María Rosa. "Estudios sobre los grabados de la novela *La Cárcel de Amor* de Diego de San Pedro." In *Estudios de iconografía medieval española*, edited by Joaquín Yarza Luaces, 429–82. Barcelona: Bellaterra, Universidad Autónoma de Barcelona, 1984.

Fuchs, Barbara. *The Poetics of Piracy: Emulating Spain in English Literature*. Philadelphia: University of Pennsylvania Press, 2013.

Funes, Leonardo. "*Cárcel de Amor*: emoción sentimental en los albores de la cultura impresa." *Páginas de guarda* 8 (2009): 129–43.

– "La impronta lírica de la narrativa de ficción sentimental del siglo XV." *Revista del Centro de Letras Hispanoamericanas* 21, no. 23 (2012): 159–76.

Gallego, Antonio. *Historia del grabado en España*. Madrid: Cátedra, 1979.

García, Dulce M. *Espada, escudo y espejo: El lenguaje como tema en las novelas de Diego de San Pedro*. New Orleans: UP of the South, 1996.

Gastañaga-Ponce de Leon, José Luis. "Diego de San Pedro y el descontento en la corte de los Reyes Católicos: Una lectura de *Cárcel de Amor*." *Bulletin of Hispanic Studies* 85, no. 6 (2008): 809–20.

Gayangos, Pascual de. *Libros de caballerías, con un discurso preliminar y un catálogo razonado*. Madrid: M. Rivadeneyra, 1857.

Genette, Gerard. *Paratexts: Thresholds of Interpretation*. Translated by Jane E. Lewin. Cambridge: Cambridge University Press, 1997.

Gerli, E. Michael. "Conflictive Subjectivity and the Politics of Truth and Justice in *Cárcel de Amor*." In *Queen Isabel I of Castile: Power, Patronage, Persona*, edited by Barbara F. Weissberger, 149–68. Woodbridge, UK: Tamesis, 2008.

– "Leriano and Lacan: The Mythological and Psychoanalytical Underpinnings of Leriano's Last Drink." *La corónica* 19, no. 1 (2000): 113–28.

– "Leriano's Libation: Notes on the Cancionero Lyric, Ars Moriendi, and the Probable Debt to Boccaccio." *Modern Language Notes* 96, no. 2 (1981): 414–20.

– "Metafiction in the Spanish Sentimental Romances." In *The Age of the Catholic Monarchs, 1474–1516: Literary Studies in Memory of Keith Whinnom*, edited by Alan D. Deyermond and Ian R. Macpherson, 57–63. Liverpool: Liverpool University Press, 1989.

Ghisalberti, Alberto Maria. *Dizionario Biografico degli Italiani*. Rome: Istituto della Enciclopedia Italiana, 1960.

Giannini, A. "La *Cárcel de Amor* y el *Cortegiano* de B. Castiglione." *Revue Hispanique* 46 (1919): 547–68.

Gil Sáenz, Daniel. "Reading Diego de San Pedro in Tudor England." *Revista alicantina de estudios ingleses* 17 (2004): 103–15.

Gilkinson, Jean. "Language and Gender in Diego de San Pedro's *Cárcel de Amor*." *Journal of Hispanic Research* 3 (1994–5): 113–24.

Gilman, Stephen. *The Spain of Fernando de Rojas: The Intellectual and Social Landscape of "La Celestin*a." Princeton, NJ: Princeton University Press, 1972.

Gillespie, Alexandra. *Print Culture and the Medieval Author: Chaucer, Lydgate, and their Books*. Cambridge: Cambridge University Press, 2006.

Ginzburg, Carlo, and Carlo Ponti. "The Name and the Game." In *Microhistory and the Lost Peoples of Europe*, edited by Edward Muir and Guido Ruggiero, 1–10. Baltimore: Johns Hopkins UP, 1991.

Goldberg, Harriet. "Cannibalism in Iberian Narrative: The Dark Side of Gastronomy." *Bulletin of Hispanic Studies* 1 (1997): 107–22.

Gómez-Bravo, Ana. *Textual Agency: Writing Culture and Social Networks in Fifteenth-Century Spain*. Toronto: University of Toronto, 2013.

Grafton, Anthony, and Lisa Jardine. *From Humanism to the Humanities: Education and the Liberal Arts in Fifteenth- and Sixteenth-Century Europe*. London: Duckworth, 1986.

Grazia, Margareta de, Maureen Quilligan, and Peter Stallybrass. "Introduction." In *Subject and Object in Renaissance Culture*, edited by Margareta de Grazia, Maureen Quilligan, and Peter Stallybrass, 1–16. Cambridge: Cambridge University Press, 1996.

Grendler, Paul F. "Form and Function in Italian Renaissance Popular Books." *Renaissance Quarterly* 46, no. 3 (1993): 451–85.

Grieve, Patricia E. *Desire and Death in the Spanish Sentimental Romance, 1440–1550*. Newark, DE: Juan de la Cuesta, 1987.

Griffin, Clive. "*Celestina*'s Illustrations." *Bulletin of Hispanic Studies* 78, no. 1 (2001): 59–79.

– *The Crombergers of Seville: The History of a Printing and Merchant Dynasty*. Oxford: Oxford University Press, 1988.

Grigley, Joseph. *Textuaterity: Art, Theory, and Textual Criticism*. Ann Arbor: University of Michigan Press, 1995.

Guilbert, Nicholas. "A propos de la tapisserie: L'histoire de Lérian et Lauréolle présenté au Musée des Tissus de Lyon." *Bulletin des musées et des monuments lyonnais* 4 (1997): 30–3.

Guiffrey, Jules. "Tapisseries françaises." In *Histoire générale de la tapisserie*. 4 vols. Vol. 2. Paris: Société anonyme de publications périodiques, 1878–85.

Gumbrecht, Hans Ulrich. "The Body vs. the Printing Press: Media in the Early Modern Period, Mentalities in the Reign of Castile, and Another History of Literary Forms." Translated by Glen Burns. *Sociocriticism* 1 (1985): 179–202.

Hagan, Susan. "Visual/Verbal Collaboration in Print: Complementary Differences, Necessary Ties, and an Untapped Rhetorical Opportunity." *Written Communication* 24, no. 1 (2007): 49–83.

Hampton, Timothy. *Fictions of Embassy: Literature and Diplomacy in Early Modern Europe*. Ithaca, NY: Cornell University Press, 2009.

Hermans, Theo. "Images of Translation: Metaphor and Imagery in the Renaissance Discourse on Translation." In *The Manipulation of Literature: Studies in Literary Translation*, edited by Theo Hermans, 103–35. London: Croom Helm, 1985.

– "Renaissance Translation between Literalism and Imitation." In *Geschichte, System, Literarische Übersetzung / Histories, Systems, Literary Translations*, edited by Harald Kittel, 95–116. Berlin: Erich Schmidt, 1992.

Herrero Carretero, Concha. *Tapices de Isabel la Católica: Origen de la colección real española*. Madrid: Patrimonio Nacional, 2004.

Hill, Bert. *Weapons and Warfare in Renaissance Europe: Gunpowder, Technology, and Tactics*. Baltimore: Johns Hopkins University Press, 1997.

Hilton, Ronald. "Review of *A Catalogue of Hispanic Manuscripts and Books before 1700 from the Bodleian Library and Oxford College Libraries, Exhibited at the Taylor Institution, 6–11 September*." *Modern Language Review* 59, no. 2 (1964): 302–3.

Hirsch, Rudolf. *Printing, Selling and Reading, 1450–1550*. Wiesbaden, Germany: Harrassowitz, 1974.

Hirschfeld, Heather. "Early Modern Collaboration and Theories of Authorship." *PMLA: Publications of the Modern Language Association of America* 116, no. 3 (2001): 609–22.

Houdoy, Jules. *Les tapisseries de haute-lice, histoire de la fabrication lilloise du XIVe au XVIIIe siècle*. Lille, France: L. Danel, 1871.

Howsam, Leslie. *Old Books and New Histories: An Orientation to Studies in Book and Print Culture*. Toronto: University of Toronto Press, 2006.

Huston, Lorna. *The Usurer's Daughter: Male Friendship and Fictions of Women in Sixteenth-Century England*. New York: Routledge, 1994.

Hutcheon, Linda. *A Theory of Adaptation*. New York: Routledge, 2006.

Ihrie, Maureen. "Discourses of Power in the *Cárcel de Amor*." *Hispanófila* 125 (1999): 1–10.

Indini, Maria Luisa, and S. Panunzio. "Modelli e registri nelle traduzioni romanze della *Cárcel de Amor*." *Tradurre, Annali Di Bari* 3, no. 2 (1980): 87–114.

Infantes de Miguel, Víctor. "La prosa de ficción renacentista: Entre los géneros literarios y el *género editorial*." In *Actas del X Congreso de la Asociación internacional de hispanistas*, vol. 1, edited by Antonio Vilanova, 467–74. Barcelona: Promociones y Publicaciones Universitarias, 1992.

Ivers, Christina. "Risky Collaboration in Fifteenth-Century Printing and *Cárcel de Amor*." *La corónica* 43, no. 2 (2015): 85–109.

Inglis, Erik. "A Book in the Hand: Some Late Medieval Accounts of Manuscript Presentations." *Journal of the Early Book Society* 4–5 (2002): 57–97.

Jager, Eric. "The Book of the Heart: Reading and Writing the Medieval Subject." *Speculum* 71, no. 1 (1996): 1–26.

Johnson, Alfred. F. *The Italian XVI Century*. Periods of Typography. London: Ernest Benn, 1926.

– *French Sixteenth Century Printing*. Periods of Typography. London: Ernest Benn, 1928.

Joubert, Fabienne. *La tapisserie médiévale au Musée de Cluny*. Paris: Réunion des Musées Nationaux, 1987.

Joyner, Charles. *Shared Traditions: Southern History and Folk Culture*. Urbana-Champaign: University of Illinois Press, 1999.

Kany, Charles. *The Beginnings of the Epistolary Novel in France, Italy and Spain*. Berkeley, CA: University of California Press, 1937.

Kelly, Louis G. *Twenty-Five Centuries of Language Teaching (500 BC–1969)*. Rowley, MA: Newbury House, 1969.

King, John N. *English Reformation Literature: The Tudor Origins of the Protestant Tradition*. Princeton, NJ: Princeton University Press, 1982.

Kinney, Arthur F. *Continental Humanist Poetics: Studies in Erasmus, Castiglione, Marguerite de Navarre, Rabelais, and Cervantes*. Amherst: University of Massachusetts Press, 1989.

– *Humanist Poetics: Thought, Rhetoric, and Fiction in Sixteenth-Century England*. Amherst: University of Massachusetts, 1986.

Knecht, R.J. "Introduction." In Thomas Wall, *The Voyage of Sir Nicholas Carewe to the Emperor Charles V in the Year 1529*. Edited by R.J. Knecht, xi–xxxviii. Cambridge: The Roxburghe Club; Cambridge University Press, 1959.

– *Renaissance Warrior and Patron: The Reign of Francis I*. Cambridge: Cambridge University Press, 1994.

Kolsky, Stephen. "Before the Nunciature: Castiglione in Fact and Fiction." *Rinascimento* 29 (1989): 331–57.

– *Courts and Courtiers in Renaissance Northern Italy*. Aldershot, UK: Ashgate, 2003.

– "Lelio Manfredi traduttore cortigiano: Intorno al *Carcer d'Amore* e al *Tirante il Bianco*." *Civiltà mantovana* 29, no. 10 (1994): 45–69.

– *Mario Equicola, the Real Courtier*. Geneva: Droz, 1991.

– "Women through Men's Eyes: The Third Book of *Il Cortegiano*." In Kolsky, *Courts and Courtiers in Renaissance Northern Italy*, 41–91.

Kruells-Hepermann, Claudia. "Aggression and Annihilation: Spanish Sentimental Romances and the Legends of the Saints." *Fifteenth-Century Studies* 27 (2002): 177–84.

Lawrance, Jeremy. "Nuevos lectores y nuevos géneros: Apuntes y observaciones sobre la epistolografía en el primer renacimiento español." In *Literatura en la Época del Emperdaor*, edited by Víctor García de la Concha, 81–100. Acta Salamanticensia 5 ed. Salamanca, Spain: Universidad de Salamanca, 1984.

Le Coq, Anne-Marie. *François Ier Imaginaire: Symbolique et politique à l'Aube de la Renaissance française*. Art et Histoire. Paris: Macula, 1987.

Lefevere, André. "Translation: Its Genealogy in the West." In *Translation, History and Culture*, edited by Susan Bassnett and André Lefevere, 14–28. London: Cassell, 1995.

Lefevere, André, ed. *Translation/History/Culture: A Sourcebook*. Translation Studies. London: Routledge, 1992.

Lehmberg, Stanford. "Carew, Sir Nicholas (b. in or before 1496, d. 1539)." In *Oxford Dictionary of National Biography*, edited by H.C.G. Matthew and Brian Harrison. Oxford: Oxford University Press, 2004. http://www.oxforddnb.com/index/101004633/Nicholas-Carew.

León, Pedro R. "Brief Notes on some 16th Century Antwerp Printers with Special Reference to Jean Steelsius and his Hispanic Bibliography." *De Gulden Passer* 54 (1976): 77–92.

Leproux, Guy-Michel. "Les peintres et l'enluminure à Paris au XVIe siècle." In *Peindre en France à la Renaissance: Les courants stylistiques au temps de Louis XII et de François 1er*, edited by Frédéric Elsig, 59–70. Biblioteca d'arte vol. 32. Milan: Silvana, 2011.

Lindquist, Sherry C.M. "'Parlant de moy': Manuscripts of *La Coche* by Marguerite of Navarre." In *Excavating the Medieval Image: Manuscripts, Artists, Audiences; Essays in Honor of Sandra Hindman*, edited by David S. Areford and Nina A. Rowe, 197–221. Aldershot, UK: Ashgate, 2004.

López Alemany, Ignacio. *Ilusión áulica e la imaginación caballeresca en El cortesano de Luis Milán*. Chapel Hill: North Carolina Studies in the Romance Languages and Literatures, 2013.

López-Vidriero, María Luisa, and Pedro Cátedra. *La imprenta y su impacto en Castilla*. Salamanca: 1998.

Losse, Deborah N. "From Auctor to Auteur: Authorization and Appropriation in the Renaissance." *Medievalia et Humanistica* 16 (1988): 153–63.

Love, Harold. *Attributing Authorship: An Introduction*. New York: Cambridge University Press, 2002.

Lucía Megías, José Manuel. *Imprenta y libros de caballerías*. Madrid: Ollero & Ramos, 2000.

Luteran, Paula. *The Theory of Translation in the Sixteenth Century: Analyzing Nicholas Herberay des Essarts' "Amadis de Gaule."* Lewiston, NY: Edwin Mellin, 2005.

Lyell, James P.R. *Early Book Illustration in Spain*. 1926. Reprint, New York: Hacker Art Books, 1976.

– *La ilustración del libro antiguo en España*. Edited by Julián Martín Abad. Translated by Héctor Silva. Madrid: Ollero y Ramos, 2012.

Mandrell, James. "Author and Authority in *Cárcel de Amor*: The Role of el Auctor." *Journal of Hispanic Philology* 8, no. 2 (1984): 99–122.

Marichal, Paul, ed. *Catalogue des actes de François Ier*. Tome V. Collection des ordonnances des dois de France. Paris: Académie des Sciences Morales et Politiques, 1892.

Marín Pina, María Carmen. "La *Cárcel de Amor* zaragozana (1493), una edición desconocida." *Archivo de filología aragonesa* 51 (1995): 75–88.

Marino, Nancy. "The Cancionero de Valencia, *Question de Amor*, and the Last Medieval Courts of Love". In *Cultural Contexts/ Female Voices*, edited by Louise M. Haywood, 41–9. London: Deparment of Hispanic Studies, Queen Mary & Westfield College, 2000.

Márquez Villanueva, Francisco. "*Cárcel de amor*, novela política." *Revista de Occidente* 14 (1966): 85–200.

Martín Abad, Julián. *Los primeros tiempos de la imprenta en España, c. 1471–1520*. Madrid: Ediciones del Laberinto, 2003.

Martín Baños, Pedro. *El arte epistolar en el renacimiento europeo*. Bilbao: Universidad de Deusto, 2005.

Matulka, Barbara. *The Novels of Juan de Flores and Their European Diffusion. A Study in Comparative Literature*. Geneva: Slatkine Reprints, 1974.

Mazzocchi, Giuseppe. "Los manuscritos y la definición de un género: El caso de la novela sentimental." In *Los códices literarios de la Edad Media: Interpretación, historia, técnicas y catalogación*, edited by Pedro Cátedra, Eva Belén Carro Carbajal, and Javier Durán Barceló, 195–205. Salamanca: Cilengua, 2009.

McDonald, Peter. "Implicit Structures and Explicit Interactions: Pierre Bourdieu and the History of the Book." *The Library* 19, no. 2 (1997): 105–21.

McGann, Jerome J. *The Textual Condition*. Princeton, NJ: Princeton University Press, 1991.

McHale, Brian. "Narrativity and Segmentivity; or, Poetry in the Gutter." In *Intermediality and Storytelling*, edited by Marie-Laure Ryan and Marina Grishakova, 27–48. New York: De Gruyter, 2010.

McKenzie, D.F. *Bibliography and the Sociology of Texts*. Cambridge: Cambridge University Press, 2004.

McKenzie, D.F., Peter D. McDonald, and Michael F. Suarez, eds. *Making Meaning: "Printers of the Mind" and Other Essays*. Amherst: University of Massachusetts Press, 2002.

McKitterick, David. *Print, Manuscript and the Search for Order, 1450–1830.* Cambridge: Cambridge University Press, 2003.

Menato, Marco, Ennio Sandal, and Giuseppina Zappelli, eds. *Dizionario dei tipografi e degli editori italiani. Il Cinquecento.* Milan: Editrice Bibliografica, 1997.

Menéndez Pelayo, Marcelino. *Orígenes de la novela.* Edición nacional de las obras completas de Menéndez Pelayo. Edited by Enrique Sánchez Reyes. Vol. 2. Madrid: CSIC, 1961.

Meyer, G.J. "The Newest Profession" In *The Borgias: The Hidden History,* 351–64. New York: Bantam Books, 2013.

Middlebrook, Leah. "'Tout Mon Office:' Body Politics and Family Dynamics in the Verse *Épîtres* of Marguerite De Navarre." *Renaissance Quarterly* 54, no. 4 (2001): 1108–41.

Milsom, John. "Songs and Society in Early Tudor London." *Early Music History* 16 (1997): 235–93.

Miguel-Prendes, Sol. "Las cartas de la *Cárcel de Amor." Hispanófila* 34, no. 3 (1991): 1–22.

– "Reimagining Diego de San Pedro's Readers at Work: *Cárcel de Amor." La corónica* 32, no. 2 (2004): 7–44.

– "Otra frontera de la ficción sentimental: la *Consolatio Philosophiae* de Boecio." *eHumanista* 28 (2014): 511–35.

Miñana, Rogelio. "Auctor omnisciente, auctor testigo: El marco narrativo en *Cárcel de Amor." La corónica* 30, no. 1 (2001): 133–48.

Minervini,Vincenzo, and Maria Luisa Indini, eds. *Càrcer d'amor, Carcer d'amore: Due traduzione della "novela" di Diego de San Pedro.* Fasano, Italy: Schena, 1986.

Mitchell, W.T.J. *Picture Theory: Essays on Verbal and Visual Representation.* Chicago: University of Chicago Press, 1995.

Moliner, Emilie. "Les tapisseries des Ducs de Lorraine." *Bulletin archéologique du Comité des travaux historiques et scientifiques* (1885): 468–76.

Moll, Jaime. "Amberes y el mundo hispano del libro." In *Encuentros en Flandes: Relaciones e intercambios hispanoflamencos a incios de la Edad Moderna,* edited by Werner Thomas and Robert A. Verdonk, 116–31. Louvain: Leuven University Press, 2000.

Moreau, Brigitte. *Inventaire chronologique des éditions parisiennes du XVI siècle.* Vol. 4. Paris: Service des travaux historiques de la ville de Paris, 1972–92.

Moretti, Franco. "Conjectures on World Literature." *New Left Review* 1 (2000): 54–68.

Müller, Jan-Dirk. "The Body of the Book: The Media Transition from Manuscript to Print." In *Materialities of Communication,* translated by William Whobrey, edited by Hans Ulrich Gumbrecht and Ludwig K. Pfeiffer, 32–44. Stanford, CA: Stanford University Press, 1994.

Munjic, Sanda. "Diego de San Pedro's *Cárcel de Amor:* Allegorizing the Role of
Poets in a Well-Ordered State." *Revista Hispánica Moderna* 65, no. 1 (2012):
81–97.

Nichols, Stephen G. "Picture, Image, and Subjectivity in Medieval Culture."
Modern Language Notes 108, no. 4 (1993): 617–37.

Nichols, Stephen G., and Siegfried Wenzel, eds. *The Whole Book: Cultural
Perspectives on the Medieval Miscellany.* Ann Arbor: University of Michigan
Press, 1996.

Nida, Eugene. "Principles of Correspondence." In *The Translation Studies
Reader,* edited by Lawrence Venuti, 126–40. New York: Routledge, 2004.

Norton, Glyn P. *The Ideology and Language of Translation in Renaissance France
and Their Humanist Antecedents.* Geneva: Librairie Droz, 1984.

Ong, Walter. "Orality, Literacy, and Medieval Textualization," *New Literary
History* 16, no. 1 (1984).

Orth, Myra D. "Manuscript Production and Illumination in Renaissance Paris
(1500–1565)." *Journal of the Early Book Society* 6 (2003): 125–35.

– "Manuscrits pour Marguerite." In *Marguerite de Navarre (1492–1992):
Actes du colloque international de Pau,* edited by Nicole Cazauran and James
Dauphiné, 85–105. Mont-de-Marsan, France: Editions Interuniversitaires, 1995.

– "'The Prison of Love': A Medieval Romance in the French Renaissance
and Its Illustration (B.N. MS Fr. 2150)." *Journal of the Warburg and Courtauld
Institutes* 46 (1983): 211–21.

– "Progressive Tendencies in French Manuscript Illumination, 1515–1530:
Godefroy le Batave and the 1520's Hours Workshop. (Volumes—III)." PhD
diss., New York University, 1976. ProQuest (AAT 7619530).

– *A Survey of Manuscripts Illuminated in France. Renaissance Manuscripts. The
Sixteenth Century.* 2 vols. London: Harvey Miller, 2015.

Pallarés, Miguel Ángel. *"La Cárcel de Amor" de Diego de San Pedro, impresa
en Zaragoza el 3 de junio de 1493; membra disjecta de una edición desconocida.*
Zaragoza: Centro de Documentación Bibliográfica Aragonesa, 1994.

Pallotta, Augustus. "The Prologues to the Spanish Texts Printed in Italy in the
Sixteenth Century." *Symposium* 48, no. 3 (1994): 216–28.

– "Venetian Printers and Spanish Literature in Sixteenth-Century Italy."
Comparative Literature 43, no. 1 (1991): 20–42.

Parent, Annie. *Les métiers du livre à Paris au XVIe siècle (1535–1560).* Geneva:
Droz, 1974.

Parrilla, Carmen. "Acrescentar lo que de suyo está crescido: El cumplimiento
de Nicolás Núñez." In *Historias y ficciones: Coloquio sobre la literatura del siglo
XV,* edited by Rafael Beltran, 241–53. Valencia: Universitat de Valencia,
1990.

- "La arenga de Leriano en la *Cárcel de Amor:* Una noticia sobre su difusión."
  Revista de Poética Medieval 16 (2006): 171–8.
Pedraza Gracia, Manuel José. "La función del editor en el libro del siglo XVI."
  Titivillus 1 (2015): 211–26.
Peeters-Fontainas, Jean. "L'officine espagnole de Martin Nutius à Anvers."
  De Gulden Passer 35 (1957): 1–104.
Perea Rodríguez, Oscar. "Valencia en el *Cancionero general* de Hernando del
  Castillo: Los poetas y los poemas." *Dicenda: Cuadernos de Filología Hispánica*
  21 (2003): 227–51.
Pérez-Romero, Antonio. *The Subversive Tradition in Spanish Renaissance Writing.*
  Lewisburg, PA: Bucknell University Press, 2005.
Perry, Anthony. "A French ("françois") Reading of a Spanish Text: Paratexts in
  La Prison Damour." Paper presented at the University of Western Michigan
  International Medieval Congress, Kalamazoo, 11 May 2014.
Perugini, Carla. "Las fuentes iconográficas de la *Editio Princeps* de la *Lozana
  andaluza.*" *Salina: Revista de la Facultat de Lletres de Tarragona* 14 (2000): 65–72.
Petrucci, Armando, ed. *Libri, editori e pubblico nell'Europa moderna: guida storica
  e critica.* Rome: Laterza, 2003.
- *Libros, escrituras y bibliotecas.* Edited by Francisco M. Gimeno Blay.
  Translated by Francisco M.Gimeno Blay, and María Luz Mandingorra
  Llavata. Salamanca: Universidad de Salamanca, 2011.
Pettegree, Andrew. "Translation and the Migration of Texts." In *Borders and
  Travellers in Early Modern Europe*, edited byThomas Betteridge, 113–28.
  Aldershot, UK: Ashgate, 2007.
Pianigiani, Ottorino. *Vocabolario Etimologico Della Lingua Italiana.* La Spezia,
  Italy: Melita, 1990.
Pinet, Simone. "The Knight, the Kings, and the Tapestries: The *Amadis* Series."
  Revista Canadiense de Estudios Hispánicos 30, no. 3 (2006): 537–54.
Plummer, John, Gregory Clark, and Pierpont Morgan Library. *The Last
  Flowering: French Painting in Manuscripts, 1420–1530; From American
  Collections.* New York: Pierpont Morgan Library, 1982.
Potter, Ursula. "Tales of Patient Griselda and Henry VIII." *Early Theatre* 5, no.
  2 (2002): 11–28.
Pratt, Mary Louise. "Arts of the Contact Zone." *Profession* (1991): 33–40.
Price, Leah. "Reading Matter." *PMLA: Publications of the Modern Language
  Association of America* 121, no. 1 (2006): 9–16.
Pym, Anthony. "Alternatives to Borders in Translation Theory." *Athanor* 12
  (2001): 172–82.
- *Negotiating the Frontier: Translators and Intercultures in Hispanic History.*
  Manchester: St Jerome, 2000.

Quondam, Amadeo. "'Mercanzia d'onore / Mercanzia d'utile' Produzione
    libraria e lavoro intellectual a Venezia nel Cinquecento". In *Libri editori
    e pubblico nell'Europa moderna. Guida storica e critica*, edited by Armando
    Petrucci, 53–103. Rome: Laterza, 1977.
Randall, Dale B.J. *The Golden Tapestry: A Critical Survey of Non-Chivalric Spanish
    Fiction in English Translation (1543–1657)*. Durham, NC: Duke University
    Press, 1963.
Rawles, Stephen. "The Earliest Editions of Nicolas de Herberay's Translations
    of *Amadis de Gaule*." *The Library* 3, no. 2 (1981): 91–108.
Rebhorn, Wayne A. *The Emperor of Men's Minds: Literature and the Renaissance
    Discourse of Rhetoric*. Ithaca, NY: Cornell University Press, 1995.
Rees, Ronald. *Interior Landscapes: Gardens and the Domestic Environment*.
    Baltimore: Johns Hopkins University Press, 1993.
Reiss, Timothy J. *Knowledge, Discovery and Imagination in Early Modern
    Europe: The Rise of Aesthetic Rationalism*. Cambridge Studies in Renaissance
    Literature and Culture 15. Cambridge: Cambridge University Press, 1997.
Rener, Frederick M. *Interpretatio: Language and Translation from Cicero to Tytler*.
    Amsterdam: Rodopi, 1989.
Reynier, Gustave. *Le Roman sentimental avant "L'Astrée."* Paris: Armand Colin,
    1908.
Richardson, Brian. *Manuscript Culture in Renaissance Italy*. Cambridge:
    Cambridge University Press, 2009.
Richie, Joy, and Kate Ronald. "Introduction." In *Available Means: An Anthology
    of Women's Rhetoric(s)*, edited by Joy Richie and Kate Ronald, xv–xxxi.
    Pittsburgh: University of Pittsburgh Press, 2001.
Rico, Francisco. *Texto y contextos. Estudios sobre la poesía Española del siglo XV*.
    Barcelona: Crítica, 1990.
Rohland de Langbehn, Regula. "Nicolás Núñez y la tradición alemana de
    Cárcel de Amor." *Medievalia* 27 (1998): 1–6.
Ross, Jill. "The Dazzling Sword of Language: Masculinity and Persuasion
    in Classical and Medieval Rhetoric." In *The Ends of the Body: Identity and
    Community in Medieval Culture*, edited by Suzanne Conklin Akbari and Jill
    Ross, 153–17. Toronto: University of Toronto Press, 2013.
Rothstein, Marianne. *Reading in the Renaissance: "Amadis de Gaule" and the
    Lessons of Memory*. Newark: University of Delaware Press, 1999.
Rouse, Richard H., and Mary A. Rouse. *Manuscripts and Their Makers:
    Commercial Book Producers in Medieval Paris, 1200–1500*. Turnhout, Belgium:
    Harvey Miller, 2000.
Rubio Tovar, Joaquín. *El vocabulario de la traducción en la Edad Media*. Alcalá de
    Hernares, Spain: Universidad de Alcalá, 2011.

Ruiz Casanova, José Francisco. "Introducción." In Diego de San Pedro, *Cárcel de Amor, Arnalte y Lucenda, Sermón*, 6th ed., 9–60. Madrid: Cátedra, 2011.

Rumeu de Armas, Antonio. *Alfonso de Ulloa, introductor de la cultura española en Italia*. Madrid: Gredos, 1973.

Russell, Jocelyne. *Diplomats at Work: Three Renaissance Studies*. Stroud, UK: Allan Sutton, 1992.

Rust, Martha D. *Imaginary Worlds in Medieval Books: Exploring the Manuscript Matrix*. Basingstoke, UK: Palgrave Macmillan, 2007.

Salzburg, Rosa. "'Per le Piaze & Sopra il Ponte': Reconstructing the Geography of Popular Print in Sixteenth-Century Venice." In *Geographies of the Book*, edited by Charles W.J. Withers and Miles Ogborn, 111–32. Farnham, UK: Ashgate, 2010.

Schlauch, Margaret. *Antecedents of the English Novel*. Warsaw: PWN-Polish Scientific Publishers, 1963.

Schleiermacher, Friedrich. "On the Different Methods of Translating." In *Western Translation Theory: From Herodotus to Nietzsche*, edited by Douglas Robinson and translated by James Hankins, 225–38. Manchester: St Jerome, 1997.

Sears, Elizabeth. "Portraits in Counterpoint: Jerome and Jeremiah in an Augsburg Manuscript." In *Reading Medieval Images: The Art Historian and the Object*, edited by Elizabeth Sears and Thelma K. Thomas, 61–74. Ann Arbor: University of Michigan Press, 2002.

Seres, Guillermo. "La llamada ficción sentimental y el humanismo vernáculo del siglo XV: Un ejemplo." *Insula: Revista de letras y ciencias humanas* 651 (2001): 12–14.

Severin, Dorothy Sherman. *Del manuscrito a la imprenta en la época de Isabel La Católica*. Kassel: Reichenberger, 2004.

– "The Sentimental Genre: Romance, Novel, or Parody?" *La corónica* 31, no. 2 (2003): 312–15.

Sharrer, Harvey L. "La *Cárcel de Amor* de Diego de San Pedro: La confluencia de lo sagrado y lo profano en 'la imagen femenil entallada en una piedra muy clara.'" In *Actas Del III Congreso De La Asociación Hispánica De Literatura Medieval*, edited by María Isabel Toro Pascua, 983–96. Salamanca: Biblioteca española del siglo XV, Departamento de literatura española e hispanoamericana, 1994.

Shire, H.M. "The Function of Translated Literature within a National Literature: The Example of Renaissance England and Scotland." In *Literature and Translation, New Perspectives in Literary Studies*, edited by James S. Holmes, José Lambert, and Raymond van den Broeck, 177–80. Leuven, Belgium: ACCO, 1978.

Smith, Helen, and Louise Wilson. "Introduction." In *Renaissance Paratexts*, edited by Helen Smith and Louise Wilson, 1–14. Cambridge: Cambridge University Press, 2011.

Solís de los Santos, José. "Ulloa, Alfonso de." *Diccionario biográfico español* 48. Madrid: Real Academia de la Historia (2009): 595–8.

Sosa Velasco, Alfredo J. "La producción del espacio en la *Cárcel de Amor* de Diego de San Pedro: Apuntes sobre el desarrollo de una economía capitalista." *eHumanista* 12 (2009): 127–44.

Spicer, Joaneath. "The Renaissance Elbow." In *A Cultural History of Gesture*, edited by Jon Bremmer and Herman Roodenburg, 84–128. Ithaca, NY: Cornell University Press, 1991.

Sponsler, Claire. "Text and Textiles: Lydgate's Tapestry Poems." In *Medieval Fabrications: Dress, Textiles, Clothwork, and Other Cultural Imaginings*, edited by E.J. Burns, 19–34. New York: Palgrave, 2004.

Stack, Lotus. *The Essential Thread: Tapestry on Wall and Body*. Minneapolis: Minneapolis Institute of the Arts, 1988.

Stallybrass, Peter. "Afterword." In *Renaissance Paratexts*, edited by Helen Smith and Louise Wilson, 204–19. Cambridge: Cambridge University Press, 2011.

Standen, Edith A. "Studies in the History of Tapestry 1520–1790." *Apollo* 113, no. 233 (1981): 6–54.

Starn, Randolph. "Seeing Culture in a Room for a Renaissance Prince." In *The New Cultural History*, edited by Lynn Hunt, 205–32. Berkeley: University of California Press, 2003.

Stierle, Karlheinz. "Translatio Studii and Renaissance: From Vertical to Horizontal Translation." In *The Translatability of Cultures: Figurations of the Space Between*, edited by Sanford Burdick and Wolfgang Iser, 55–67. Stanford, CA: Stanford UP, 1996.

Sumillera, Rocío. "Language Manuals and the Book Trade in England." In *Translation and the Book Trade in Early Modern Europe*, edited by José María Pérez Fernández and Edward Wilson-Lee, 61–80.

Cambridge: Cambridge University Press, 2014. Surtz, Ronald E. "The Reciprocal Construction of Isabeline Book Patronage." In *Queen Isabel I of Castile: Power, Patronage, Persona*, edited by Barbara F. Weissberger, 55–70. Woodbridge, UK: Tamesis, 2008.

Tahir-Gürçağlar, Şehnaz. "What Texts Don't Tell: The Uses of Paratexts in Translation Research." In *Crosscultural Transgressions: Research Models in Translation Studies II: Historical and Ideological Issues*, edited by Theo Hermans, 44–60. Manchester: St Jerome, 2002.

Taylor, Barry. "Learning Style from the Spaniards in Sixteenth-Century England." In *Renaissance Cultural Crossroads: Translation, Print and Culture in Britain, 1447–1640*, edited by S.K. Barker and Brenda M. Hosington, 63–78. Leiden, Netherlands: Brill, 2015.

Tilley, Arthur A. *Studies in the French Renaissance*. New York: Barnes & Noble, 1968.

Torrego, Esther. "Convención retórica y ficción narrativa en la *Cárcel de Amor*." *Nueva Revista de Filologia Hispánica* 32, no. 2 (1983): 330–9.

Trachsler, Richard. "How to do Things with Manuscripts: From Humanist Practice to Recent Textual Criticism." *Textual Cultures* 1, no. 1 (2006): 5–28.

Tymozco, Maria. "Western Metaphorical Discourses Implicit in Translation Studies." In *Thinking through Translation with Metaphors*, edited by James St André, 109–43. Manchester: St Jerome, 2010.

Van Eck, Caroline. *Classical Rhetoric and the Visual Arts in Early Modern Europe*. New York: Cambridge University Press, 2007.

Venuti, Lawrence. *The Scandals of Translation: Towards an Ethics of Difference*. New York: Routledge, 2006.

– *The Translator's Invisibility: A History of Translation*. London: Routledge, 1995.

Waley, Pamela. "Love and Honor in the *Novelas Sentimentales* of Diego de San Pedro and Juan de Flores." *Bulletin of Hispanic Studies* 63 (1966): 253–75.

Wardropper, Bruce W. "Allegory and the Role of *El Autor* in the *Cárcel de Amor*." *Philological Quarterly* 31 (1952): 39–44.

Warner, Lyndan. *The Ideas of Man and Woman in Renaissance France Print, Rhetoric, and Law*. Farnham, UK: Ashgate, 2011.

Webb, Ruth. *Ekphrasis, Imagination and Persuasion in Ancient Rhetorical Theory and Practice*. Surrey, UK: Ashgate, 2009.

Weigert, Laura. "Tapestry Exposed." *Art Bulletin* 85, no. 4 (2003): 784–96.

– *Weaving Sacred Stories: French Choir Tapestries and the Performance of Clerical Identity*. Ithaca, NY: Cornell University Press, 2004.

Weiss, Julian. "What Every Noblewoman Needs to Know: Cultural Literacy in Late Medieval Spain," *Speculum* 81, no. 4 (2006): 1118–49.

Weissberger, Barbara F. "The Gendered Taxonomy of Spanish Romance." *La corónica* 29, no. 1 (2000): 205–29.

– *Isabel Rules: Constructing Queenship, Weilding Power*. Minneapolis: University of Minnesota Press, 2003.

– "The Politics of *Cárcel de Amor*." *Revista de Estudios Hispánicos* 26, no. 3 (1992): 307–26.

– "Resisting Readers and Writers in the Sentimental Romances and the Problem of Female Literacy." In *Studies on the Spanish Sentimental Romance (1440–1550): Redefining a Genre*, edited by Joseph J. Gwara and E. Michael Gerli, 173–90. London: Tamesis, 1997.

Whinnom, Keith. "*Autor* and *Tratado* in the Fifteenth Century: Semantic Latinism or Etymological Trap?" *Bulletin of Hispanic Studies* 59 (1982): 211–18.

- "Cardona, the Crucifixion and Leriano's Last Drink." In *Studies on the Spanish Sentimental Romance (1450–1550): Redefining a Genre*, edited by Joseph J. Gwara and E. Michael Gerli, 207–15. Rochester: Tamesis, 1997.
- "Introduction." In San Pedro, *Obras completas II: Cárcel de Amor*, 49–52.
- "Lucrezia Borgia and a Lost Edition of Diego de San Pedro's *Arnalte y Lucenda*." *Annali – Sezione Romanza* 13 (1971): 143–51.
- *The Spanish Sentimental Romance, 1440–1550: A Critical Bibliography*. London: Grant and Cutler, 1983.
Wiesner, Merry E. "Beyond Women and the Family: Towards a Gender Analysis of the Reformation." *The Sixteenth Century Journal* 18, no. 3 (1987): 311–21.
Wildenstein, Guy, et al. *The Arts of France from François Ier to Napoléon Ier: A Centennial Celebration of Wildenstein's Presence in New York*. New York: Wildenstein, 2005.
Wilson, Timothy, ed. *The Battle of Pavia*. Oxford: Ashmolean Museum, 2003.
Wittlin, Curt. *De la traducció literal a la creació literària: Estudis filològics i literaris sobre textos antics catalans i valencians*. Valencia: Institut Interuniversitari de Filologia Valenciana, 1995.
Wyatt, Michael. *The Italian Encounter with Tudor England: A Cultural Politics of Translation*. Cambridge: Cambridge University Press, 2005.
Ynduráin, Domingo. "Las cartas de Laureola (beber cenizas)." *Edad de Oro* 111 (1984): 299–309.
Yoon, Sun-Me. "La continuación de Nicolás Núñez a *Cárcel de Amor*." *Dicenda: Cuadernos de Filología Hispánica* 10 (1991–2): 327–39.
Zilli, Carmelo. "Notizia di Lelio Manfredi, letterato di corte." *Studi e problemi di critica testuale* 27, (1983): 39–54.
Zöhl, Caroline. *Jean Pichore: Buchmaler, Graphiker und Verleger in Paris um 1500*. Ars Nova. Turnhout, Belgium: Brepols, 2004.
Zumthor, Paul. "The Great Game of Rhetoric." Translated by Annette and Edward Tomarken. *New Literary History* 12, no. 3 (1981): 493–508.

Bibliographies and Databases

Biblioteca Nacional de España. *Catálogo Automatizado de la Biblioteca Nacional*. Madrid: Biblioteca Nacional de España.
Bibliotheca Bodmeriana. *Manuscrits Français du Moyen Âge*. Cologny-Geneva: Fondation Martin Bodmer, 1975.
Bibliothèque de Genève. *On-Line Digital Catalogue*. Geneva: Bibliothèque de Genève.

Bibliothèque nationale de France. *Catalogue des actes de François Ier.*
   Gallica: Bibliothèque Numérique. Vol. 5. Paris: Bibliothèque nationale de
   France.
– *Gallica: La Bibliothèque Numérique de la BnF.* Paris: Bibliothèque nationale de
   France.
Bodleian Library. *On-Line Library Catalogue.* Oxford: University of Oxford.
British Library Board. *Catalogue of Books Printed in Spain and of Spanish Books
   Printed Elsewhere in Europe before 1601 Now in the British Library.* 2nd ed.
   London: The British Library, 1989.
Brunet, Jacques-Charles. *Manuel du Libraire et de l'Amateur des Livres.* Geneva:
   Slatkine, 1990.
Cátalogo de obras medieval impresas en castellano hasta 1600 (COMEDIC. http://
   comedic.unizar.es/index/index/id/60.
De Bure, Guillaume, and Joseph Van Praet. *Catalogue des livres de La Bibliothèque
   De Feu M. Le Duc de la Vallière.* Vol. 2. Paris: Guillaume de Bure, 1783.
Delisle, Léopold. *Le cabinet des manuscrits de la Bibliothèque Impériale: Catalogue
   des Manuscrits Français.* Paris: Imprimerie Impériale, 1868.
Duff, Gordon. *A Century of the English Book Trade. Short Noticed of all Printers,
   Stationers, Book-Binders, and Others Connected with it from the Issue of the First
   Dated Book in 1457 to the Incorporation of the Company of Stationers in 1557.*
   London: The Bibliographical Society, 1948.
EEBO. *Early English Books Online.*
EDIT 16. *Censimento nazionale delle edizioni italiane del XVI secolo.* Instituto
   Centrale per il catalogo unico delle biblioteche italiane e per le informazione
   bibliografiche. http://edit16.iccu.sbn.it/.
Folger Shakespeare Library. *On-Line Digital Catalogue.* Amherst, MA: Amherst
   College.
Fondation Martin Bodmer Bibliothèque et Musée. *On-Line Digital Catalogue.*
   Cologny, Switzerland.
Haebler, Konrad. *Bibliografía ibérica sel siglo XV.* Vol. 2. Madrid: Ollero &
   Ramos, 1997.
Harvard Library. *On-Line Archives and Manuscripts.* Boston: Harvard
   University.
Hispanic Society of America. *On-Line Digital Catalogue.* New York: The
   Hispanic Society of America.
Huntington Library. *On-Line Digital Catalogue.* San Marino, CA: Huntington
   Library.
Martín Abad, Julián. *Post-incunables ibéricos.* Madrid: Ollero & Ramos, 2001.
– *Catálogo bibliográfico de la colección de incunables de la Biblioteca Nacional de
   España.* Madrid: Biblioteca Nacional de España, 2010.

Moreau, Brigitte. *Inventaire chronologique des éditions Parisiennes du XVI siècle*. Vol. 4. Paris: Service des travaux historiques de la ville de Paris, 1972–92.

Norton, F.J. *A Descriptive Catalogue of Printing in Spain and Portugal 1501–1520*. Cambridge: Cambridge University Press, 1978.

OCLC Online Computer Library Center. "*Worldcat*." OCLC Online Computer Library Center 2014. https://www.worldcat.org.

Pächt, Otto, Jonathan J.G. Alexander, and Bodleian Library. *Illuminated Manuscripts in the Bodleian Library, Oxford*. Vol. 2, *Italian School*. Oxford: Clarendon Press, 1970.

Palau y Dulcet, Antonio. *Manual del librero hispanoamericano. Post-Incunables Ibéricos*. Edited by Julián Martín Abad. Vol. 19. Madrid: Ollero & Ramos, 2001.

Pastorello, Ester. *Tipografi, editori, librai a Venezia nel secolo XVI*. Florence: Olschki, 1924.

Peeters-Fontainas, Jean. *Bibliographie des Impressions Espagnoles des Pays-Bas Méridionaux*. Edited by Anne-Marie Frédéric. Vol. 2. Nieuwkoop, Holland: B. de Graaf, 1965.

Pettegree, Andrew, Malcolm Walsby, and Alexander S. Wilkinson, eds.. *French Vernacular Books: Books Published in the French Language before 1601 = Livres vernaculaires français: livres imprimés en français avant 1601*. Leiden: Brill, 2007.

Real Academia Española. *Catálogo automatizado de la Real Academia*. Madrid: Real Academia Española.

Russell, Peter. *A Catalogue of Hispanic Manuscripts and Books before 1700 from the Bodleian Library and Oxford College Libraries, Exhibited at the Taylor Institution, 6–11 September*. Oxford: Primer Congreso Internacional de Hispanistas, 1962.

Salvá y Mallen, Pedro. *Catálogo de la biblioteca de Salvá* "Sección Novelística; Libros De Caballerías." Vol. 2. Valencia: Ferrer de Orga, 1872.

Sánchez Fernández, Juan M. *Bibliografía aragonesa del siglo XVI*. Vol. 2. Madrid: Imprenta clásica española, 1913–14.

Simón Díaz, José. *Bibliografía de la literatura hispánica*. Vol. 2. Madrid: CSIC, 1956.

Toda y Güell, Eduart. *Bibliografia espanyola d'Italia dels origins de la impremta fins a l'any 1900*. Vol. 5. Vidall Güell: Castell de Sant Miquel d'Escornalbou, 1927.

Universal Short Title Catalog. St Andrews, Scotland: University of St Andrews. http://ustc.ac.uk/index.php.

Vindel, Francisco. *Manual gráfico descriptivo del bibliófilo Hispano-Americano 1475–1850*. London: Magg, 1930.

Index

Abad, Julián Martín, 262n21
Abril, Pedro Simón, 133
actio, 39, 99, 157, 159, 163
adaptation, 3–4, 6, 15–16, 25, 27,
    45–6, 80–1, 83, 142, 145, 171, 179,
    181, 183, 191, 199, 208, 210–11, 219,
    222, 241n2, 266n75
agency: authorial, 69, 138; editorial,
    137; female, 221; human, 107;
    individual, 26; interpretive, 142;
    textual, 107, 125, 259–60n3
Akbari, Suzanne Conklin, 256n2
d'Alançon, Françoise, 60, 121,
    184, 191
Albericus, Philippus, 186
d'Albret, Henri, 57, 190
Aletiphilo, Lelio, 53, 56, 76. *See also*
    Manfredi, Lelio
Alexander VI, Pope, 95
allegorization. *See* allegory
allegory, 89, 92, 220, 224; of
    authorship, 248n29; concretization
    of, 102, 147, 160; discursive mode
    of, 95; intertwining ekphrasis and
    exegesis with, 93; of lovesickness,
    6, 94, 128, 167; and medieval
    medical theories, 257n11; political,
10, 16, 194, 217, 219; prison, 145,
    193; textual, 93; as theatre of
    memory, 17
ambassadors, 11, 37, 43, 63–5,
    116, 128. *See also* diplomats;
    negotiation, diplomatic
de Angoulême, Marguerite, 190, 196
annotation, 104, 110, 140–1
anthologies, 42, 123, 125–7, 133, 191
Aretino, Bernardo Accolti, 50
Aretino, Pietro, 250n9
Armstrong, Guyda, 131, 141
Arnoullet, Olivier, 120, 179
ars dictaminis, 10, 42, 140, 248n36
art: of the ambassador, 65; art-
    historical perspectives, 179;
    figurative, 197, 214; love, 8, 34;
    memory, 8, 94; and reality, 247n25;
    Renaissance, 213; temporal and
    spatial peregrinations of, 13;
    viewer of, 244n33; xylographic,
    143
D'Assy, François: appropriation
    of San Pedro by, 37; authorial
    role of, 62, 68, 82; as courtier,
    66; dedication, 28, 59–60, 121,
    128, 180–2, 187–8, 191, 194, 220,

Studies in Book and Print Culture

General Editor: Leslie Howsam